CW00816484

Fulham Strikers

Fulham Strikers

A celebration of post-war goalscoring

Martin Plumb and Ken Coton

Edited by Robert Fennell

ASHWATER
PRESS

Ashwater Press

Established 1992

21 years of Fulham books

Fulham Strikers

Limited Edition

November 2013

© Copyright Martin Plumb and Ken Coton, 2013

The right of Martin Plumb and Ken Coton to be identified as the authors of this work has been asserted by them in accordance with the Copyright, Designs and Patent Act 1988.

Designed and published by Ashwater Press
68 Tranmere Road, Whitton, Twickenham, Middlesex, TW2 7JB

www.ashwaterpress.co.uk.

Printed and bound by Berforts Information Press, Eynsham, Oxfordshire, England

ISBN 978-0-9927119-0-0

Contents

From the Boardroom
The Manager's Notes
Teamsheet
Pre-match Warm-up

Acknowledgements

Sincere thanks to all who have helped during the production of this book. In particular Robert Fennell, Javier Garcia, Dave Wilson, Alan Pinnock, Graham McDermott, Alex White, Dennis Turner, Ken Simpson.

Picture Credits

Ken Coton, Javier Garcia, Daily Mail/Solo Syndication (front cover, 218, 221, 224), Ashwater archive.

Cover picture: Brian McBride celebrates another Ashwater book.

From the Boardroom

For many years, players have been identified by squad numbers, keeping the same number on their shirt throughout a season. It's not possible from a player's number to determine where he plays in the team. Given the convention that the main goalkeeper is usually allocated the number 1, another goalkeeper could have any other number, so you wouldn't be able to tell from his number alone that he was a goalkeeper. However, clubs do seem to reserve the number 9 shirt for their principal striker. At Fulham, Bobby Zamora had the number 9 shirt, as did Andy Cole, as does Dimitar Berbatov. So what's going on with the number 9?

Time for a bit of history, whilst asking forbearance from our older readers. Here are the teams as printed in a Fulham programme of the 1950s.

THE COTTAGERS' JOURNAL   7

FULHAM
White Shirts, Black Knickers.

R   BLACK   L

2   3
CHENHALL   LAWLER

4   5   6
HILL   BRICE   LOWE,

8   10
ROBSON   HAYNES

7   9   11
STEVENS   JEZZARD   MITTEN

Referee—   Linesmen—
Mr. R. H. MANN   Mr. C. H. HAYWARD
(Worcester)   (Yellow Flag)
                                  Mr. W. C. WEIR
                                           (Red Flag)

11   9   7
OSCROFT   FINNEY   MALKIN

10   8
MARTIN   BOWYER

6   5   4
SELLARS   THOMSON   MOUNTFORD

3   2
McCUE   BOURNE

L   ELLIOTT   R

STOKE CITY
Red and White Striped Shirts, White Knickers, White Stockings with Red Tops.

Patrons will be advised of any change in the above teams.

The eleven players are numbered from 1 to 11, as they were for every match. (In the illustration the goalkeepers' number 1 is taken for granted.) Thus, in different matches a player could well wear a different number. The line-up of the players on the pitch was somewhat different from today's formations. Rarely did we see 4–4–2 or 4–3–3 or 4–5–1. In fact the established formation – one that persisted for many years – was 2–3–5. In front of the goalkeeper were two full backs – a right back and a left back (numbers 2 and 3). In front of them were three half backs – a right half, a centre half and a left half (numbers 4, 5 and 6). And there were five forwards, numbered from 7 to 11 – outside right, inside right, centre forward, inside left and outside left. Numbers 7 and 11 tended to be wingers; numbers 8 and 10 (the inside forwards) tended to be the goal suppliers, and they usually played slightly behind the number 9, who was the principal striker. Actually the word 'striker' was hardly used in those days; the number 9 player was simply the centre forward or the target man, meaning he was there primarily to score goals.

That's why the number 9 on a player's shirt still tends to be associated with a team's principal goalscorer.

Life seemed so much simpler in those days when footballers wore stockings and knickers…

The Manager's Notes

Centre forwards, goalscorers, number nines, front men – we're talking strikers. Actually it's not easy to pin down exactly what we mean by strikers! Some supporters may possibly disagree with the inclusion of some of the players featured in this book – or may grumble about those who are not included. Indeed, a bit of artistic licence has been taken with regard to who is actually included, but rest assured that great thought lies behind all decisions! Every post-war forward who scored fifty or more goals for the club has been included.

We've concentrated on those players who have represented Fulham since the Second World War up to the end of season 2012–13. This covers almost seventy years and we've come up with seventy-five strikers across the eight decades. Consideration has been given to those who didn't fare so well (yes, we have had some of those…) as well as to the successful and prolific scorers. We have split these seventy-five into fifty principal strikers (indicated thus: ✦) and twenty-five other players (✦). One of the reasons we have opted for this split is that the goalscoring exploits of the 'others' often produce abnormal statistics which compare unrealistically with those of Fulham's real stalwarts – and these 'others' have consequently been omitted from some of the statistical tables.

The seventy-five players form the main body of the book. We then list twenty-five other forwards who have worn the number nine shirt for Fulham, bringing our total of strikers to a satisfying one hundred. This is followed by lists of midfield players, wingers and defenders who have also occasionally played 'centre forward' for Fulham for some reason or another.

Except where a player *has* to go in due to the sheer number of goals scored for Fulham, we have limited our main text to the 'central front player' and not those in other positions. So, in this volume the likes of Alan Mullery, Gary Barnett, Robert Wilson, Simon Morgan and Steed Malbranque are not included, despite their goalscoring figures. Do we see another book: 'Midfield Maestros'?

Almost all the principal strikers in this book have worn the coveted 'number nine' shirt at least once, or have played in what would be considered the centre forward position. The only exceptions are the specialist inside forward/half back Bobby Robson, and wingers Trevor Chamberlain and Jimmy Conway.

The text and images concentrate on the player's Fulham career. They focus on goals, but attempt also to paint a picture of what was happening at the club at the time, what the player was like in terms of style – and in some cases what kind of person he was.

To give the book a more rounded approach, we also discuss each player's early years, the clubs he played for before joining Fulham, where applicable, and his success there, as well as the clubs he played for after leaving Fulham, also where appropriate. Where information is known, each player's profile includes details of what the player did after retiring from football. Overall we believe that interesting information is included here that has not been covered in previous Fulham publications.

General statistics are included with each player profile and there is a whole range of statistics at the end of the book which throw up some quite interesting, even fascinating, facts.

Our fifty principal strikers have made over 8,000 appearances for Fulham and scored over 2,400 goals. In their careers, they have made over 16,500 league appearances (average 330 each) and scored over 5,200 league goals (average 105 each).

To put things into context, in the history of the Premier League (more than twenty years now) only one player has scored over 200 league goals. Within this book we have three players from Fulham's post-war history who have scored more than 200 league goals in their career.

Likewise, at the time of writing, only twenty-four players have managed to score 100 or more Premier League goals (of these, three just about make the grade with 100 or 101 goals). Fulham FC can boast twenty-six players (more than half of the principal strikers within this book) who have achieved more than 100 career league goals.

Whilst it is acknowledged that some of Fulham's goalscorers' efforts were not in the top tier, these statistics remain remarkable achievements. Perhaps we didn't do too badly with the 'number 9s' that have passed through Craven Cottage.

Martin Plumb
Ascot, November 2013

Teamsheet

Les BARRETT ☆	82	George JOHNSTON	114
Rod BELFITT	130	Allan JONES	64
Roy BENTLEY	51	Peter KITCHEN ☆	152
Dimitar BERBATOV ☆	246	Frank LARGE ☆	100
Luis BOA MORTE ☆	204	Graham LEGGAT ☆	58
Gary BRAZIL ☆	170	Dirk LEHMANN	191
Bobby BROWN	66	Malcolm MACDONALD ☆	103
Viv BUSBY ☆	125	Brian McBRIDE ☆	218
Johnny BYRNE ☆	98	Doug McGIBBON	16
Trevor CHAMBERLAIN ☆	44	Tony MAHONEY	131
Allan CLARKE ☆	87	Steve MARLET ☆	213
Andrew COLE ☆	226	Rodney MARSH ☆	71
Dean CONEY ☆	156	Teddy MAYBANK ☆	133
Mike CONROY	178	Dave METCHICK	67
Jimmy CONWAY ☆	91	John MITCHELL ☆	120
Maurice COOK ☆	54	Paul MOODY ☆	182
Roger CROSS ☆	117	Bobby MOSS	95
Gordon DAVIES ☆	140	Erik NEVLAND ☆	237
Brian DEAR	111	Paul PESCHISOLIDO ☆	185
Clint DEMPSEY ☆	233	Chris PIKE	166
John DOHERTY	50	Sir Bobby ROBSON ☆	22
Roy DWIGHT ☆	47	Ronnie ROOKE	12
Steve EARLE ☆	78	Leroy ROSENIOR ☆	162
Sean FARRELL ☆	176	Arthur ROWLEY	20
Joe GILROY ☆	96	Louis SAHA ☆	209
Chris GUTHRIE ☆	148	Facundo SAVA ☆	216
Kelly HAAG	173	Andy SAYER	167
Vic HALOM ☆	107	Tony SEALY	164
Barry HAYLES ☆	197	Phil STANT ☆	174
Johnny HAYNES ☆	35	Arthur STEVENS ☆	13
Heidar HELGUSON ☆	230	Reg STRATTON	65
Jackie HENDERSON	69	Jeff TAYLOR	29
Jimmy HILL ☆	30	Dale TEMPEST	159
Geoff HORSFIELD ☆	193	Bob THOMAS	16
Bobby HOWFIELD	76	Tony THORPE	189
Bedford JEZZARD ☆	17	Alan WARBOYS ☆	137
Collins JOHN ☆	223	Bobby ZAMORA ☆	239
Andrew JOHNSON ☆	242		

☆ Ashwater's 50 principal strikers

Pre-match Warm-up

 Principal strikers (see *The Manager's Notes*)   ⭐ Other strikers

The book is divided into eight decades.

The date given at the top of each player's profile is the date of his Fulham debut rather than his signing.

The statistics of career goals and appearances relate to English football only, and thus exclude Scottish, Welsh, Irish and overseas careers.

The book also does not include any statistics relating to appearances for non-league sides.

League appearances include those as a substitute.

The statistics of total career goals and appearances (as opposed to Fulham career goals and appearances) relate to *league* appearances and goals only. This is the accepted convention in almost all articles, books and publications. It would have been a monumental, and probably impossible, task to ascertain all FA Cup and League Cup appearances and goals for all players involved. This means that in a few cases a player's total league appearances and total league goals may appear as *less* than his appearances and goals for Fulham, as the Fulham totals contain cup competition figures as well.

Any Fulham goals scored in FA Cup matches on neutral grounds are classified as away goals. Goals scored at Loftus Road when the club re-located there for two seasons are classified as home goals.

Fulham appearances comprise the domestic Football League and Premiership programmes, the FA Cup, the League Cup, the Intertoto Cup and the Europa League. Other competitions (such as the Anglo-Scottish or the Anglo-Italian tournaments) are excluded. Various other minor tournaments may be mentioned throughout the text.

The League Cup is referred to as such throughout and encompasses all its incarnations, such as the Littlewoods Cup or the Milk Cup.

Where individuals are still playing, career statistics are 'to date' (up to the end of the 2012–13 season).

Often the text refers to a brace, being the usual expression for two goals scored by one player in a game.

Where match scores are quoted, Fulham's score is always given first.

Please note

The names of the top four tiers of English football have changed over the years, as shown below. Where appropriate, the official names of the four divisions are used in the text. However, in an attempt to avoid confusion, references from 1992 sometimes use the lower-case names 'first division', 'second division', 'third division' and 'fourth division' to indicate which of the four divisions is being referred to. Similarly, the phrases 'first (or top) tier', 'second tier', 'third tier' and 'fourth tier' are sometimes used.

Tier	Seasons		Official name
First	1946–1992	–	First Division
	1992–present	–	The Premiership
Second	1946–1992	–	Second Division
	1992–2004	–	Division One
	2004–present	–	Championship
Third	1946–1958	–	Third Division (North & South)
	1958–1992	–	Third Division
	1992–2004	–	Division Two
	2004–present	–	League One
Fourth	1946–1958	–	*Did not exist*
	1958–1992	–	Fourth Division
	1992–2004	–	Division Three
	2004–present	–	League Two

Neville Plumb

January 1926 – September 2013

This book is dedicated to my wonderful Dad, without whose endless giving of time, encouragement, humour and love, I would never have achieved anything.

The book starts in 1946, and this picture is from the same year.

Martin

The 1940s
(post war)

Having set this book's parameters as post-war strikers (1946 onwards), we immediately go against our own rules by starting off with a player who made his Fulham debut in 1936. Ronnie Rooke played for the club throughout the war and carried on his goalscoring exploits after the war, and that is one of the reasons why he is included here.

November 1936

Ronnie Rooke

Fulham's all-time top goalscorer.

Ronnie Rooke is, on the most literal interpretation, Fulham's leading goalscorer of all time, eclipsing both Gordon Davies and Johnny Haynes. The reason he is not at the very top of the official statistics is that his best years came during the war when only unofficial statistics were kept.

He originally joined **Stoke City** as a youth after playing for Woking and Guildford, but returned to London with **Crystal Palace**. He failed to play regularly at Selhurst Park despite scoring prolifically for the reserves, and was picked up by **Fulham** manager Jack Peart in November 1936 for the princely sum of £300. His effect was immediate, scoring a hat-trick on his debut in a 5–0 win over West Ham. He netted three more hat-tricks in his first season. He was top scorer in all his eleven seasons at Craven Cottage. He holds a Fulham record as the only Fulham player ever to score six goals in a match. He managed that feat in an FA Cup tie against Bury in January 1939 when Fulham won 6–0.

During the war years, sides were put together as scratch teams and games were played with a mixture of Fulham players and guest players, but that does not lessen Rooke's phenomenal goalscoring record. He managed to score over thirty goals in a season five times during the war. He was a ruthless finisher with both feet and good in the air, despite all of which he was awarded just a single wartime international cap.

Such was his goalscoring prowess that he managed no fewer than *ten* four-goal games and *sixteen* hat-trick games during his eleven seasons. He averaged over a goal a game during the war with 209 goals

from 199 appearances. In all (including the war years) he scored 287 goals in 309 appearances. (Outside the war years, his Fulham statistics are seventy goals from 105 appearances.)

He was leading the charts again in the first proper season after the war with thirteen league goals when he suddenly departed to **Arsenal** in December 1946 for £1,000 plus two Arsenal players. Both those players failed to make an impact at Fulham, but Rooke became a sensation in the First Division. His goals saved Arsenal from relegation, and the next season he was top scorer in the league, his thirty-three goals helping Arsenal to the championship. He was in his mid-thirties at the time. He was still playing for **Crystal Palace** at almost forty, before later playing for and managing **Bedford Town**. He died in 1985.

RONNIE ROOKE				
Post-war Fulham career – all competitions				
Season	Appearances	Goals	Home	Away
1946–1947	18	13	6	7
Total	18	13	6	7

*Total post-war career **league** appearances–151, and post-war career **league** goals–107.*

Arthur Stevens

A fine club servant for twenty years, Stevens was a Fulham team regular for eleven seasons.

Arthur Stevens was born in Wandsworth in 1921. He played for Isthmian League amateurs Wimbledon before the Second World War in 1937, for First Division Brentford in 1938 and 1939 and for Sutton United in the early war year of 1940, before joining **Fulham** as an amateur in 1941. He signed professional forms two years later. He would have played more games but the war saw him on active service overseas. He earned the nickname 'Pablo' due to his dark hair, dark complexion and European look.

Although he spent most of his career in the right-wing shirt, he was equally at home at centre forward. He took part in Fulham games during the war, and made his proper league debut in September 1946 in a Second Division 2–2 away match at Plymouth Argyle, when he was already twenty-five. His first goal followed two games later in a 4–2 victory over Leicester City at Craven Cottage. The following season, 1947–48, he went though a mid-season spell of eight goals in seven games and notched the first Fulham hat-trick of his career in a 5–2 FA Cup win over Bristol Rovers. He ended up top scorer that season with fifteen.

He was ever present in the 1948–49 Second Division championship season and netted another hat-trick in a 5–0 demolition of Queens Park Rangers in October.

Stevens shoots for goal during the home game against Chelsea in January 1952. The Chelsea player putting in a strenuous tackle is the left back, Sid Tickridge.

Goal! Bedford Jezzard looks on as Stevens beats Derby County goalkeeper Brown with a close-range shot in the First Division match at the Cottage in January 1951.

He would go on to miss just twelve league games in five seasons.

Stevens was a regular in the Fulham side for eleven seasons and, although he scored a third career hat-trick in a 3–1 win over Grimsby Town in October 1956, was more of a steady and regular scorer than a prolific one. He scored goals in every one of those eleven seasons, reaching double figures in six of them. In that 1956–57 season he finished as second-highest scorer behind goal-machine Roy Dwight.

His final full season was 1957–58 and, although he scored only four league goals, he scored five in the FA Cup including both semi-final matches against Manchester United. His goal in the 3–5 semi-final defeat at Highbury was his final Fulham goal.

Stevens was a very skilful player, some say as good as Stanley Matthews. He should have received more credit at Fulham for, apart from being a goalscorer, he regularly created goals for the other forwards. He had pace, two good feet and was exceptionally good in the air for a winger. He was also lightning quick over the first ten yards.

He had a rather peculiar running style but was very direct in approach, often hugging the touchline, but was also capable of cutting inside and letting fly at goal. When out on the wing he was an expert at hard, low crosses even at full speed which were difficult to defend against.

He finally lost his place when Fulham signed Graham Leggat, and played only three games in the

Stevens scores his final goal for the club, shooting past Manchester United's goalkeeper Harry Gregg in the FA Cup semi-final replay at Highbury in March 1958, which Fulham lost 3–5.

side that won promotion from the Second Division in 1958–59. He played his final game in a 0–1 home defeat by Liverpool at the age of thirty-seven! Because of his long and faithful service with his only club, he was awarded a joint testimonial match with equally long-serving full back Joe Bacuzzi in 1960.

Following the end of his playing career, Stevens remained at Fulham as trainer and coach for a further five years. For a brief spell of five weeks he was also caretaker manager following the resignation of Bedford Jezzard in 1964. He was badly treated and unceremoniously removed by incoming manager Vic Buckingham during his 'purge' of 1965.

Stevens gave Fulham twenty-five years service, making over 400 appearances, and his appearance total puts him inside the top ten Fulham players of all time. At that time he also became only the third player in the club's history to score over 100 goals for Fulham. He continued to have close connections with the club in his later years. Arthur Stevens died in 2007 at the age of eighty-six.

FULHAM F.C. SUPPORTERS CLUB

Souvenir Programme

GRAND TESTIMONIAL MATCH

for

J. BACUZZI

and

A. STEVENS

FULHAM v. ALL STAR XI

Wednesday May 4th 1960

Kick off 7.0. p.m.

6d

ARTHUR STEVENS
Fulham career – all competitions

Season	Appearances	Goals	Home	Away
1946–1947	16	5	3	2
1947–1948	28	15	10	5
1948–1949	43	12	11	1
1949–1950	41	5	2	3
1950–1951	47	12	10	2
1951–1952	40	7	3	4
1952–1953	36	13	10	3
1953–1954	35	11	6	5
1954–1955	23	9	5	4
1955–1956	30	9	6	3
1956–1957	42	17	9	8
1957–1958	29	9	4	5
1958–1959	3	0	0	0
Total	**413**	**124**	**79**	**45**

*Total career **league** appearances–**386**, and **league** goals–**110**.*

Doug McGibbon

His debut hat-trick was Fulham's first post-war treble.

Doug McGibbon was signed by **Fulham** from **Southampton** in January 1947. He scored a hat-trick on his debut in a 3–1 home win over Plymouth Argyle (Fulham's first treble after the cessation of hostilities) and netted eight goals in just seventeen league starts that season. He is one of only two Fulham players to score a hat-trick on their debuts, Ronnie Rooke being the other. He also made a dynamic start to the 1947–48 season, with six goals in the first three games, including a second hat-trick in a 5–0 win over Brentford on the opening day.

He remained at Fulham that season, but was in and out of the side. He felt he didn't get the service he needed at Fulham, and in the close season he joined **Bournemouth**, where he scored a spectacular sixty-five goals in just 103 league games. His Fulham record was eighteen goals in forty-two appearances. He died in 2002.

	DOUG McGIBBON *Fulham career – all competitions*			
Season	**Appearances**	**Goals**	**Home**	**Away**
1946–1947	17	8	4	4
1947–1948	25	10	4	6
Total	42	18	8	10

*Total career **league** appearances–**158**, and **league** goals–**92**.*

Bob Thomas

The top scorer in the 1948–49 promotion season.

Bob Thomas was signed from **Plymouth Argyle** for £4,000 in the summer of 1947 and scored on his debut for **Fulham** against Brentford in August 1947, but managed only six goals in all competitions that season. Feeding off Arthur Rowley, he subsequently flourished and in Fulham's 1948–49 promotion season scored twenty-three league goals, finishing top scorer. Goals were tougher to find back in the First Division in 1949–50, but once again he finished top scorer with eleven goals.

In the 1950–51 season, he topped the goalscorer charts for the third season in a row, netting double figures again with fourteen. Despite scoring a number of braces, he never scored a hat-trick for Fulham. He scored only three goals in the 1951–52 relegation season before joining **Crystal Palace** where he scored thirty-one goals in ninety-six league games. He ended up with fifty-seven goals in 176 appearances for Fulham. He died in 1990.

	BOB THOMAS *Fulham career – all competitions*			
Season	**Appearances**	**Goals**	**Home**	**Away**
1947–1948	41	6	3	3
1948–1949	41	23	15	8
1949–1950	44	11	5	6
1950–1951	38	14	8	6
1951–1952	12	3	1	2
Total	176	57	32	25

*Total career **league** appearances–**204**, and **league** goals–**103**.*

Bedford Jezzard

Thirty-eight league goals in one season – will that post-war record ever be beaten?

Bedford Jezzard was born in Clerkenwell in London and played football as a junior with Croxley Boys and later made sporadic appearances for Edgware Town. He appeared as an amateur for League South Watford in the 1944–45 season. After Jezzard's army service in India, manager Jack Peart snatched him from under Watford's nose and he joined **Fulham** in 1948. Originally he joined in an amateur capacity combining football with a role as a local club secretary, and remained a part-time player until the 1950–51 season when he signed professional forms.

Although a prime centre forward, he made his debut for Fulham as an amateur at inside left (10) in the 1948–49 season, the number nine shirt being held by the experienced Arthur Stevens and later Arthur Rowley. In his first season he was an integral part of the side that won promotion as champions of the Second Division. After just three games for the reserves he made his Second Division debut in a 1–2 defeat at Cardiff City but retained his place for the rest of the season. Despite being a natural goalscorer, he had to wait until his sixth game for his first goal in a 2–1 victory over Sheffield Wednesday at Hillsborough. His first home goal arrived the following week.

Still finding his feet in top-class football, he scored six goals in his first season, and finished fourth highest scorer behind Bob Thomas, Rowley and Stevens. Fulham's first season back in the top flight, 1949–50, was a difficult one and Fulham scored just over forty goals all season. The young Jezzard, however, was second highest goalscorer with a respectable eight. The next season was very similar and a struggle for goals especially after Rowley's departure, and Jezzard finished with nine goals. After three seasons he had never scored more than one goal in a single game.

The 1951–52 season saw Fulham relegated. Jezzard, now wearing the number 9 shirt, was injured for part of the season and played only twenty-seven league games, but still managed to finish as top scorer with eight goals; he also netted the first brace of his career in a 5–0 home win over Stoke City.

Back in the Second Division in 1952–53, he was ever-present and his skills really came to the fore and although Fulham finished eighth they scored over eighty goals and Jezzard's contribution was thirty-five, over 40% of Fulham's total. This included his first hat-trick in a 4–1 home win over Rotherham United in February and nine games where he scored twice.

The following season proved to be 'Jezzard's year'. Due to their continuing defensive deficiencies, Fulham once again finished only eighth. However, they scored a massive 107 goals. Jezzard was again ever-present and scored a post-war record of thirty-eight goals, 35% of the total. It is a total unlikely to be equalled or beaten in modern-day football. He actually scored in twenty-five of the forty-two league matches (60%). Prompted by the emerging skills of Johnny Haynes, this amazing tally included four goals in a 5–2 win over Derby County at Craven Cottage in October, a second hat-trick in a 3–1 home win over Plymouth Argyle in December and eight further games where he scored twice.

In the year between March 1953 and April 1954 he represented the Football League in three games. The Football League won them all with Jezzard scoring three times. His goalscoring feats led him to being awarded an England cap in May as a Second Division player. He took part in the 1–7 annihilation of the England team by the majestic Hungarian team in Budapest. After the 3–6 humbling by the 'Magnificent Magyars' at Wembley the year before, it seemed poor judgment to have pitched this youngster into his first international and he had little chance to show his skills. Jezzard was also included in the 1954 World Cup squad of twenty-two, and like Johnny Haynes was one of the five players held in reserve at home in case of injury. Neither player had to travel.

Jezzard was only five foot ten, and weighed just a little over twelve stone, but he was immensely strong, determined and difficult to knock off the ball. Even on heavy, muddy Fifties pitches he was extremely quick off the mark and over the ground, and often just out-ran Second Division defenders. With Haynes' quick thinking and through passes, Jezzard was adept at springing the offside trap of opposing defences and running half the length of the field to round the goalkeeper and score. Like most quality spearheads, he scored effortlessly with either foot. For a small centre forward he was strong and powerful in the air, unsettling the strongest defences. Ninety minutes against him was apparently like 'repeatedly jumping into a brick wall'.

Undaunted by his England disappointment, Jezzard maintained his exuberant goalscoring form in 1954–55. He missed only three league games and scored another twenty-three goals, the same number as the talented Bobby Robson. He scored in all of the opening seven matches of the season and registered ten goals in the first ten league games. Included in this season was his third hat-trick, in the 5–1 win over Swansea Town in April.

Towards the end of the season he made his first appearance for the England 'B' team and responded with a hat-trick in a 4–0 trouncing of West Germany in the Glueckauf Stadion in front of 42,000. Two months later he played again and scored in a 2–1 victory over Yugoslavia.

In the 1955–56 season, Jezzard missed just four league games and plundered another twenty-seven goals. He scored in the opening three fixtures and this included a four-goal haul against Barnsley in

Jezzard (seated) greets a young Johnny Haynes in the Fulham dressing room in the early 1950s. Also in this typical hand-coloured picture of the era is left-winger Charlie Mitten.

a 5–1 home victory. In October he went one better, scoring all five goals in a 5–0 walloping of Hull City at the Cottage, writing himself into the club's record books. The season also included another five braces. Although not realised at the time, he scored his final goal in what proved to be his last match, fittingly an exciting 4–3 victory over Nottingham Forest at the Cottage.

Once again he was way ahead in being top scorer. The brilliant triumvirate of Robson (8), Jezzard (9) and Haynes (10) was now the envy of most clubs in the land. Jezzard's *anni mirabiles* were between 1952 and 1956 and during that time, being fed by the passes of Johnny Haynes and Bobby Robson, he scored a phenomenal 123 times in 161 league matches (an average of over thirty goals every season). Despite this, in his entire career Jezzard never scored an FA Cup goal for Fulham.

In October 1955, Jezzard had won his third cap for the England 'B' team, scoring twice in a 5–1 victory against Yugoslavia. He also represented the London XI (in what was the forerunner of the Inter-Cities Fairs Cup) with Bobby Robson and Charlie Mitten and scored twice against Frankfurt at Wembley in a 3–2 London victory. A month later, he was awarded his second England cap, playing alongside Johnny Haynes in a 3–0 win over Northern Ireland at Wembley. He should have been awarded more caps, but found it difficult to displace a front line assembled from the talents of Tom Finney, Stanley Matthews, Nat Lofthouse and Tommy Taylor.

Alongside Haynes, he journeyed to South Africa in the summer of 1956 as part of an FA XI on a goodwill tour. Tragically, during a rough and tumble match against South Africa, whilst running at full tilt Jezzard was badly tackled by a full back, fell and fractured his ankle. He spent time in hospital in South Africa and returned to England in plaster and on crutches. It was originally thought that Jezzard would recover, but in the ensuing months it became clear that he would never be the player he was and, after turning his ankle again in a pre-season match in August 1957, he immediately announced his retirement. Fulham rewarded him with a job as youth team coach straight away. He was coach for just a year and, when the wife of manager Dugald Livingstone failed to settle in the south, Jezzard was appointed Fulham manager in August 1958.

He was just thirty-one and the promotion was a gamble, but he was a genial, ethical man and popular amongst the players and supporters alike. With an attack-minded team, he returned Fulham to the First Division in 1958–59 at his very first attempt and to tenth position the year after. He was manager through some tough times but also took Fulham to the 1962 FA Cup semi-final. He enabled Fulham to retain their First Division status in his six full seasons in charge. A modest and unassuming man, he enjoyed the role and was able to radiate a quiet authority and to command respect from all the senior players at the club.

With the abolition of the maximum wage, Fulham were unable to compete with salaries offered by other clubs and often needed transfer funds. In March 1964, Fulham sold the outstanding young, home-grown player, Alan Mullery, to Tottenham Hotspur without consulting the manager. For Jezzard, who was a man of principle, this was the beginning of the end. Six months later, he resigned from the job and walked away from football completely, disenchanted with changes in the game. He retired to the licensing trade and ran the Thatched House public house in Hammersmith for a number of years.

Sadly, in his later years Beddy Jezzard suffered from Alzheimer's disease and died in May 2005 aged seventy-seven, just six months before the death of his friend Johnny Haynes.

Fulham v Bristol City, September 1955, and Jezzard challenges for the ball with City's left half, Alan Williams. The original caption to this picture identified Jezzard as the London club 'raider' – a description of a number 9 player that Ashwater hadn't thought of!

BEDFORD JEZZARD
Fulham career – all competitions

Season	Appearances	Goals	Home	Away
1948–1949	31	6	3	3
1949–1950	41	8	4	4
1950–1951	38	9	5	4
1951–1952	28	8	8	0
1952–1953	43	35	22	13
1953–1954	45	38	24	14
1954–1955	40	23	12	11
1955–1956	40	27	22	5
Total	306	154	100	54

*Total career **league** appearances–292, and **league** goals–154.*

Arthur Rowley

The League's highest-ever scorer, with hat-tricks during his brief spell with Fulham.

Arthur Rowley was signed by **Fulham** from **West Bromwich Albion** in December 1948 in a deal that saw that saw Ernie Shepherd going in the opposite direction.

Rowley was a one-man goal machine. He was the missing link in the team that won promotion that season, scoring an incredible nineteen goals in twenty-two league matches. This included eight in three games in January with a four against Bury and a hat-trick against Plymouth, and there were three braces as well, including one in a 2–0 win over West Ham United in the final game that guaranteed the championship.

Rowley found it much harder in the First Division with only seven goals. At the end of the 1949–50 season he was transferred to **Leicester City**, for whom he scored 251 league goals.

He subsequently netted 152 goals for **Shrewsbury Town** as player/manager.

He holds the record for the most goals in the history of English league football, scoring 433 from 619 league games, though the vast majority of these goals were scored outside the top flight of English football.

He died in 2002.

ARTHUR ROWLEY
Fulham career – all competitions

Season	Appearances	Goals	Home	Away
1948–1949	23	19	13	6
1949–1950	36	7	5	2
Total	59	29	18	8

*Total career **league** appearances–**619**, and **league** goals–**433**.*

Seated behind the Division Two trophy, Rowley poses proudly in Fulham's championship-winning team of 1948–49.

The 1950s

Sir Bobby Robson

A much respected player and manager – a true Fulham legend.

Sir Bobby Robson CBE was born in Sacriston, County Durham, the fourth of five sons born to Philip and Lilian Robson. When he was a few months old, Robson's family moved to the nearby village of Langley Park where his father was a coal miner. He grew up in tough living and working conditions, and as a boy he was often taken by his father to watch Newcastle United, an afternoon requiring a thirty-four-mile round trip. He grew up watching the skills of inside forwards Len Shackleton and Jackie Milburn who were his role models.

Robson attended the Waterhouses Secondary School, and as the school team were not in a league he began to play instead for Langley Park Juniors on Saturday mornings at the age of eleven. By the time he was fifteen, he was representing the club at U-18 level. Robson left school aged fifteen to start work as an electrician's apprentice for the National Coal Board in the Langley Park colliery.

In May 1950, Fulham manager Bill Dodgin Snr made a personal visit to the Robson household to offer Bobby a professional contract. Despite being offered a contract by nearby Middlesbrough, and attracting some degree of interest from Newcastle (both of the First Division), the offer made by Dodgin was too attractive to turn down, so he signed for **Fulham** and moved to London playing as an inside forward. He moved into digs and established a life-long friendship with Fulham defender Tom Wilson. One reason for the move was that he considered he would have an improved chance of a league breakthrough with Fulham who were also at the time in the First Division.

Although Robson had signed professionally, his father strongly advised that he should continue his work as an electrician. Therefore, he spent the day working at the Festival of Britain site whilst training three nights a week at Craven Cottage. Eventually this took its toll and he gave up his trade to concentrate on full-time professional football.

In April 1951, Robson made his first-team debut for Fulham at eighteen, in a 2–2 draw at Sheffield Wednesday, his only appearance in that 1950–51 season. The following season he made sixteen league appearances playing at both inside left and inside right with a single appearance on the wing. He scored his first Fulham goal back in the north-east against Newcastle rivals Sunderland in a 2–2 draw, and added two more in the final three matches of the season. However, it was not enough to save Fulham who finished bottom of the table and were relegated.

From the start of the 1952–53 season Robson became a regular, settling into and making the number

eight shirt his own. He made a terrific start with eight goals in the first eight league games, including three braces. He was still under twenty and the pace of goals reduced for a while, but he came back with three more braces in his final six league games. His total for his first full season was an impressive nineteen, second leading scorer behind goal-machine Jezzard.

He missed a quarter of the 1953–54 season, but still managed double figures again. He scored twice on the opening day in a 4–4 draw with Bristol Rovers and scored twice on two further occasions. He also opened his account in the FA Cup with a goal against Leyton Orient. He was third highest scorer with fourteen and the trio of Jezzard, Haynes and Robson had scored seventy-one goals between them. A relatively poor defence meant that the Fulham side still finished mid-table.

A high point of Robson's career at Fulham came in the following season, 1954–55, when he was joint

top scorer with Jezzard with twenty-three goals, which included four braces. Once again the powerful front three had scored over fifty goals but Fulham still languished in the bottom half of the Second Division table.

In the 1955–56 season Robson, for the fourth season running, scored double figures, netting ten including two braces. His final goal and appearance came in March, in a 1–2 defeat at Leicester City. He had also won an England U-23 cap by now, scoring on his debut in a 5–1 win over Denmark, England's other four goals coming from Johnny Haynes (2) and Alf Stokes (2). (Stokes would later join Fulham.) Fulham by this time were short of money and, having turned down offers for about three years, finally capitulated and Robson was back in the First Division with **West Bromwich Albion**. He was signed by Vic Buckingham who would later manage Fulham. The transfer fee was £25,000 and was a club record for Albion at the time.

He made his Albion debut in a 4–0 home defeat by Manchester City the following week, but added just one goal in the ten games before the end of the season. In 1956–57 season he managed double figures again with thirteen. His top-scoring season for Albion was 1957–58 when he was the club's leading league goalscorer; his tally of twenty-seven goals in all competitions included four in a 5–1 win against Burnley. During this season he won his first England cap when, playing alongside Johnny Haynes, he scored twice in a 4–0 friendly victory over France. He was however omitted from the next game. He won two more caps prior to the World Cup in 1958 and represented England in two of the group stage matches. England were knocked out of the competition at the group stage by Russia in a play-off match.

Vic Buckingham considered Robson as more of a playmaker and sought to pull him back into midfield and eventually Robson settled into the half-back line as number 4 or number 6 (right half or left half). His goal totals diminished immediately and he scored only four league and one FA Cup goal in 1958–59. It continued the same way: in 1959–60 he missed just one league game and scored six; in 1960–61, now as captain of the Albion side, he missed just two games and scored five. In this season he also won the majority of his England caps winning ten between May 1960 and May 1961. Included in that set are Robson's other two England goals, one in a 9–3 thrashing of Scotland at Wembley in the Home International Championship and another a month later against Mexico.

In his final season at the Hawthorns, 1961–62, he missed only three matches scoring four goals. He

also won his last five England caps, the last of the twenty being against Switzerland in May 1962. In total, Robson played 257 games for West Bromwich Albion scoring sixty-one goals. In six and a quarter seasons, he missed just twenty-three league games in all, thirteen of those in one season. Robson was selected by England for the 1962 World Cup finals too, but an ankle injury sustained in a club friendly game in Chile meant that he could not take part. A young player, a certain Bobby Moore, replaced him and Robson didn't play for England again.

Former Fulham player Archie Macaulay had replaced Buckingham at the Hawthorns and following Johnny Haynes' pay rise to £100 per week (after the abolition of the maximum wage brought about by Jimmy Hill) Robson as captain of the Midlands side tried to re-negotiate his own contract. Vice-chairman Jim Gaunt would not budge and Robson put in a transfer request, as a result of which he was stripped of the captaincy and not supported by Macaulay. He was also refused a testimonial.

Although Steve Earle scored a memorable hat-trick at Northampton in the relegation clash in April 1966, it was Robson who set Fulham on the way to victory with this superb long-range shot. Robson is way out of the picture.

Fulham came to the rescue and with the help of fans' money, Robson returned to Craven Cottage in August 1962 for a fee of £20,000 with Fulham doubling his £25 per week wage. Robson was approaching thirty now and slowing a little and was used by Fulham as a general midfield player, with as much emphasis on defence as attack. In 1962–63 he scored just twice and only once in the league. Fulham stuck around the lower-middle of the First Division the following season and Robson netted just once, on Boxing Day in the 10–1 win over Ipswich Town. During this time, Robson took his coaching badges and (with Fulham's blessing) did some preliminary coaching work with Oxford University.

In 1964–65 Robson, now thirty-two, played in all of Fulham's forty-seven competitive games, scoring just once in a critical 3–2 win over Blackburn Rovers in April which helped secure points that would save Fulham from the drop. Following the sale of Jim Langley to QPR, Robson became the Fulham penalty taker in the 1965–66 season. Fulham were in the mire again but eventually escaped with a late run. Robson scored six that season, one against his old West Bromwich Albion club. His goals were now mainly penalties or long-range shots. His last ever goal for Fulham was appropriately against Newcastle United on Tyneside on the final day of the season.

Bobby Robson was almost six feet tall, and could head a ball, but he was mainly noted for his ball play and midfield skills. When in the forward line, he had an eye for goal and many of his efforts were spectacular. But it was his general play in the middle of the field that took the eye. He was a strong tackler, an accurate passer but most of all an intelligent reader of the game. His elegant control and running made him such a fine all-round player. He was also extremely fit

and could keep up the quality of his play for the full ninety minutes.

Off the field at Fulham, he was renowned for his humour and geniality and frequently attended Fulham social functions. His humble roots made it very easy for him to get close to the fans with whom he enjoyed a good relationship.

The 1966–67 season saw Bobby Robson miss just one of Fulham's forty-seven competitive games and he failed to score in a season for the first time in his career. Fulham played some attractive stuff and finished clear of the drop. Fulham had made a quick trip to the USA that season and Robson had played in Canada as a close-season guest during his playing career. He had been approached over a coaching role in Canada and decided towards the end of that season to cease playing. The Fulham crowd were disappointed but understood and the thirty-four-year-old played his final game on the last day of the season when Fulham lost 2–3 at home to eventual runners-up Nottingham Forest.

It brought to an end a seventeen-year career of 627 games and 141 goals. Although he admitted to having been fortunate in respect of long-term injuries, in his fifteen full years as a professional (starting 1952–53), Robson missed just sixty-four league games out of a possible 630, which means he played in almost 90% of all league games, a remarkable record. However, just like his good friend Johnny Haynes he had nothing to show for his club career – a fourth-place finish with West Bromwich Albion and a cup semi-final with the same club were the closest he ever came to glory.

Despite the offer of a player/manager role at Southend United, Robson left Fulham in the summer and accepted a three-year deal with Canada's

Robson played his last match for the club against Nottingham Forest on the final day of the 1966–67 season. Here he leaves the pitch surrounded by players and supporters, facing a change of career and destined to become an illustrious manager of clubs and country.

Vancouver Royals. He was to be player/manager in their inaugural 1968 season in the North American Soccer League (NASL). He persuaded a number of English players to follow him including his ex-Albion team-mate Bobby Cram and young Fulham player Henry Hill. What had seemed at first glance to be a great adventure and a golden opportunity quickly turned sour, with players and staff not being paid.

The position proved difficult; a long-distance joint-ownership agreement gave the Hungarian footballer Ferenc Puskás control over the San Francisco section of the squad, while Robson took care of the Vancouver squad. Robson was dissatisfied by this situation and the unstable control over coaching and team selection.

In January 1968 manager Vic Buckingham's tenure was extinguished at Craven Cottage and Fulham offered Robson a way out and a route back home with a contract as manager which he gladly accepted. He returned to England having never kicked a ball in six months abroad.

Fulham were already looking dead and buried in the 1967–68 campaign and Robson could not save them; a number of quality players – Langley, Mullery and Leggat – had gone, he himself had retired, George Cohen had been lost to injury and players such as Johnny Haynes and Tony Macedo were at the tail end of their careers. He started with a nervous 4–2 FA Cup win over non-league Macclesfield Town and his first league game in charge was a 2–7 defeat at Upton Park. Fulham were relegated and lost star forward Allan Clarke.

The 1968–69 season started well, but a goal drought and loss of form left the team struggling in the relegation spots before November. With little cash available and only a few real assets at his disposal,

Robson needed time to rebuild, but a cowardly Fulham board led by the unpopular Eric Miller denied him that opportunity and dispensed with his services far too quickly. Robson was devastated and learned of his dismissal after just ten months via a newspaper billboard. Miller was proven wrong inasmuch as both Johnny Haynes and Bill Dodgin Jnr were unable to save the club from a second successive relegation.

Fortunately Robson wasn't unemployed for long. Whilst doing some temporary scouting work for Chelsea under former Fulham coach Dave Sexton, he met Ipswich directors at Portman Road, and after discussions was offered the manager's post there. After four mediocre seasons, albeit in the First Division, Robson led Ipswich to fourth place in the league and success in the Texaco Cup in the 1972–73 season. In the following nine seasons, Ipswich only once finished lower than sixth place in the First Division, in the 1977–78 season.

However, that season was a success too with a 1–0 victory over Arsenal in the FA Cup final. His reign at Ipswich lasted for thirteen years, during which time the club twice finished as League runners-up, and made regular appearances in European competitions, winning the UEFA Cup in 1981 with a 5–4 aggregate victory over Dutch side AZ 67 Alkmaar. During his thirteen-year tenure, he brought in only fourteen players from other clubs most notably Allan Hunter, Bryan Hamilton and Paul Mariner, relying instead on players developed through Ipswich's youth programmes. This included a host of players who would become seasoned internationals, such as Terry Butcher, Mick Mills and John Wark. Robson showed what a tactical genius he was, displaying a talent for developing new players, with his good interpersonal skills, caring attitude, hard work and enthusiasm helping them to achieve their very best.

Robson's achievements with Ipswich earned him a job offer from the Football Association for the position of national coach, and with a heavy heart he declined an offer of a ten-year contract extension and increased salary from Ipswich director Patrick Cobbold. In July 1982, two days after England were knocked out of the World Cup, he succeeded former Fulham team-mate Ron Greenwood as England's coach, selecting former West Bromwich Albion team-mate Don Howe as his chief assistant.

It was not all plain sailing in the early stages and, when Robson's team failed to qualify for the European Championships in 1984, he honourably offered his resignation and it was declined. However, England did qualify in style for the World Cup in 1986. A shoulder injury to namesake skipper Bryan Robson and the sending-off of Ray Wilkins didn't give England a good start, but England qualified at the group stage by beating Poland, and then Paraguay in the knock-out stages, but were eliminated by the 'Hand of God' goal from Argentina's Maradona which disgusted Robson.

England qualified for the 1988 European Championships with impressive form, but had a disastrous tournament losing all three group stage matches. Some months later, a disappointing draw in a friendly with Saudi Arabia prompted Robson once again to offer his resignation, but it was again declined.

Robson led England through qualification for the 1990 World Cup without conceding a goal. They were one of six seeded teams and were once again placed in a group with the Netherlands and Ireland, with Egypt the fourth side. As in the 1986 World Cup, Robson was denied the services of captain Bryan Robson. England topped their qualifying group, gaining four points from their three games.

This success was followed by victories over Belgium and Cameroon during the knock-out stages to set up a semi-final with West Germany. England lost the match in a penalty shoot-out, after the score had been tied at 1–1 after extra time, Germany's goal being an own goal deflected in by former Fulham defender Paul Parker. Robson remains only the second coach after Sir Alf Ramsey to take England to a World Cup semi-final, and the only coach to do so on foreign soil. He was awarded the CBE that year.

The FA informed Bobby before the tournament that his contract would not be renewed. Therefore he moved to Holland to coach PSV Eindhoven succeeding manager Guus Hiddink. It was a culture shock and an adventure. Despite Robson having to handle some difficult players, PSV won the Dutch league in both the 1990–91 and 1991–92 seasons. However, this still wasn't enough; the team had not made the progress expected by the board in European competitions and Robson was informed that he would be leaving the club at the end of his second season.

Robson moved on to Sporting Lisbon in the summer of 1992, where his Portuguese interpreter was a young

Manager Robson chats with new signing Reg Matthewson in the Fulham dressing room in February 1968. Not even the arrival of the class defender could save Fulham from relegation at the end of the season.

José Mourinho. The club was in a poor condition, but Robson guided them to a third-place finish in his first season in charge (1992–93). However, he had a poor relationship with the club's president who wanted control of players and team affairs, and Robson was sacked after just eighteen months, with the Lisbon club at the *top* of the league table. The club president cited the club's early exit from the UEFA Cup as the reason for the dismissal.

Sporting's rivals, FC Porto, moved quickly to employ Robson, with Mourinho appointed as his assistant manager. Porto were another club in a poor state and in decline when Robson arrived and the average attendance had dwindled to 10,000. The club promptly went on to beat Sporting in the Portuguese Cup final. This achievement was followed with successive league titles in the 1994–95 and 1995–96 seasons, as Robson once again demonstrated his coaching prowess. It was at this time that cancer began to affect him and he missed some months of the second season with melanoma. Such was the strength of the team put together by Robson that after his departure Porto won three more *successive* championships.

A chance phone call during the summer of 1996 from Barcelona to discuss a player became an offer of employment with the Spanish club. Robson took over in July and made Mourinho's move with him to the club a condition of his employment. One of the key decisions Robson made during his brief tenure at Barcelona was the US$20m signing of Ronaldo. The player was influential in a season when Barcelona won the Spanish Cup, the Spanish Super Cup and the European Cup Winners Cup. Robson himself was voted European manager of the year for 1996–97. The

Author Martin Plumb had the pleasure of meeting Sir Bobby whilst researching Ashwater's book on Johnny Haynes. The great man afforded Martin hours of his time, and was knowledgeable and gracious.

next season saw him moved upstairs to the position of general manager, with Louis Van Gaal taking over the managerial role, but he stayed in this position for only one season.

The lure of coaching and managing proved too much and Robson returned to the Netherlands and his previous club PSV Eindhoven on a one-season deal. PSV missed out on the league title in 1998–99, finishing third behind Feyenoord and Willem II. However, Robson still led the club to victory in the Dutch Supercup and also to qualification for the Champions League on the final day of the season.

After almost a decade abroad, Robson returned to England where he was expected to take up an appointment with the FA, but following the resignation of Ruud Gullit, he took over as manager of his hometown club Newcastle United in September 1999. In his first match in charge, bottom of the league Newcastle faced second bottom Sheffield Wednesday, and thrashed them 8–0. Although they didn't pull up any trees, the Geordies finished a comfortable eleventh in the 1999–2000 season, a position they repeated in 2000–01.

In 2001–02 Newcastle, having at one stage been bottom of the Premier League, finished in fourth place, qualifying for the Champions League. The season culminated with Robson being knighted for his services to football. In 2002–03 Newcastle went one better, finishing third, thus ensuring qualification for the Champions League for the second consecutive year. However, Robson was unable to guide Newcastle through the Champions League qualifying rounds and the club dropped back into the UEFA Cup during the 2003–04 season. During this time, Robson was inducted into the English Football Hall of Fame in recognition of his impact as a football manager. At the end of that season, Newcastle United finished fifth in the table, five points short of the Champions League qualifying fourth place, but reached the semi-finals of the UEFA Cup, before losing to Marseilles.

He held the Newcastle post for virtually five years, when he was controversially dismissed in a shabby fashion by Freddy Shepherd, after a poor start to the 2004–05 Premier League season, Shepherd citing this and an alleged 'discontent' in the dressing room. Even a genial man like Robson was scathing over the actions of Shepherd and fellow director Douglas Hall with regard to their running of the club, in particular his being kept in the dark as to the management of the finances and contracts at St James' Park. Despite the poor treatment meted out to Robson by the Newcastle directors he remained a hero amongst the fans.

Robson's last real involvement with football was as consultant to Steve Staunton, the manager of the Republic of Ireland. He held that post for almost two years, standing down in November 2007 after the Republic's final match in their unsuccessful qualifying campaign for the 2008 European Championships.

It was an open book that Bobby Robson had been fighting cancer for over fifteen years. He had suffered bowel cancer, melanoma and lung cancer. He had had several operations and fought back each time and appeared to be in fairly decent health. He had a brain tumour removed which left him partially paralysed and although he continued to fight, work and act as he always had, by 2007 he knew he had a terminal prognosis. His illness was controlled by chemotherapy and he spent his remaining time campaigning and raising huge sums of money for research and treatment of the condition. By March 2013, the foundation had raised over £5m.

When Sir Bobby Robson died on 31st July 2009, a huge outpouring of grief came from every area of the game and every corner of the globe. The footballing fraternity had lost a loved genius and the world had lost a very special person whose humanity, compassion, honesty, manners and basic human qualities had shone out throughout his life. A thanksgiving service was held in September 2009 at Durham Cathedral. One thousand invited guests attended the service, which was also broadcast live on national television, as well as to Newcastle United's St James' Park, Ipswich Town's Portman Road ground, and Craven Cottage.

In May 2011 a memorial garden which had been created on a spot close to the St James' Park stadium was unveiled. Part of the garden consists of five carved stones with each one representing an era of Sir Bobby's life.

During his lifetime in football he won many awards, too many to be detailed here, but amongst them are:
• a life-size statue placed outside Ipswich Town's Portman Road ground;
• being made the honorary president of Ipswich Town Football Club;

- the re-naming of the North Stand at Portman Road the Bobby Robson Stand;
- the Freedom of the town of Ipswich;
- the Freedom of the city of Durham;
- the Freedom of the city of Newcastle upon Tyne;
- a life-size statue placed outside Newcastle United's St James' Park ground;
- the awarding of the Emerald UEFA Order of Merit award, given to 'individuals who have dedicated their talents to the good of the game';
- a Lifetime Achievement Award at the BBC's Sports Personality of the Year in recognition of 'his contribution as both player and manager in a career spanning more than half a century'.

Posthumous awards and dedications include:
- the FIFA fair play award, for the 'gentlemanly qualities he showed throughout his career as a player and coach';
- the East Coast train operating company naming one of its Class 91 electric locomotives the *Sir Bobby Robson*, which was unveiled at Newcastle Central station;
- the Port of Tyne Authority naming its new work boat the *Sir Bobby Robson*.

SIR BOBBY ROBSON
Fulham career – all competitions

Season	Appearances	Goals	Home	Away
1950–1951	1	0	0	0
1951–1952	16	3	1	2
1952–1953	36	19	11	8
1953–1954	34	14	9	5
1954–1955	43	23	12	11
1955–1956	27	10	5	5
1962–1963	38	2	2	0
1963–1964	42	1	1	0
1964–1965	47	2	2	0
1965–1966	39	6	2	4
1966–1967	47	0	0	0
Total	370	80	45	35

*Total career **league** appearances–**583**, and **league** goals–**133**.*

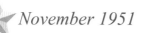

November 1951

Jeff Taylor

A non-regular player who netted two Fulham hat-tricks.

Jeff Taylor was a skilful inside forward who was signed from **Huddersfield Town** in November 1951, but he was kept out of the side because of the emerging talent that was Bobby Robson. He scored two hat-tricks for **Fulham**, the first against Middlesbrough in a 6–0 home win just a month after joining, and two years later in the remarkable 5–5 third-round FA Cup match at Grimsby. He made thirty-five appearances and scored eighteen goals, one every other game. He moved on to **Brentford** in 1954. He scored almost eighty league goals for the three league clubs that he represented. He is one of only seven post-war Fulham players to score an FA Cup hat-trick. He died in 2010.

JEFF TAYLOR
Fulham career – all competitions

Season	Appearances	Goals	Home	Away
1951–1952	21	5	4	1
1952–1953	2	1	0	1
1953–1954	12	12	7	5
Total	35	18	11	7

*Total career **league** appearances–**195**, and **league** goals–**75**.*

 *March 1952*

Jimmy Hill

Probably the most influential footballing figure of the twentieth century.

Jimmy Hill was born in Balham, south London, into a middle-class family. He attended the Henry Compton Grammar School in Clapham from 1939 to 1945, and after leaving school he worked as a clerk in the Stock Exchange. He was then called up for his national service as a clerk in the Royal Army Service Corps in which he attained the rank of corporal and was considered a potential candidate for officer training. He was a good footballer and during his time in the army he was, fortunately, pitched in with nine professional footballers 'on enforced sabbatical'. He held his own alongside these players who taught him the ropes and gave him a grounding in professional football.

Above: Roy Bentley evades Bristol Rovers goalkeeper Ron Nicholls and passes the ball to Jimmy Hill who scores in the 3–2 victory at the Cottage in March 1957.

After national service, he decided to leave the Stock Exchange and give football a try. During his army days he had been noticed by **Reading** manager Ted Drake (later to work at Fulham) who encouraged Hill to come to Elm Park. After a trial game against Brentford, Hill spent six months as an amateur at Third Division Reading mostly playing for the third XI or the reserve XI. At that time Hill wanted to remain an amateur and earn his living outside the game.

Reading declined to sign him anyway as a professional, and quoted cost reduction as well. So Hill decided to visit Second Division **Brentford** as Drake said that they might be interested. The Bees immediately offered Hill a professional contract which he accepted. For the next four years, Jimmy Hill played as a wing half and occasional forward for Brentford and during his time at Griffin Park scored ten goals in eighty-three league games. After a day's training, he would still busy himself taking his coaching badge, coaching the Oxford and London University football sides and writing a column for the local paper.

In March 1952, Hill joined **Fulham** in a transfer that took Fulham player Jimmy Bowie in the opposite direction to Brentford. Initially it was not viewed as a popular signing, but gradually Jimmy won the home crowd over. He made his First Division debut and scored in a 2–4 defeat at Blackpool, his only goal in six appearances. Fulham were relegated that season. The following season, 1952–53, playing as a half back, he did not find the net at all in thirty-one games.

During the following three seasons, goals were equally elusive, but Hill was then more of a provider, putting long passes forward for the front three of Robson, Jezzard and Haynes. He felt he could do better as an inside forward and the latter stages of the 1955–56 season saw him playing in the number 8 shirt. Those three seasons saw him net just nine goals in 102 appearances.

However, the departure of Bobby Robson to West Bromwich Albion and the career-ending injury to Jezzard saw Hill given a more permanent opportunity in the forward line. His 1956–57 season was pretty barren with five goals in total, but he managed three goals in the final seven matches. In the following season, however, he was prominent with twenty-two goals from forty-four appearances, ending the season as second-highest scorer behind the free-scoring Roy Dwight. During that season, in a great run of form for both Hill and the team, he netted five goals in a 6–1 win at Doncaster Rovers, just one of two players in Fulham's history to score five goals in one away match. (The other is Steve Earle in the match at Halifax Town in September 1969.) He also played a major role in Fulham's run to the FA Cup semi-final with six goals in seven matches, scoring in the semi-final.

Goals were again scarce the following season when Fulham won promotion. Hill couldn't 'buy a goal' and the crowd were getting at him. However, in probably the most important match of the 1958–59 season against promotion rivals Sheffield Wednesday at Craven Cottage over Easter, with Fulham desperately hanging on to a 3–2 lead, Jimmy Hill netted a late hat-trick, all headed goals, to give the Cottagers a resounding 6–2 victory, a result that went a long way to guaranteeing the team promotion.

Due to his prominent chin and a beard, Jimmy Hill earned the nickname 'The Rabbi' at the Cottage, and the chant 'Give it to the Rabbi' was often heard. By his own admission he was not the most skilful of players, but he made up for this by the sheer effort and bustling style he put into a game. He was very fit and would run and run for the full ninety minutes tiring out defences. He knew his limitations and stuck to them.

He was always one of the most positive people around, and his game revolved around energy and

boundless enthusiasm. He was always looking to support team-mates when he didn't have the ball, never shirked a tackle and was constantly searching for a bit of space in which to play. One of his key attributes was his tireless ability to run 'all over the place' covering acres of ground. He rarely kept to his position on the field and would often be found out on the wing or at centre forward. This often confused Second Division defenders, who would follow him to mark him, but with the defenders being drawn out of position, extra space would be created for Johnny Haynes and his slide rule passes that brought many goals. Sometimes it would be frustrating for Haynes as passes forward to where Hill should have been often went astray as Jimmy had undertaken one of his decoy runs. He was also a very versatile player who appeared in seven different shirt numbers during his time at the Cottage.

His time in the First Division in 1959–60 was going pretty well with six goals up to January when he received a bad right-knee injury in a 1–4 defeat at Luton Town which virtually ended his season. He had surgery but his appearances the following season were sporadic with just thirteen, and he scored just one goal, in a 4–1 win over Blackpool, his penultimate league game. His right knee was injured again the following week at the end of a 0–1 defeat at Everton and at thirty-three he didn't play league football again. He had made just under 300 appearances for the Whites in his ten seasons.

With his educated schooling background and eloquent speaking, Jimmy had taken on the mantle of being Fulham's PFA representative when Norman Smith retired; he had also performed the same role at Brentford. Whilst at Fulham during an upheaval within the PFA, Hill had found himself elected as chairman in 1957. It was a role he took seriously.

It is probably after his retirement from playing that Jimmy Hill is best remembered. In 1961, not long after retiring, he led a potential players' strike against the maximum wage (then £20 per week). He received 100% backing from his union members and the crisis reached Government level (Ministry of Labour) as it threatened the entire league programme and the football pools. After lengthy brinkmanship, the authorities caved in and his militant efforts that year won the right of players to be released from restrictive contracts. This to some degree has led to the kind of salary that players today, particularly those in the Premiership, now receive.

In November of the same year, Hill became manager of Coventry City. His time at the club was marked by great changes, an era called 'The Sky Blue Revolution'. He changed the home kit's colours to sky blue, the team coining the obvious nickname 'The Sky Blues'. He also penned the club song 'The Sky Blue Song', sung to the tune of the 'Eton Boating Song'. Among his other innovations were the first full-fledged matchday magazine in English football, and pre-match entertainment to encourage fans to arrive early. His partnership with chairman DH Robbins also led to a redevelopment of the Highfield Road stadium, with two new stands being built.

Hill was always happy to talk to the press. Here he holds forth in one of the club's hospitality lounges in the 1970s. The journalist on the right is Tony Stenson, who edited the Fulham programme for a number of years.

Hill arrived at Coventry with the club in the doldrums and sixteenth in the Third Division table. Two seasons later, in 1963–64, they won the Third Division championship, and three seasons after that the Second Division title, taking Coventry City into the First Division for the very first time. It was then a huge surprise when Hill quit before the start of Coventry's first campaign in the top flight.

After leaving Coventry in 1967, Hill moved into broadcasting, acting as technical adviser to the BBC before becoming head of sport at LWT (London Weekend Television) from 1968 to 1972. He also fronted their 1970 World Cup coverage which, at his suggestion, used the first ever panel of four opinionated football pundits. This in itself spawned an entire mini football industry of football debate. During this time he co-hosted the Sunday afternoon soccer television programme *The Big Match* with Brian Moore.

In 1972 he even found himself running the line in a First Division match between Arsenal and Liverpool when linesman Dennis Drewitt pulled a muscle and was unable to continue and no replacement was present. Hill was a spectator at the game and, as a qualified referee, was able to see the game through to its conclusion, dressed in a sky-blue track suit. Around the 1972–73 period, Hill returned to Fulham to assist Alec Stock in a part-time capacity re-vamping the club's commercial operation following the construction of the new Riverside stand.

He was briefly LWT's deputy controller of programmes, before joining the BBC to present *Match of the Day* replacing David Coleman.

Hill racked up 600 appearances on the show over fifteen years, and became a television icon, instantly recognisable by his long chin and distinctive beard. As a presenter or analyst, he worked on every major international championship for over thirty years from 1966.

Hill had returned to Coventry City in April 1975 as managing director before becoming chairman. Although the reign was less successful, Coventry were able to retain their top-flight status. His part-time role there lasted for over nine years before he left again in 1983.

He then had a short spell as chairman of Charlton Athletic in 1986, before attending to his most important role. He returned as chairman of Fulham in 1987 with the club facing bankruptcy and extinction, having been sold out by Ernie Clay. The club had been acquired by Marler Estates, a group of property companies run by David Bulstrode who wanted to demolish the Craven Cottage site for property development and merge Fulham with Queens Park Rangers, whose ground his company also owned, to form the ludicrous 'Fulham Park Rangers'.

Jimmy bought back the club (but not the ground) from Bulstrode, and formed a new company, Fulham Football Club (1987) Ltd. He spent the next decade, accompanied by a strong band of professional assistants and willing volunteers, all of them long-term Fulham fans, foiling all attempts to eradicate Fulham from the footballing map. It was a long road with a number of bumps along the way, but at the end of that time Fulham were once again a strong and going concern. When Mohamed Al Fayed arrived and completed the last piece of the jigsaw with the purchase of the ground from the Royal Bank of Scotland along with ample funds, Fulham's future was assured and Jimmy could finally be relieved of his duties. It is likely that none of the 'Premiership Experience', currently being enjoyed by Fulham, would have ever happened without the efforts of Jimmy Hill.

In 1999, Hill moved from the BBC to Sky Sports where he featured on initially *The Last Word* and subsequently *Jimmy Hill's Sunday Supplement*, a weekly discussion show between Hill and three football journalists conducted over a Sunday breakfast in a fake kitchen in Sky's studios in Osterley. In

2007, he was replaced by his co-presenter Brian Woolnough and the programme was renamed *Sunday Supplement*.

Sometimes an acquired taste, Jimmy Hill was often controversial with his views and opinions and he didn't always get it right, but the majority of his views on the game were spot on. His almost hectoring style on television made for compelling viewing and he wasn't afraid to cross swords with anyone when he considered that the good of the game was at stake. But he was a deep thinker and an all-round innovator who in the end won the respect of all in football.

Jimmy Hill will go down as probably the most influential individual in the world of football of the twentieth century. He pioneered the first all-seater stadiums, put forward and championed the cause of three points for a win, now adopted all over the world, and encouraged positive football by opting for goals scored rather than goal difference or goal average as being the main criterion for promotion for teams finishing on equal points.

He understood publicity and the power of television and public relations and was never shy in coming forward with opinions, but on the other side of the coin he did not take himself too seriously either, often appearing in adverts, comedy and quiz shows and sending himself up. Even the adult comic *Viz* runs sketches where Jimmy appears in a cartoon frame in the most inexplicable places! Most of all he is remembered also as being a thoroughly decent and kind man whose deep involvement in a number of charities is legendary. He has been a trustee of the Stable Lads' Association and a patron of the Labrador Rescue South East and Central.

Until age finally caught up with him, he was a very good tennis player and golfer and also loved horse riding. In 1999, Jimmy Hill was presented with a Lifetime Achievement award by the Royal Television Society. He received the Professional Footballers Association Merit Award in 2001, and is now also Jimmy Hill OBE. In 2011, a seven-foot bronze statue of Jimmy Hill costing £150,000 was unveiled at Coventry City's Ricoh Arena by Hill himself as a tribute and lasting monument to the work he did at the club.

JIMMY HILL
Fulham career

Season	Appearances	Goals	Home	Away
1951–1952	6	1	0	1
1952–1953	31	0	0	0
1953–1954	36	3	2	1
1954–1955	33	1	0	1
1955–1956	33	5	4	1
1956–1957	39	5	3	2
1957–1958	44	22	11	11
1958–1959	36	8	5	3
1959–1960	26	6	5	1
1960–1961	13	1	1	0
Total	297	52	31	21

*Total career **league** appearances–359, and **league** goals–51.*

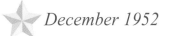

Johnny Haynes

The Maestro.

Johnny Haynes was born in Edmonton, north London, and was a schoolboy prodigy, winning honours with England Schoolboys and England Youth. He shot to fame in a rare televised match in 1950 between England Schoolboys and Scotland Schoolboys. The English demolished the Scots 8–2. Haynes scored two, created the majority of the rest and was an overnight sensation. He was coveted by all the big First Division clubs including Arsenal and Tottenham, but the north London boy chose homely **Fulham**, a Second Division team, simply because his schoolboy friend, Trevor Chamberlain, had joined the club and was happy there.

He started as an office boy and then eventually moved on to the groundstaff. To increase his experience and to toughen him up, he was sent out on loan to non-league sides like Feltham, Woodford Town and Wimbledon. He quickly turned professional and due to injuries within the team made his debut on Boxing Day 1952 in a 1–1 home draw against Southampton. His first goal came after a long wait, and it was fourteen league games before he scored in a 2–3 home defeat to West Ham United.

The next season, 1953–54, he missed just one game and scored a remarkable eighteen goals. The Fulham teams of the day were regularly scoring one hundred goals or more a season. He scored his first Fulham hat-trick in this first full season in a 5–1 win over Luton Town at the Cottage and managed three braces. He finished as second highest scorer behind the prolific Jezzard.

The following season he scored six in the first seven games and finished with nine overall. So good was the trio of Bobby Robson, Bedford Jezzard and Johnny Haynes that First Division Newcastle United bid £60,000 for the three players, an amount of money unheard of at the time. Both Robson and Haynes were then still under twenty years of age. Haynes was already attracting attention and was given his first England cap at the age of nineteen in a 2–0 win over Northern Ireland in October, scoring on his debut.

The next season, 1955–56, Haynes found his scoring boots again, finishing with nineteen goals, missing only two league games. A second Fulham hat-trick at Notts County came his way in a 4–3 win and there were also three braces. His rapid progress was to be curtailed somewhat by the sale of Bobby Robson to West Bromwich Albion and the career-finishing injury to Bedford Jezzard. Haynes was already being talked about as the best inside forward in the country, despite playing in the Second Division. His passing of the ball, reading of the game and his fitness made Fulham the envy of almost every other club. Haynes had become the first footballer to appear for England in every class of football available – Schoolboy, Youth, Under-23, England 'B' and full international.

Haynes had now been given the Fulham captaincy. He was just twenty-one but was beginning to experience problems with injury and was in and out of the side for the first half of the 1956–57 season, netting only three times before Christmas and finishing with a disappointing five from thirty-five games. Up to

Haynes scores the first goal in Fulham's 4–2 defeat of Lincoln City at the Cottage in September 1958. The other Fulham player in the picture is Jimmy Hill. Oh, and Haynes scored the other three goals that day as well.

– 35 –

Haynes' debut match.

now these Fulham sides had all finished around mid-table in the Second Division despite the high level of goalscoring, and this was down to defensive weaknesses.

The following season Fulham were a much improved side and just missed out on promotion due to severe fixture congestion at the end of the season. They also reached the semi-final of the FA Cup as a Second Division team. Haynes missed just four of the forty-nine games, hitting sixteen goals in the process. Despite these sixteen goals he was only third highest scorer, behind Roy Dwight and Jimmy Hill. He scored four in the first seven games and then scored fairly regularly throughout the season, mainly single goals. He then played in the 1958 World Cup in Sweden where he was exhausted and felt the backlash from a fickle press after England had failed to get through the group stages.

The 1958–59 campaign proved to be a highlight for Fulham and for Johnny Haynes as Fulham were promoted back to the First Division as runners-up and Haynes scored for fun, finishing with twenty-six in thirty-four league games. He was far and away top scorer. In a remarkable season, he netted a four-goal haul against Lincoln City at the Cottage (4–2) and three more hat-tricks, all at home, against Sunderland in September (6–2), against Leyton Orient in February (5–2) and to round it off on the final day against Rotherham United (4–0) in April. His remarkable talents had the press running out of superlatives, considering his efforts to be almost superhuman.

He was also a success in the England side, and he responded to press criticisms the only way that he knew by scoring a hat-trick for the national side against the Russians in a 5–0 demolition at Wembley. At this stage Haynes had made thirty-two of his fifty-six appearances for England whilst Fulham were playing in the Second Division. No English player has appeared as many times for the national team when playing outside a country's top tier.

Haynes was one of the most remarkable players of the era. Although he was quick over a few yards, he wasn't the fastest over distance, and heading the ball wasn't a speciality. He wasn't tall either and posed little aerial threat, but what he did on the ground was outstanding. He was probably the finest post-war passer of a football from distances of six to sixty yards. He had a stocky build and very strong thighs which made him very solid and difficult to knock off the ball. Although at times a prolific goalscorer, he is remembered by the football world at large mainly for creating goals for others. He was a superb reader of the game and knew what he would do with the ball

before it reached him, often being three passes ahead of everyone else. He trained harder than anyone else, was a superb athlete and a great competitor.

He was a great sports all-rounder and could have been a professional golfer or tennis player. He was an also an excellent all-round cricketer, like a number of Fulham players. He was an able wicket-keeper/batsman and had been offered professional terms by Middlesex Cricket Club.

On the field he was known to be demonstrative and tetchy, with icy stares, gestures and withering words towards team-mates who weren't as good as he was, but really it was borne out of frustration during the heat of the game. Off the field he was totally different, a shy, polite and retiring person who didn't like to stand out from the crowd and who was held in the highest regard by his playing colleagues. He thoroughly enjoyed being with Fulham supporters and would attend almost all social functions.

Life was tougher for Haynes in the First Division during the 1959–60 season, and early on he missed two months due to injury. He finished with ten goals (including one brace) as Fulham finished in their highest position ever at the time, tenth in Division One. He was also made captain of the England team.

It became even tougher in the 1960–61 season. Haynes missed only three games and netted nine

The classic picture of Haynes' frustration with his colleagues, or himself, as he wonders what's going on in the match against Nottingham Forest in March 1962. The stubborn stance was enough to make the picture a part of the campaign years later to keep Fulham alive and staying put at Craven Cottage.

including two braces, but Fulham finished a disappointing seventeenth. Haynes probably had his mind on other things as there had been a massive offer of £100,000 from AC Milan to take him to Italy. But Haynes' Fulham playing colleague Jimmy Hill successfully negotiated the abolition of the maximum wage of £20 per week and Haynes became the first player ever to be paid £100 per week. Chairman Tommy Trinder was content to pay such a sum to his 'favourite son'. Remarkably Haynes turned down a life of luxury in Italy to remain with lowly Fulham.

The form of the England side had received a real upturn under Haynes' captaincy. At one stage in 1960–61, England scored forty goals in just six matches! Included in that sequence of results was a massive 9–3 win over Scotland at Wembley, eleven years to the day after he had done the same to Scotland as an England schoolboy. Once again Haynes scored twice and created most of the other goals.

Season 1961–62 was even more trying and Fulham at one stage looked like relegation certainties, but Haynes' play pulled them round to escape relegation by the skin of their teeth. He had scored just twice up to the end of January and finished with only six, but he played a captain's role in guiding Fulham to their second FA Cup semi-final in four years.

After this demanding season, Haynes captained England in the 1962 World Cup finals in Chile. They reached the quarter-finals, but were eliminated by the eventual winners Brazil. Haynes was again not at his best, and the press had a field day. At this juncture, he became only the fourth player ever to have been awarded over fifty England caps. The Brazil elimination proved to be his final cap (fifty-six) and the last of his twenty-two games as captain. He had scored eighteen goals for his country.

At the start of the 1962–63 season and at the height of his fame, one wet and windy August evening Haynes broke curfew and was with a lady friend when his sports car, which she was driving, was involved in a collision on Blackpool promenade. Haynes damaged his knee extensively and broke bones in both legs. Doctors said it was the end of his career, but he doggedly fought back, working tirelessly on his own for fitness. On his comeback he was injured again, and played only nine games that season, failing to score at all. Fulham were in trouble in the league yet again, but under Jim Langley's temporary captaincy they prospered and survived comfortably.

Haynes recovered enough to miss just two league games in 1963–64, and some thought him good

Haynes wasn't always grumpy! Here he celebrates a Fulham goal.

Concentration from the Maestro against Nottingham Forest.

enough to play for England again, but new manager Alf Ramsey considered that he wasn't the same player since the car accident and never picked him. Haynes had lost some of his pace and mobility but was still an outstanding player. He was much more a creator than a scorer now as he approached thirty, but he still managed to net eight single goals as Fulham maintained their top status quite comfortably. He added one unwelcome statistic when he became the first Fulham player to be sent off for twenty-five years following a clash with Bertie Auld in a 0–0 draw with Birmingham at St Andrews just before Christmas.

1964–65 was a tough season for Haynes as his friend Beddy Jezzard had resigned as Fulham manager and the club had denied Haynes the opportunity to join Spurs for £100,000. Haynes missed just three league games, two due to suspension, but netted only five single goals. Fulham just clung on in the First Division, but it went to the last week before safety was confirmed. In 1965–66, the team's position was even worse, and relegation looked an absolute certainty by February, but the arrival of coach Dave

Sexton and young strikers Steve Earle and Les Barrett saw Haynes produce some of his best form for years despite being thirty-two. Fulham survived once again but it went down to the wire once more. Haynes netted seven goals including one brace.

The 1966–67 campaign was a season of consolidation under new manager Vic Buckingham. Haynes missed just nine league games and weighed in with a respectable seven goals, and despite a poor second half to the season Fulham remained in the First Division quite comfortably.

However it was all over the following season. With the departure of internationals Bobby Robson and Graham Leggat, as well as the career-ending injury to World Cup hero George Cohen, Haynes had little left to support him. Once again he scored seven goals, but age was beginning to catch up with him and Fulham were relegated.

The 1968–69 season was worse and, following Bobby Robson's sacking, Haynes reluctantly agreed to become Fulham's player/manager. The arrangement lasted just seventeen days and four games before

Haynes takes a throw-in at a sun-dappled Craven Cottage. The picture gives a glimpse of the flags flying along the riverside, representing all the clubs in the First Division.

he stepped down. This Second Division Fulham side was even worse than the previous season's and was relegated again. Haynes failed to score at Craven Cottage at all and netted just twice all season. Following a 0–6 thrashing by Bristol City at Ashton Gate in March, new manager Bill Dodgin withdrew

Cup and caps.

Haynes from the team to spare the Maestro further humiliation. Haynes was awarded a well-earned testimonial at the end of the season.

Amazingly he stayed at Fulham, his only club, and celebrated twenty years at the Cottage by starting the 1969–70 season as a Third Division player. He scored Fulham's first league goal in the Third Division. He was ever-present too right up to the time of an injury. He scored only three goals, the final one being at Brighton in November in a 1–2 defeat, and he made his last Fulham appearance in a dismal 1–1 draw with Stockport County in January 1970.

Despite his loyalty, manner, prowess and abundant skill, Haynes finished playing in this country without a single medal, trophy or domestic honour of any kind on the field. Even worse, he was not afforded any recognition off the field either, a fact that many today, both inside and outside the game, still consider a national disgrace.

Many thought he would stop playing in 1970, but he amazed everyone by going to South Africa and continuing his playing career for a further five years. It was a controversial move at the time given Haynes' fame and the political situation in South Africa surrounding sport and apartheid. In South Africa, he teamed up with former Fulham colleagues Tony Macedo, Bobby Keetch and Johnny Byrne and won two championships and three other cup trophies with Durban City, his only medals. He finally retired with

Maritzburg at the age of forty-one, having played top-level football non-stop for a quarter of a century!

Haynes remained a bachelor until he was thirty-eight, marrying and divorcing twice whilst in South Africa and also meeting his third partner Avril. He remained in that country for fifteen years. After a short spell of coaching in South Africa, he returned to live in Scotland with Avril, happily assisting in the running of her business operations, watching Hearts and Scottish rugby whilst enjoying golf and

Haynes scores his last goal at Craven Cottage in the 4–3 defeat of Plymouth Argyle in September 1969.

holidays. He was never seriously involved with football again, except for the occasional cameo television appearance.

However, Haynes never forgot Fulham and theirs was the first result he looked for. During the late Eighties and early Nineties he campaigned vigorously when Fulham's very existence was under threat and it looked as if Craven Cottage itself would disappear to the builders. In 2002, Haynes became an inaugural inductee to the English football Hall of Fame in recognition of his football talents and impact on the national game. (On the day of the formal induction, our revered editor was interviewed on BBC TV News to give his opinion as to why the Maestro deserved to be honoured in this way. Never at a loss for words, he filled his fifteen seconds of fame to the full.)

Tragedy struck on the afternoon of his seventy-first birthday in 2005, when Johnny Haynes suffered a stroke whilst driving in Edinburgh and his car ploughed into a light goods vehicle. Haynes lost his life and Avril was badly injured. His funeral in Scotland was attended by the luminaries of the day including Sven Goran Eriksson, Bobby Charlton, Dave Mackay and his old friend Sir Bobby Robson. Within months, the Stevenage Road Stand at Fulham was re-named in his honour.

Words of consolation from Haynes for Les Strong in the Wembley dressing room in 1975. Les had to miss the FA Cup final due to injury, having played in all the previous eleven cup matches.

JOHNNY HAYNES
Fulham career – all competitions

Season	Appearances	Goals	Home	Away
1952–1953	19	1	1	
1953–1954	44	18	11	7
1954–1955	38	9	5	4
1955–1956	42	19	7	12
1956–1957	35	5	3	2
1957–1958	45	16	12	4
1958–1959	38	26	20	6
1959–1960	33	10	6	4
1960–1961	41	9	8	1
1961–1962	45	6	2	4
1962–1963	9	0	0	0
1963–1964	43	8	7	1
1964–1965	43	5	4	1
1965–1966	38	7	6	1
1966–1967	41	7	3	4
1967–1968	42	7	3	4
1968–1969	31	2	0	2
1969–1970	31	3	2	1
Total	**658**	**158**	**100**	**58**

*Total career **league** appearances–**594**, and **league** goals–147.*

In 2008, a full-size bronze statue of the Maestro, commissioned by chairman Mohamed Al Fayed, was unveiled outside the Johnny Haynes Stand, and so the greatest Fulham player of all time now has a permanent place at Craven Cottage looking down on all visiting home and away supporters.

Trevor Chamberlain

Scored with his first kick and famous for his lethal shot – and for bringing Johnny Haynes to Fulham.

Trevor Chamberlain was born in Camden, north London. As a left winger he played for Middlesex, London and England boys. In a cup final played at Craven Cottage in 1948 with his local club side White Lion Play Centre, he impressed Fulham manager Jack Peart, and he joined the **Fulham** groundstaff upon leaving school in 1949. He gained England Youth honours. Chamberlain was key in bringing his close friend Johnny Haynes to Fulham in 1950. He signed professional forms in 1951, but then embarked on the mandatory two years of national service.

On his return, he made his league debut against Second Division Lincoln City in November 1954 where he scored with his first kick in professional football inside the first minute, Fulham winning 3–2. It was his only goal in the five league games he played that season. He had to wait until midway through the next season to get into the team again, but he responded in fine style with eleven league goals in twenty-one games including a hat-trick in a 4–0 win over Doncaster Rovers in the penultimate league match.

In February of the 1955–56 season he scored another hat-trick in one of the most exciting games ever seen at Craven Cottage when Fulham played FA Cup holders First Division giants Newcastle United in a fourth-round tie at a misty Craven Cottage. Fulham were three goals down in twenty minutes but, inspired by Haynes, and Chamberlain's three goals, at one stage led 4–3, only for Newcastle finally to win 4–5, thanks to a controversial late winner when goalkeeper Ian Black was bundled into the net by Vic Keeble. Of Chamberlain's fourteen goals that season, thirteen came at the Cottage.

For the next two seasons he was an automatic choice as the direct replacement for Charlie Mitten, and he registered another fifteen goals from the left wing during season 1956–57, including his third hat-trick in a 7–2 thrashing of Blackburn Rovers at Craven Cottage just before Christmas. In 1957–58 he missed a quarter of the season through injury, but still notched up a one-in-two record with thirteen goals in twenty-seven matches. He played an important role in Fulham's FA Cup run, scoring in the 3–5 defeat to Manchester United at Highbury in the semi-final replay.

In the 1958–59 promotion season he started with a flourish with six goals in the first twelve games, but due to injury played only four of the next half-season's worth of matches, adding just one more goal. However, he returned to the side for the final promotion push. He was a regular in the first season back in First Division, but found defences a lot tougher to crack and he netted just six times.

His role in his final five playing years was more as a back-up and during those seasons he made fewer

than fifty appearances, adding just another five goals as his place came under threat initially from Graham Leggat and then from a young Brian (Pat) O'Connell. He made eight appearances in the 1964–65 season scoring his final goal in a 3–3 draw with Blackpool at the Cottage in November. His final appearance was in a Boxing Day 0–4 trouncing at Burnley. During his later years at Fulham he was also a sports instructor and coached football at the Elliott school in Putney.

Trevor was a victim of the 1965 Vic Buckingham purge and was given a free transfer. He signed for **Dover Athletic** in the Southern League and later had a spell at **Gravesend and Northfleet**.

Nicknamed 'Tosh', Chamberlain was one of Fulham's great characters and had a warm relationship with the home crowd. Football then was all about entertainment and pleasing the supporters. Although he was one of life's jokers, that often overshadowed the fact that he was a good, skilful winger with pace and a ferocious shot. The fact that he scored forty-three goals from the left wing in three seasons is a testament to his shooting ability.

He often drove Johnny Haynes to distraction when he failed to read the Maestro's passes down the wing and the verbal interchanges between the pair of them were amusing and colourful. Apocryphal stories about Tosh are legendary. He once let a Haynes pass to the wing bounce out of play because he wasn't watching and was chatting to spectators. In one game during a break in play, he passed time by having a cigarette with a member of the crowd. When play resumed Tosh hared off down the wing with ball, still with the ciggie in his hand. His cannonball powerful shooting was also legendary. One shot against Leicester City carried the England goalkeeper Gordon Banks into the net with it and one back-pass to his own goalkeeper Tony Macedo was hit so hard that it broke his ribs.

Tosh retained his close, brotherly friendship with Johnny Haynes right up until Haynes' untimely passing in 2005. Now seventy-nine, he retains a deep affection for the Whites, his only club, and still occasionally attends matches at Craven Cottage.

TREVOR CHAMBERLAIN
Fulham career – all competitions

Season	Appearances	Goals	Home	Away
1954–1955	6	1	1	0
1955–1956	22	14	13	1
1956–1957	41	15	8	7
1957–1958	33	14	7	7
1958–1959	24	7	3	4
1959–1960	29	7	2	5
1960–1961	13	1	1	0
1961–1962	16	2	2	0
1962–1963	4	0	0	0
1963–1964	7	2	2	0
1964–1965	9	1	1	0
Total	204	64	40	24

*Total career **league** appearances–187, and **league** goals–59.*

Roy Dwight

A spectacular goalscorer, he hit five hat-tricks over a period of just thirty league games.

Roy **Dwight** (full name Royston) was born in Dartford and was an England Youth international winger. Following the early death of both his parents, he was raised principally by his grandparents.

Roy was more of a winger than a striker initially but his quick thinking and explosive shooting meant that as he matured he was equally at home in the centre-forward position. He served a brief non-league apprenticeship with Hastings United, before joining **Fulham** alongside Johnny Haynes in the summer of 1950 aged seventeen.

Due to the prolific scoring form of Bobby Robson, Bedford Jezzard and Johnny Haynes, Dwight had to wait patiently for his debut. He first appeared intermittently in season 1954–55 (four games) making his Second Division debut against Birmingham City in a 2–3 defeat in March. He scored in that game and in his next one too against Middlesbrough.

The next season was equally frustrating due to Jezzard's tremendous form, but an injury near the end of the season allowed Dwight his chance which he took with both feet. He scored five league goals in just four games, starting with a hat-trick against Liverpool at the Cottage. Fulham won all four of those games, scoring fourteen goals in the process.

The career-ending injury to Jezzard in the summer of 1956 gave Dwight a permanent opportunity of which again he took full advantage. In all competitions in the 1956–57 season he scored twenty-six goals in just thirty-six appearances. This included scoring in all of the first seven league games of the season.

In one spell, bridging the previous season, by early February, Dwight had scored five hat-tricks in just thirty league games, a goal-scoring feat that even the likes of Jezzard, Haynes and Gordon Davies never matched. In that season he scored a hat-trick in both matches against Swansea Town (7–3 home and 5–4 away). Four players scored over ten league goals that season, but unsurprisingly Dwight finished as top scorer in his first full season, way ahead of the rest.

He then proved that this was no fluke by repeating the feat in the 1957–58 season. In this season he also scored in the opening four matches. Despite missing a number of matches, he scored twenty-two league goals in just thirty matches and this included a four-goal haul in a 6–3 win over Sheffield United. His goals also helped Fulham to an FA Cup semi-final. Four players again netted double figures, but Dwight was once more top scorer. During this season, alongside Johnny Haynes, he also represented the London XI that beat Lausanne Sports 2–0 at Highbury (in a forerunner of the Inter-Cities Fairs Cup).

His final goal for Fulham came in a 2–2 draw at Bristol Rovers in April, and his final appearance was at the end of the month in a 1–1 home draw with Blackburn Rovers.

After two spectacular seasons, it seemed impossible that Fulham would sell their top scorer, but they were offered a 'significant fee' for Dwight by First Division **Nottingham Forest** which they accepted. Fulham had already signed a replacement in Scotsman Graham Leggat.

Dwight scored on his debut for Forest and in his first full season, 1958–59, scored twenty-six goals in fifty league and FA Cup appearances. This included two hat-tricks, one at Leicester (3–0) and one in the FA Cup in a 5–0 demolition of Birmingham City.

Nottingham Forest reached the FA Cup final that year and played Luton Town. Dwight scored the first goal of the final in just under ten minutes. Forest then scored again; however, Dwight's joy was short-lived

Season	Appearances	Goals	Home	Away
1954–1955	4	2	1	1
1955–1956	4	5	4	1
1956–1957	36	26	20	6
1957–1958	36	24	10	14
Total	80	57	35	22

ROY DWIGHT
Fulham career – all competitions

Total career ***league*** *appearances–154, and* ***league*** *goals–85.*

as he broke his leg in a tackle with Luton's McNally around the half-hour mark and had to listen to the conclusion of the final from a hospital bed. This pre-dated the use of substitutes, so his team-mates had to battle on for an hour with just ten men. To Dwight's delight, though, Forest clung on to win the final 2–1.

Dwight missed virtually the whole of the following season recovering from the severe injury and scored on his first match back with Forest in March 1960. Sadly it was clear that he probably was now not fit enough for First Division football and he played just two more games for Forest.

He was released by Forest and returned to his native Kent dropping into non-league football with **Gravesend and Northfleet** for the 1960–61 season to work his way to better fitness. He scored ten goals that season. Former Fulham team-mate Jimmy Hill was then in charge at **Coventry City** after retiring from playing, and in January 1962 he persuaded Dwight to try his luck again, this time at Third Division level. He was Hill's first Coventry signing.

In the 1961–62 season he managed seven goals in eighteen league appearances, but in the following season made only thirteen league appearances scoring just once. He did however play his part in helping to propel the Sky Blues up the league towards the First Division. Dwight left Coventry to return to London for two seasons at Third Division **Millwall**, but managed just seven league starts, scoring two goals, and in that first season Millwall were relegated to the bottom tier.

After retiring from league football in 1965, he spent a short time playing for **Dartford**, and then followed a period in the late Sixties in the USA as assistant coach to his former Millwall team-mate Len Julians at the Detroit Cougars.

In the Seventies, he tried his hand at local football management, starting off with Erith and Belvedere. He then went on to manage London's Tooting and Mitcham, who had been Nottingham Forest's third-round opponents in their winning 1959 FA Cup run. He managed Tooting in their great FA Cup run of 1975–76 when the non-leaguers reached the fourth round proper. They beat Swindon Town in a replay

before bowing out to Bradford City. He later had brief spells in management with Dartford and Tilbury.

During this time, he also taught physical education at Forest Hill Boys Secondary School. A heart operation in the early Eighties then forced an early retirement. Later in life, he took up a position in the greyhound racing industry of assistant racing manager at Catford Stadium in south London. Roy Dwight died in London in 2002 aged just sixty-nine. Outside of football, Roy is forever associated with the music industry as he was the cousin of Reginald Dwight, more familiarly known as Elton John. Roy's father Edwin and Elton's father Stanley were brothers.

John Doherty

A skilful and versatile forward who looked set for the big time.

John Doherty was born in Stoneleigh and joined Chelsea in 1953 as a seventeen-year-old amateur. He failed to break through at Stamford Bridge and moved to **Fulham** a year later. A talented youngster, he seemed to be a very bright prospect. As a young player he didn't feature in either the 1954–55 or the 1955–56 season.

He made his debut the following season on the left wing against Huddersfield Town at Craven Cottage where Fulham won 1–0. He then switched to inside left and played four games in the number 10 shirt deputising for the Maestro Johnny Haynes. His sixth game was at inside right. He failed to break his scoring duck that season.

In 1957–58, he once again deputised for Haynes for one match, but then moved to centre forward. In his second game in the number 9 shirt he scored his first Fulham goal in a 2–0 win at home to Swansea Town just before New Year. He then scored again the following week with an FA Cup goal in a 4–0 win over non-league Yeovil in the third round. In all competitions, he had played six matches and scored two goals.

Doherty was a skilful player, a deep-lying and scheming forward who could pass, dribble and shoot. He sometimes had the urge to take on too much himself or to try too many fancy tricks when a simpler pass was on. He also had quite a volatile temperament which didn't stand him in good stead with some of the

senior players. He was also a confidence player and sometimes became despondent when he didn't score as often as he should.

In the promotion season of 1958–59, he deputised for Haynes with distinction in seven games, as well as having another spell at centre forward. He scored two more goals in 5–2 home wins over Barnsley in November and Leyton Orient in February; in all he made eleven league appearances.

The first season back in the First Division, 1959–60, saw Doherty awarded his best run in the side and he started the first ten league games, mainly at centre forward. He scored twice, in a 3–1 win over league champions Wolves, and three days later in a 4–2 win over Luton Town. He made five more league appearances and one further FA Cup match without adding to his goal tally. When he played against Bolton in February on the right wing, he had shown his skill and versatility by appearing in all five forward line positions.

His final two seasons were disappointing. He appeared in just four league games in 1960–61, scoring once in a 2–7 defeat early in the season at Newcastle, and in the 1961–62 season he started in four of the opening five games, scoring the winner in the 2–1 win over Everton. After that he made just four further appearances, his final outing being a 1–1 home draw with Nottingham Forest in March.

Doherty had been at Fulham for eight years and had made only fifty-one appearances. He decided to move to Australia to continue his career, and played for **South Coast United** in the New South Wales League Division One. He played three seasons for them from 1962 to 1964. Whilst in Australia, he won NSW representative honours in 1964 playing for the 'New Caledonia' side.

He returned to England in the summer of 1964 in time for the 1964–65 season, signing for Fourth Division **Aldershot**. He played for two seasons with the Hampshire club, but represented them on just eighteen occasions, scoring a solitary goal. He was released at the end of the 1965–66 season. He then moved into non-league football and later spent one season with **Fleet Town** (1967–68) and finally one with **Guildford City** (1968–69).

On his retirement from football, he became a successful accountant and was last reported to be living in the Stoneleigh/Ewell area.

JOHN DOHERTY
Fulham career – all competitions

Season	Appearances	Goals	Home	Away
1956–1957	6	0	0	0
1957–1958	6	2	2	0
1958–1959	11	2	2	0
1959–1960	16	2	2	0
1960–1961	4	1	0	1
1961–1962	8	1	1	0
Total	**51**	**8**	**7**	**1**

*Total career **league** appearances–**67**, and **league** goals–**8**.*

Roy Bentley

A vastly-experienced Fulham legend who had a passing connection with Chelsea…

Roy Bentley was born in Bristol and played briefly for both Bristol clubs. After leaving the Royal Navy, he joined First Division **Newcastle United** for £8,000 and spent eighteen months on Tyneside, scoring twenty-two league goals in forty-eight appearances.

To improve his health, he moved south to join First Division **Chelsea** for £12,500 as a replacement for Tommy Lawton but his career in London in his first part-season was slow to get off the ground.

However, in his first full season, 1948–49, he was top scorer with twenty-one goals and earned his first England call-up against Sweden. In the next season, he scored twenty-three goals for Chelsea. He was part of the England side that were embarrassed 0–1 by the USA in Brazil in the 1950 World Cup.

Although Chelsea's league form during his time there was often patchy, Bentley played a key part in their first major FA Cup run for almost two decades in 1950. They reached the semi-final before being beaten by Arsenal after leading. Two years later came another semi-final loss in 1952, again versus Arsenal.

Ted Drake then arrived as Chelsea's manager and, within three years, Bentley had achieved one of the highlights of his playing career, captaining Chelsea in 1954–55 to their first ever First Division title. In addition to being captain, he scored twenty-one league goals during the season, including a hat-trick against Newcastle United and two crucial strikes in a 4–3 win against principal title rivals Wolves.

In that excellent season, he also scored a hat-trick for England against Wales in November. In all, Bentley won twelve England caps scoring nine goals.

Bentley remained with Chelsea for only one more full season (1955–56) and was one of the first to leave as the ageing championship-winning side was gradually broken up by Drake. During this season he represented the London XI in the Inter-Cities Fairs Cup in October as they beat Frankfurt 3–2 at Wembley, where he was playing alongside Fulham's Bobby Robson, Bedford Jezzard and Charlie Mitten.

Having scored 150 goals in 367 appearances, Bentley currently lies fifth in Chelsea's all-time goalscorers list, level with Peter Osgood. He was top scorer at the club in *every one* of his eight full seasons at Stamford Bridge, and only once failed to achieve sixteen goals in a season.

After just four games in the 1956–57 season and aged thirty-two, Bentley joined Second Division **Fulham** who were reeling from the loss of Bedford Jezzard and Bobby Robson. He would partner Roy Dwight up front and use his significant experience to mentor the up-and-coming Johnny Haynes.

Bentley made his debut in September, scoring in a comfortable 3–1 win over Rotherham United. After missing the next game, he played in all the remaining matches that season and scored regularly. Despite scoring fifteen goals that season in all competitions, he was still only joint third highest goalscorer. The goals included a hat-trick in a 6–3 win over Port Vale in February and three two-goal games.

Bentley was an early exponent of the deep-lying centre forward position, an unorthodox tactic which often unsettled opposing defenders. He was also an intelligent player using stealth, guile and experience to out-manoeuvre opponents. These skills, combined with a very strong heading ability, great acceleration and a powerful shot, made him a very potent centre forward.

The 1957–58 season was just as fruitful with five single strikes in the first sixteen league games. Fulham manager Dugald Livingstone then decided, as Bentley was now a little slower, to convert him to a half back and then finally a centre half, mainly for his class but also for his experience. This would help mentor a young George Cohen and improve on the Edwards/Stapleton half-back pairing. From this position he could still assist and advise Johnny Haynes.

Bentley added three more goals from defence/midfield that season, but experienced heartbreak for the third time when Fulham were beaten at the semi-final stage of the FA Cup. He had played thirty-nine games. In 1958–59, Bentley played a key role in Fulham's calm defence that saw them promoted, missing just seven league games all seasons as pivot. However, he added no further goals.

Despite now being thirty-five, Bentley was still a star back in the First Division in 1959–60, many considering that he was skilful enough and had the class still to be playing for England. Fulham finished tenth at the end of the season and Bentley had added another thirty-one appearances in all competitions. He scored only two more goals from defence, both being against his former clubs, Newcastle United and Chelsea.

Bentley pictured during his debut for the club, a 3–1 victory against Rotherham United in September 1956. It was an important signing for Fulham, as Bentley added experience to the youthful skills of new Fulham captain Johnny Haynes.

He was a regular starter in the next season too, making sixteen appearances, until he suffered a bad leg muscle injury during a 1–5 defeat by Blackburn Rovers at Ewood Park in early December. It took time to heal and Eddie Lowe and Derek Lampe began to take over the position. It proved to be Bentley's final game. He was given a free transfer by Fulham in the summer of 1961, a move that surprised many, and the players pleaded with Fulham's management for his retention, even though he was aged thirty-seven, but in the end he left.

He continued his playing career, dropping down to the Third Division to join his third west London club **Queens Park Rangers**, missing only one league game out of forty-six in the 1961–62 season as the Loftus Road side missed out on promotion by just three points. His final career tally shows more than 650 appearances and more than 200 goals.

Following his retirement from playing, Bentley moved into management. He took over at Reading (1963–69) and later Swansea City (1969–72), winning promotion to the Third Division with the latter. He returned to Reading in 1977, this time as club secretary, leaving seven years later to perform the same role for Aldershot.

Roy Bentley, now almost ninety, lives in quiet retirement near Reading. Until recently he was still actively involved in the corporate side of his former club Chelsea, and also gave inspirational talks to the young players at the club.

ROY BENTLEY
Fulham career – all competitions

Season	Appearances	Goals	Home	Away
1956–1957	34	15	9	6
1957–1958	38	8	3	5
1958–1959	39	0	0	0
1959–1960	31	2	0	2
1960–1961	16	0	0	0
Total	158	25	12	13

*Total career **league** appearances–559, and **league** goals–175.*

Maurice Cook

A versatile, old-fashioned centre forward with almost 100 Fulham goals – and top scorer in two seasons.

Maurice Cook was born and raised in Hemel Hempstead and played county football for Hertfordshire. He grew up in a tough level of football with **Berkhamsted Town**. He was also an accomplished cricketer for the local side Potten End and won many awards and trophies with the club with both bat and ball. So good was he that he represented Hertfordshire County Cricket Club as an amateur.

Cook joined Third Division South side **Watford** as an amateur in 1952 following national service, turning professional at the end of the 1952–53 season. He made his debut in Watford's first game of the 1953–54 season at Southampton. His first professional goal came exactly one month later, giving Watford a 1–0 win at Coventry City. Playing forty-five of a possible forty-seven games, Cook finished the season with nine goals as Watford ended up in fourth place.

His career took off the following season. One of three players in 1954–55 to play in all fifty of Watford's fixtures, he finished as the club's top scorer

with thirty-one goals in all competitions, more than twice as many as his nearest competitor. Like Johnny Haynes he continued with cricket in the summer, even though he was now a professional footballer.

Cook scored fifteen and sixteen goals in 1955–56 and 1956–57 respectively, and then added ten in thirty Watford games in the first six months of 1957–58. By then, Cook had made 218 appearances in the Football League and FA Cup, scoring seventy-seven goals and missing just four games. He had also represented the Third Division South's divisional team. Despite his goals, Watford remained at best a mid-table side.

He was transferred to Second Division **Fulham** for a fee of £15,000 in February 1958. It was at the time the largest fee Watford had ever received. Initially Cook knew little about the transfer. The Watford supporters were angry too as Cook was considered to be their best player at the time, and were only appeased months later when they signed Arsenal's Cliff Holton (also a good cricketer) to replace him.

Maurice Cook was the epitome of the old-fashioned battering-ram centre forward, but he was a versatile player who could occupy any position in the forward line; he was also competent as a half back and had even played in goal. During his earlier career it was rumoured that he had played in every outfield position. He was never blessed with great pace nor great ball skills; often he would look heavy-footed, ungainly and even clumsy. He was sometimes Johnny Haynes' whipping boy and was regularly on the end of icy stares and withering words from the Maestro for not reading his intentions.

To make up for this he had a number of attributes. He was strong and physical and any defender playing against his bustling style was always going to be in for a tough afternoon. Also, although he disliked hard training and didn't keep the healthiest of lifestyles, he could run and run for ninety minutes. He was an excellent target man with a real nose for goal, and very good with his heading. He was very brave and committed to the cause. He tended to be under-rated but he made a valuable contribution to the Fulham side. His work-rate and distracting style often took the weight off the more gifted players like Haynes, Leggat and Rodney Marsh. He also fitted in well at Fulham. A thoroughly nice and good-natured man, with a ready smile, good sense of humour and waspish wit, he blended immediately with the other Fulham 'characters'.

He was cup-tied and couldn't join in the 1958 Fulham run to the semi-final of the FA Cup, but he made a useful contribution in the league. He made his debut in a 2–2 draw with West Ham, and scored in

just his second game, a 6–0 demolition of Grimsby Town, and in that third of the season he netted nine goals in just fifteen games. Fulham just failed to get promotion.

The following season, Maurice hit a hat-trick against Stoke City on the opening day in a 6–1 win. He scored seventeen goals in his first full season that saw Fulham promoted to the First Division. In that momentous season however, he was still only the third highest scorer – behind Johnny Haynes (26) and Graham Leggat (22), sixty-five goals being not a bad haul for just three players. Probably the most important goals he scored were the brace at Hillsborough over Easter that secured Fulham a valuable 2–2 draw against their fierce rivals which effectively sealed promotion.

In the First Division in 1959–60, his first season was a lot tougher as he had competition from youngster John Doherty, and he had injuries too, but finished with a very respectable nine goals in just nineteen starts. The following season, 1960–61, he was a regular starter and scored thirteen in all competitions in thirty-four appearances. He also made history that season when he became the first player ever to score a goal in the Football League Cup. He scored in the ninth minute away at Second Division Bristol Rovers, in a match that had started fifteen minutes earlier than nearly all the other ties. In true Fulham style the team eventually lost 1–2. He scored a hat-trick in a 4–2 away victory at Molineux on the final day of the season against a strong Wolves side that had finished

Cook scores his hat-trick goal in Fulham's 5–2 defeat of Sheffield United in March 1962.

third in the table and for whom this was only their second home defeat of the season.

In the 1961–62 season, Cook's goals were important in the FA Cup run to the semi-final including the important winner in the sixth-round replay against Blackburn Rovers at Ewood Park. His best ever match was probably against Burnley in the semi-final. He led the line skilfully having two headers from Jim Langley's long throws saved on the line and then, in the closing minutes, he was through with only goalkeeper Adam Blacklaw to beat. Maurice was

flattened by the custodian and it was as clear a penalty as anyone could wish for, but the referee refused to give the decision thus depriving Fulham of the chance of a Wembley appearance. It is an incident that is still discussed fifty years on. Cook picked up another hat-trick in a 5–2 victory over Sheffield United at the Cottage. He also settled the nerves with the important first goal in a 2–0 win over Manchester United in the final home game that effectively saved Fulham from relegation. He ended as top scorer with nineteen goals in all competitions.

A flying header from Cook crashes against the bar in the 2–1 victory over Birmingham City in September 1960.

In the next season, 1962–63, he repeated his top-scoring feat and netted fifteen goals in thirty-nine games including his third hat-trick in the 4–1 win over Sheffield Wednesday in Fulham's first ever game under floodlights at Craven Cottage. The following season he was not as prolific, with just six goals as his place began to come under threat from youngsters like Steve Earle, Rodney Marsh and Dave Metchick. In his final season, 1964–65, he was no longer an automatic choice but when called upon scored freely. In the second half of the league season, having been recalled to the side, he responded by scoring seven goals in eleven matches. His final goal was the clincher in a 2–0 win over Sheffield Wednesday at the Cottage in March, and his final appearance came a month later on the last day of the season in a 1–1 draw at home to Aston Villa.

Maurice was now thirty-three and new Fulham manager Vic Buckingham had already decided Cook's fate and let him depart to Third Division **Reading** at the end of the season for a nominal fee of £5,000. Cook did not really want to leave the Cottage and was disappointed with the manager's hasty decision to let him go. Although he had sometimes been on the receiving end of criticism from Fulham supporters, many considered that he had been released too early. It was a shame too as he had amassed just three goals short of a century to join an elite Fulham few.

His stay at Reading was brief, just one season where he made just twelve appearances scoring twice. After leaving league football, he spent one season at **Banbury United** as player-coach guiding them to the Southern League for the first time in their history.

After hanging up his boots, Maurice moved to Berkhamsted and took over the Old White Hart pub (now sadly a car park). He set up a local team in Potten End and continued to play there. The club and team he created still survives today. He ran another two public houses before retiring. He later spent some time working in security at The Oval cricket ground. He maintained his interest in both cricket and football for the remainder of his life.

Maurice Cook died on New Year's Eve in 2006 aged seventy-five, on the very eve of a game between the two clubs he had represented with such distinction, Fulham and Watford. At the beginning of the match, a minute's silence in his honour was immaculately observed by both sets of supporters. At his funeral, at the Holy Trinity Church in Potten End, the church was full to overflowing and many stood outside in the rain listening to a relay of the service for their friend and colleague. He is buried in the local churchyard.

MAURICE COOK
Fulham career – all competitions

Season	Appearances	Goals	Home	Away
1957–1958	15	9	5	4
1958–1959	45	17	13	4
1959–1960	19	9	4	5
1960–1961	34	13	3	10
1961–1962	45	19	14	5
1962–1963	39	15	9	6
1963–1964	32	6	6	0
1964–1965	19	9	7	2
Total	248	97	61	36

*Total career **league** appearances–441, and **league** goals–159.*

Graham Leggat

Showing his usual formidable athleticism, Leggat scores the first goal of his hat-trick against Leicester City in December 1966.

One of Fulham's favourite strikers, he scored over 100 goals in the top flight, holds the post-war record of eight hat-tricks – and was sold for a pittance.

Graham Leggat was born in Aberdeen and began his football career with the youth team Torry Former Pupils winning a Scottish Youth cap, before signing with the top youth team Banks O'Dee where he stood out as a prodigious talent. Leggat started his professional career at his home town club as a right winger whilst also at the same time being employed as a trainee graduate PE teacher at Jordanhill College in Glasgow. In the summer of 1953, he was pitched straight into the **Aberdeen** side with scarcely any junior matches and just one reserve game behind him.

He possessed all the attributes – speed, natural ability, dribbling skills coupled, with mental and physical agility. Many at Pittodrie consider that he was 'the complete player' and almost solely responsible for transforming Aberdeen from a 'nearly' team to one that achieved. They reached the Scottish Cup final in 1954, Leggat scoring in the 6–0 semi-final victory

over Glasgow Rangers, but they were edged out 1–2 in the final against Celtic. The Dons then took the Scottish League title in 1955. The next season, 1955–56, Aberdeen won the Scottish League Cup. Leggat scored nine goals in the ten ties, including the winner against St Mirren in the final at Hampden Park. In the league that season, Leggat notched twenty-nine goals in just twenty-nine games. He also netted six goals playing for the Scottish League in a mere five appearances.

At twenty-one he made his full Scotland debut in 1956 against the 'auld enemy' England. He scored a superb lobbed goal in the second half and Scotland were only denied their first win over England in twenty years by an equaliser a minute from time from Johnny Haynes. A second cap against Wales followed in October and Leggat looked to be cemented into the Scottish side, but injuries followed and he did not play again for Scotland until October 1957, where once again he scored, in a 1–1 draw against Northern Ireland. Disaster followed weeks later, when he broke his leg playing for Aberdeen which kept him out most of the 1957–58 season.

He was written off by some critics, but being superbly fit and a trained instructor, Leggat confounded the media by returning fit and ready for the 1958 World Cup in Sweden. He competed in two pre-tournament friendlies against Hungary and Poland and on the strength of those performances booked his place. Although Scotland did not progress, Leggat played in two of the three group games.

Despite missing three-quarters of one season, by the summer of 1958, Leggat had scored sixty-four goals in 109 league appearances for Aberdeen and an astounding ninety-two goals in 152 matches in all competitions, almost two every three games. His form and appearances for Scotland attracted scouts from south of the border and after having initial approaches rebuffed, **Fulham** secured Leggat's signature in the summer of 1958 for an incredibly low £17,000. The fee was probably recouped by Roy Dwight's transfer to Nottingham Forest.

At Fulham he was an instant success. The beginning of the 1958–59 season showed the Cottage crowd what they could expect. Fulham won all six of the opening league games netting twenty-three goals. Leggat scored in every one of those matches, seven in total. At the end of October came his first hat-trick in a

3–2 victory at Middlesbrough. He showed initial signs of his versatility too by playing a number of games on the left wing equally effectively. At the end of the season Fulham were promoted and Leggat had scored twenty-one goals in just thirty-six games. He was second highest scorer as Johnny Haynes had, for one season, been top scorer. During that promotion campaign and in the ensuing close season, Leggat won five more Scottish international caps, scoring three times.

Naturally the going was tougher in the first season back in the top flight, but Leggat, despite injuries, again scored regularly, including five in the first four home matches. His ability to play anywhere in the front line showed when he was asked to play at centre forward at Old Trafford and in his very first game in that position fired a hat-trick in an entertaining 3–3 draw. Later in the season he went one better with four goals in a 5–0 victory over Leeds United at Craven Cottage. There were a further four braces in the total for that season. Despite missing a third of the league season, Leggat finished the 1959–60 season as top goalscorer with twenty goals in league and FA Cup. He then won six further Scottish international caps scoring in three of the matches, including another goal against England. Yet, at the height of his career, he was never selected for his home country again, due to the selectors always preferring to pick players plying their trade in Scotland.

Watched by a crowd of nearly 40,000, Leggat shoots on goal in the match at home to Leeds United on Good Friday 1966.

Leggat looks more bemused than inspired by manager Vic Buckingham's team talk pictured here in the dressing room at Blackpool at the beginning of the 1965–66 season.

Many believe that Leggat was the first of the modern forwards, not very tall but quick and difficult to shake off the ball. He had a great shot with both feet and was also very good with his head. Being a PE teacher he was very fit. He had superb balance with a very correct body position that made volleying the ball look effortless. Some called him the 'Scottish Jimmy Greaves'. Many of his goals were opportunist efforts and the majority were scored within the six-yard box. He had the striker's happy knack of being in the right place at the right time to finish off good approach work. He had that ruthless streak like Allan Clarke. He was also tough and a hard player, never afraid of getting injured which he often was with breaks and fractures. His style of play also won Fulham a considerable number of (perfectly valid!) penalties. Most of all, considering that he was essentially a winger, his goals to games ratio was outstanding.

Season 1960–61 was to prove no different for Leggat. Fulham as a team struggled in the league, but Leggat, supplied by Haynes' passes, remained scorer supreme. He netted five in the first eight games and in an amazing thirty days bridging October and November, Leggat netted in five consecutive games, nine goals in total including his fourth and fifth hat-tricks, against Bolton Wanderers (3–0) and Leicester City (4–2). By this third season he had also appeared at inside right and inside left, meaning that he had played in all five positions in the forward line. For the second consecutive season he finished as leading scorer with twenty-three goals in thirty-six games.

In 1961–62 he wasn't so prolific, being second highest scorer behind Maurice Cook but still added fourteen goals. In the 1962–63 season he once again netted double figures with ten further goals. As he approached thirty he began to slow a little and injuries took their toll.

He played in just over half the season's matches of the 1963–64 season, but still managed, for the third time in five years, to be top scorer. Some of this total was due to the remarkable match that occurred on Boxing Day 1963, when Fulham slaughtered Ipswich Town 10–1 on a muddy pitch. After Maurice Cook had opened the scoring on the quarter-hour, Leggat fired a hat-trick timed at just under four minutes, as Fulham led 5–1 at half time. It was the fastest First Division hat-trick in history and a statistic unlikely ever to be broken. He claimed a fourth too with a long-range shot near the end. It was his sixth game with three goals or better.

Season 1964–65 was a poor one for Leggat as injuries saw him play only seventeen league games in which he added just four further goals to his total. Under manager Vic Buckingham, Leggat had an in-

You can hear the crowd baying for a penalty, but surely this blocked shot by Sunderland defender Hurley in March 1966 was too close to be a deliberate handball.

and-out start to the following season, but added a seventh hat-trick in a strange league game against Aston Villa at Craven Cottage in September. Fulham recovered from being two goals down with a Leggat hat-trick which put the home side ahead, only for comical goalkeeping and defending by the Cottagers to allow Villa to snatch four late goals to win 3–6. Fortunately for Fulham, Leggat returned to form and fitness in the 'great escape', netting eight goals in the last fifteen matches, some of those goals proving crucial in helping Fulham avoid relegation. Despite missing almost a third of the season, he finished as top scorer for the fourth time in seven seasons with another fifteen goals.

In the close season, Fulham toured Asia alongside Sheffield Wednesday, playing six matches. Leggat scored in every game, ending up with eleven. The locals marvelled at his shooting and his eye for a goal. The modest Leggat said, 'The team scores the goals, I just put my name on 'em.'

In 1966–67 Leggat, now thirty-two, started well, and in the first eleven games (ten league and one League Cup) put away a further five goals. Manager Buckingham, trying to lower the age of the side, then dropped him and Leggat very reluctantly asked for a transfer. The Scotsman had the final word when recalled to the side at Christmas due to an injury to Steve Earle. He responded with a superb hat-trick in a 4–2 home victory over Leicester City – his eighth

treble. His eight hat-tricks remain a post-war highest total. Just to emphasise the point, in the next game four days later on New Year's Eve, Leggat scored two more and his third shot was defected in, during a 4–1 win over Stoke City. The statistics today would probably show it as a hat-trick. This cut no ice with Buckingham who, thinking he had younger replacements in Steve Earle and Allan Clarke, promptly sold Leggat to Second Division **Birmingham City** just a couple of days later for a giveaway fee. Fulham supporters were stunned and devastated.

Leggat will be remembered as the only Fulham player ever to score over a century of league goals all in the top division of the league. He also managed to reach double figures in terms of goals in seven out of the eight seasons he was with Fulham.

Leggat's return to the Second Division with the Blues was a big disappointment. Given the role of slotting in behind the front three strikers, his goal production failed to meet expectations, he scored just once in nine games in the remainder of that 1966–67 season. In the opening game of the following season Leggat found himself in the reserves and despite scoring five goals in one second-team game he saw only sporadic action in the first team, with three goals in seven games. A serious back injury led to him leaving St Andrews at the end of that season with a free transfer.

He signed for Third Division **Rotherham United** for the 1968–69 season and although his playing time was limited, he managed seven goals in thirteen starts, still almost one in two at the age of thirty-five. Leggat retired from professional football at the end of that season. He was briefly back in the Midlands initially as coach at Aston Villa under Tommy Docherty (his Scottish international team-mate) and then, after being prised out of playing retirement, for a short playing spell with non-league **Bromsgrove Rovers** in 1970.

There followed a complete one-year's break from football when he joined Rank Xerox as a salesman. In 1971 he emigrated to Canada with his family as player/coach of the **Toronto Blizzards** (aka Toronto Metros) in the NASL. He put on his boots again and made eleven appearances, scoring two goals with two assists. He was almost thirty-eight by this time. He parted company with the Metros in the middle of 1972, and this paved the way for an unlikely career in television.

In a country where football was regarded as a foreign sport, Leggat's Scottish accent and knowledge of the European game made him a popular pundit at CBC, who covered everything from the World Cup to the European championships and then the Olympic Games. During this busy time, Leggat even found time to be vice-president and managing director of the NASL's Edmonton Drillers team for two years (1979–80).

When CBC dropped soccer coverage in 1986, Leggat became the popular host of TSN's (The Sports Network) programmes *Soccer Saturday* and *World of Soccer*, the country's weekly magazine programme. He became a household name, the 'voice of soccer', Canada's answer to Archie Macpherson, with whom he had studied PE at Jordanhill College.

During his broadcasting years, Leggat entertained viewers with his unbiased and knowledgeable approach to the sport. Many said his colloquialisms and panache could only have come from someone familiar with being on the pitch and living the football life. He was still broadcasting into the twenty-first century.

Graham Leggat was inducted into the Canadian Soccer Hall of Fame in 2001 as a 'builder', which means a key figure of the development of the sport in that country.

He has now retired and lives quietly at his Canadian home with his wife, near to Niagara Falls. Tragedy has also hit the family. Leggat's son, also called Graham, was executive director of, and a leading figure in, the San Francisco Film Society; he passed away with cancer aged just fifty-one in 2011.

GRAHAM LEGGAT
Fulham career – all competitions

Season	Appearances	Goals	Home	Away
1958–1959	40	22	13	9
1959–1960	30	20	13	7
1960–1961	36	23	11	12
1961–1962	39	14	8	6
1962–1963	35	10	5	5
1963–1964	28	16	10	6
1964–1965	19	4	3	1
1965–1966	37	15	8	7
1966–1967	16	10	9	1
Total	280	134	80	54

*Total career **league** appearances–285, and **league** goals–138.*

The 1960s

Allan Jones

Scored with his first kick, but three goals in seven matches are the sum of his Fulham career.

Allan Jones was born in Paddington and joined Fulham as a seventeen-year-old in April 1958. He didn't make an appearance in the 1958–59 promotion team, but received an early opportunity up front when he made his First Division debut against Bolton Wanderers in February 1960. He made a dream start at centre forward too, scoring with his first kick of the ball in just thirty-five seconds in a 1–1 draw at the Cottage. He played five games out of six before returning to the reserves. Near the end of the season he was recalled again and scored in two consecutive matches, a 3–0 win over Arsenal and a 2–1 win over West Bromwich Albion, to make it three goals in only seven matches.

He looked a promising young player, but was given a hard time by Johnny Haynes in the team, and disillusioned he quit league football at the end of that season. However, his love of football remained and he joined non-league side **Dover Athletic** in the close season. He spent the next three seasons there, being top scorer in each of those seasons.

He moved on to have a partial season at **Ramsgate**, before joining **Margate**. He remained there for two seasons making eighty-six appearances and scoring thirteen goals.

He then had a season at **Tonbridge** before joining **Canterbury** where, apart from a season at **Gravesend** (when he broke a leg), he spent the remainder of his career.

He retired in 1974 having scored eighty-four Southern League goals for Canterbury and then joined the club's coaching staff. In later years, he went on to become manager at Dover, Faversham, Sheppey and Folkestone before being appointed Canterbury's secretary. Outside of league football, he worked as an executive in a London advertising agency.

ALLAN JONES
Fulham career – all competitions

Season	Appearances	Goals	Home	Away
1959–1960	7	3	3	0
Total	7	3	3	0

*Total career **league** appearances–7, and **league** goals–3.*

Reg Stratton

An Amateur Cup winner and England youth player who was an honest trier for Fulham.

Reg Stratton was born in Kingsley (near Alton) in Hampshire. He was an England youth player and an England amateur international, playing three games against Germany, Ireland and Switzerland in 1957. He played as an amateur for **Woking** and, aged just eighteen, helped them to lift the FA Amateur Cup in 1958 by scoring the second goal twelve minutes from time in the 3–0 win over Ilford in front of 71,000 at Wembley. At Woking, Stratton had been a regular scorer, with sixty-four goals in 123 games. He joined **Fulham** in the close season in 1959.

Amateur Reg Stratton made his debut in a 2–4 defeat at Stamford Bridge in the 1959–60 season playing on the left wing in place of Trevor Chamberlain. It was his only game that season. The following two seasons, 1960–61 and 1961–62, he failed to make a first-team appearance at all. In 1962–63 he made three league appearances in mid-season replacing the injured Brian O'Connell.

In 1963–64 he made two early appearances on the wing and later that season he was awarded a decent run in the side with nine (including eight consecutive) games at centre forward. He scored his only league goal for Fulham during that run, the winner in the 1–0 victory over eventual champions Liverpool, in Alan Mullery's final game before his controversial transfer to Tottenham.

He made six further league appearances in the latter stages of the 1964–65 season, a couple on the left wing but mostly at centre forward. He did not add to his league goal tally, but he scored twice in the 3–3 home draw with Fourth Division Millwall in the third round of the FA Cup. His final game was a 0–3 defeat at Blackpool in March.

Stratton was an honest trier but was somewhat out of his depth in the top two divisions of English football. Like many others, he was an early victim of the Vic Buckingham purge and left at the end of the 1964–65 season on a free transfer when he joined Fourth Division **Colchester United**.

Stratton rediscovered his scoring touch with Colchester. He made his United debut in August 1965, a 1–0 away defeat at Port Vale, and opened his scoring account with two goals in early September in the League Cup as United beat Exeter City 2–1 at Layer Road. In his first season he scored eighteen league goals, was top scorer and helped the club to promotion to the Third Division at the end of that season. The following two seasons he repeated the top-scoring feat with twenty-four league goals in 1966–67 and nine goals in 1967–68 respectively. In 112 league games he scored fifty-one times (fifty-six in all competitions). However, in the close season of

1968 and after refusing new contract terms he was placed on the transfer list and briefly joined **Vancouver Royals** in the NASL where he made four appearances before the team folded.

Stratton then returned to England at thirty and played out the remainder of his career with non-league clubs **Brentwood Town**, **Basingstoke Town** and **Dover Athletic**. Stratton is great-uncle to Manchester United and England player Tom Cleverley.

REG STRATTON
Fulham career – all competitions

Season	Appearances	Goals	Home	Away
1959–1960	1	0	0	0
1960–1961	0	0	0	0
1961–1962	0	0	0	0
1962–1963	4	0	0	0
1963–1964	11	1	1	0
1964–1965	8	2	2	0
Total	24	3	3	0

Total career league appearances–133, and league goals–52.

Bobby Brown

A former amateur with an impressive strike rate, and released too early by Fulham.

Bobby Brown was born in Streatham. He started as an amateur with non-league **Barnet**, for whom he scored twice in the 1959 Amateur Cup final against Crook Town but finished on the losing side 2–3. He also won England amateur caps whilst with Barnet. In the summer of 1960, he represented England at football in the summer Olympic Games playing three games and scoring four goals. He got two of them in the 3–4 defeat to a Brazil side that included Gerson and scored one in the 1–1 draw with Italy who fielded the fabulous Gianni Rivera and the recent Irish manager Trapattoni.

Brown moved into the Football League with First Division **Fulham** in September 1960, but continued to play initially as an amateur, making his debut the following month in a 3–0 win at Bolton. He played the next game too. He returned after an absence of four games to play three more and in the second of those two games had his best day with Fulham scoring twice at Craven Cottage in a very exciting 4–4 draw with Manchester United. He won more England amateur caps too, making it fourteen in total.

In the close season of 1961, the six-foot Brown was one of five amateur players chosen for an FA tour of Singapore, Hong Kong and New Zealand over May and June. He played three matches, netting a hat-trick in *each* of them, a 10–0 win over Otago, a 13–0 win over Minor Provinces and an 8–0 win over Auckland. In the 1961–62 season, Brown played in three matches early in the season, and scored two further goals to make it four in eight for Fulham. The 2–2 draw with Bolton proved to be his final goal and his final game for the Cottagers.

Strangely, he was never picked again despite his promise, and Fulham allowed Brown to leave for Third Division **Watford**. Over a period of two years he played twenty-eight league games for the Hornets scoring ten goals. Over Christmas 1963 he left Watford to join Second Division **Northampton Town**. The Cobblers were a side on the up and Brown was an astute signing. He did not score that season, but in the following season his thirteen goals (making him equal leading goalscorer with Don Martin and Tommy Robson) propelled Northampton into the top flight.

He was also Town's top scorer in the following season, 1965–66, with nine goals but Northampton were relegated. Three of those nine goals were scored against Fulham. In a match where goalkeeper Tony Macedo broke his jaw and Rodney Marsh played in goal, Brown smashed a hat-trick to remind Fulham what they had let get away.

After relegation, Brown was allowed to leave and moved to Second Division **Cardiff City** in October 1966 for a fee of £15,000. He was a Welsh Cup winner with them in 1967 and he took part in the Bluebirds' 1967–68 European Cup Winners Cup campaign. He had already scored an impressive twenty-four goals in just fifty league games for Cardiff when he injured his knee during a 3–0 win over Aston Villa on Boxing Day 1967 and was forced into retirement at the premature age of twenty-seven. Over his career he had scored almost sixty league goals in under 140 games, almost a goal in every other game, a ratio better than the majority of strikers.

BOBBY BROWN
Fulham career – all competitions

Season	Appearances	Goals	Home	Away
1960–1961	5	2	2	0
1961–1962	3	2	1	1
Total	**8**	**4**	**3**	**1**

*Total career **league** appearances–**136**, and **league** goals–**59**.*

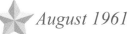

Dave Metchick

He once scored six goals in the opening four matches of a season.

Dave Metchick was born in Bakewell near Derby, and started as a youth player with **West Ham United** where he won England youth caps. One of only a small number of Jewish players in the game, Metchick turned professional in 1961, signing for **Fulham**. A little too small to be a central striker, Metchick was definitely more of an inside forward, but scored a number of goals, especially from long range. In his later career at Leyton Orient he became known as the 'Mighty atom'.

After joining Fulham in the close season of 1961, he made his debut in his first month in a 1–2 defeat at Manchester City. He enjoyed a decent run in the side and his first goal came in September in his fourth game, a 1–1 draw at Sheffield Wednesday, with another a month later in the 3–1 home win over Aston Villa. His third goal came in a 2–0 away win at Walsall in an FA Cup fourth-round replay. In all competitions, Metchick made twenty-three appearances in his first season.

The following season, 1962–63, he played twelve matches in all, but he was used more as a back-up forward. His only goal of the season came in a League Cup tie with Hull. The next season saw a similar pattern. Metchick appeared sporadically early in the season, with a few appearances late on. His only league goal was against Leicester City, but he managed two in Fulham's 3–5 defeat at Colchester United in the League Cup. He was a versatile player, happy at inside forward or, slightly less so, on the left wing.

He made an outstanding start to the 1964–65 season with Fulham, with six goals in the first four league games, scoring in every one. This included a hat-trick in a midweek 3–1 home victory over Birmingham City. They proved to be his last goals for the club. He played in eleven out of the first twelve league games, his last one being a 0–3 defeat at Tottenham in October. Despite his good start, he was a **Leyton Orient** player two months later.

At Second Division Orient, he played for the best part of three seasons and was a popular player, making seventy-five appearances and scoring fifteen goals. Unfortunately, the O's were relegated at the end of his

Metchick scores with a diving header – one of his three goals against Birmingham City at Craven Cottage in September 1964.

second season. With considerable financial problems on and off the field, Leyton Orient sold Metchick around the transfer deadline in March 1967 to Third Division **Peterborough United**.

In a season and a quarter with the Posh, Metchick was a regular, scoring six goals in forty-one matches in all competitions, including three in consecutive matches midway through that period. He moved back to London with First Division **Queens Park Rangers** in the summer of 1968. For Rangers it was a disastrous season, and Metchick made just two substitute appearances for the team that finished bottom of the table, the first of those appearances in October. He could also manage only one substitute appearance the following season too, against Charlton Athletic in October, but scored his only Rangers goal.

This was followed by a move to **Arsenal**. At Arsenal he never played a competitive match for the first team, but was a stalwart of the reserve side, helping to develop and coach the younger players in the squad, many of whom would star in the Arsenal double-winning side the following season.

Like a number of players at the time, Metchick left these shores to play in the emerging NASL, and initially joined the **Atlanta Chiefs**, playing twenty games and scoring eight goals with six assists in his first season (1970) and eight games with three goals the next. He then had a season with **Miami Gatos** making nine appearances, with no goals but one assist (1972). He returned to the Atlanta team, now re-named **Atlanta Apollos**, where he played eighteen games, scoring two goals with three assists (1973).

In the summer of 1973, Metchick returned to England, and at aged thirty, joined his fifth London club, Fourth Division **Brentford**. In a season and a half there, he again proved himself a popular, regular and hard-working player, making sixty-one appearances scoring four goals. He was also sent off in a match at Plymouth Argyle.

Near the end of that second season, he left Griffin Park to join Isthmian League **Hendon**. His time there was brief, before moving back to West London to join **Hillingdon Borough**, at that time a very strong non-league side. In his two years at Hillingdon, he made eighteen appearances scoring three goals; they also enjoyed some FA Cup giantkilling, winning at Torquay

United. Towards the end of his second season he left to finish his career by the coast with sixteen matches for **Weymouth** in the Southern Premier League.

Like a number of his team-mates, Metchick enjoyed boxing and would often be found in the company of Bobby Keetch and Johnny Haynes at London bouts. After finishing with football, Metchick took 'the knowledge', as did several other Fulham players, and became a London taxi driver.

	DAVE METCHICK			
	Fulham career – all competitions			
Season	Appearances	Goals	Home	Away
1961–1962	23	3	1	2
1962–1963	12	1	0	1
1963–1964	10	3	1	2
1964–1965	11	6	4	2
Total	56	13	6	7

*Total career **league** appearances–**224**, and **league** goals–**35**.*

Jackie Henderson

A lively, classy player, and experienced Scottish international.

– 69 –

Jackie **Henderson** was born in Glasgow and was a junior with the Kirkintilloch Boys Club but signed for First Division giants **Portsmouth** initially as a seventeen-year-old amateur, before signing professional forms. After completing his national service, he made his Portsmouth debut against Sunderland in January 1951. Initially a centre forward, Henderson was known for his versatility and his ability to play the role of a deep-lying inside forward and also that of a left winger, often called a 'one-man forward line'. A physical player known for his direct running, pace and fierce shot, he was a regular goalscorer for Pompey for seven years.

Four times in six seasons he netted double figures for the south-coast club with the two other seasons ending in eight goals; in 1955–56 he netted sixteen goals. After just two years with Portsmouth, his goalscoring and raw courage attracted the attention of the Scotland national side management and in 1953 he played two games, scoring his only Scotland goal in

Henderson came up against his former team-mates when Fulham entertained Arsenal in September 1962, but finished on the losing side, with Fulham defeated 1–3.

a 3–1 win over Northern Ireland in October. In 1954 he was awarded two further caps and was selected for the 1954 Scottish World Cup squad, but in the end remained in Scotland 'on reserve'. He was awarded one more cap in 1955.

After making over 200 league appearances for Portsmouth, Henderson moved to First Division **Wolverhampton Wanderers** in March 1958 for £16,000, but never really settled. Wolves won the First Division title that season, but Henderson played just one game and did not qualify for a medal. He began the following season, 1958–59, still at Molineux, and appeared in eight early games scoring three goals in what would be another championship-winning campaign for the Midlands side.

Unable to hold down a first-team place at Wolves, he moved on to **Arsenal** in October 1958 for a significant fee of £20,000, and made his debut against West Bromwich Albion at Highbury, where he scored twice with flashing headers in a thrilling 4–3 win. A month later he won his final cap for Scotland against Northern Ireland. Injury marred his initial season with the Gunners, although he still scored twelve times. He returned to become a first-team regular in the 1959–60 and 1960–61 seasons, scoring seventeen goals in those two campaigns.

Arsenal under George Swindin were usually a mid-table side and the manager's constant experimenting with the Arsenal attacking line-up meant that the versatile Henderson was unable to hold down any particular position in the side, and midway through the 1961–62 season he was transferred to First Division **Fulham** for £14,000. He had played over 100 league games for Arsenal.

He made his Fulham debut in a 3–4 home defeat by Chelsea in January. His first goal came two weeks later in a 2–2 home draw with Walsall in the fourth round of the FA Cup. Fulham were deep in relegation trouble when Henderson signed, and the club saw an

upturn in form in the final three months of the season. He scored a precious goal as Fulham secured a point in a 1–1 draw with Nottingham Forest and after that Fulham won five of the next seven league games. He ended the season with five goals from only eighteen starts and he also played a significant role in Fulham's journey to the FA Cup semi-final.

In season 1962–63 Henderson was ever present in the league during the first half of the season, but managed just three goals in all competitions, his final goal being in the 2–1 away victory over Aston Villa in the November of that season. Sadly, he broke a leg in a 1–0 away win at Blackburn in March and missed the remainder of that season. Despite working very hard on a comeback, he played only four Fulham games late in the 1963–64 season without scoring, his final game being in March, a 0–2 defeat at Nottingham Forest. He quickly realised he could no longer compete at the top level and left Fulham at the end of the season. He had played fourteen seasons in his career, *all* of them in the First Division.

After leaving professional football, he signed for Southern League side **Poole Town**. Straight away he was hugely influential as Poole gained promotion to the Southern League Premier Division. After four years with Poole, Henderson began four years of sterling service with **Dorchester Town** of the Western League, not ending his playing days until 1971, when he was nearing forty. A lively and pleasant character, he had always been keen to put back something into the game at the lower levels.

After his retirement from playing, he left the game completely, settling in Dorset, and for thirty years he worked as a storeman for a local builders merchant. He still attended Portsmouth's reunions until near to the time of his death in 2005, at the age of seventy-three.

JACKIE HENDERSON
Fulham career – all competitions

Season	Appearances	Goals	Home	Away
1961–1962	25	6	3	3
1962–1963	26	3	1	2
1963–1964	4	0	0	0
Total	55	9	4	5

Total career **league** *appearances–* ***374***, *and* **league** *goals–* ***108***.

Rodney Marsh

A born entertainer who was Fulham's top goalscorer in 1964–65, and scored over 170 career goals.

Rodney Marsh was born in Hatfield in Hertfordshire, but he grew up in the tough areas of east London around Stepney. He was named after *HMS Rodney* by his father, who served on the battleship. He played for Hackney boys and joined West Ham United as an amateur aged fifteen whilst continuing to study. Three years later, after leaving technical college with a creditable four 'A' levels, he joined the groundstaff at **Fulham**.

After scoring forty goals for the Fulham juniors, he made an outstanding Fulham debut at eighteen scoring the only goal in the 1–0 defeat of Aston Villa at Craven Cottage in February 1963. He injured himself soon after, breaking his toe and chipping a bone whilst doing extra training and that meant that the Villa game was his only league game of the season.

At the start of the 1963–64 season, he got back into the side, but in his third outing, whilst scoring the winning goal with his head against Leicester City at Filbert Street in a 1–0 victory, he collided with the goal post and a defender, broke his jaw and was badly injured. The injury resulted in permanent deafness in his left ear. It also badly affected his vision and his balance, and it was a long time before he could even walk properly again. At one stage it looked as if his fledgling career might be over. Specialists worked on him for ten months and would not let him do even light training for a long spell. He appeared only once more that season.

He worked exceptionally hard during the close season and at the start of the 1964–65 season came back to claim a regular spot in the Fulham side. He did very well too scoring twelve goals before Christmas, including two in a 3–2 victory at Nottingham Forest, Fulham's only away win that season, and two in a 5–2 home victory over Leicester City. In the second half of the season he scored five in nine games in a purple patch. In his first full season, he was top scorer for the First Division side with seventeen goals.

Rodney Marsh loved to entertain, and winning or losing took second place in his eyes. Even if Fulham had lost he would think wasn't it a great game though? He was tall, blond and well built and had pace too. The main part of Rodney's game was his ball skill, and there was almost a Brazilian quality to some of his play. He loved to beat players and humiliate them. He had a number of party tricks and skills and loved to play to the crowd. Nutmegs, drag-backs, overhead kicks – he had them all.

He was the ultimate showman who always played with a smile on his face. He was capable of superb individual goals, but sometimes these were at the expense of team play. In today's game it would probably be described as showboating, but he was very popular with supporters. However, sometimes the over-elaboration and showing off irked some of the senior Fulham players. He had almost ridiculous natural ability, and could make the ball do whatever he wanted it to do, but it also looked on occasions as if he only really played when he wanted to. When he wanted to play, he was a world beater; when he didn't, he could appear just lazy and half-hearted.

Regrettably his sometime lack of seriousness and his clowning did not go down very well with new manager Vic Buckingham. The feeling was mutual and occasionally Marsh would be sent off in training, and quite often there were verbal confrontations.

Typical flamboyant style from Marsh in the 0–3 defeat against Chelsea in August 1965.

In the 1965–66 season it took him eleven games to get off the mark – in a 1–1 draw with Nottingham Forest. In November he actually played in goal for the majority of a match when Tony Macedo was injured against Northampton; Fulham lost 1–4 at home. The following week he scored two superb goals in a 2–3 defeat at Stoke City, but they were to be his last. He played his final game for Fulham during a forgettable 1–3 defeat in an FA Cup third-round tie at Sheffield United, cutting a lonely figure out on the wing in a number 7 shirt.

He was labelled 'a clown' by Buckingham who consigned him to the reserves as a tagged misfit, and by the transfer deadline he had moved across west London to join **Queens Park Rangers**, then in the Third Division, for a paltry fee of just £15,000. It would go down as one of Fulham's costliest ever mistakes, and it was remarkable that a top scorer in the top flight (today's Premiership) was virtually given away to a side two divisions lower – and Marsh was just twenty-one years of age! It took a little time for Marsh under the attacking ethos of wily manager Alec Stock to acclimatise himself with that level of football, but he still managed eight goals in the sixteen remaining league games of the season. His form prompted First Division Newcastle to make a bid for him that was flatly turned down by QPR chairman Jim Gregory.

The next season, 1966–67, was a remarkable one for both Marsh and QPR; they took the division by storm, winning the league championship by a clear twelve points (when it was only two points for a win). They also became the first ever Third Division

side to win the Football League Cup when they beat First Division West Bromwich Albion 3–2 in front of 100,000 at Wembley. Rangers came from two goals down at half-time to win, with Marsh scoring a spectacular solo-run equaliser. He scored forty-four goals that season and was the highest goalscorer in the country. Thirty goals were scored in the league and fourteen more in cup competitions.

The following season, 1967–68, was almost as good and QPR were promoted again to the First Division. It was a bittersweet moment for Marsh, for as his QPR side were being promoted they were replacing Fulham who were going in the opposite direction. Marsh's contribution was fourteen goals in twenty-five league games. His talent was recognised at international level too, and he won two England U-23 caps, scoring in both games.

Alec Stock left the club in the close season, and QPR lasted just one season in the top flight, 1968–69, as they just did not have the quality or depth of squad to remain. They won only one league game after Christmas and finished with just eighteen points. Marsh's contribution was a meagre four goals, but he had been injured for a significant percentage of the season. Included in the defeats was a 1–8 trouncing by Manchester United.

Back in the Second Division, the illegal and foul tackles that Marsh had to contend with to stop him playing were becoming worse and he was being booked regularly for retaliation. He still played well, and registered twelve league goals in thirty-eight appearances during the 1969–70 season. It looked as

More acrobatics from Marsh (in dark shirt), but to no avail as Fulham lost this encounter at Tottenham in October 1964.

if Rangers would be promoted but they stumbled in a poor run and ultimately finished ninth, prompting Marsh to ask for a transfer in his quest for First Division and international football. He relented a month later and signed a new contract.

The following season, 1970–71, was just as mediocre for the QPR team as they finished eleventh following a dismal start. Marsh's contribution however was again significant with twenty-one goals in thirty-nine appearances, including a spectacular televised hat-trick in a 5–2 destruction of Birmingham City. In 1971–72 QPR fell just short of promotion finishing two points away in fourth place.

Marsh had been on great form and could not be ignored at international level with Alf Ramsey awarding the forward his first cap against Switzerland in October in a European Championship qualifying match that ended 1–1. Once again Marsh had added significant goals to his Rangers total with another seventeen in thirty league games. During his time at QPR he scored at a rate of a goal every other game.

At the transfer deadline he was transferred to **Manchester City** for a fee of £200,000 just £20,000 short of the British transfer record at that time. City were top of the First Division at the time, four points clear and looking odds-on to win the title. But Marsh was overweight and not fully fit when joining City, and it was a controversial move. The flamboyant assistant manager Malcolm Allison wanted him, the wily old-stager and manager Joe Mercer did not. Mercer's view was 'if it ain't broke, don't fix it', but Allison insisted on thrusting Marsh into their free-flowing side. Rodney's individualistic style did not fit in easily and City finally finished fourth in the title race, albeit just one point short in a very tight finish. Marsh took a great deal of the blame for that eventual collapse.

During this period, Ramsey gave Marsh his second England cap in a defeat by West Germany, but substituted him after an hour. He played in the return 0–0 draw in Germany and in the Home International Championship where he scored his solitary goal for England against Wales.

The 1972–73 season proved to be a good one for Marsh as he scored nineteen league goals for City and finished as top scorer, dazzling the crowd with his skills. Allison was a strong defender of the player's style and City's fans, like those at Loftus Road, took Rodney to their hearts. It was a turbulent season for Marsh at international level. After seven consecutive England appearances, Ramsey grew tired of the 'lazy' and carefree, irreverent style of Marsh's play and following a verbal confrontation with the England manager was never picked for his country again.

The following season, 1973–74, was disappointing for City as well as Marsh. Nevertheless he helped them reach the League Cup final. He starred in that match but the team didn't perform. They lost 1–2 to Wolves and a disconsolate Marsh didn't even collect his runners-up medal on the day. He had managed just nine goals in his thirty-five games.

In 1974–75 the City managership was passed to former defender Tony Book, whose defensive and workmanlike style was alien to the maverick Marsh, who was now captain. City finished eleventh and Marsh felt stifled. It was a relationship that was never going to work and following a physical bust-up with Book early in the 1975–76 season, Marsh was placed on the City transfer list. When all is said and done though, Marsh had contributed forty-seven goals in all competitions in 150 matches for the Manchester club. Following his departure, the Manchester City board received 7,000 letters of complaint from admiring Marsh supporters.

Disillusioned with English football and now thirty-one, Marsh cashed in on his career. He went to America, but before that played three games in Ireland for **Cork Hibernians**, which almost bankrupted them. He joined **Tampa Bay Rowdies** in the NASL in January 1976 for just £40,000 and was introduced to the crowd in March. He responded with twelve goals in just twenty-three matches along with nine assists.

Even this was not without incident. He got star billing but managed to upset manager Eddie Firmani, so vowed to return to England for one last shot.

And it was to his first side, **Fulham**, that he went home, to play alongside his friends George Best and Bobby Moore in the 1976–77 season. Rodney looked past his best, carrying a little too much weight, and not fully fit. In the sunshine of summer and early autumn, however, he contributed to a carnival atmosphere at Craven Cottage, after a stale and colourless 1975–76 season. He scored in his third league game, a 2–0 win at Luton Town, and the season peaked in the amazing and legendary 4–1 televised victory over Hereford United, where he scored twice. But as the cold set in and the heavy pitches came to the fore, Marsh's influence waned, his lack of fitness and apparent lack of interest costing him his place in the struggling team. His final goal came in a shambolic 3–3 January home draw in the FA Cup with Third Division Swindon Town. His final game was just a month later, a 1–2 home reverse against Luton Town. In all he managed

Marsh celebrates his goal at Luton in September 1976, where Fulham won 2–0.

just twenty-two starts and six goals. It was no real surprise that his return to English football looked destined to be no more than a passing farewell and he was released in March.

Firmani had now departed the Rowdies, so Marsh was more than happy to return to the USA and the Florida sunshine. He would grace American football and be a star, feeling unrestricted and able to play his 'normal' game away from the violence and stifling tactics in England. Over the course of the next three seasons, he made eighty-seven appearances for the **Rowdies** with forty-one goals and even more assists. He finally hung up his boots and retired in 1979 aged thirty-five.

Immediately after retiring he remained in the USA, and spent six years as a coach, initially with New York United, then with Carolina Lightnin' and finally with Tampa as coach in 1984 for their final season in the NASL. He was head coach from 1984 to 1986 and was the club's chief executive for eleven years during various re-incarnations of the American soccer scene. He came out of retirement at forty-two to play in the American indoor league (AISA) playing twenty games and scoring thirteen goals. Despite that success overseas, Marsh never harboured any desires to coach or manage in England.

In the last twenty years, Marsh has spent his time between the UK and America. Never one to shun the limelight, he still retains his sense of humour and the ability to send himself up by appearing in numerous televisions programmes, which include *I'm a Celebrity Get me out of Here* (raising £40,000 for charity), *Come Dine with Me*, *The Alan Titchmarsh Show* and *Cash in the Celebrity Attic*.

On a more serious note, he has become a respected pundit and commentator on the modern game, attracting a reputation for his outspoken and controversial views on today's football, bringing the same instinctive flair into the studio that had served him so well on the pitch.

He was a presenter for CNN in the USA during the 1994 World Cup which led to him signing a contract with Sky Sports as an analyst on a live six-hour show, *Gillette Soccer Saturday*. Marsh went on to spend twelve years there and developed a popular repartee with presenter Jeff Stelling. He was sacked in 2005 for a broadcast remark concerning David Beckham and the tsunami (Toon army). He later apologised on air but it did not save his job.

In 2005, he joined *Talksport* to host his own daily radio show and also worked exclusively for them during the 2006 World Cup in Germany. During this time, he was hired by Yahoo! to be their football expert making match predictions for the Premiership, Champions League and the 2006 World Cup. Aside from his media career, Rod is currently chief executive officer of a successful property development business in Florida.

RODNEY MARSH
Fulham career – all competitions

Season	Appearances	Goals	Home	Away
1962–1963	1	1	1	0
1963–1964	4	1	0	1
1964–1965	44	17	10	7
1965–1966	19	3	1	2
1976–1977	22	6	5	1
Total	90	28	17	11

*Total career **league** appearances–**408**, and **league** goals–**171**.*

Bobby Howfield

A cannonball shot and a fiery temperament.

Bobby Howfield was born in Watford and began his football career with local side Bushey FC, before signing amateur terms with Millwall in May 1957. He didn't play for them and instead became a professional with Third Division **Watford** four months later. In two seasons he made forty-seven league appearances for the Hornets scoring nine goals. Howfield was an all-round sportsman and excelled at cricket, being a handy bowler.

In the close season of 1959, he made an ill-fated move to Fourth Division **Crewe Alexandra**, playing for the club for just two months and making five appearances before a £1,500 move back to the south with **Aldershot**, also of the Fourth Division. Despite missing three months of the season away from the club, he finished up as top scorer with fourteen league goals. He started 1960–61 well too with seven early goals, but after scoring twice against Barrow, he broke a leg and was sidelined for the remainder of the season. He came back strongly the following season where his powerful shooting earned him a 'Golden boy' reputation, and the twenty-three league goals he scored in the 1961–62 season were a club record for a number of years.

But he was a player of fiery temperament both on and off the field, and he repeatedly upset the club's management. Having been warned about his behaviour, he was finally suspended in March 1962 for missing training and a late arrival for a league game. Howfield decided he would only sign a monthly contract at the start of the 1962–63 campaign, so when **Watford** again showed an interest in the player, the Aldershot board accepted the Hornet's 'substantial' £4,000 offer. Howfield's second stay at Watford lasted just fifteen months, including a sending-off, where he netted thirteen times in forty-three appearances. In his two spells with Watford, he had made over 100 appearances for them.

Howfield moved to **Fulham** in November 1963 for £6,000 to replace Trevor Chamberlain and assist the young Brian O'Connell, and made his Fulham debut in the same month in a 0–2 defeat by Liverpool at Anfield, but he did score the following week on his home debut, the third in a 3–1 win over Sheffield United. He took part in the 10–1 massacre of Ipswich Town on Boxing Day and scored a hat-trick. He netted twice more in a spell of fourteen consecutive league games in the side, and he also scored another,

Howfield scores Fulham's third goal against Blackpool in the 3–3 draw at the Cottage in November 1964.

in a third-round FA Cup tie against Luton Town. By the end of the 1963–64 season, he had posted a very respectable seven goals in just sixteen matches. Although fundamentally a winger, Howfield was capable of playing as an inside forward or centre forward.

In the 1964–65 season, he made twelve more consecutive league appearances mid-season adding three more goals. He scored his final goal in a 4–1 win over Nottingham Forest at the end of January, and his last game followed a week later in the 1–3 defeat at Stoke City. It was not only Howfield's last game but also that of the great Stanley Matthews, and he also took part in one FA Cup tie and one League Cup tie.

He was yet another to be included in Vic Buckingham's purge of older players and was released on a free transfer at the end of the 1964–65 season. He had been an aggressive player with a cannonball shot, and although enthusiastic had generally looked out of his class in the higher division.

After leaving Fulham, he spent a brief period in the newborn American 'International Soccer League' playing for the **New Yorkers**, but he returned to England for the 1965–66 season. His potential as a crowd puller saw him re-sign for Fourth Division **Aldershot** where he spent the final two seasons of his league career. He managed ten goals in thirty-four appearances, mostly in that first season.

Unfortunately his bad boy image had not deserted him and although he remained at the Recreation Ground for two seasons, he was continually in conflict with the club's officials, serving internal suspensions, and finally at the end of the 1966–67 season he was released. He spent one more season in football with non-league **Chelmsford City** in the 1967–68 season.

Known for his powerful kicking and shooting, Howfield returned to America in 1968 to take up the American football sport as a 'place kicker'. Between 1968 and 1970 he played for the Denver Broncos, before moving to the New York Jets in 1971, and playing for them until 1974. After his retirement from sport, he worked in the insurance department of a Denver bank, and he still lives close to the city. His son Ian Howfield kicked for the Houston Oilers in 1991.

BOBBY HOWFIELD
Fulham career – all competitions

Season	Appearances	Goals	Home	Away
1963–1964	16	7	5	2
1964–1965	14	3	3	0
Total	30	10	8	2

*Total career **league** appearances–**232**, and **league** goals–**85**.*

February 1964

Steve Earle

Ten years service, four hat-tricks, to scorer in three seasons and scorer o over 100 goals.

Earle scores with a fine shot at Tottenham in February 1966.

Steve Earle was born and bred in Whitton (home of Ashwater Press) near Twickenham, just a few miles from Fulham's ground. He joined the **Fulham** groundstaff in 1963 after successful trials, playing alongside Rodney Marsh and John Dempsey.

After several promising displays in the juniors and reserves, and a number of goals, he made his debut in the 0–2 defeat at Nottingham Forest in February 1964 not long after his eighteenth birthday, and the following week scored in his first home match, a 1–1 draw with Blackpool. He remained in the team for the rest of the season, scoring five goals in twelve league games, including the winner in a rare victory over Chelsea (2–1) at Stamford Bridge and a goal against Manchester United.

However, his progress then faltered somewhat. Despite two goals in four appearances in the following 1964–65 season, he was largely frozen out of the side by new manager Vic Buckingham.

This changed in January 1966 when Buckingham recruited Dave Sexton as coach. With Fulham facing what seemed certain relegation, Sexton dispensed with some of the underperforming older players and brought Earle back into the side along with other young players Brian Nichols, John Dempsey and Les Barrett. It prompted a major change in Fulham's fortunes, and the team went on to win nine and draw two of their final thirteen matches and survive in the First Division at Northampton Town's expense. It was Fulham's greatest escape from relegation, ranked alongside the last-match escape at Portsmouth in 2008.

It was down to Earle's goals and those of Graham Leggat that Fulham survived. Playing alongside the Scot and Les Barrett, Earle netted eleven goals in just fifteen games, including both in the historic 2–0 win over eventual champions Liverpool, and a stunning hat-trick in the memorable 4–2 win at Northampton. At one stage he scored in five consecutive matches. Fulham netted an amazing thirty-two goals in their last fourteen matches. Steve was now a permanent fixture.

Earle was really best as a centre forward, but could also play slightly behind a striker (such as

Dazzling the Upton Park crowd.

Allan Clarke); he was also highly effective on either wing. He had superb pace and the ability to ride a tackle, excellent ball control and ball skills for beating an opponent. He was the ideal striker, able to score confidently with both feet. He was also one of the best headers of a ball in Fulham's history. He could play anywhere in the forward line with equal effect. He was capable of scoring goals from close in but also possessed an explosive shot with many twenty-five-yard specials in his repertoire. He also led the line very well and if colleagues were not available often embarked on spectacular solo runs that brought goals.

Earle was a very elegant and deceptive player, who could drift in and out of games. He had an uncanny knack of losing his marker and had that ability always to be in the right place at the right time. He was not a physical player and seemed to play better with a 'big man' (like Vic Halom) alongside him. But he was a very intelligent player and a good athlete and had the skill of being a split-second ahead of his opponent's thinking.

The following season, 1966–67, he added another thirteen goals – all single goal strikes. He finished second highest scorer behind the prolific Clarke. He also became Fulham's first-ever goalscoring substitute, twice in five days. He suffered injury at the start of the following season and scored just once before

Christmas. He also sustained a back injury in a League Cup match at Workington. He recovered to a degree but managed just seven goals in total as Fulham were relegated. It plagued him also the following season, 1968–69, to a point where his whole future career was in doubt. Fulham were relegated again, Earle making just a handful of appearances and failing to score at all. Fortunately Earle's injury was diagnosed and eventually cured by the England FA doctor Alan Bass.

Events changed dramatically at the beginning of the 1969–70 season when new manager Bill Dodgin, with a very attacking ethos, played four main forwards with Jimmy Conway on one wing and Les Barrett on the other, Vic Halom in the middle with Earle playing off the striker. Steve profited greatly from this line-up and style.

Although it was the Third Division, he scored twenty-three goals that season in the number 9 shirt, none of these being penalties. In one spell he scored ten goals in five games – all away from home. He wrote his name into the Fulham record books with five goals in an 8–0 win at Halifax Town and followed that up with a hat-trick at Stockport in a 4–1 win eleven days later. He missed just two league games and finished joint top scorer with Conway who also netted twenty-three. With a very similar line up, Earle scored a further fourteen goals in the promotion season of 1970–71, finishing second highest scorer behind Les Barrett. He missed just four league games that season.

Following Fulham's promotion to the Second Division, the going was a lot tougher in 1971–72 in terms of goals, but Earle was top scorer again with fourteen goals in all competitions despite a close call with relegation. This included another hat-trick in a League Cup tie against Cambridge United.

After Bill Dodgin's time, manager Alec Stock was well aware of Earle's attributes and he saw Steve top score again in 1972–73 with another fifteen goals from forty appearances. Stock and Dodgin had both rejected bids from First Division clubs in order to retain Earle's services. Despite being a key member of the side, Earle was not as prolific at the start of the 1973–74 season. His final goal was an excellent effort away at First Division Ipswich in a 1–2 League Cup replay defeat in November, and his final league game came ten days later, a 0–2 defeat at West Bromwich.

Fulham were going through a financial crisis carrying a burden of debt following the construction of the new Riverside stand and First Division **Leicester City** made a bid of reportedly between £80,000 and £100,000 for Earle's services.

Fulham were reluctant to sell and Earle didn't really want to leave, but Leicester's fee was crucial and they were able to offer him a better financial deal which brought improved security for his family. Because Steve had been with them for over a decade, Fulham hastily arranged a testimonial for him in 1975 against his new club.

Earle scored on his debut against Spurs and netted four in his first eight games. He returned to Fulham with Leicester just a couple of months later in a fourth-round FA Cup tie. Thankfully he didn't score in the 1–1 draw, but Fulham lost the replay 1–2. That season Earle's goals helped Leicester to reach the FA Cup semi-final. He played for the Midlands side for four seasons back in the First Division making 115 appearances in total for them and scoring twenty-six goals. His best season was 1976–77 with thirteen goals, including ten in seventeen games.

After one loan match at **Peterborough United**, he retired from the English game at the age of thirty-two. He then moved with his family to America where he still resides. He continued playing for three American sides including **Tulsa Roughnecks**. He put roots down in Tulsa where he remains. After hanging up his boots, he was assistant coach and later head coach to the Roughnecks for about a year. In the USA he worked in the insurance industry until retirement. His footballing career though has never really ended as he has continued to coach professionals and youngsters and, despite being a senior citizen himself, was still coaching young players over Christmas 2012 in a tournament in Dallas. Earle occasionally returns to England and the Cottage and still fondly remembers his time at Fulham as the 'best years of my life'.

STEVE EARLE
Fulham career – all competitions

Season	Appearances	Goals	Home	Away
1963–1964	12	5	4	1
1964–1965	4	2	1	1
1965–1966	15	11	4	7
1966–1967	43	13	7	6
1967–1968	35	8	6	2
1968–1969	17	0	0	0
1969–1970	44	23	8	15
1970–1971	49	14	13	1
1971–1972	46	14	12	2
1972–1973	44	15	8	7
1973–1974	18	3	0	3
Total	327	108	63	45

Total career **league** appearances–**391**, and **league** goals–**118**.

Evading the tackle and getting his cross in – that's the Les Barrett way.

⭐ *January 1966*

Les Barrett

Ten years service, almost 500 games, top scorer in 1970–71, there was always a buzz when he got the ball.

Les Barrett was born in Wandsworth and joined Fulham after leaving school, though he was still working part-time for the Post Office. His rise was rapid. At the beginning of the 1965–66 season, he began with the Fulham South-East Counties junior team as an apprentice. Within a couple of months, manager Vic Buckingham saw Barrett star in a 5–0 cup win over Crystal Palace and immediately offered him professional terms. By November he had already been elevated to the reserve Football Combination side. Shortly after that and following just a handful of reserve games, he was in the first team.

Fulham looked almost relegation certainties when Barrett made his debut in an inauspicious 0–0 draw with Blackpool at the Cottage in January 1966. Buckingham brought in fellow striker Steve Earle and defenders John Dempsey and Brian Nichols to try to save the day. Barrett was an instant hit and scored his first goal, a super volley, against Spurs at White Hart Lane in just his third game (3–4) in front of almost 32,000. He then scored another in a 5–2 win at Villa Park. He was a major influence in Fulham avoiding relegation and by the end of that first batch of matches he already had four goals from twelve games.

For the next decade Les would be a regular in the Fulham side, virtually making the number 11 shirt his own and becoming a true fans' favourite. His best season was his next, 1966–67. He didn't score a league goal until the end of October, having missed seven out of the first ten games, but his displays were stunning. He managed nine goals from the wing and the press were unrestrained in their praise, many telling Alf Ramsey that here was his next wide England player. At the end of that season, Les was awarded his only honour, an England U-23 cap against Greece. He also played in an England versus Young England game, giving his Fulham team-mate George Cohen a real roasting from the wing. Young England won 5–0. Allan Clarke (still with Fulham) scored twice from the penalty spot and two of the other goals came from former Fulham player Rodney Marsh.

Les was an uncomplicated winger, and one of a dying breed. He was basically right-footed but had learned to play with his left. His chief attributes were searing pace, close control and the ability to go both inside and outside the full back following quick surges down the wing. He specialised in hard, low crosses from either wing from the byline that set up numerous chances for other forwards. He also had the attributes of a goalscorer, never one to miss an opportunity to have a crack at goal.

One of his specialities was to beat the goalkeeper at the near post when many expected a cross. He was very two-footed and scored from the left wing using both feet. For a smaller player he was more than competent in the air and scored many Fulham goals with his head. Barrett was also extremely consistent and it was rare indeed to see him have an off-day. Les was one of the few Fulham players who excited the crowd when he received the ball; there was an air of expectancy that something exhilarating was about to happen.

As a man he was quite private and undemonstrative, happy to be playing football and doing his best for the Fulham team. He didn't seek any limelight in scoring or creating goals. Off the field he was the same. He was the subject of a Fulham fan club in the Swinging Sixties and even recorded a disc with his brother Paul, but it was not natural for Les to be in the spotlight.

In the 1967–68 season Fulham were relegated, but Barrett played consistently well, scoring double figures for the first time including his first brace in a 3–2 win over Sunderland in August. He missed only two out of fifty-one competitive matches. The second successive relegation in 1968–69 saw Barrett's most disappointing season, missing over a third of the league programme as different formations and players were

tried. He did have the slight consolation of scoring one of the best goals seen at Craven Cottage for years with a stunning volley at home to Cardiff City which put Fulham ahead. Regrettably, Cardiff came back with five goals of their own… Two goals in thirty-two appearances made it a miserable season.

In the Third Division in the following season, Barrett was rejuvenated under Bill Dodgin. With Jimmy Conway scoring on one side and Steve Earle in the middle, Barrett tore the defences apart causing havoc. As the Earle/Conway partnership took the limelight, Barrett scored just once before Christmas. Then after almost five months without a goal and with Fulham in full flow he netted six in eight games. Regrettably, Fulham finished just two places outside the promotion slots. Once again he had missed just three matches (the first three of the season) and played in the next forty-seven.

There would be no mistake in the following season, 1970–71. Fulham were in the promotion places virtually all season and Barrett's goals were the springboard for promotion. Rare as it was for a winger, Barrett was top scorer with eighteen in all competitions. He had five in the first month or so, scoring the winner on the opening day in a 1–0 victory at Barnsley. Goals came regularly throughout the season, but this season he would score two goals in a match four times. Quite a few of the single goals were important match-winners. Remarkably he played in all fifty-three games. Club scouts were eyeing him and there was talk about either Manchester United or Spurs signing him.

Back in the Second Division life was tougher the next season, but he still weighed in with eight precious goals as Fulham clung on to survive. Once again he showed his consistency by being ever present for the second consecutive season, playing in all forty-

The first of Fulham's four goals without reply against Torquay United in February 1971 was this cracking shot by Barrett.

Les evades a flying tackle from a Newcastle defender at home in February 1967, a match which Fulham won 5–1. The Cottagers played in their red away kit because Newcastle had neglected to bring their change strip.

seven matches. It was a time of strife for Fulham and Barrett asked for a transfer mid-season. The big clubs hovered, but in the end Les agreed to stay.

Alec Stock, Dodgin's successor, also appreciated Barrett's skill and he became a mainstay of Stock's team. He was more of a creator, and scored just twice before Christmas but ended the 1972–73 season with six goals. When he missed the goalless draw with Portsmouth at the Cottage in November, it broke a run of 168 consecutive matches covering three and a half seasons. Once again Les missed just three out of forty-seven games. At the end of that season and along with team-mate and centre half Paul Went, Les Barrett played in Gibraltar for an FA XI under the guidance of Alf Ramsey. (They won 9–0.)

1973–74 was just as remarkable. Although Fulham finished mid-table, Barrett was yet again ever present over forty-nine games. He scored in the opening two matches that were both won, and scored regularly throughout the season reaching double figures for the third time with eleven (single goals) in all competitions.

In the next season league goals were hard to come by with just two in the first five months, but he scored a brace in a League Cup tie at First Division Wolves in September as Fulham won 3–1 knocking out the cup holders. As Fulham progressed through the FA Cup, Barrett was outstanding in the 2–1 win over Everton at Goodison Park in the fifth round, and then had the satisfaction of scoring the toe-poked goal that gave Fulham victory in the 1–0 win at Carlisle in the quarter-final. Alongside forwards Jimmy Conway, Viv Busby and John Mitchell, Barrett represented Fulham with honour in the 1975 FA Cup final against West Ham at Wembley. With amazing consistency Les played in fifty-three matches, missing just one league game all season!

The 1975–76 season was a bit of an anti-climax and although Fulham once again finished halfway in the league table, Barrett scored in the second game, against Carlisle in a 3–0 win at Craven Cottage, but failed to find the net again. He was still first-choice winger after a decade at the club.

The FA Cup side was broken up quite quickly and it was a dark period at the club. Barrett respected Alec Stock and when the manager left, Barrett was likely to follow. He scored four times in the first seven matches of the 1976–77 season, but was in and out of the side after that. His last goal came as an equaliser in a 2–2 home draw with Burnley in January 1977. His final game was six weeks later in a dismal 0–1 defeat at Hereford United. Fulham survived in the Second Division and Barrett remained at the club but

did not play again under Bobby Campbell. However in 1976 he was awarded a testimonial by Fulham after ten years of loyal service, and West Ham sent a strong team to play at Craven Cottage, winning the match 5–2.

He was still in the Fulham squad at the start of the 1977–78 season, but now being pushed for his spot in the team by young John Margerrison. After eleven full seasons, Barrett left Fulham in October 1977 to join Second Division **Millwall** for £12,000. At almost thirty and having hared down the left touchline for most of that time, Les had begun to lose a little pace but was still a very potent player. His time at Millwall however was short and unhappy. He played just ten games in total for the Lions, scoring once, leaving on a free transfer at the end of the season.

Like a number of players at the time, Les left these shores for a spell in the USA and the NASL. He played over two USA seasons with **California Surf** – in 1978 with three goals and three assists in twenty games, and in 1979 with three goals and one assist in twenty-four games.

He returned to England in 1979 to join non-league **Woking** under manager Fred Callaghan, his team-mate at Fulham. After Callaghan left, Barrett had a season with **Slough Town** (1981–82) scoring five goals in a busy fifty-eight game season schedule. Later he returned to **Woking** where Callaghan had become assistant manager. Les was now just using his experience and playing in defence as full back or

August 2013 in the Fulham dressing room, and memories flood back for John Fraser and Barrett, as they recall the FA Cup run in 1975. Les is getting ready to read all about himself in the Ashwater book about the Wembley campaign.

sweeper. He carried on playing and coaching until not far short of his fortieth birthday making a total of 179 appearances for the Cards, including a couple of local cup finals.

After hanging up his boots, Les worked for British Telecom for a number of years, and later assisted his wife in the running of a market garden/flower shop close to Earlsfield Station. He is now in retirement and visits the Cottage whenever possible.

Even though he played for just eleven years, he managed to appear in 491 Fulham matches and remains to this day third in the overall list of appearances of any Fulham player in history, behind Johnny Haynes and Eddie Lowe. His total of ninety goals for a winger is stunning, considering that he never played in the middle at all, and is a record unlikely to be broken. Despite that goal total, he never scored a hat-trick for Fulham. From August 1969 to May 1975, Les Barrett missed just *four* out of a possible 300 games. Over eleven and a quarter seasons that works out as almost forty-four matches a season, *every* season.

LES BARRETT
Fulham career – all competitions

Season	Appearances	Goals	Home	Away
1965–1966	14	4	1	3
1966–1967	39	9	6	3
1967–1968	49	10	7	3
1968–1969	32	2	2	0
1969–1970	47	7	4	3
1970–1971	53	18	9	9
1971–1972	47	8	5	3
1972–1973	44	6	2	4
1973–1974	49	11	6	5
1974–1975	56	8	3	5
1975–1976	35	1	1	0
1976–1977	26	6	4	2
Total	**491**	**90**	**50**	**40**

*Total career **league** appearances—**432**, and **league** goals—75.*

This typical poacher's goal from Clarke gave Fulham hope at Southampton in March 1967, but the visitors lost 2–4.

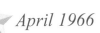 *April 1966*

Allan Clarke

Top scorer in two years at Fulham, a lethal striker who scored 223 career league goals.

Allan Clarke was born in Willenhall, Staffordshire. He came from an amazing footballing family and was one of five brothers. His older brother Frank played for various clubs including Shrewsbury Town, QPR and Ipswich, younger brother Derek for Oxford United and Orient, Wayne for Wolverhampton Wanderers, Birmingham City, Everton and Leicester amongst others, and Kelvin for Walsall. In fact four of the brothers played for Walsall at some stage of their careers.

Even as a youngster he was probably the star of the five and represented Birmingham Schools and South East Staffordshire Boys before joining **Walsall** as an apprentice on leaving school in 1961. He turned professional in 1963. He made his debut for Walsall not long after his seventeenth birthday in the physically very tough days of the Third Division.

In his first full season for Walsall (1964–65) he was the club's top scorer aged just eighteen with twenty-three league goals. He was also their player of the year. By the time he joined Fulham part way through the 1965–66 season, he had already netted over forty league goals for the Saddlers.

At this time Fulham were involved in their annual relegation dogfight but had turned the corner. They had Steve Earle, Les Barrett and Graham Leggat (who was now over thirty) in attack, but Fulham manager Vic Buckingham decided that a younger additional

forward was required. Clarke himself did not think he was quite ready to step up two divisions, but a number of clubs were now courting him. Fulham manager Vic Buckingham was persistent in his quest. Clarke twice turned him down, but finally on the transfer deadline day of 1966, Clarke agreed to join **Fulham**.

Such was the interest in Clarke that Fulham were forced to pay a club record fee in order to secure his signature. £35,000 was a great deal of money for the club at the time. To put it into context the fee was more than it had cost to build the entire Hammersmith End Stand six months earlier!

As the club were in the midst of a winning streak, he didn't go straight into the side. He was substitute for a few games, judging the pace of the division, and came on in the second half of the home game against Leeds United which Fulham lost 1–3. He then stayed in the side for the remainder of the season. Given his prowess, his first goal surprisingly didn't come until his seventh game. It was a scrappy goal too, bundled in unceremoniously from a yard out following a goalmouth mêlée against Stoke City, but it was a critically important goal. It earned Fulham a 1–1 draw and it ensured safety from relegation.

In his first full season, 1966–67, Clarke struggled for goals early on, and by the end of September had scored just twice in his first eighteen games and some Fulham supporters were openly questioning whether it had been cash wisely spent! However, everything changed in October. He was selected for the England U-23 side against Wales at Molineux and responded by scoring four in an 8–0 massacre, and then the Fulham goals began to flow.

He scored twelve goals in his next nine home games at Craven Cottage, scoring twice in five of them. During that time he also scored twice at Anfield, where Fulham secured an excellent 2–2 draw. He continued to score regularly in the second half of the season too, including a sparkling hat-trick against Newcastle United. In that first season with Fulham he played in all but one game in all competitions. He finished as leading scorer with twenty-nine goals and was amongst the highest scorers in the First Division. He was still just twenty.

Clarke really played in just one position, the pinpoint centre of attack, a genuine centre forward, despite the fact that with vagaries of team numbering, he usually wore the number 10 shirt. He would rarely be found outside the penalty area or out on the wing. He didn't really resemble a footballer early on. He was tall and very slender, of slight build, often described as 'lanky' or 'gangling'. He was thin-legged and pale of complexion – you wouldn't have thought he could survive as a footballer! He was affectionately known as 'Twiggy' at Fulham.

Because of his skill, he was targeted by unscrupulous defenders, especially those tackling from behind. His ankles and knees were often kicked and it was not unusual to see him prostrate in a heap on the ground. But, due to hard upbringing in the Third Division, he gave as good as he got, resulting in a sending-off (against Arsenal) and several bookings. He certainly was not averse to handing out some stick of his own, and opponents did not take too many liberties with him, as he could be mean and nasty to those who fouled him frequently. He did not mind giving referees, opponents and team-mates alike some verbal rockets. Yet off the field he was quite quiet and a bit of a loner. He was a rural lad from the Black Country area of the west Midlands who never really settled in the south and did not hanker for the bright lights of London.

The only thing Clarke lacked was true pace, but he rarely needed it. He was skilful with the ball at his feet and could beat opponents with ease. He was a player who had only one thing on his mind – finding the net. He would shoot at every opportunity and was selfish in the box; he would often say: 'Ditherers don't score often.' He had a finely attuned sense of being in the ideal position to score.

Clarke had many attributes. He had the ability to ride a tackle, together with excellent ball control and first touch. He was the ideal striker, able to score effortlessly with both feet. He was also one of the best headers of a ball in Fulham's history. He was fearless and got in where it hurt. He specialised in overhead kick goals and even took the team's penalties. He was one of those players who could always seem to

find that extra half-yard of space in the box. He could also perform solo runs from the halfway line if the situation demanded it.

He joined on a fairly low wage and almost left the club during that first close season. Clarke knew his worth and his abilities and said he would ask for a transfer if he was not given a wage rise. It caused problems in the boardroom, but the club recognised their prize asset and Clarke got his increase.

The following season he was even better and he won four more England U-23 caps and represented the Football League. He was clearly a player destined for the very top. Fulham's ageing side struggled unsuccessfully against relegation in 1967–68, but

Clarke is pulled down in the Tottenham penalty area during the match at White Hart Lane in February 1967. The offender is former Fulham player Alan Mullery. Referee's verdict: no foul...

Clarke shone out like a beacon. He was once again the clear top scorer with twenty-seven goals in a mediocre team; nobody else managed double figures in the league. In one match he scored four goals – a League Cup replay against Workington at Craven Cottage. He was once again, at just twenty-one, one of the top scorers in the First Division. His final goal, another fine solo effort, came at Liverpool, Clarke scoring Fulham's only goal in a 1–4 defeat. He missed the final league game and his last was the penultimate game of the season, a 2–2 home draw with Southampton.

His final haul for Fulham was a total of fifty-seven goals in exactly 100 games. This included one four-goal game, one hat-trick and fourteen two-goal matches (an average of a goal every 1.75 matches, or four in seven). One amazing statistic was that in those two seasons in all competitions, Clarke scored against *every* team in the First Division at that time except for Chelsea and the team he would ultimately join, Leeds United.

After relegation, Fulham at first insisted that Clarke would stay as he was under contract. However, all the top clubs were chasing him by now including Manchester United, Liverpool and Nottingham Forest. Clarke had nothing but affection for Fulham who had given him his big chance in football, but recognised that his international ambitions would be hampered by playing in the Second Division. Fulham also realised they could not really hold him and could do financially very well by agreeing to the transfer.

It started a ferocious bidding war, and First Division clubs were all over themselves trying to sign him.

Major clubs offered two and sometimes three players in exchange; others offered large cash sums plus players, some straight cash. At the time, Fulham manager Bobby Robson described some of the offers as astounding, many never reaching the ears of the press. In the end, it led to a valuation of Clarke of £150,000. Clarke was expected to join a big club, but **Leicester City** manager Matt Gillies was first off the mark on the eve of the FA Cup final and persuaded Clarke to join. It seemed a strange decision by the hard-nosed Clarke, but his wife Margaret was from the west Midlands and she favoured a return nearer home. Fulham received £150,000 for Allan Clarke in 1968, a British transfer record at the time. This was actually £100,000 in cash plus a Leicester forward, Frank Large, valued at £50,000. Fulham's profit was £115,000, then a huge sum.

He stayed at Leicester for just one season, and although they reached the FA Cup final they were a poor side and Clarke experienced relegation from the First Division for the second consecutive season. Once again, though, he was the club's top scorer with fifteen goals in all competitions. It was inevitable that he would move again, and this time it was to a big club, **Leeds United**. For the second season running, Allan Clarke broke the British record transfer fee, Leicester forcing Leeds to pay a record £165,000 for him in 1969.

He was really the missing piece in the jigsaw for Leeds United who wanted someone up front to partner Mick Jones who had joined from Sheffield United. Clarke scored twenty-six goals in his first season at

Leeds and earned the nickname Sniffer, because of his predatory instincts in front of goal – if there was even the remotest goal-scoring opportunity, Clarke would sniff it out.

With Leeds United, Clarke won the Inter Cities Fairs Cup in 1971, the FA Cup in 1972 (where he headed the winning goal) and the First Division title in 1974 when Clarke was once again top scorer. He was involved in many other cup and European finals and close calls with the league title, but also suffered plenty of heartbreak when Leeds failed at the final hurdle, such as the FA Cup final of 1973 against Sunderland, and the 1975 European Cup final (Champions League) against Bayern Munich.

During his time at Leeds United he was part of Sir Alf Ramsey's 1970 World Cup squad and played in that tournament, scoring a pressure penalty on his debut against Czechoslovakia (1–0). He played nineteen times for England, scoring ten goals. This included the England team that failed to overcome Poland and qualify for the 1974 World Cup. He remained at Elland Road for nine years, scoring over twenty goals a season four times, and being Leeds' top scorer on four occasions. By the time he left in 1978 he had made 351 appearances and scored 151 goals, but by then a knee injury was beginning to curtail his ability to play at top-flight level.

He was transferred for £45,000 and took part in a season with Fourth Division **Barnsley** as player/manager adding a further fifteen league goals, winning promotion in his first year. He went on to manage Leeds United for two years but was sacked when Leeds were relegated. He then managed Scunthorpe United to promotion but resigned along with the chairman following relegation the next season. He returned to Barnsley for another four years but they were just short of the play-offs, and after one poor start to a season Clarke was sacked. His final flirtation with football was a six-month stint at Lincoln City.

He broke all ties with football in 1990 and has not been involved in the game since. Although he attends Leeds United reunions, he remains fiercely critical of the modern game and refuses any significant media role, but does some after-dinner speaking. Clarke probably never made the money he should have done during his time in football and returned to ordinary work, latterly as a travelling salesman for a plant hire company based in Wakefield.

ALLAN CLARKE
Fulham career – all competitions

Season	Appearances	Goals	Home	Away
1965–1966	8	1	1	0
1966–1967	47	29	21	8
1967–1968	45	27	16	11
Total	100	57	38	19

*Total career **league** appearances–**510**, and **league** goals–**223**.*

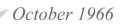

Jimmy Conway

Ten years service, an Irish international, a scorer of almost 80 goals.

Jimmy Conway was one of a family of seventeen from Dublin. He received many honours and represented his country at schoolboy, youth and amateur levels. At a young age he had already been playing youth football with Stella Maris boys and senior soccer with Bohemians. In the summer of 1966 aged just nineteen, he journeyed across the sea with his

colleague Turlough O'Connor, to join **Fulham**. There was a minimal transfer fee involved. He joined the club in time to get accustomed to his new colleagues with a tour of the Far East.

After just a handful of games for the reserves in the 1966–67 season, Conway made his debut in a League Cup match against Wolves in October. He crowned an impressive debut by scoring the third and best goal of the night in a 5–0 win, a solo run and a thirty-yard drive. From that moment on, he was virtually a permanent fixture in the Fulham line-up for the next decade.

He played his first league game in a 2–2 draw at Anfield and scored his first goal a month later in a 5–1 thrashing of Aston Villa at Craven Cottage.

This was followed by another in a 3–1 victory over Southampton a month after that. His introduction to the team coincided with the best form Fulham had shown for some time. So impressive was his play that his first international cap for Eire arrived just weeks after his Fulham debut. It was the first of four European Nations Cup (now the European Championship) qualifiers he would take part in over the next year or so. The next season, 1967–68, he scored just four goals including Fulham's last in the First Division in a 1–5 defeat at Everton. He played in all of the fifty-one games that season.

Conway was initially an attacking half back or wing half. He wore the number 6 shirt for quite a while. He was a pocket-sized dynamo, always fit, busy and involved in the game for the full ninety minutes. He seemed to possess endless energy. He was more than a midfield player – he was a genuine all-rounder in defence, midfield and attack, often called a utility player. He had many attributes including pace and excellent control and ball skills for beating an opponent. This was combined with smooth passing and an eye for goal.

Jimmy cemented Fulham's midfield, playing alongside some of the greatest names in Fulham's history like Bobby Robson, Johnny Haynes and Alan Mullery. He was a two-footed player and considering his diminutive stature was good in the air, scoring a number of headed goals. He was very adaptable, could play on both sides of midfield and even deputised for World Cup winner George Cohen at full back.

In 1968–69, when Fulham were relegated again, Conway scored just five goals, but still ended up as joint second highest scorer. In this turbulent season, he wore six different shirt numbers. Conway's career changed dramatically at the beginning of the 1969–70 season when he was converted to a right winger by manager Bill Dodgin. He became an overnight sensation, and alongside Les Barrett on the other wing, terrorised Third Division defences with speed and trickery. He was also appointed the club's penalty taker. Together with Steve Earle, scoring freely from their crosses, they became known as the 'three musketeers' and Jimmy finished with twenty-three goals and was joint

top scorer with Earle. For the second time in three seasons, Conway was ever present and played in all fifty games. Earle and Conway were amongst the Third Division's leading scorers.

That form continued into the 1970–71 season with Conway once again creating and scoring goals regularly. So impressive was his form that high-flying Leeds United were reportedly ready to pay £80,000 to Fulham to take him back to the First Division.

Sadly, the gifted Fulham players were targeted by tough Third Division defenders and Conway missed three critical months of the season with a knee injury that ultimately required cartilage surgery. He returned successfully to play a significant role in Fulham's promotion back to the Second Division contributing a further ten goals from his thirty-one appearances.

Fulham struggled after their promotion in 1971–72 and Conway, not fully fit, played just twenty-five games. Despite this he weighed in with another nine precious goals as Fulham retained their Second Division status by their fingertips. When fit, he scored seven goals in a seven-game spell that once again coincided with Fulham's best form that season.

The arrival of Alec Stock as manager in 1972–73 changed little, as Conway was regarded by Alec as a valuable member of the Fulham team. As his pace began to drop a little, he combined his role as a right winger with that of a scheming inside forward. He was still hampered by injuries and made just fourteen appearances that season scoring four goals. After limping out of the first game of the season, he missed four months. On his return, he netted his four league

Conway's flying header produces one of the four goals which Fulham scored without reply against Cardiff in August 1974.

goals in five games. During this brief return Fulham were unbeaten, which easily demonstrated his value to the side. When he was injured again, the team's fortunes dipped.

That injury hoodoo persisted through the 1973–74 season. Conway was now concentrating on midfield and only managed to start in half the games after missing three months early on, and his haul of three goals in twenty-nine games was to prove his leanest spell in a Fulham shirt. However Conway helped to consolidate Fulham's position in the Second Division after a decade of instability.

Fortunately he returned to full fitness in 1974–75 and played forty-five games that season scoring five times. He was influential in the league, but even more

so in the FA Cup, scoring the important goal against Hull City in the first game in the third round. In later rounds, he created goals in the 2–1 victory over Nottingham Forest, the 2–1 victory over First Division leaders Everton and was involved with the goal in the 1–0 win at Carlisle United. After playing his part in the semi-final, Conway represented Fulham in the FA Cup final against West Ham United at Wembley and although Fulham finally lost 0–2, he played with distinction alongside Alan Mullery and Alan Slough in the Fulham midfield.

Although Fulham didn't set the league alight in 1975–76, Conway played in forty-three more games missing just three in total whilst adding another very respectable nine goals to his total. His final goal was a winner in the 1–0 victory over Oldham Athletic in March and his final game was the penultimate league game of that season, a nondescript 0–0 home draw with Plymouth Argyle.

During that summer, and after a decade of loyal service to the Whites, Jimmy finally moved to rejoin coach Bill Taylor at First Division **Manchester City** for a fee of £30,000. However, his stay there was a brief one. He was at Maine Road for just eighteen months, making only a handful of appearances and scoring just one goal. The Conway family then moved to Oregon in the USA.

Conway represented the Republic of Ireland in twenty-three matches: four World Cup qualifiers, six European Championship qualifiers, nine friendly internationals and four amateur/unofficial matches. (Apart from one whilst at Manchester City, all these caps were gained during his time at

A goal against high-flying Millwall in March 1969.

This cracking shot from Conway at Halifax in March 1971 goes just wide.

Fulham.) He scored three goals in an international career spanning thirteen years. The Republic played only around sixty games in those thirteen years, so he appeared in more of a third of them, and this percentage would have been significantly higher had it not been for knee injuries and cartilage operations.

Conway finished his playing career with three seasons in American football at **Portland Timbers**.

After hanging up his boots, the family remained abroad and Jimmy coached soccer for a number of years and was highly respected. He returned to England briefly in 1995 to take part in the 'replayed' 1975 cup final against the Hammers at Craven Cottage and delighted fans by showing that he had lost none of his enthusiasm or skills.

Jimmy Conway's Fulham career shows that, despite significant injuries, he made 360 appearances for the Cottagers in less than ten seasons and scored seventy-six goals, an excellent return for a wide-right midfield player. Despite the total he never scored a hat-trick. His loyalty through the tough times, his skill and work-rate make him a Fulham icon and a firm favourite. Those appearance and goal totals rank him among the top twenty-five players ever to play for Fulham.

JIMMY CONWAY
Fulham career – all competitions

Season	Appearances	Goals	Home	Away
1966–1967	34	4	3	1
1967–1968	51	4	1	3
1968–1969	37	5	2	3
1969–1970	50	23	14	9
1970–1971	31	10	5	5
1971–1972	25	9	3	6
1972–1973	15	4	3	1
1973–1974	29	3	3	0
1974–1975	45	5	5	0
1975–1976	43	9	6	3
Total	**360**	76	45	31

*Total career **league** appearances–**329**, and **league** goals–**68**.*

Bobby Moss

Early Fulham promise, but a one-season career.

Born in Kenton in Middlesex, **Bobby Moss** was one of **Fulham's** 'nearly' men. He came through the apprentice ranks, playing regularly for the junior South Eastern Counties League. He joined at fifteen, signing professional forms at seventeen. He was a prolific scorer who quickly caught the attention of the Fulham management. Essentially he was a winger, but scored the number of goals that a striker would be proud of.

Certainly he could have never been called a target man. He was extremely small, just five feet five and lightly built. Having a number of forwards with injuries or knocks, manager Vic Buckingham pitched Moss in for a first-tcam debut aged just eighteen in October 1967 in a midweek First Division game at Sheffield Wednesday along with Irishman Turlough O'Connor. Probably out of necessity Buckingham used him in a more central role.

He did enough in that game, despite a 2–4 defeat, to keep his place. On his home debut at the weekend, he wrote himself into folklore with a bullet header in the dying seconds that enabled Fulham to record a 2–1 win over star-studded Everton. He played the next three games (all lost) and a League Cup game before drifting back into reserve football.

Buckingham brought him back into the team at Christmas and Moss responded by scoring in both games, and again they were two quality goals, one at Molineux in an unlucky 2–3 defeat, and the other, his final goal, a scorching volley that earned a point in a 2–2 draw with neighbours Chelsea at the Cottage.

After Buckingham lost his job a month later, Moss was strangely overlooked, despite scoring regularly in the reserves. He made just one more first-team start, at Southampton. He was snubbed by Bobby Robson, by player-manager Johnny Haynes and then finally by Bill Dodgin. It was thought that he was too small to be a striker and he had suffered a couple of injuries.

Certainly in the 1968–69 relegation season from the Second Division, Fulham were in dire need of goals, but they never once turned to Moss.

Despite his early promise, he was given a free transfer by Fulham at the end of the 1968–69 season and was quickly snapped up by Fourth Division **Peterborough United**. The Posh decided to revert Moss back to his winger's role and he found some success. Over the next two and a half seasons he played regularly making over 100 appearances, scoring nineteen goals in all competitions.

He left Peterborough at the end of the 1972–73 season, and joined Southern League side **Wealdstone** helping them to promotion in his first season. He continued to play regularly for the next six seasons notching around fifty goals for the side. Very early on at Wealdstone he teamed up with Johnny Haynes and former Fulham and Spurs forward Terry Dyson. He hung up his boots at the relatively early age of thirty.

BOBBY MOSS
Fulham career – all competitions

Season	Appearances	Goals	Home	Away
1967–1968	10	3	2	1
Total	10	3	2	1

*Total career **league** appearances–**113**, and **league** goals–**20**.*

Composite picture from two negatives.

Moss (here wearing number 8) has just headed a dramatic winner in the last seconds at home to Everton in September 1967.

Joe Gilroy

Unlucky but skilful Scottish forward, a strong goalscorer in a poor Fulham side.

Joe Gilroy was born in Glasgow and began his career with **Queen's Park** where, at sixteen years of age, he made a handful of appearances alongside Alex Ferguson. Studying at The Scottish School of Physical Education with Craig Brown and Andy Roxburgh, he played for the Scottish amateur team against Ireland. During this time he gained his full SFA coaching badge and was a staff coach in 1963. He became a school teacher of physical education and played football part-time. That year he signed for **Montrose**. In his one season there he played thirty-one games scoring six goals.

Joe then joined **Clyde** in 1964 still as a part-timer and his very impressive haul of forty-four goals in 106 league games during just over three seasons saw him sign for **Fulham**, where for the first time he became a full-time professional. Like his Scottish predecessor Graham Leggat, Gilroy was very mobile and very strong, possessed a good footballing brain and was very good in the air. He had refused a new contract with Clyde, and had only re-signed with them on the understanding that he would be released if a reasonable offer were forthcoming from an English club; he had also considered going to America in the close season. Buckingham had only seen Gilroy play once, but had received complimentary reports about him from Scottish scout Jackie Cox.

Fulham were in trouble at the bottom of the First Division when Gilroy signed on a Friday night in October 1967 for a reasonable fee of £20,000, and he was pitched into the team at Arsenal the next day. Although Fulham lost 3–5, he did well and was unluckily denied a goal in the first ten minutes by a last-ditch goal-line clearance. Unlike some from Scotland, Gilroy took to the English game straight away, scoring in his next game, a diving header in a 3–0 win at Coventry. In November and December he scored five more, one very important headed goal to

keep Fulham in the League Cup in a 1–1 draw with Huddersfield, and two goals over Christmas which each earned a merited point against Chelsea at the Cottage (2–2) and at White Hart Lane (2–2). After netting a crucial fourth against Macclesfield Town in the FA Cup (4–2), he sustained a nasty injury against Burnley that kept him sidelined for several matches. Gilroy's arrival in the side had seen Fulham show their best form in a dismal season. Once he was injured the team slumped again. He returned with a crucial goal in the 3–2 win over Sheffield United at Bramall Lane which kept survival hopes alive, but it was not to last. Gilroy's final two goals that season were in Fulham's last home game in the top flight for thirty-three years in a 2–2 draw with Southampton. His goal return of ten goals in twenty-two games in a poor and struggling side showed that Vic Buckingham had been a good judge and that Gilroy was a bargain.

He started the next season well scoring Fulham's winner in a 1–0 win over Bristol City on the opening day but it was to prove to be his last goal. Fulham had made buys to solve their goalscoring crisis on Allan Clarke's departure following relegation, including Frank Large, Don Kerrigan, Vic Halom, Johnny Byrne and Cliff Jones. With this congestion Gilroy was in and out of the team. His manager at Clyde, John Prentice, was now managing **Dundee** and had problems with goalscorers, and with Fulham being in free-fall he made an enquiry and terms were quickly agreed. Fulham recouped their outlay and Gilroy returned to Scotland, his last game being a 2–2 draw at Blackpool in September. It was a pity as it looked as if he could have blossomed into a good if unspectacular forward.

In three seasons at Dundee he scored a modest thirteen goals in fifty-two games. In the twilight of his career he went to South Africa and joined **Highland's Park** in 1972 to help win the league and the National Castle Cup.

Returning to Scotland, Gilroy was appointed coach of Falkirk with John Prentice as manager. He then

Above: a fairly ordinary picture of Gilroy in action is enhanced by the official in the background – Jack Taylor, acclaimed World Cup referee.

coached at the Valur club in Iceland for a season. Returning to Scotland again, he was appointed manager of Morton in October 1975, and in a difficult few months he nevertheless managed to steer the team clear of First Division relegation at the death. He was still combining this role with that of a PE teacher and he found this a burden as it was putting pressure on his family, so he resigned in June 1976. He joined Queen's Park still in a part-time capacity but the job was nearer his home.

He coached/managed the team for three seasons and they finished 5th, 7th and 13th under his guidance. After leaving Queen's Park, he emigrated with his family to Australia. There he managed the Brisbane Lions and Brisbane City in the National League and then coached the Queensland team until 1997. He is still in Australia but occasionally returns to England and Scotland.

On an anecdotal note, whilst with Fulham, he and a number of Fulham and Chelsea players were selected to make an advert for Bilsland bread. There was a delay and the players went to the pub. Apparently the 'acrobat' hired to do the overhead kick finale couldn't seem to do it. Don Kerrigan offered Gilroy with, 'Nae bother, Joe does it every day in training.' Fortified with lunch-time drink, Gilroy sent a number of overhead kicks acrobatically flying into the net. They were used in the advert (shown in Scotland appropriately) and Joe's face and kick made him a household name!

JOE GILROY
Fulham career – all competitions

Season	Appearances	Goals	Home	Away
1967–1968	22	10	6	4
1968–1969	6	1	1	0
Total	28	11	7	4

*Total career **league** appearances–**24**, and **league** goals–**8**.*

Johnny Byrne

Experienced England international, brought to Fulham in a 'British Rail' deal, he struggled to inspire.

Johnny Byrne was a youth player with Guildford City before signing a professional contract with Fourth Division **Crystal Palace** on his seventeenth birthday. He quickly won England youth caps and England U-23 caps. He made his first-team debut the following October against Swindon Town, at the age of seventeen. After two or three steady seasons, he became a regular for Crystal Palace and in the 1960–61 season scored thirty-one of the 110 goals that enabled them to win promotion. His strike partner Roy Summersby scored twenty-five, meaning that the two had scored over half of Palace's final total!

In the Third Division in November 1961, he was called up to the England squad, one of only five post-war players at the time to be called up for the national side when playing for a team two divisions outside the top flight. He made his England debut in a 1–1 draw against Northern Ireland at Wembley in 1961.

After 220 appearances and a spectacular goal haul of ninety-six in all competitions, he left Palace in the spring of 1962. Such was his skill in the lower leagues that First Division **West Ham** paid a then record £65,000 fee for a Third Division player to lure him from Selhurst Park. Many thought him unfortunate not to be included in the 1962 World Cup squad.

He was a very modern type of attacker for the early Sixties, and at only five feet eight inches and weighing just over eleven stone, he was never a target man. He was adept at dropping off his marker, finding space, and either launching a colleague with an inspired pass, or using his own pace, skill and powerful right foot to set off for goal himself.

He continued to star in the First Division too where he linked up to form a formidable strike partnership with Geoff Hurst. He played in the 1964 FA Cup final which saw the Hammers win 3–2 against Second Division Preston North End. He was the West Ham player of the year in 1963–64, when he was also top scorer with thirty-three goals in all competitions. He was injured though and replaced by Brian Dear in their European Cup Winners Cup side that beat TSV Munich 2–0 at Wembley in 1965.

He was awarded eleven England caps, scoring eight goals. He scored twice in an 8–1 victory over Switzerland and he scored a hat-trick too in 1964 in a remarkable 4–3 win over an emerging Portugal team containing Eusebio. He was part of Alf Ramsey's original 1966 World Cup squad, but did not make the final cut. In just five years at Upton Park, Byrne added another seventy-nine league goals and over 100 in all competitions. This included four hat-tricks and twelve two-goal hauls. He was also an expert penalty taker. His career total in all competitions was already over 200.

At only twenty-seven, and at the height of his fame and ability, his career began to decline rapidly as a result of off-field alcohol abuse. He was a very genial and sociable man who liked to engage with football friends and supporters, and found it hard to decline a drink. He was nicknamed 'Budgie' Byrne because of his chatty style and incessant wit.

With his weight increase, his performances began to dwindle, but he was very surprisingly sold back to **Crystal Palace** in February 1967 for £45,000 to aid their promotion push from the Second Division. This campaign eventually fizzled out but he did manage five goals which took him to over a century for Palace.

Generally, he never recaptured his earlier form and was surprisingly transferred back to the First Division with **Fulham**. The Crystal Palace team were returning from an away match on the same 6.26 train from Manchester as Fulham, and manager Bobby Robson quickly agreed terms between the clubs at £17,000, and the deal was concluded just an hour before the midnight transfer deadline. He made his debut the following week in a 1–3 home defeat by Arsenal.

Byrne could not prevent Fulham falling into the Second Division, and played sporadically the following season, 1968–69. Again the Fulham team struggled and Byrne, looking well past his best, managed just two goals, at home to Huddersfield Town (4–3) and away a week later at Charlton (3–5). He suffered many minor injuries and seemed unfit and lacking in mobility. The last of the nineteen games he played for Fulham was ironically against Crystal Palace at Selhurst on the final day of the season. Fulham were already relegated and Palace came from two goals down at half-time to win 3–2 and clinch promotion to the First Division for the first time.

After this game, a disillusioned Byrne quit English football and moved to South Africa, playing for

and managing **Durban City**, and he was a major influence in tempting Fulham's Johnny Haynes to play in South Africa. In this reduced quality league, Byrne and Haynes were a major success with many honours between them. After leaving Durban City he coached the South African team Hellenic for a significant time.

Byrne chose to live and remain in South Africa for the rest of his life. Unfortunately he also continued with the drinking lifestyle that he enjoyed in England. He died of a sudden heart attack at the age of just sixty in October 1999.

JOHNNY BYRNE
Fulham career – all competitions

Season	Appearances	Goals	Home	Away
1967–1968	5	0	0	0
1968–1969	14	2	1	1
Total	19	2	1	1

*Total career **league** appearances–414, and **league** goals–171.*

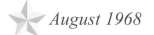

Frank Large

**A bold, bustling centre forward, part of a record transfer, he scored goals for fun at
every club he played for – except Fulham.**

Frank Large was born in Leeds and joined **Halifax Town** of Division Three (North) in 1957. There he spent five years learning his trade. He made his debut at eighteen and in four seasons with the Shaymen he made almost 150 appearances, scoring fifty-two goals.

In the 1962 close season, he made his first move – and his first to London – with a transfer to Third Division **Queens Park Rangers**, where he netted seven goals in just twenty-one appearances. But he didn't even complete that first season there, as in March 1963 he

was on the move again with the first of three spells at **Northampton Town**. Northampton were a team on the up and Large's goal tally of eighteen in his first twenty games contributed richly to their promotion from Division Three as champions. In Division Two, his goals consolidated the Cobblers' position in that division. His total was an impressive thirty goals in just forty-seven appearances.

However, he started to become a 'Have boots – will travel' centre forward and on the transfer deadline of March 1964, Bert Head of Division Two **Swindon**

Town paid Northampton £10,000 to bring Large to the County Ground. He was brought in to replace young star Bobby Woodruff who had joined Wolves for £35,000. Large scored twice on his debut against Plymouth Argyle and four times in ten games before the season closed. However, he failed to score in the opening seven games of the following 1964–65 season, was omitted from the side and was on his way again, dropping down a division to **Carlisle United**.

Carlisle had been promoted from Division Four the previous season and Frank Large was the missing piece of their jigsaw. He made his debut at home to Bournemouth, partnering Hugh McIlmoyle up front. In that season, Large netted sixteen goals as United won the Division Three championship and a second successive promotion. But by the end of the year he was on the move again, once again dropping down a division to join **Oldham Athletic** for £7,000.

He scored eighteen goals in thirty-four matches for the Latics, and this scoring rate attracted his former club **Northampton Town** and he answered their SOS, returning there in December 1967 with a £14,000 move. Northampton Town had experienced one unsuccessful season in the top division, and despite Large's eight goals in twenty-one games, he could not prevent Northampton slipping down to Division Three. Then came a very surprising move. First Division **Leicester City** were struggling in the lower reaches of the table and gambled with a £20,000 transfer for Large. It would be his one and only crack at the First Division.

He was an immediate hit. The fans loved his bravery, and his bustling, aggressive, no-nonsense approach intimidated defenders. He scored eight league goals in twenty-six matches, goals which eventually dragged Leicester City clear of any relegation worries. He also scored three in six FA Cup ties. This included a fourth-round replay against league champions Manchester City at Filbert Street where Leicester were 1–3 down at one stage. A storming second-half display by Large saw him score twice and create another as Leicester recorded an historic 4–3 win.

After just a few months at Leicester, he was involved as makeweight in the British transfer record deal that took **Fulham**'s Allan Clarke to Leicester City. Fulham had just been relegated and, on losing their prime forward, manager Bobby Robson needed strength, height and goals and gambled that the 'blond bomber' Large was the man to provide them. He was valued at £50,000 in the £150,000 record transfer. Large was happy at Leicester and didn't really want to come south again.

Frank Large was the epitome of the Fifties and Sixties rugged, battering-ram centre forward. He was big, strong and very brave, and would run himself ragged, charging up and down the field to score. An absolute bull of a man he endeared himself as a chaser of lost causes who would give 100% for the full ninety minutes. Although he was a good player who had shone in the lower divisions, he certainly was not the most gifted in terms of touch, control or finesse. Large had the unenviable and some say impossible job of replacing Clarke at Fulham and it showed. It was also unfortunate for him that he was playing in probably one of the poorest sides ever to represent Fulham.

The harder Large tried to score the more frustrating it became. He made his debut against Bristol City on the opening day of the 1968–69 season. It took him twelve games to find the net, scoring twice in a 4–5 defeat away against Birmingham City, the longest spell without a goal in his entire career. He clearly was not the classy striker that Robson and Fulham needed and his cumbersome touch and his failure to convert chances had the boo-boys quickly on his back. After four more goalless games he was dropped. He made only sporadic appearances for the rest of the season. He was recalled on the final day after Fulham's second successive relegation and scored his only other Fulham goal in a 2–3 defeat against promoted Crystal Palace.

After just a couple of games in the Third Division in the 1969–70 season, it was clear that Large was unhappy at Craven Cottage and that a move would benefit both parties. His 'home' club **Northampton Town** came to the rescue again and he joined them for the third time in September 1969, for £14,000. It was probably one of the worst pieces of transfer business Fulham had done and was possibly one of the factors that cost Robson his job. It was a shame, as Large was a very good man and a 'great lad', popular with team-mates, a genial guy who fitted in everywhere he played.

Predictably, Large found his shooting boots immediately after returning to the County Ground. In three full seasons now in the Fourth Division he scored forty-three league goals in just 125 games. In one bizarre game though, against Swansea at the Vetch Field, he was sent off for brawling with a spectator whose comments had annoyed him! After eleven goalless games at the start of the 1972–73 season, Large made one final league move, when he went up a division in November to join **Chesterfield**.

In a calendar year at Saltergate bridging two seasons, Large added yet another fifteen league goals in his lengthy league career of sixteen years. Like a number of players towards the end of their careers in the Seventies, he then spent a year in the USA with the **Baltimore Comets**. He made seventeen appearances, scoring nine goals with two assists. On his return to England, he was signed by young manager Ron Atkinson, then in charge of **Kettering Town** of the Southern League, to bolster their promotion push for the Football League. He played the 1974–75 season for them predominantly at centre half as he no longer had the pace to be a forward. He is fabled for knocking out then non-league Wimbledon's Roger Connell following a foul with a fine punch, and had sent himself off and down the tunnel before the referee could get his notebook out!

Big Ron who worked with some of the biggest and best talent around had this to say about a warrior after his own heart: 'Frank was terrific to work with; he was as strong as a lion and as competitive as any player I've ever known. He worked on the building sites and I remember him coming in one day when he had dropped a hod of bricks on his foot and broken his big toe. He knew we were a bit short, so he just cut a chunk out of his boot to make it a bit more comfortable so he could play.'

Following his retirement from playing, Frank and his wife, Aileen, were the owners of a bed and breakfast establishment in County Mayo in Ireland. He helped his son Paul manage footballing sides Westport United and Ballina Town in County Mayo, and he also played cricket for County Mayo Cricket Club. A smoker for most of his life, Frank Large died at just sixty-three in Louisburgh Mayo in 2003 following a long battle with cancer. After his three spells and numerous exploits with Northampton, there is now a road named after him in the town – Frank Large Walk.

FRANK LARGE
Fulham career – all competitions

Season	Appearances	Goals	Home	Away
1968–1969	26	3	0	3
1969–1970	2	0	0	0
Total	28	3	0	3

*Total career **league** appearances–**562**, and **league** goals–**208**.*

Malcolm Macdonald

Natural goalscorer, given away by Fulham, scored almost 200 career league goals, and later became the club's manager.

Malcolm Macdonald was born in Fulham, just a stone's throw from the ground and was introduced to Craven Cottage by his father when he was just five years old. As a boy he could regularly be seen near the ground trying to get the autographs of his heroes.

He was not immediately snapped up by a league club and he started out as a full back with non-league **Tonbridge**. Recommended by **Fulham** coach and scout Harry Haslam, new Fulham manager Bobby Robson paid the princely sum of £1,000 to bring Macdonald to Craven Cottage in the summer of 1968, just after the club's relegation from the First Division. He had been set to join Crystal Palace, but Bobby Robson was his boyhood hero and that was enough to persuade him.

He did well immediately in the full back position, but due to injuries was played up front in the reserves as an experiment by Bobby Robson, and he responded with a few goals. After relegation, Fulham were in poor shape and along with injuries to the first-team players they were going through a significant goal drought. Robson took a gamble and thrust the eighteen-year-

old Macdonald into the first team at Oxford United in a September televised game. Fulham lost 0–1, but Macdonald had two goals disallowed and did well enough to keep his place.

On Friday the thirteenth the following week, Macdonald scored the winner against high-flying Crystal Palace in a 1–0 win. His inexperience showed and he missed three or four other chances, but at least he was shooting and getting in the right positions. He was a revelation and after seven league games already had five goals under his belt, scoring in four consecutive games. He looked a real prospect.

Macdonald's main ability was that he was a natural goalscorer, and like Allan Clarke was a selfish 'shoot on sight' kind of player. Although not tall at five feet ten inches, he was well built and barrel-chested, strong as an ox and very difficult to knock off the ball. There was also something of the Bedford Jezzard about him. Despite his bandy-legged gait, he had tremendous pace to accompany his strength and ran directly at and through defenders, shooting powerfully with both feet. For a smaller man he was also strong in the air. Such was his athleticism that he

Macdonald is here pictured (all in blue) in his first full start for the club, at Oxford United in September 1968. He is about to dispossess 'Big Ron' Atkinson.

Macdonald pounces on a shot from Haynes (in background) and crashes the ball in the net for Fulham's goal in the 1–1 draw against Blackburn Rovers in September 1968.

could run 100 yards in 10.7 seconds, a good enough time to qualify him for the Olympic Games. He was also immensely competitive, a gap-toothed, snarling and tigerish powerhouse.

Things went catastrophically wrong for Macdonald following Bobby Robson's sacking in early November 1968. Johnny Haynes as caretaker thought him arrogant and inexperienced and when Bill Dodgin took over he limited Macdonald to just two more games in a side already looking doomed to a second successive relegation. Macdonald's final game was in a dire 0–2 home defeat by Carlisle United in February. Back in the reserves, Macdonald scored for fun in a second-string team, netting seventeen goals in only twenty games as the team were runners-up to Arsenal for the Football Combination title. Malcolm's Fulham career was over after just thirteen games. It had been such a poor 1968–69 season for Fulham that, with those five goals, Macdonald still managed to become joint second-highest scorer.

Harry Haslam and Roy McCrohan had both left Fulham and gone to Third Division **Luton Town** where the experienced Alec Stock was in charge. Stock had watched Macdonald and on the recommendation of the coaches snapped up the forward for just £17,500. Macdonald had already spoken to Bill Dodgin and Tommy Trinder and asked for a move after heated exchanges. It looked as if Fulham had made a good one-year profit on the young player, but they soon came to regret it, and it proved to be another of Fulham's worst ever transfer mistakes. It was the second time in three years that Alec Stock had pilfered a top Fulham forward for next to nothing.

In his first season with Luton, 1969–70, Macdonald prospered at Kenilworth Road and was the division's top scorer. His goals were sufficient to propel Luton Town to promotion to the Second Division at the first attempt. To rub salt into the wounds, Luton beat Fulham twice that season, with Macdonald scoring the only goal in both games, the second of those encounters at Craven Cottage effectively ending Fulham's own promotion challenge.

Those goals were no flukes and back in the Second Division in the 1970–71 season Luton finished a very creditable sixth, a few points off a second consecutive promotion. Macdonald had been ever-present in the side over both seasons and had scored forty-nine goals in just eighty-eight league games, sixty-one in all competitions.

His goals caught the eye of **Newcastle United** manager Joe Harvey, and in the summer of 1971 he signed Macdonald for £180,000. Thus was he thrust, at twenty-one, into the First Division for the first time. At Newcastle he quickly became a favourite of the fans, earning the nickname Supermac and scoring a hat-trick on his home debut against star-studded Liverpool (3–2); he was the club's top scorer for *all* of his five seasons on Tyneside. He missed just twenty-three league games in those seasons and was twice ever-present. He formed effective goal-scoring partnerships with both John Tudor and Alan Gowling.

After just four months at Newcastle, he was given his First England U-23 cap and scored on his debut against Wales in a 2–0 win. In 1971–72 he scored twenty-three goals in all competitions. During the close season he made his debut for England against Wales in May 1972 when England won 4–0. He played in all three Home International matches. Early in the following season, 1972–73, he was awarded his fourth England U-23 cap and responded with a hat-trick against Wales. Once again Newcastle finished only mid-table but Macdonald bagged seventeen goals and they won the Anglo-Italian Cup.

Manager Macdonald imparts football knowledge to new Fulham captain Les Strong.

The 1973–74 season was just as disappointing as Newcastle slumped to fifteenth in the table. They did however reach the FA Cup final with Macdonald scoring in every round up to the final but they were soundly beaten 0–3 by Liverpool, and Malcolm hardly got a kick. There were still fifteen more league goals to add to his tally, and three more England caps in the summer.

The 1974–75 season was a personal triumph for Macdonald as he finished as the First Division's leading scorer with twenty-one goals, though Newcastle finished a dismal fifteenth. By March, Don Revie had taken over as England manager and awarded Macdonald another cap, and he scored his first goal for England in a 2–0 win over world champions West Germany. But it was a month later that Malcolm Macdonald would write his name into the record books when he scored all five of England's goals in a 5–0 victory over Cyprus. It is a record that still stands today, almost forty years on.

In his final season on Tyneside, 1975–76, he scored nineteen league goals, but for the third year in a row, Newcastle finished an unflattering fifteenth in the table. They also reached the League Cup final but lost 1–2 to Manchester City. In the early months of the season he was awarded his final three England caps making a total of fourteen. Macdonald and other players like Alan Ball fell out with manager Revie and he was not picked for England again.

Macdonald left Newcastle in 1976 after manager Harvey's departure. The new Magpies manager Gordon Lee disliked Macdonald's superstar status, and the pair fell out irrevocably during a pre-season tour of Majorca, prompting Macdonald to submit a transfer request. To the dismay of the Geordie fans he returned to London and signed for **Arsenal**, who had offered Newcastle a third of a million pounds. Arsenal wrote a cheque for £333,333.33 but realised that they were short-changing the sellers by a fraction of a penny, so wrote a new cheque for £333,333.34. Macdonald left Newcastle with a total in all competitions of 138 goals in 257 games.

Malcolm played two full seasons for Arsenal, striking up a fine relationship with Frank Stapleton and being the club's top scorer in both seasons 1976–77 and 1977–78. In that first season, he was once again the First Division's top scorer with twenty-five. In the second season he scored just fifteen goals and his knee was beginning to trouble him. This showed when Arsenal reached the FA Cup final in 1978 but were beaten 0–1 by Ipswich Town; Macdonald had a poor game and his last chance for silverware had vanished.

After two goals in four starts at the beginning of the next season, Macdonald suffered a bad knee injury in a meaningless League Cup match against Rotherham United from which he was unable to recover completely. He spent ten months trying to get fit, but it was an uphill task and he did not play in the Arsenal first team again. After having spent a couple of months in Sweden with **Djurgårdens IF** with a couple of goals in nine appearances, he realised his playing days were over and he announced his retirement at the premature age of twenty-nine in August 1979. He had scored forty-two goals for Arsenal in eighty-four league appearances and fifty-seven goals for them in total. In his career he achieved the unusual statistic of scoring on average a goal every other game for all the clubs he had played for.

A month after retiring, he was back at his first club Fulham, working behind the scenes in marketing as part of the commercial department, eventually becoming commercial manager. It was something of a sensation when, following the sacking of Bobby Campbell in October 1980, Macdonald took over as Fulham's team manager the following month. The charismatic Londoner immediately began to transform relegated Fulham's fortunes bringing a rich vein of young talent into the side to accompany some astute signings.

In his first full season as Fulham manager, 1981–82, he won promotion to the Second Division on the final evening in the classic match at home to Lincoln City. He then became a Fulham director. The next season was even better and, with the immense help of the coaching skills of Ray Harford, his young colts came within a whisker of a second successive promotion back to the First Division in 1982–83, halted only by a little loss of form at the death, and the final day Derby County debacle.

Things then began to go wrong for Supermac, and the Fulham team fared less well in 1983–84. Towards the end of the season, following revelations about his personal life which were alien to a club like Fulham, Macdonald resigned and was replaced by Harford. Macdonald's marriage broke up following his relationship with a young hotel manager Nicky Thompson. They married and set up a licensee business in Worthing which ultimately failed and he was made bankrupt.

Macdonald then returned to football management in 1987 with eight months at Huddersfield Town as manager. It was a disastrous time where little went right and the Yorkshire side was relegated from the Second Division, his reign having included a 1–10 loss to Manchester City.

Following the failure of his second marriage, Macdonald moved to Milan in the early 1990s after meeting an Italian interpreter, Vania, while working in Geneva. Whilst in Italy, Macdonald tried to set up a phone-line business with David Sullivan, owner of the *Daily Sport*. However, the business never fully got off the ground; he returned from spending Christmas in the UK one year to find that the Italian government had closed the whole phone-line industry down. There was little he could do to recoup his business losses. So he returned to the UK virtually penniless.

The pain in his injured knee had become harder to cope with and Macdonald found solace with the whiskey bottle, drinking a bottle a day. His descent into alcoholism has been well documented. This culminated in an arrest for drink-driving in 1997 whilst working for a Newcastle radio station. However, following financial help from the PFA and encouragement from his former Newcastle playing pal Micky Burns, Macdonald had an operation that significantly decreased his pain. Life was tricky for a while, but Macdonald conquered his demons and got his life back.

He was married for a third time to Carol Johnson who was divorced from Brian Johnson, the Geordie lead singer of rock band AC/DC, and she helped Macdonald to dry out. Carol used the experience from her battle with cocaine and whiskey as a teenager on tour with AC/DC to help Malcolm pull through a drying-out programme.

Since then Carol has helped him rebuild his life and a career as a soccer pundit in the north-east, augmented by radio and phone-in programmes. He is also in demand on the after-dinner circuit, and he writes a regular column for the retro football magazine *Backpass*.

MALCOLM MACDONALD
Fulham career – all competitions

Season	Appearances	Goals	Home	Away
1968–1969	13	5	4	1
Total	13	5	4	1

*Total career **league** appearances–372, and **league** goals–191.*

Vic Halom

A charismatic striker with a long career, an FA Cup winner, scorer of over 130 career league goals.

Vic Halom was born in Swadlincote, Derbyshire. His maternal grandfather was a Cossack murdered by the Bolsheviks and his parents met in a concentration camp. With a mother born in the Crimea and a father from Budapest, Halom, who grew up in a home where German was the language of choice, would have been eligible to play for England, Hungary or the USSR.

A **Charlton Athletic** colt, signing in January 1966, he could not really establish himself at centre forward ahead of the likes of veterans Eddie Firmani and Ron Saunders, although he did make his debut at seventeen and played twelve games for Second Division Charlton in the 1966–67 season without finding the net.

After a season and a half at the Valley, he joined Third Division **Orient** in the close season of 1967, initially on loan, but the move was made permanent a couple of months later. After a slow start, Halom forged a decent partnership with Roy Massey and later Micky Bullock and the goals began to flow. At the start of the 1968–69 season, Vic began to score regularly and was amongst the league's leading scorers

and after fifty-three games and twelve goals joined **Fulham** in November 1968 for £30,000, a sizeable fee that allowed Orient to fund their own promotion a year later. He made his league debut in a 2–2 draw with Portsmouth at the Cottage.

He opened his account in his third game. Fulham were going through one of the worst seasons in their history and struggling desperately in front of goal. He scored in a 4–3 win over Huddersfield Town on a day when three players scored their first goals for the club (Cliff Jones and Johnny Byrne being the others), and followed this up a week later with another against former club Charlton.

He seemed to be getting into form with a third goal against Birmingham City on Boxing Day, but he was injured in a disastrous 1–5 defeat at Bury two days later. The injury was slow to heal but on recovery Bill Dodgin did not select him even though he was scoring freely for the very successful Fulham combination side.

Season 1969–70 continued the same way, Halom making only sporadic appearances, not looking

Signing for Fulham in November 1968 warranted a happy posed picture of Halom with partner and car.

particularly fit and not scoring. This led to a showdown near Christmas where he publicly spoke of his wish to leave as he felt a change would benefit him. With Fulham going downhill fast and with a doomsday scenario of three consecutive relegations looming, Dodgin bought Halom back into the side and his return galvanised the team.

Fulham began scoring for fun and went on an incredible run of fifteen unbeaten matches during which the club rose from sixteenth in the Third Division to fourth place, just missing out on promotion. Vic Halom's contribution was eleven goals in eighteen games.

The following season, 1970–71, the side carried on where they had left off. Halom scored another eight league and cup goals before Christmas as Fulham scored freely. Once again Halom suffered an injury around Christmas which saw Fulham's form dip but he returned to play his part in the successful campaign that saw Fulham promoted back to the Second Division.

However, after scoring in a League Cup tie against Cambridge United early in the 1971–72 season, it was a big surprise when the nomadic Halom moved on, being transfer-listed in September. His final game was against Norwich at the end of August. Fulham signed Roger Cross from Brentford for £30,000 and Alec Stock, then **Luton Town** manager, made another of his several 'raids' on Craven Cottage by paying that

same sum for Halom. Fulham did not therefore make a profit or loss on the deal. Halom's total at Fulham was seventy-seven games and twenty-five goals.

Vic Halom was a player in the truest Fulham tradition, a real character and a crowd-pleaser. He played football with a smile on his face and was always ready to share a joke with his team-mates or the home crowd. His favourite 'tricks' were to hide the ball from the referee and to harass over-protected goalkeepers by standing in front of them or trying to knock the ball out of their hands. He was also one for winding up opponents with plenty of back-chat, and his response to heavy, clogging tackles was always a sarcastic smile and a word that seemed to rile them further.

Not blessed with great pace or technique, he was nonetheless a players' player. He had a big, powerful physique and was difficult to knock off the ball. He was also as strong as an ox, brave as a lion and would run all day for the team. Many forwards would comment on how much 'weight' he took from them by his unselfish, bustling hold-up play. Although not a prolific goalscorer, he possessed a powerful shot and was very good in the air. He was a far better player than a lot of people gave him credit for and was always missed when not in the side.

He was also a very likeable and personable guy who just wanted to be a down-to-earth person; he had a very good rapport with supporters at all clubs and enjoyed their company at social events and on the street.

Vic Halom's stay at Kenilworth Road was brief. He stayed just eighteen months and Luton Town finished in mid-table in the Second Division in both of those seasons (1971–72 and 1972–73). He still scored regularly though and notched up another seventeen goals in fifty-nine games.

In February 1973, Halom's skills caught the eye of Harry Catterick, manager of high-flying Everton in the First Division and they lodged a bid which Luton accepted (£35,000). However, Halom had a chance encounter with Bob Stokoe, the Sunderland manager, at a Middlesbrough match. Stokoe knew Halom, and had been his coach as a youth at Charlton, and he convinced Halom to come to Roker Park – despite the fact that **Sunderland** were in the bottom six in the Second Division! The move changed Halom's career. He travelled to Elm Park where Sunderland were playing an FA cup-tie against Reading and he signed immediately after the match.

He proved to be the 'missing piece in the jigsaw', his non-stop bustling style allowing the gifted Bobby Kerr, Billy Hughes and Dennis Tueart to play their football. In the fifth-round FA Cup replay against Manchester City, Halom wrote his name into folklore with one of finest volleyed goals seen at Roker Park as the First Division side were humbled 3–1 in front of 54,000. His status was further enhanced when he scored the first Sunderland goal in the semi-final against the mighty double-winners Arsenal. Following this 2–1 success, Halom went on to be an

A corking header, one of Halom's two goals in the 4–0 victory at Reading in March 1970.

integral part of the legendary team that conquered the mighty Leeds United 1–0 at Wembley to lift the trophy.

He also scored a memorable second-half hat-trick in a League Cup tie against then league champions Derby County, a team that contained the then England international Roy McFarland at centre half. Sunderland were finally promoted back to the First Division as champions in the 1975–76 season. Halom then departed the club, having amassed thirty-five goals in 113 games for the Rokerites. Forty years on, he still retains his iconic status on Wearside.

Vic moved on to **Oldham Athletic** in the Second Division during the close season and remained at Boundary Park for four seasons, adding forty-three goals in 123 league appearances. In February 1980, he signed for Third Division **Rotherham United**, and played twenty games for them scoring just twice, but his league career ended on a happy note as Rotherham were promoted as champions in 1981.

Vic dropped into non-league with a spell at **Northwich Victoria**, but he played just six games scoring once. It is thought he then moved on to get his first coaching and managerial experience under his belt with a season with Bergsøy in Norway (1982–83).

For the 1983–84 season, he was appointed player/manager of non-league **Barrow** (a former league club). He played thirty-seven games scoring three goals. He took the club to the Northern Premier League title at the first attempt, lifting them into the Vauxhall Conference League. However, his managerial talents were being noted in the Football League and after just one year at Barrow he departed, along with top scorer Barry Diamond, to join Fourth Division Rochdale as manager.

After some initial success, the Lancashire team went into steep decline. At the end of the season, despite Rochdale having escaped re-election by just one point, Halom was retained. However, he was told by chairman Tommy Cannon (of comedy duo Cannon and Ball fame) to sell those players who were on expensive contracts. This seriously weakened the side and by December 1986 the club had sunk to bottom of the league. Halom was sacked and after becoming disillusioned with the politics in football never managed a league club again except for a very brief spell with his home-town Burton Albion in 1988. Halom did though, during his time at Rochdale, coerce Les Strong into signing for them and playing one game!

In 1992 he stood as a Liberal Democrat candidate for Sunderland North in the General Election; he finished third, but took 10.7% of the votes cast (over 5,000).

His only involvement in football after that was a brief scouting job for Sunderland's rivals Newcastle United in 1999–2000.

He worked in public relations for a customer service company based in Oldham and the latest news is that he works with AMEC utilities based in Bulgaria working on house building contracts.

VIC HALOM
Fulham career – all competitions

Season	Appearances	Goals	Home	Away
1968–1969	11	3	2	1
1969–1970	25	11	8	3
1970–1971	42	10	5	5
1971–1972	4	1	1	0
Total	82	25	16	9

*Total career **league** appearances–452, and **league** goals–131.*

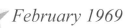

Brian Dear

Prolific scorer in the First Division, top scorer in 1968–69, his career finished too early.

Brian Dear was born in Plaistow very close to the West Ham United ground. He began his career with First Division **West Ham**, joining the club at the age of fifteen. He made his debut against Wolves in August 1962. Over the next six seasons he was in and out of the team, but he always found it difficult to dislodge strikers Johnny Byrne and Geoff Hurst and scorers like Martin Peters and winger Peter Brabrook. He also lived life his way and often found himself at odds with opponents and team-mates alike.

However, when he did play he usually made an impact. He holds the record for the quickest ever five goals in an English game, scored in just twenty minutes either side of half-time in a home game against West Bromwich Albion in April 1965 (6–1). Dear opened his tally a minute before half-time before adding goals in the 53rd, 56th, 59th and 64th minutes.

Although he made just eighty-two appearances in that time in all competitions he scored a noteworthy thirty-nine goals, including five against Leicester City over Christmas 1967, a hat-trick on the Boxing Day (4–2) and a brace in the return game (4–2) four days later.

Dear was also a member of the famous West Ham team that won the European Cup Winners Cup in

1965 in front of 100,000 at Wembley, a 2–0 victory over TSV Munich.

Some thought that Dear did not take the game seriously enough and that he led a rather excessive lifestyle off the pitch which gave him a slightly portly appearance. He briefly joined Third Division **Brighton and Hove Albion** on loan in March 1967 (being Albion's first-ever loanee) where he scored five goals in just seven appearances. He was expected to move permanently during the close season but declined a transfer to the south coast, and the Seagulls baulked at the £20,000 fee demanded.

He did however join **Fulham** in February 1969 for that same fee. Fulham were struggling badly and having one their worst ever seasons when Dear joined along with Stan Horne and Wilf Tranter. He was linking up again with former West Ham team-mate Johnny Byrne who had joined Fulham a year earlier.

He made his debut against Preston North End at Craven Cottage that resulted in a rare victory (2–1). His first goal came in his third game and was a close-range effort that secured a point against Aston Villa (1–1), and he netted again the following week when Fulham lost 2–3 at Bolton. He helped Fulham beat table-toppers Millwall the following week (2–0) and then followed that up with two goals against high-

Dear's only goal for the club at Craven Cottage was this shot against Aston Villa in the 1–1 draw in March 1969.

flying Cardiff City at Ninian Park, Fulham's only away success all season. Three wins and a draw in six matches represented Fulham's best form that season.

Dear scored two further goals to secure a point against Blackburn Rovers at Ewood Park (2–2) and scored in the last game (also his last game) of the season at Selhurst Park (2–3) by which time Fulham had been relegated. If Dear had been signed at the beginning of the season, maybe Fulham would have stayed up, as his seven goals in thirteen games in a poor side was an excellent return. Although he played just those thirteen league games, he was Fulham's top goalscorer that season!

He was a hard player who possessed a rocket shot and like most good strikers seemed always to be in the right place in the penalty area at the right time, and he was quick at putting away chances with his 'shoot on sight' attitude. However, his weight was an issue and he was generally rather slow and cumbersome.

It was a major surprise when he moved on again in the close season to Second Division **Millwall** in a double swap deal valued at £20,000. Manager Bill Dodgin acquired an experienced right back in John Gilchrist and also obtained youth forward Danny O'Leary in exchange for Dear and Fulham's Brendan Mullan. Dear would have been happy to stay at Fulham but Millwall manager Benny Fenton, who admired the player, swung the deal.

Dear was not keen on the move and in his one season at the Den made just six appearances for Millwall,

failed to score and was a given a free transfer at the end of the season. Although he still had a liking for alcohol, Brian Dear was given a second chance by manager Ron Greenwood in October 1970 and rejoined **West Ham United**. He had been casually playing non-league football with Woodford Town. However in the three months up to Christmas, Dear played just four league games, again failing to score.

The following month, he and West Ham team-mates Bobby Moore, Jimmy Greaves and Clyde Best, along with the club's trainer, were all fined a week's wages and banned for two games by Greenwood after going out drinking in a nightclub until the early hours of the morning prior to an FA Cup third-round tie away against Blackpool. West Ham lost 0–4. Dear never played again and was given a free transfer at the end of the season. Greaves' contract was also not renewed the following year. Moore lost the West Ham captaincy and would move to Fulham within three years.

After hanging up his boots, Dear worked as an Essex publican for a number of years; however he continued to drink and reached rock bottom with alcoholism. To his credit, and without the use of AA, he stopped drinking and got his life back on track. Known as 'The Stag', he returned to football as catering manager with Southend United and was later involved in their commercial department. He retired in 2008 after fifteen years with the Shrimpers. He still attends social functions at West Ham.

BRIAN DEAR
Fulham career – all competitions

Season	Appearances	Goals	Home	Away
1968–1969	13	7	1	6
Total	13	7	1	6

*Total career **league** appearances–95, and **league** goals–45.*

The 1970s

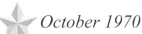 *October 1970*

George Johnston

Scored vital goals in Fulham's promotion season of 1970–71.

George Johnston was born in Glasgow and began his football career as a junior at Second Division **Cardiff City** after being spotted playing for local side Maryhill Harp. He turned professional in 1964, making his debut at the end of the 1964–65 season at the age of seventeen. He was part of Cardiff's 1965 Welsh Cup winning team. The following season he was a regular in the Bluebirds side and, playing alongside the likes of veteran international John Charles and the young John Toshack, he finished as the club's top scorer with a total of twenty-three goals in all competitions.

In March 1967 Johnston played in a benefit match for victims of the Aberfan mining disaster against **Arsenal** and scored twice against them, which persuaded the London side to offer £20,000 to Cardiff to sign him. He made his debut for Arsenal on the opening day of the 1967–68 season against Stoke City and made seventeen appearances in his first season,

which included a marvellous late winner in a thrilling 4–3 win over Leeds United.

However, he could not hold down a place in the 1968–69 season and dropped to the reserves, where he won a Football Combination winners medal and was way out in front as Arsenal's top scorer with sixteen in just twenty-one games, turning down a loan move to Second Division Charlton Athletic during the season. Out of the limelight, he joined Second Division **Birmingham City** in the close season of 1969 for a fee of £30,000. In total, he made only twenty-five appearances for Arsenal and scored three goals.

Signed as a replacement for former England international Fred Pickering, he again failed to hold down a first-team place, making just nine appearances in the 1969–70 season and scoring one goal. In the early stages of the following season, the Blues loaned Johnston to Third Division **Walsall** and in that month he made five appearances for the Saddlers scoring once. Once the loan expired, Third Division **Fulham** stepped in with a £6,000 bid to bring him to Craven Cottage.

Bill Dodgin Jr had watched Johnston at Fulham in a reserve game the month previously and saw him as a replacement for Jimmy Conway who had a long-term injury. Johnston's principal asset was his goalscoring; he was not tall and he was very stocky, and pace and mobility were certainly not his main assets. However, he had experience, good skill and close control, played using his brain and, above all, had an eye for goal.

Fulham began the 1970–71 season with a run of fifteen unbeaten league games. Johnston made his debut in the next game, a televised match at Torquay United. On a windy afternoon Fulham lost 1–3, but Johnston scored a neat goal. He took a while to settle in but then scored regularly. He showed very neat approach work and also set up a number of vitally important goals. His main input was in April when he scored two of the three goals at Bradford City in the match that saw Fulham promoted back to the Second Division.

Bill Dodgin maintained that Johnston had been one of the principal reasons for the promotion and dedicated it to Johnston who had netted ten goals in only twenty-seven matches. In the following season, 1971–72, Johnston scored on the opening day in

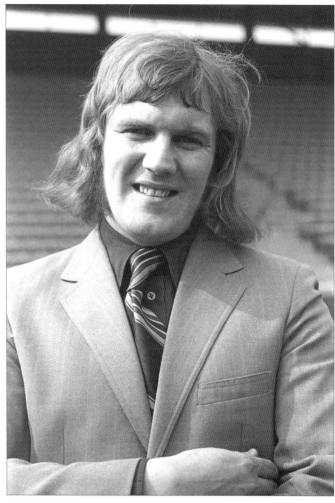

Johnston just fails to score with this effort against Luton in January 1972, but still got two goals in the 3–1 victory.

Johnston heads his second goal, and Fulham's third, in the dramatic 3–2 win at Bradford City in April 1971. The victory secured the club's promotion to Division Two after two seasons in the third division.

a 3–0 win over Watford, but after five games and with Fulham struggling, he disappeared from view especially after the signing of Roger Cross. His final goals were a brace in a very important 3–1 win over Luton Town in January and he also made a couple of cameo appearances towards the end of the season. His final appearance was as a substitute in a dismal 1–3 defeat at Carlisle United.

In the summer of 1972, he returned west to join Fourth Division **Hereford United** making eighteen appearances and scoring five goals, helping them

to achieve promotion to the Third Division. In the summer of 1973 he joined Fourth Division **Newport County**, but made only three appearances for them. The following summer, Johnston decided to quit professional soccer altogether, aged just twenty-six.

He then played football for fun only and had spells in the Welsh League with Caerau Ely and Llanishen Wanderers, turning out with his friends. Johnston settled in Cardiff and worked for a marine engineering maintenance company as a storekeeper before retiring.

GEORGE JOHNSTON
Fulham career – all competitions

Season	Appearances	Goals	Home	Away
1970–1971	27	10	2	8
1971–1972	15	3	3	0
Total	**42**	**13**	**5**	**8**

*Total career **league** appearances–**154**, and **league** goals–**42**.*

Roger Cross

A Fulham character with a cannonball shot, but only a few goals for the Whites.

Roger Cross was born in East Ham in London and joined **West Ham United** as an apprentice at sixteen in July 1964. He was a fairly prolific scorer for West Ham's colts and as he progressed he became the top scorer for the reserve side for two consecutive seasons. As with others at West Ham though he had found his opportunities limited by having the likes of Hurst, Byrne, Dear and Brabrook ahead of him in the pecking order. Like Fulham's Maurice Cook and Johnny Haynes before him, Roger was also a very useful cricketer and was on the books of Essex County Cricket Club, and there was a strong possibility that he could have made a career in the first-class game.

He started the 1968–69 season in the West Ham first-team squad and made his First Division debut against Burnley (5–0) in August as a substitute. He was then loaned to Third Division **Leyton Orient** in October 1968 as a stop-gap signing to replace Vic Halom who had just joined Fulham. At Brisbane Road he scored twice in six games, but by December he was back at Upton Park, though he was not picked again for the first team that season.

At the beginning of the 1969–70 season, Cross started a clutch of First Division matches for the Hammers. He scored in just his second game, a 1–1 draw with Arsenal. However, he returned to the reserves after just seven league games and one League Cup game, not adding to his goal total.

As a recall to the first team seemed remote, Cross joined Fourth Division **Brentford** on a permanent basis for a fee of £12,000 at the close of the 1970 transfer deadline. He became quite a cult hero at Griffin Park in a short space of time, and scored twenty-one goals in just over one and a half seasons. His scoring rate attracted **Fulham** who were struggling for goals in the Second Division after promotion and they signed him to replace Vic Halom who had just departed to Luton Town. Fulham paid £30,000 for Cross's services in November 1971.

He made his debut immediately in a 0–2 defeat against Burnley at the Cottage. He hardly made a great start to his Fulham career, experiencing a number of near misses but no luck. It was not until his eleventh game that he broke his duck in a 2–1 victory at Ashton Gate against Bristol City. He followed that with a goal the following week, a trademark thirty-yard screamer against Cardiff City in a 4–3 victory. A third came before Christmas with a headed goal against Middlesbrough, but on the whole goals were hard to come by. It was not helped by the fact that this was a struggling Fulham side on the edge of the Second Division relegation zone.

Roger Cross's main claim to fame at Fulham was scoring two goals in an FA Cup third-round replay against Queens Park Rangers at Craven Cottage. Both were thunderous shots and described as 'world class'.

Cross scores his final goal for Fulham in the 2–1 victory at Middlesbrough in August 1972.

Cross crashes home the second of his two memorable goals in the 2–1 defeat of QPR in an FA Cup replay in January 1972.

He also scored twice in the famous 1972 friendly with Benfica, played to celebrate the opening of the new Riverside stand (Fulham won 3–2).

Roger Cross was also a character in the true Fulham mould. He possessed a mane of long hair, and the long sideburns of the day. He also was one of the first players to wear non-black boots; along with Arsenal's Alan Ball, he sometimes wore white ones. Through his connections with Harry Redknapp at West Ham, he owned and bred boxer dogs that were good enough for Crufts.

Cross was a strong and sturdy striker, who could trap long goal kicks on his chest. He also possessed a very long throw (like Chelsea's Ian Hutchinson) which Fulham used to good effect. His main asset of course was his powerful shooting; he had a kick like a mule with his left foot but was less happy with the right. Long-range shooting was his speciality.

Whilst he always gave of his best, he lacked any real pace and on occasions seemed slow and cumbersome on the ball, often being robbed by defenders, and he never really looked settled in the team. He managed just nine goals in thirty-eight league and cup appearances although Fulham finally escaped from relegation on the last day of the 1971–72 season.

The arrival of Alec Stock as Fulham manager changed the team's structure and although Cross made four more starts netting one more goal at the beginning of the season 1972–73 season, he did not really seem to fit into Stock's plans. Following the emergence of John Mitchell and after making just one further appearance as a substitute against QPR in October, Cross was back at **Brentford**, now in the Third Division, after the clubs had agreed a transfer fee of £16,000.

He once again enjoyed a great relationship with the Brentford fans and scored a number of spectacular goals. In his four years there he made 145 appearances scoring fifty-two goals. Surprisingly, Brentford decided to release him and in January 1977 he moved from west London to east, joining Second Division **Millwall** for £8,000.

After a few appearances and with injuries taking their toll, Cross took a sabbatical from Millwall and travelled to play in the North American Soccer League for **Seattle Sounders** in 1978. He made eight appearances for Seattle, scoring twice and with three assists. He rejoined **Millwall** in 1979 but decided to hang up his boots shortly afterwards at the age of just thirty. In the two split seasons with Millwall he had made eighteen appearances but not scored.

Immediately after retirement, he was appointed youth team coach at Millwall and then reserve team coach under George Petchey. When Petchey left, Cross worked for a succession of managers at Cold Blow Lane, including George Graham and John Docherty. In 1982 he was briefly caretaker manager following the departure of manager Peter Anderson.

After a considerable time with Millwall, Cross moved to Queens Park Rangers to work under Trevor Francis, and later Don Howe and Gerry Francis. Following two seasons there, Gerry Francis left to take over at Tottenham Hotspur, and took Cross along as his assistant. After around five years at Tottenham he had worked under numerous managers including Christian Gross and Ossie Ardiles.

He then rejoined Gerry Francis at Queens Park Rangers and this coach/assistant manager appointment lasted four years. In 2001, Cross found his way back home after taking a call from old friend Harry

ROGER CROSS
Fulham career – all competitions

Season	Appearances	Goals	Home	Away
1971–1972	38	9	7	2
1972–1973	8	1	0	1
Total	46	10	7	3

*Total career **league** appearances–**266**, and **league** goals–**84**.*

A Cottage portrait of Roger and his lady.

Redknapp and he returned to West Ham as reserve team coach. When asked by new manager Alan Pardew to combine that role with that of chief scout, it proved to be too much, so in the end he stopped coaching and became a full-time scout. He held this position for over a decade until he was unceremoniously sacked by the Hammers as part of a ruthless cost-cutting exercise in 2011.

John Mitchell

He scored goals that took us to Wembley, was top scorer for three seasons, and scored two hat-tricks.

John Mitchell was born in St Albans and played youth football with Carlton Youth Club and won an early medal at eighteen by winning the FA County Youth Cup in the Hertfordshire side that beat Cheshire 2–1. He initially played for Hertford Town but then joined **St Albans** in a semi-professional capacity whilst carrying out an apprenticeship in the print trade. His goal return at St Albans was excellent, with twenty-five in forty-seven games.

Mitchell had trials for both Watford and Wolves, but was spotted when Fulham played St Albans in a pre-season friendly match in 1972. He was invited for trials at Craven Cottage and played a few games, but initially nothing seemed to come of it and he returned to St Albans.

However a few weeks later, he received another call and returned to **Fulham** as an amateur at the beginning of the 1972–73 season. Under new manager Alec Stock Fulham were short of goals and, with Roger Cross seemingly out of favour, Stock was left with Steve Earle as the single central striker. After Mitchell had scored six goals in the reserves early on, Stock almost in desperation thrust the twenty-year-old into the first team.

He made his debut in a 1–1 draw with Huddersfield Town at home in September and did very well, being unlucky not to score. He opened his account in just his third game with a diving header in the second minute at Millwall where Fulham won 3–1. From then on he was an instant hit. Mitchell signed as a professional and St Albans received a nominal fee. The goals came thick and fast including braces against Hull and Bristol City. He had eight in his first fifteen games and was receiving great reviews from the press. Fulham's form improved tremendously.

He was used to the rough and tumble of non-league football and relished the competitive, physical side of the game. He was going to make the most of his chance in football and his exuberant displays seemed to rub off on others. He was an extremely enthusiastic player who was all elbows and legs, but did not give defenders any peace.

As he became better known, defenders tried illegal means to stop him and he spent a lot of time on the deck. He was always in the thick of the action and regularly popped up in the box to convert chances. Mitch would score with his shoulder, knee and shin but was capable of quality strikes as well and was a

handful in aerial duels. In summary, he was a brave battler who would give all he had for ninety minutes.

Seeing as it was his first season he should have played only a handful of games, but so good was he and Fulham so improved that he played in thirty-seven league games. At one stage Fulham were third in the table and looking a good outside bet for promotion. At the end of that season he was already valued at £60,000 and had netted eleven league goals, being second top scorer behind Steve Earle.

There were great expectations for him, but in the next season, 1973–74, he didn't score until October, and by the beginning of December his season was effectively over through injury. His campaign finished with just two goals in eleven league games. Sadly that continued throughout the majority of the next season too, as back, knee and pelvic injuries plagued him. By March, he had played just two league games and was in danger of becoming Fulham's forgotten man.

But he fought his way back to fitness as Fulham progressed up the league and into the later stages of the FA Cup. He began to be picked again and he scored two good goals against high-flying Norwich City at Carrow Road (2–1) over Easter, and it prompted Stock to gamble with the striker for the FA Cup semi-final against Birmingham City. It worked and Mitch scored a beauty. Although Fulham were the better side, they had to be content with a 1–1 draw at Hillsborough. In the semi-final replay at Maine Road, he scored the winner off his chest and shoulder in the last seconds of extra time to send the Whites to Wembley for the first time and to write himself into Fulham folklore.

He scored another brace against Portsmouth before the final, finishing the season with seven goals in league and FA Cup in only thirteen games. Alongside Conway, Busby and Barrett, Mitchell was a member of the team that played in the FA Cup final against West Ham United.

In 1975–76 he started with a bang with three goals in the first six games, but the injury jinx returned again and he missed virtually three months between October and Christmas. He returned to a purple patch with five goals in five games but the season fizzled out and the Cottagers finished in mid-table. However, for the first time John Mitchell was top scorer with ten goals.

In 1976–77 the arrival of Best and Marsh and more particularly Teddy Maybank raised Mitchell's game to a new level. Although the team struggled for most of the season Mitchell scored regularly and having finally shrugged off the injury hoodoo missed just four league games and scored twenty-one goals in all competitions. He saved the best until the final home game where a 6–1 victory over Orient finally dispelled any threats of relegation. Mitchell scored a career-best four goals and Maybank the other two. Fulham were actually six ahead by half time. These figures made him top scorer for the second season running.

Thankfully the injury problems stayed away the following season. Mitch started well with seven goals

before Christmas including a hat-trick against Notts County in September in a 5–1 win at the Cottage. He missed only three league games in all, but finished with nine goals. He had lacked support following the departure of Teddy Maybank to Brighton.

He also added an unwanted statistic when he was sent off during a violent 1–1 draw with Crystal Palace at the Cottage in February, following a clash with Palace defender Billy Gilbert. Otherwise it was a beige kind of season and although Fulham were pulling up no trees they finished comfortably in mid-table and, despite his relatively low total of nine goals, Mitchell was top scorer for the third consecutive season. Fulham's goals were spread across fourteen players that season. Mitch's final goal for the club came in a 2–2 draw at Sunderland on April 1st. His final game was the last match of the season against divisional champions Bolton Wanderers in a 0–0 draw at Burnden Park in front of 34,000.

However it was a turbulent time at Craven Cottage. His mentor Alec Stock had now gone, and when Second Division **Millwall** came in with a £100,000 bid for him in the summer of 1978 the club, now beginning to be asset-stripped by Ernie Clay, accepted the offer from George Petchey. Mitchell was Millwall's first ever £100,000 transfer fee. He would be greatly missed by both team-mates and supporters alike.

In three years at the Den, Mitchell made eighty-one appearances scoring eighteen goals for the Lions. They

This header is one of Mitchell's four goals in the 6–1 defeat of Orient in May 1977. The other two goals were scored by Teddy Maybank – and all six goals came in the first half.

were relegated in his first season there. Towards the end of his time in south London, once again a number of injuries limited his playing time and when a knee injury could not be overcome Mitchell announced his retirement. He was still under thirty, and his league career had lasted just nine years.

After his retirement, John worked in the sports equipment industry and then prospered in his own sports business, later teaming up with his former Fulham playing colleague Bobby Moore as Mitchell-Moore Associates, a sports marketing company. This was highly successful and amongst other dealings it went on to arrange Mastercard's sponsorship of the World Cup.

He maintained an interest in non-league football and returned to assist St Albans following the club's relegation to the Second Division of the Isthmian League in 1982–83. In the following season he returned as joint manager with John Butterfield, and a few months later he took over the reins fully. The club took an upward turn from that point and were promoted back to the First Division.

Their first season back there, 1984–85, saw them finish a creditable seventh. In the following season more success followed under Mitchell's managerial skills and the Hertfordshire club was promoted back up to the Premier League. In 1986–87 it was tougher going and Mitchell resigned to become a club director, with former Fulham playing colleague centre half John Lacy taking over as manager.

Yes! That's the way to do it! Mitchell celebrates one of his two goals against Oldham in December 1976. Fulham won 5–0.

Three years later Mitchell once again became manager. By the end of the 1991–92 season, it seemed as though he was steadily assembling a team capable of possibly winning the league title, even though they had only improved a couple of places on the 1990–91 season. Whilst lying second in the table, the officials from the Conference inspected the ground and concluded that it was not up to standard, because of two oak trees including one that was on the terrace. It was decided to leave the trees standing. To add insult to injury, the club finished the season as runners up. The ground of the eventual champions Chesham United was also deemed to be not up to standard which meant had it not been for the oak tree, City under Mitchell could have been promoted to the Conference. Mitchell had been so disgusted at the Conference's decision not to promote St Albans City that he resigned as manager.

Later on in his career, in the mid-Noughties, John Mitchell joined local team Luton Town initially as a director in 2004 and then again in 2006 as part of a consortium attempting to assist the Hatters during administration. He became CEO in December 2006. It was a complex and unhappy time for Luton Town with a number of personnel issues behind the scenes. There were also financial problems. In the end a number of directors including Mitchell were fined and banned from football because of financial irregularities; although John was guilty only of a single minor charge, he was not suspended and was fined just £250. A number of FA charges against the club in general were upheld and they suffered a severe points deduction from which they did not recover and the Hatters dropped out of the Football League at the end of the 2008–09 season.

John Mitchell still fondly remembers his time at the Cottage and visits whenever possible usually with his friend Les Strong. He will always be very popular with the fans. His never-say-die attitude was always apparent and made him a much admired player at Craven Cottage.

JOHN MITCHELL
Fulham career – all competitions

Season	Appearances	Goals	Home	Away
1972–1973	37	11	7	4
1973–1974	18	2	2	0
1974–1975	23	7	2	5
1975–1976	31	10	6	4
1976–1977	43	21	12	9
1977–1978	42	9	7	2
Total	194	60	36	24

*Total career **league** appearances–251, and **league** goals–75.*

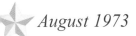

Viv Busby

An elegant goalmaker and goalscorer, was top scorer for two seasons.

Viv **Busby** was born in Slough. After leaving school, he was happily engaged in a fledgling career as a cost accountant and supplemented this by playing for then non-league (Isthmian) team **Wycombe Wanderers**. He joined their youth team at seventeen in 1966. Quite quickly he forced his way into the reckoning for the senior side. Three years later he had an unsuccessful trial at Fulham.

He was not always a regular in the Wycombe side either and, despite playing in most of the forward line positions in three and a half seasons there, made just fifty appearances scoring nineteen league goals; he also added eight in sixteen FA Cup games. Luton manager Alec Stock watched Busby bag a hat-trick in a county cup tie and offered him a trial at Kenilworth Road. Initially he turned the idea down, but after advice from his father decided to give it a go; he did well and was offered a professional contract.

At **Luton Town** in January 1970 he linked up with ex-Fulham centre forward Malcolm Macdonald and it was the start of a successful partnership that saw Luton promoted to the Second Division at the end of that 1969–70 season. He netted four in his first nine matches. The following season was less prolific with eight goals in twenty-eight appearances.

He struggled to find any form in 1971–72 and spent a short period out on loan at First Division **Newcastle United**, teaming up once again with Malcolm Macdonald. He scored twice in four league games at

St James' Park. In his one FA Cup tie for Newcastle he was in the team beaten 1–2 by non-league Hereford United in one of the biggest cup shocks of the century. His loan was not extended; he managed just two goals all season for Luton. The next season, 1972–73, he found goals just as hard to come by with again just two in twenty-seven appearances.

After three and a half seasons and seventy-seven appearances for the Second Division Hatters, Busby moved on. Alec Stock had left Luton Town the season before when he had resigned to become the manager of **Fulham**. At the start of his second season in charge, 1973–74, Stock made a significant outlay to bring Viv and the Luton midfielder Alan Slough to Craven Cottage, Busby being valued at £25,000 in a £70,000 double transaction.

Busby made his debut for Fulham on the opening day of the 1973–74 season in a 2–0 home win over Millwall. However, it was not until the seventh game that he registered his first goal, in a 1–0 win over Bolton Wanderers. Initially he lacked confidence and by the end of January 1974 had netted only five times. His form improved dramatically when he scored a hat-trick and took home the match ball following a 4–1 win over Sheffield Wednesday in February. He finished this first season with eleven league goals from thirty-eight matches and as leading scorer.

Viv started the following season in fine style with six in his first eleven matches. In one match in August

Busby nets Fulham's third goal in the 3–0 victory at Sheffield Wednesday in December 1973.

against Cardiff City at the Cottage, Busby scored one of the greatest Fulham goals ever seen. Taking possession on the wing on the halfway line he beat five Cardiff players on a magnificent solo run along the touchline before beating the keeper with a fine drive; Fulham went on to win 4–0. After this purple patch he did not get another league goal for three months.

But things were beginning to happen for him in the FA Cup. He scored twice in the third-round replay away at Hull City, including the equaliser in the last seconds to keep Fulham in the competition (2–2). In the fourth-round third replay against Nottingham Forest he scored both goals to see Fulham through (2–1). Days later came his biggest occasion when he netted both Fulham goals in the cup shock of the day, a 2–1 victory over First Division league leaders Everton at Goodison Park. The six goals were major contributions towards Fulham's visit to Wembley in 1975. The goals began to flow more regularly in the league as well. Viv was a member of the Fulham team that lost bravely 0–2 to West Ham in the FA Cup final.

In 1975–76 he started the season with a bang with four in his first eight games, but once again the goalscoring touch almost disappeared completely and he scored in just one further league match all season, both goals in a 2–0 victory over Sunderland. It was probably time for another move and, following the return of Rodney Marsh and the arrival of George Best early in the 1976–77 season, after five games without a goal Viv Busby signed for First Division **Norwich City** for £50,000 in September 1976.

Viv Busby was an elegant but enigmatic forward who never really fulfilled his promise at Fulham. Some days he would look like a world-beater, on other occasions the game would pass him by. He could delight and frustrate in equal measure. He could score spectacular goals, yet blast over the bar from two yards.

He was just as much a goal-maker as a goal-taker and his link-up play was always good. He formed a

very good partnership with John Mitchell. He was very flexible and could play anywhere up front and was just as much at home on the right wing where he had started his career. He had two quick feet, good pace on the ball and an eye for goal but never really converted enough chances to put him in the bracket of the great Fulham goalscorers.

Never the most physical player, some say he was too nice to be a footballer, and he relied a lot on confidence. When this was high, he could score at will, when it was low, the goal seemed only one foot wide and the ball would never go in. Wherever he went in his career, however, it was unanimously agreed that he was a very intelligent lad and one of the nicest people you could ever meet in football, a player who always had time for the supporters.

At Carrow Road he was following a difficult act in Ted MacDougall who had just left to join Southampton. Busby was signed by John Bond as a direct replacement and made his usual fine start with eleven goals in his first eighteen games, but history repeated itself as the goals dried up. Amongst those initial goals was a hat-trick scored against Leicester City on New Year's Day in 1977 (3–2). Norwich were quite an unstable club at the time and Busby was dropped from the side. He made just five appearances the following season and after a falling out with the management he was transfer-listed and on his travels

Another Busby goal against Sheffield Wednesday, this one part of a hat-trick at home in February 1974.

again in November to Second Division **Stoke City**. His stay at Norwich had been a mere fifteen months.

In his first part-season Busby netted just four in twenty-four appearances. However, the second season, 1978–79, was more successful, with seven goals in twenty-two matches. His experience, effort and goal-making were also invaluable as Stoke secured promotion back to the First Division. He was a regular in the Potters side early in the following season, but once again found difficulty scoring, and after netting just once in fourteen games was dropped. During the period out, he was allowed to spend a

short spell on loan to Third Division **Sheffield United** in January. He scored once in three games for the Blades. Big wages had not arrived in football at this time and, being out of the team, Busby supplemented his income by selling shoes from the boot of his Ford Capri.

On his return from Sheffield, he made a temporary move to the USA and played for **Tulsa Roughnecks** in the NASL. Viv played nineteen matches, but netted only once with two assists. After the season finished, he remained in America joining the Oklahoma team for the indoor league, scoring eight

A Busby goal fondly remembered by Fulham fans lucky to be present at the 4–0 demolition of Cardiff City at home in August 1974. Viv leaves City defenders floundering as he triumphantly rounds off a mazy run.

Coach Bill Taylor presents Busby with the match ball following his hat-trick against Sheffield Wednesday in February 1974. Also in the picture are, left to right, Alan Slough, Les Strong, Les Barrett and John Fraser.

times and achieving five assists in the seven games he appeared in. He did not appear again for Stoke and his total return for the club was just twelve goals in sixty appearances.

After a year in the USA, Busby signed a good deal with Second Division **Blackburn Rovers**. He remained there for the rest of the 1980–81 season, but he made only eight appearances, scoring just once. There is no reference to Busby appearing at all for Blackburn in the 1981–82 season, and at the end of that season he made his final move, to Fourth Division **York City**. In the 1982–83 season he made sixteen appearances scoring four goals. The following season Busby was combining playing with coaching and made just five appearances for the Minstermen, but had the satisfaction of seeing his career close on a high as York were promoted as champions at the end of that 1983–84 season, accruing over one hundred points.

As a coach and assistant manager, Busby stayed at York for almost five years working alongside his former Stoke City team-mate Denis Smith. Smith departed York in 1987 and took Busby with him, and there was another five-year stint and association at Sunderland, taking them to a play-off final. His next job after 1992, and six months out of the game, saw his first role as a manager with a brief and unspectacular eight-month stint during a time of turmoil at Hartlepool United. He then worked as a coach at one of his previous clubs, Sheffield United, assisting another former Stoke team-

mate, Howard Kendall; this was another five-year assignment. Once again he helped to take the team to the play-off finals. Kendall left Bramall Lane to return to Everton as manager for a third spell in the summer of 1997 and took Busby with him. However, the pair spent just a year at Goodison Park before heading out to Greece for a six-month stint with Athens-based Ethnikos Piraeus in 1998.

After Greece, Busby held a temporary scouting post for Sheffield United. He only did this for three months before returning to former club Fulham as assistant and coach alongside Paul Bracewell. Sadly progress was not swift enough for Mohamed Al Fayed and just

Busby leaps high to celebrate his second goal in the epic 2–1 victory at First Division Everton in the FA Cup in 1975.

VIV BUSBY
Fulham career – all competitions

Season	Appearances	Goals	Home	Away
1973–1974	42	11	9	2
1974–1975	53	18	6	12
1975–1976	41	7	4	3
1976–1977	7	0	0	0
Total	143	36	19	17

*Total career **league** appearances–**301**, and **league** goals–**74**.*

six months later the pair left Craven Cottage. Soon after this, former Sunderland and Derby defender Colin Todd appointed Busby as youth team manager at Swindon Town in 2000.

This is where Viv had the biggest battle of his life when, after feeling ill for a couple of weeks, he was diagnosed with acute myeloid leukaemia. His family were told to prepare for the worst and he spent a harrowing year in hospital and saw his weight plummet by four stone while he underwent five gruelling sessions of chemotherapy. He was also kept in isolation because of dangers to his immune system, but he finally managed to conquer the disease.

Amazingly, in September 2004 he returned to the game as assistant manager at York City, now in the Conference. Busby became caretaker manager at York in November, but left the club by mutual consent just three months later. His next spell in early 2007 took him north of the border to Scottish club Gretna who were on the verge of a financial revolution. He was appointed as youth academy manager, but this also ended in controversy when he was savagely axed as part of a drastic cost-cutting exercise as the Gretna 'dream' imploded. His final footballing post was a happy four-year spell as assistant manager at non-league Workington Town.

Following divorce, and calling time on forty-five years in the game, Viv Busby emigrated to Spain with a new partner in 2011. He is the older brother of Martyn Busby who played around 200 professional games for Queens Park Rangers, Portsmouth and Burnley.

Rod Belfitt

A definite also-ran in our list of Fulham strikers.

Rod Belfitt was born in Bournemouth and spent his formative years with his family in South Africa and India before they settled in Doncaster. Rod attended the local secondary modern school and then Doncaster Technical College before serving an apprenticeship as a draughtsman.

He joined Arsenal as an amateur from Doncaster United but things did not work out and he returned north to play for Doncaster United and then Retford Town. He was offered a contract by Second Division **Leeds United** in July 1963 when he was ready to turn professional aged seventeen. During his eight years at Elland Road, Belfitt was playing for one of

This is it! Belfitt's only goal for Fulham, fired in from close range in the 1–1 draw at Nottingham Forest in December 1974.

the dominant teams in Europe and he could not hold down a regular first-team place, competing with the likes of Alan Peacock, Peter Lorimer, Allan Clarke and Mick Jones.

However, Belfitt still scored thirty-three goals from 128 appearances in all competitions for Leeds including a hat-trick in an Inter Cities Fairs Cup semi-final against Kilmarnock and two goals against Derby in the League Cup semi-final. He also appeared for Leeds as a substitute in the League Cup final of 1968 against Arsenal. A tall, elegant and intelligent striker, he would probably have been a regular in most other First Division sides. He was a willing runner, and often made goals for his more illustrious colleagues.

After his service at Leeds, he joined Bobby Robson's First Division **Ipswich Town** in 1971 and

over a season and a part-season made forty league appearances scoring thirteen goals. He scored in his first two games for the club and finished the season as equal leading scorer with seven goals in twenty-six games. The next season he was already leading goalscorer with nine. Then in a shrewd transfer, Robson exchanged his top scorer plus £40,000 in cash for a relatively unknown twenty-one-year-old English forward David Johnson of Everton. Johnson went on to play for England and have a flourishing career with the East Anglian side and with Liverpool.

Belfitt played just sixteen league games in eleven months for First Division **Everton** scoring twice, enduring a difficult time before a mid-season move to Second Division **Sunderland** where he stayed for two years. He managed only four goals in thirty-nine league games with the Wearsiders during that period.

In his second season he was transfer-listed, and was loaned to **Fulham** in November 1974, as a short-term replacement for Viv Busby, making his debut in a 1–0 win over Blackpool. He scored in his second game, an equaliser in a 1–1 draw away at Nottingham Forest. He played a further four league games without scoring, and Fulham as a team netted only once in that period. After six games he returned to Sunderland.

In February 1975, he was loaned out to Third Division **Huddersfield Town** and scored twice in six matches for the Terriers, but they were relegated to the bottom division. In the close season of 1975, he made a permanent move to Leeds Road where he stayed for a season scoring six league goals in twenty-eight appearances.

He decided to hang up his boots at the relatively early age of thirty and played non-league football mainly for fun, firstly with **Worksop Town** and then **Frickley Colliery**, before joining up with his former Leeds colleague Mick Bates at **Bentley Victoria**. He returned to his original career as a draughtsman for ten years, later becoming a financial advisor before running his own insurance business.

ROD BELFITT
Fulham career – all competitions

Season	Appearances	Goals	Home	Away
1974–1975	6	1	0	1
Total	6	1	0	1

*Total career **league** appearances–**210**, and **league** goals–**45**.*

Tony Mahoney

A competitive player who should have scored more goals.

Tony Mahoney was born in Barking and joined a **Fulham** youth squad which contained a number of players who would go on to have long first-class careers. He became an England youth international in 1977, playing alongside Fulham colleagues goalkeeper Perry Digweed and centre back Tony Gale.

Mahoney was one of Fulham's youngest ever debutants, being just a month past his seventeenth birthday when making his first start against Cardiff City in November 1976. He also made one other substitute appearance that season.

His first start of the 1977–78 season was also against Cardiff and his first goal followed a few days later when he scored in the 4–1 home win over Burnley, just days after his eighteenth birthday. He scored the following week too, saving a point at the Cottage in a 1–1 draw with Blackpool. Later on that season, after the departure of Alan Warboys and Teddy Maybank, he had a run of nine games in the side and scored his third goal to win the match against Luton Town 1–0. That season he appeared seventeen times.

In the next season, he had a run of early league games once more, but managed only one league goal in a 2–0 home win over Sheffield United and a League Cup goal against Darlington. He played just twice more that season being substituted both times, a

disappointing season ending with only nine appearances in all competitions.

The 1979–80 season followed a fairly similar pattern. An early run of six games failed to produce a goal and, as Fulham's form stuttered, Tony disappeared from the side. With Fulham virtually relegated, manager Bobby Campbell brought him back into the squad for the final seven games. He played in five, scoring in the final two games of the season.

Mahoney was a tall, upright striker who had scored a significant number of goals in junior and reserve football. He was well built for a young man and although not the best on the floor, scored some vital headed goals. He also enjoyed the physical, competitive side of the game, not being intimidated by older, bigger players.

That physical side showed up in the first game of the 1980–81 season at the Cottage. In a League Cup match against Peterborough United, Mahoney was sent off in a 1–1 draw, and less than two months later he was sent off again at the Cottage during a bad-tempered 3–1 win over Burnley. He seemed also to 'get involved' in other matches too, earning himself a reputation as a bit of a hothead.

But in that season he enjoyed his best form. He played in ten out of eleven league games around the start of the season, but only scored once in the league. He also scored the winner in a 2–1 victory over Reading in the first round of the FA Cup at Elm Park. From December to February he enjoyed his best Fulham scoring spell, with four goals in six games. His final goal came in a 2–0 win over Blackpool at Bloomfield Road.

His final game for Fulham was the last league game that season, a 2–4 defeat at Leeds Road versus Huddersfield Town. In all though, he had played twenty-nine games that season and scored six goals. He remained at Fulham for the following season, 1981–82, going out on loan to Fourth Division **Northampton Town** for six games in October.

He found it difficult to dislodge Gordon Davies and the emerging

talents of Dean Coney and Dale Tempest. He was not selected by new manager Macdonald at all that season, so it was not a surprise when he moved to Third Division **Brentford** in the summer.

In the 1982–83 season, things went very well at Brentford for a few months, with Mahoney forming a very effective goalscoring partnership up front with Francis Joseph. However, in an FA Cup replay against Swindon Town at Griffin Park, Mahoney broke his leg following a horror tackle from a Swindon player. He was out for some time, but managed to get fit and return to the Bees side the following season. He appeared not to be the player he had been, and that summer joined Second Division **Crystal Palace**, having scored twelve goals in forty-one appearances for Brentford. He played twenty-four games in all competitions and scored five goals for the Eagles.

He was released by Crystal Palace at the end of the season, and pursued a non-league career back in his native Essex, with significant spells at **Grays Athletic** and **Canvey Island**. Since then, there have been some reports that Tony's health has suffered recently and that he has been diagnosed with multiple sclerosis.

Mahoney gets a header on target in the last match of the 1979–80 season, away at Shrewsbury. He didn't score with this effort, but he did net one of Fulham's two goals that day. Unfortunately, Shrewsbury scored five.

TONY MAHONEY
Fulham career – all competitions

Season	Appearances	Goals	Home	Away
1976–1977	2	0	0	0
1977–1978	17	3	3	0
1978–1979	9	2	2	0
1979–1980	12	2	1	1
1980–1981	29	6	2	4
Total	69	13	8	5

*Total career **league** appearances–**124**, and **league** goals–**26**.*

Teddy Maybank

A proven goalscorer and a colourful character, Maybank was never afraid to get in where it hurt.

Teddy Maybank was born in Lambeth and attended the same school as Ray Lewington. He lived in a Chelsea catchment area alongside the likes of Ray Wilkins, Tommy Langley, John Sparrow and Lewington, and he attended Chelsea training twice a week at Stamford Bridge. He became, along with those players, a member of the crack Senrab Sunday youth team, and honed his skills on Hackney Marshes.

He joined **Chelsea** and made his First Division debut as an eighteen-year-old in April 1975 against Tottenham in a 0–2 defeat, and managed a goal in three league appearances that season. The following season (1975–76) he scored five goals in twenty-six matches including two beautifully headed goals in a televised game against Carlisle United early in the season. The following season though he made just three appearances for the Blues. There were

occasional rumours that some of his family could sometimes be found on the 'wrong side of the law' and his early career was dogged by an accusation of receiving stolen property. Perhaps this hastened his departure from Stamford Bridge.

Surprisingly, he joined a struggling **Fulham** on a month's loan in November 1976, after the departure of Viv Busby, and made a useful Second Division debut in a 2–3 defeat at Blackpool linking up well with John Mitchell. On his home debut he scored twice in an emphatic, televised 5–0 win on a frozen pitch against Oldham Athletic, and in his fourth game he secured a 2–0 win against Blackburn Rovers with another goal. Fulham hoped to extend the loan period but he returned to Chelsea.

With Fulham looking to be heading for certain relegation it was a surprise and a relief when, along-

Maybank puts a flashing header just wide, but he scored later in the 1–1 draw at home to Charlton in August 1977.

side Peter Storey from Arsenal, Maybank made a return in a permanent transfer in March 1977 for between £65,000 and £75,000. It was a bargain; Fulham's form immediately improved with Maybank in the side and the team secured five wins and four draws in the final twelve games to stay up. In one game he won and converted a penalty against Sheffield United and then added Fulham's third in a 3–2 win that secured two precious points. He was also delighted to play a pivotal role in the 3–1 downfall of his former club Chelsea at the Cottage on Good Friday. Fulham had also signed Alan Warboys and, in this final third of the season, were effectively playing with three centre forwards in Mitchell, Warboys and Maybank.

He was the ideal foil for John Mitchell, and this was emphasised in the final home match of the season when Fulham demolished Orient 6–1 at Craven Cottage with all six Fulham goals coming in the first half. John Mitchell scored four with Maybank contributing the other two. He finished the season with eight goals from just fifteen matches.

Teddy was big, blond and burly and was as brave as they come, often ducking into flying boots to get his head to a cross. He was a super header of the ball and as a target man created many goals for others. His physique and awkward style were ideally suited to hold-up play, and his ability always to give opponents a busy afternoon made space for Mitchell's more silky and fluid skills. He had an unusual running style and walking gait that earned him a nickname of 'The

Penguin'. Although not blessed with great pace or brilliant technique, Maybank more than made up for it by giving one hundred per cent in every game. He was a players' player and his work-rate was appreciated by his team-mates.

He was also a player in the true Fulham tradition, unpredictable but always playing with a smile on his face. He had the ability to chat back to referees and wind up opponents in equal measure. He was a bit of a 'wide boy' in his early career but his infectious swagger and cheeky style of play made him an instant hit with the Cottage faithful.

His second season, 1977–78, also got off to a bang with another seven goals in the first ten matches. This included a brace in a tempestuous 3–2 derby victory over Crystal Palace at Selhurst Park that saw Tony Gale score his first senior goal. Maybank was sent off later in the match and the Palace centre half Ian Evans broke a leg in a tackle with George Best. Another thriller happened at the Cottage a month later in a topsy-turvy match with Sunderland which ended 3–3. With Fulham trailing 2–3 they were awarded a penalty that Maybank confidently took and missed. But he redeemed himself with a brilliant and brave diving header in the last seconds to save a point.

Two games later and Maybank had played his final game, a comfortable 2–0 win over Hull City at the Cottage. Ex-Fulham player Alan Mullery was now in charge of a revitalised Second Division **Brighton and Hove Albion** team and was a big admirer of

the blond bomber. With Fulham going through one of their seemingly regular financial crises, he bid an amazing club record £238,000 to take Maybank to the Goldstone Ground. At that time it was a record transfer between two Second Division sides. Within a month Teddy Maybank returned to the Cottage with Brighton. Fulham were playing well and although Maybank inevitably scored near the end, Fulham won the match 2–1. Maybank played his part in a good Brighton team that missed out on promotion to the top flight on goal average. He did however net six for the Seagulls in half a season.

The next season (1978–79), however, with Peter Ward up front, Brian Horton in midfield and Mark Lawrenson at the back, Brighton were promoted as runners-up into the First Division for the first time

ever. During that season Maybank also hit a hat-trick in a 5–0 demolition of Cardiff City on Boxing Day. One near miss against Sunderland with an acrobatic overhead kick that hit the bar was described as 'possibly being the goal of the century' if it had gone in. He once again showed another side of his character by being sent off in under ten minutes for punching a Sheffield United opponent. He was also showing signs of injury and his own season was curtailed at the beginning of April when he was carried off with a knee injury against Notts County. He scored ten goals in thirty-five appearances in that promotion season

Teddy Maybank also had the distinction of scoring Brighton's first ever goal in the First Division at Villa Park. Despite promotion, the supporters amazingly did not really take to Maybank. He never worked out a great understanding with Peter Ward who was the darling of the home fans. His hold-up play was recognised but he did not seem to score enough goals. Some also did not warm to him as they considered him too 'flash' for

Brighton. He appeared to be struggling for fitness and occasionally needed cortisone injections for his knee. Brighton were languishing in the lower reaches of the First Division and Maybank was receiving increased criticism from the fans, and Mullery thought the best thing he could do was try to re-coup some of the fee he had paid out. Fulham were in even more trouble in the Second Division, and Maybank re-signed for **Fulham** for £150,000 and made his third Fulham debut on Boxing Day 1979 at Cardiff. Apart from one spell of three goals in five games, Teddy seemed to have lost some pace and spark and was possibly too similar a player to Chris Guthrie, his then strike partner. He played nineteen league games but failed to halt Fulham's slide into the Third Division.

It was not really a major surprise when a player of his quality left the club, and he was signed in the close season by Dutch side **PSV Eindhoven**. Fulham again received a significant fee reported to be around £250,000. Sadly his knee was a problem and after just six games and no goals for PSV he sustained another knee injury which effectively finished his playing career. After just five seasons, his colourful time as a footballer was over at twenty-five, but he did receive a sizeable compensation payout. Fulham made a profit of well over £250,000 in transfer dealings involving Maybank.

Teddy was a larger than life character and a 'decent bloke' who always had time for the fans. He demonstrated his lighter side by appearing as a contestant on Cilla Black's *Blind Date* TV programme as 'our Edward from Brighton'; he also appeared on (and won) an episode of *The Weakest Link* in 2008. Anne Robinson made many tongue-in-cheek references to living in Brighton as it was a town with a significant gay community but Teddy would not bite at the remarks! He also possessed a decent singing voice and YouTube has some entertaining Maybank karaoke clips.

In his later working life, Teddy went into construction and maintenance and focused on flooring, with areas like squash courts and other sports facilities being the speciality. He still lives in the Brighton area.

TEDDY MAYBANK
Fulham career – all competitions

Season	Appearances	Goals	Home	Away
1976–1977 (loan)	4	3	3	0
1976–1977	11	5	5	0
1977–1978	14	8	5	3
1979–1980	21	3	1	2
Total	50	19	14	5

*Total career **league** appearances–**138**, and **league** goals–**39**.*

Alan Warboys

Full of endeavour, too few goals for Fulham, but nearly 140 career goals.

Born in Goldthorpe near Barnsley, **Alan Warboys** began his career at **Doncaster Rovers** learning his trade from experienced professionals like Alick Jeffrey and Laurie Sheffield. He made his debut in April 1967, just after his seventeenth birthday, in a 1–4 defeat at Leyton Orient in the Third Division and scored his first league goal against Scunthorpe United a couple of weeks later. He initially played as an amateur, training on Tuesday and Thursday nights while working at the Goldthorpe pit. In the mid-Sixties mining was all there was, and Doncaster's offer of professional football had come out of the blue.

Rovers were relegated at the end of that season but finished midway in the Fourth Division in his second season. Alan managed eleven goals in his initial stint of forty games at Belle Vue. After just fourteen months, he moved across Yorkshire joining First Division **Sheffield Wednesday** for £40,000 in the summer of 1968.

He remained at Hillsborough for just over two seasons. It was a very big step up from the Fourth Division and he was also trying to fill the boots of experienced striker John Ritchie who had returned to Stoke City. He did fairly well but Sheffield Wednesday were relegated at the end of that second season, so his third season was played out in the Second Division. Thus, even at a young age, Warboys had already played in all four divisions of the Football League. He added thirteen goals in almost seventy appearances.

Following Wednesday's relegation, he joined Second Division **Cardiff City** for a club record fee of £42,000 in November 1970, as a direct replacement for John Toshack who had recently joined Liverpool for £110,000 to link up with Kevin Keegan.

On his Boxing Day home debut for the club, Warboys scored twice against the team he had just left, Sheffield Wednesday, and went on to finish the season with thirteen goals in seventeen league games, including scoring four times in one match in the 4–0 win over Carlisle United in March 1971. They were all left-footed shots and Warboys holds the record for the fastest ever hat-trick for Cardiff, the first three goals coming inside the first ten minutes and the fourth before half time. This was despite the fact that he was playing with a leg injury and with his thigh heavily strapped. The club missed out on promotion by just one place.

After spending one more year at Cardiff, he returned to Yorkshire early the following season to join First Division **Sheffield United** for £20,000 in September 1972. Warboys was never really given sufficient recognition at Cardiff where his strike rate was at least equal to that of Toshack. He scored twenty-seven goals over just sixty games.

The spell with Sheffield United proved to be brief with Alan making just seven appearances and failing to find the net. Just six months later, he joined Third Division **Bristol Rovers**, then managed by former Fulham boss Bill Dodgin senior, for another sizeable fee of £35,000. In his five seasons at the club, he forged a lethal forward pairing with fellow Yorkshireman Bruce Bannister which would be much celebrated, taking Rovers to promotion to the Second

Division and earning the duo the nickname 'Smash and Grab' in reference to Warboys' physical battering-ram playing style and Bannister's ability to grab the resulting chances thus created. In the 1973–74 season the pair scored forty goals between them and gained Rovers promotion from the Third Division. It included a period of thirty-two unbeaten games for Rovers. He and Bannister were both included in the inaugural PFA team of the year for the Third Division, the only time two Rovers players have received this honour in the same year.

One amazing game saw Rovers win 8–2 at Brighton and Hove Albion, then newly managed by Brian Clough. Brighton were already reeling from having been dumped out of the FA Cup 0–4 on their own ground by non-league Walton & Hersham and, when bad weather forced the postponement of many top-flight games, 10,000 fans plus the press and cameramen flocked to the Goldstone Ground. Rovers were 4–1 ahead after just over thirty-five minutes with Bannister claiming a hat-trick, and Warboys scored the final four goals in the rout. Rovers were promoted as runners-up. Warboys spent almost three more seasons at Eastville with Bannister although Rovers were never much above a mid-table Second Division side. His final record at Bristol Rovers was fifty-three goals from 144 appearances.

During that final season, he signed for **Fulham** for £30,000 in February 1977. The decision to buy him was a strange one, but Fulham were struggling badly in the relegation places in the Second Division and although John Mitchell and later Teddy Maybank provided a lot of finesse in the forward line, Fulham seemed to lack physical presence up front, and needed something of a 'nuisance player' who would soak up the physical knocks.

He made his debut in a 1–5 defeat at Wolverhampton, and scored in the following home match against Luton Town but it was another loss, 1–2. There was a third defeat against Hereford by a single goal but after that, Warboys' presence seemed to have an effect, and Fulham lost only two games in the next eleven, winning five, to secure safety. His only other goal in a Fulham shirt was the first in the memorable 3–1 victory over local rivals Chelsea on Good Friday. Warboys played in all of the last fifteen games.

Warboys was perhaps never the most gifted of footballers, but what he lacked in ability he more then compensated for with endeavour. He had a good touch and decent pace with the ball at his feet, but could sometimes look awkward and clumsy. He was burly, ungainly and hard but a great target man who relished the physical side of the game. He had a typical Seventies style too with long, jet-black hair and sideburns that seemed longer than his shorts! He enjoyed playing alongside the gifted George Best and Rodney Marsh and always had good things to say about Fulham and their manager at the time, Bobby Campbell.

Warboys played just the first four league games for Fulham in the 1977–78 season, making nineteen in total, when the lure of returning north proved too great and he moved on to Second Division **Hull City** for £25,000. Hull were having a poor run, but Warboys became an instant hero scoring the two goals that defeated Tottenham Hotspur in their one season in the Second Division. He stayed for two seasons, but with his pace slowing managed just nine goals in forty-nine appearances. He teamed up again with Bannister at Hull.

He finally returned to his first Fourth Division club, **Doncaster Rovers**, taking a pay cut to play there. In

Warboys scores on his home debut in February 1977, a match that Fulham lost 1–2 to Luton Town.

his first season back he received the club's Player of the Year award and in the second season Rovers were promoted to the Third Division. In his third and final season under Billy Bremner, he moved into the centre of the team's defence, working as a mentor for the younger professionals like Glyn Snodin.

He missed a fair bit of that third season with back trouble, and following an operation to remove a disc from his back, he finally retired in 1982. Alan Warboys scored his last career goal in 1981 against Cambridge United in his final Doncaster game. He was awarded a testimonial by Doncaster in 1983. His final spell was still pretty impressive with twenty-one goals in eighty-nine games.

He was keen to go into a management/coaching role with Rovers after retiring, but the job that he was promised never materialised. Disillusioned, he lost interest and broke all ties with football. He subsequently ran a public house in Swinton for a number of years and then worked as a lorry driver and for a scaffolding firm before retiring. He stays in touch with supporters from both Bristol and Doncaster and still looks out for the scores of all the teams he played for. Warboys was a true hard-working professional who was down to earth and happy to be amongst the supporters, never forgetting his roots.

ALAN WARBOYS
Fulham career – all competitions

Season	Appearances	Goals	Home	Away
1976–1977	15	2	2	0
1977–1978	6	0	0	0
Total	21	2	2	0

*Total career **league** appearances–479, and **league** goals–136.*

Gordon Davies

A Fulham favourite – and the club's all-time top goalscorer, including four hat-tricks.

Gordon Davies, nicknamed Ivor, was born in Merthyr Tydfil in Wales. He played in the local league for Georgetown Boys Club and gained schoolboy Welsh international honours. He had initially signed schoolboy forms for Manchester City at fourteen and spent two years at Maine Road but his potential was not recognised and he was released, being told he would not make the grade.

He returned to Wales where he played a significant part in helping Hoover Sports win the coveted South Wales Amateur League title. Hoover Sports (now Merthyr Saints) shared the use of Penydarren Park, the home of Merthyr Tydfil FC. After some decent displays for Hoover and a brief spell at Ebbw Vale, nineteen-year-old Gordon was recruited by **Merthyr Tydfil** manager Emrys Evans. Gordon played weekend football for Merthyr whilst studying at Madeley College for a teaching qualification.

Upon finishing his studies, Davies returned to South Wales to do his teaching practice, and was signed on a £12 per week wage for the Merthyr club, good wages for the time. He continued to play for Merthyr on a semi-professional basis whilst teaching geography and PE at the local Gwernllwyn School in Dowlais. During this time at Merthyr, Davies initially played as a right winger, where he had not played before, but he still managed thirty goals. An injury within the Merthyr squad led to Evans switching Gordon's position from a winger to a central striker. This proved to be a masterstroke and his scoring prowess (thirty-five goals by February) and impressive displays alerted league clubs.

In the 1977–78 season **Fulham** came calling. Although Cardiff City and Swansea City had both shown an interest, Fulham had a reputation for attacking football and giving players an opportunity. They paid a fee of £8,000 with the addition that in the event of any transfer to another club, Merthyr would receive 10% of the transfer fee. Fulham also played two friendly games at Merthyr. Gordon actually signed for the Cottagers in November 1977 but, at the request of manager Evans, and with Fulham's consent, he remained at the Valleys-based club until March 1978 as Merthyr reached the quarter-finals of the FA trophy.

By March in this partial season, Davies had already netted twenty goals in twenty-five games.

It was a wrench to leave Wales and his teaching career, but it was a once in a lifetime opportunity to turn professional which Gordon took. He did not expect to play in his first season, but he was included in the squad against Mansfield over Easter and played a few minutes as substitute. Then in April he was told a couple of hours before the away game against Blackpool that he would be playing. A late starter, Gordon would be making his Second Division debut not far short of his twenty-third birthday.

He couldn't have made a worse start, being in the wrong penalty area and conceding a spot-kick that put Fulham behind after only six minutes. After a rollicking from captain Ray Evans, Davies atoned by laying on the equaliser with a pass to Les Strong. Les then returned the compliment later in the game, setting Davies up for the winning goal in the 2–1 victory. He remained in the side for the last three league matches of the season, but did not score again.

For Gordon, the 1978–79 season was like 'stepping up five divisions' and after an early goal against Darlington in the League Cup, he struggled for goals. He broke his duck against Oldham in September, but playing with various strike partners he did not really settle into a set position or role. By Boxing Day he still had only two goals to his name. He seemed to get to the pace of the division more in the second half of the season and a goal in the 5–1 victory over Cambridge United over Christmas settled him down. This was followed by another in the 2–0 victory against Queens Park Rangers in the third round of the FA Cup. Goals began to flow and he netted his first brace in a 3–0 win over Leicester City towards the end of the season. In his first full season he finished with eleven goals, just two behind leading scorer Chris Guthrie. In the ten matches he scored in, Fulham won seven and drew the other three.

The 1979–80 season started brilliantly for him. In the opening fixture, Fulham had been torn apart by a rampaging Birmingham City side at St Andrews and were 0–3 down at the interval. However a Davies-

The Davies style – get in close with determination, and the goals will come.

inspired second half saw him net a hat-trick and Fulham came back from the dead to win 4–3. He also scored in the League Cup against First Division West Bromwich Albion. A brace against Burnley was followed by a second away hat-trick in a month in a 3–3 draw against eventual league champions Leicester City. By Christmas, he already had thirteen goals under his belt. But once again playing with various striker partners (Mahoney, Guthrie, Maybank and Kitchen) he did not truly settle into one position.

The season turned sour and the second half of the campaign brought just three goals. Fulham were relegated and it was scant consolation to Davies that he ended up as top scorer with sixteen in forty-three appearances. But he was well and truly a first-team regular now. He was also now an international player having been selected to play his first game for Wales against Turkey in a European Championship qualifier. In the summer, he received a second cap when he was selected to play against Iceland in a World Cup qualification match which Wales won 4–0.

Davies found life in the Third Division during 1980–81 slightly easier and was soon on the goal trail. It was a transitional season for Fulham following the dismissal of manager Bobby Campbell in October. For a while the team showed little cohesion, but slowly and surely their form improved. Davies had already worn every number in the forward line, but by the end of this season he seemed to have gravitated into the number 7 shirt.

Under the auspices of Ray Harford and Malcolm Macdonald, Davies started to mature into a very good player. Towards the end of the season he began

his partnership with a young Dean Coney. He had netted twelve single goals and three more braces, plus four goals in cup competitions. Davies became just the second player in eleven years (the first being John Mitchell) to score twenty goals for Fulham in a season. His final total was twenty-two and once again he was top scorer. A transitional Fulham finished in mid-table. Davies missed only one of the fifty-three fixtures that season.

It all began to click in the 1981–82 season and the Coney/Davies partnership blossomed. Davies scored on the opening day and never looked back. During October, he netted braces in three consecutive games, and had scored sixteen in all competitions by New Year. January started with Gordon's amazing 'goal from the corner flag' which won the match against Chesterfield and, although the goals dropped a little, two further braces which included the critical 3–0 win over Preston North End in the penultimate home match saw him finish the season with twenty-five goals, top scorer for the third consecutive season.

The Coney/Davies pairing had put away forty-four goals between them. Promotion was achieved on the final evening against Lincoln City and Davies was back in the Second Division. He was the Third Division's top scorer that season. He had also won his third and fourth caps for Wales during the season as a substitute, in a friendly against Spain that finished 1–1 and in a friendly against France that ended 1–0.

If that season was good, 1982–83 was even better. Once again Ivor scored on the opening day and alongside new signing Ray Houghton and with Coney's assistance began to blitz the division's

Showing typical style from our favourite striker, this picture was used as a programme cover for most of the 1981–82 season.

defences. Some of the football played was a delight and the best seen in twenty years at Craven Cottage. By the New Year, Davies had bagged another fifteen goals which had included five braces in five months. Included in these doubles was a televised 4–1 victory at Newcastle which really put this young Fulham side into the public eye. Of these five braces, four had come away from home at difficult places such as Middlesbrough, Grimsby and Wolverhampton.

A second successive promotion looked a certainty as Fulham hugged the promotion places, but a small squad suffering from tiredness plus the refusal of the chairman to buy an extra forward in Andy Thomas was their undoing. Form away from home began to falter. In the critical home match against Leicester City, Davies had a goal wrongly ruled out for a marginal offside decision. To most in the crowd it was clearly on-side and it proved crucial as Leicester won 1–0 with a breakaway goal. It seemed to knock the stuffing out of the young side. Davies had added just five in the second half of the season.

Disturbing scenes at Derby on the final day, which saw crowd invasions and Fulham players assaulted, prevented the match finishing properly and saw the season end in an awful fashion. Fulham missed out on promotion by a single point. Davies had scored twenty goals for the third consecutive season and was top scorer for the fourth time running.

There was some consolation for Gordon inasmuch as he had won five more Welsh caps during that season and the close season. He played against England in the Home International championship and Brazil in a friendly and finally scored his first international goal against Northern Ireland, the winner in a 1–0 encounter.

Gordon Davies was an intelligent player who, like Steve Earle, had the ability to be a second ahead of his opponents. He enjoyed running on to through balls but just as much being on the end of crosses. He had two quick feet, and keeping a cool head allowed him to beat opponents in the box. For a small striker he scored a significant number of goals with his head. As he had started his career as a winger he was quite comfortable playing wide and coming into the centre or to play the central striker's role.

His main attribute though was putting chances and half-chances away regularly. In the period since the war he was probably Fulham's ultimate goal poacher. He had that sixth sense of where the ball would fall and would be there to put it in the net. He had that rare skill of a sense of positioning and body position that allowed him to convert seemingly with ease. Despite the different players he teamed up with, he always found the net.

He was also a true Fulham icon, one who had come up the hard way and knew the value of being given the opportunity to play league football. He was a true character and had the principal asset that Fulham supporters admire most – playing with a smile. Whatever position the team or the game was in, Davies appeared to enjoy every minute. He always seemed to want to 'converse' with the crowd and it is probably why he developed such a deep and unique rapport with the Cottage faithful. He fell into the mould of Marsh,

Halom and Maybank, who saw football as sport and a theatre for the supporters to enjoy rather than just a drab, grey affair.

Although the 1983–84 season was a little deflationary after the sparkling form of the previous campaign, one thing stood out and that was the fact that Gordon Davies continued scoring. It was a slow start for him, not scoring until his sixth league game, but he netted a couple in a 5–0 win over Swansea and then completed his third Fulham hat-trick against neighbours Chelsea; unfortunately Fulham lost 3–5. The first of those hat-

trick goals saw Davies' 100th goal for the club. He then had a bit of a drought, possibly the worst in his career, when he netted only once in the league in almost three months.

But normal service was resumed in the second half of the season when from New Year's Eve he scored sixteen goals. This included three doubles and one fabulous four-goal haul against Manchester City at the Cottage when Fulham won 5–1. The side finished disappointingly in mid-table, but for Davies it was his best season in figures with twenty-six goals in all

Davies snaps up the only goal of the game at Chester in October 1980.

competitions. It was also the fourth season in a row he had scored twenty or more and he was top scorer for a remarkable fifth consecutive season.

During the season Gordon had been negotiating a new contract and had asked for appearance money, a mere £35 a week, but chairman Clay and the finance director vetoed it, so Davies continued on a week-by-week contract, a stand-off that would last almost a year. That season and the close season had seen four more Welsh caps awarded, a 5–0 win over Romania and all three of the Home International championship matches.

Maybe with the contract on his mind, Davies did not find the net in his first six games of the 1984–85 season, but then returned with a flourish, netting in five consecutive league fixtures, the last being in a 3–1 home win over Wimbledon in November, his last game. Chairman Ernie Clay was already showing signs of stripping the club of its assets and Chelsea came in with an offer after Clay had told a Chelsea representative that Gordon was 'available'; the eventual fee was set by tribunal. Davies did not want to leave Fulham, but signed for First Division **Chelsea** for £90,000 in November 1984. There were add-ons too; a further £35,000 for Fulham after Davies had made thirty-five first-team appearances. For Ivor, it was a chance at least to test himself at the top level. He left Fulham with 127 goals to his name in just six seasons. He had also just won his fourteenth international cap for Wales.

It was not long at Stamford Bridge before he showed why he was in demand. He scored on his debut for Chelsea in a 1–1 draw against Sheffield Wednesday at Hillsborough in early December. He would go on to score a further four goals that month, including a hat-trick against Everton in a stunning 4–3 Chelsea win at Goodison Park. He opened the scoring once more in a home game against Manchester United but the Blues eventually lost 1–3.

Despite his impressive start at Chelsea, Davies' time at the club coincided with that of several attacking

talents, including David Speedie and prolific scorer Kerry Dixon, and it proved difficult for the Welshman to dislodge those players. He would be utilised as cover for the remainder of his spell at Stamford Bridge making just eight further appearances in the latter half of the season, two of which were as a substitute. He signed off with a flourish with a goal in May at Anfield where once again Chelsea won 4–3. Six goals in twelve starts in 1984–85 would seem an impressive return, but it was not enough.

Having scored more goals during pre-season than both Speedie and Dixon combined, Davies found that Chelsea reneged on a promise to keep him in the first team at the start of the following season. He made just one further appearance for Chelsea in the 1985–86 season, and promptly put in a transfer request.

This request virtually put an end to an eleven-month career at Chelsea, and a month later he had been signed by First Division **Manchester City** for a fee of around £100,000, the club that had rejected him over ten years earlier. It was an arrangement brokered by the two chairmen, Ken Bates and Freddy Pye. Manchester City had been promoted from the Second Division at the end of the previous season but were already situated in the relegation spots. Davies made his City debut in a 2–3 defeat at Watford and his first goals came two days later in a 6–1 victory over Leeds United in the Full Members Cup, Davies scoring a hat-trick that evening. City would reach the inaugural final only to lose 4–5 to Davies' previous club Chelsea at Wembley. Gordon would also miss the occasion due to injury.

He was on target again at the end of the month in a 1–2 home loss to Arsenal in the third round of the League Cup, but had to wait until early December to get his first league goal when he nabbed the equaliser in a 1–1 draw at Leicester City. This was followed up seven days later with a brace in a 5–1 home win over Coventry City, and with results continuing to improve both the team and Gordon hit a purple patch after Christmas. With a goal in a 3–1 win at Walsall in the FA Cup third round, Davies was again on the scoresheet in the next round in a 1–1 home draw with Watford before the Blues eventually exited the competition when they went down 3–1 after a second replay. He was also in fine form in the league where he had been on the mark in three consecutive games against Tottenham Hotspur (2–0), West Bromwich Albion (2–1) and QPR (2–0) as the team climbed to eleventh in the table with six wins out of seven games.

After an injury to Davies, City's league campaign went rapidly downhill. Despite Gordon returning and scoring in three of the last four league games of the season, not a single league victory was achieved in the final thirteen games. City eventually stuttered to a fifteenth-place finish in the table with Gordon's nine goals from his twenty-six appearances only two behind top-scorer Mark Lillis (who had been Dale Tempest's striking partner at Huddersfield Town).

One of Davies's goals was nominated for *Match of the Day*'s 'Goal of the Season'. Despite this, he had not enjoyed a great relationship with City manager Billy McNeill.

With only one win in the first seven games of the following season, manager McNeill decided he had had enough and left City to join Aston Villa. Although Davies had been in the side for the opening five matches, it was clear when Jimmy Frizzell became the new manager that Gordon's days at the club were numbered, and after playing in a 2–1 win over Southend United in the League Cup it was decided he was surplus to requirements and he was allowed to return to **Fulham** in October 1986 for a fee of £50,000. In his twelve months at Maine Road he had scored a creditable fifteen goals in forty-two league and cup games, and had also earned his final two Welsh caps. He had scored his second Welsh goal in a 2–1 win over Saudi Arabia and played his final game, against the Republic of Ireland, in March.

Player/manager Ray Lewington was delighted to have the thirty-one-year-old back, and Davies knew that he would be in an environment where he was accepted, appreciated and more importantly playing every week, even though it was a drop of two divisions. He made his second debut in a 1–2 defeat at Doncaster and scored the following week but Fulham lost 1–3 at Chesterfield. After a blank week he then scored four in five matches. The goals then dried up and his sixth was in the last game of the season. He had also put away three in the FA Cup. It had been a season punctuated by injury, Ivor missing twelve games; but a partial 1986–87 season's total of nine goals was not a bad return.

A flying effort from our Welsh Wizard at Blackpool in February 1981.

Despite the maelstrom of takeovers and mergers going on around the club, the 1987–88 season provided an upturn in Fulham's fortunes. Davies had lost partner Dean Coney to QPR but had started a new one with Leroy Rosenior. Both scored twice in a 4–0 win over Doncaster Rovers in the second league game. Davies scored regularly throughout the season, finishing with thirteen league and two cup goals. Fulham finished ninth. He was second highest scorer to Rosenior who had had an excellent season with twenty-two. The season however ended in an unusual and unsavoury way. The final league game at Chesterfield, who could have been relegated if results had gone against them, suddenly developed into a war and both Gordon Davies and defender Jeff Hopkins were sent off with coach Jack Burkett also banished to the stands.

In the 1988–89 season, Fulham built on the previous season's form. For Davies it was a frustrating start as injuries halted his progress. He only started one league game before December. He also had just one goal, scoring the winner as a substitute against Southend in a 1–0 win in the second match of the season. However from December, he set about beating the records, although it was something he wasn't truly conscious of. His fifth goal of the season in a 4–1 victory over Chester City at the Cottage in January saw him breeze past Bedford Jezzard's total of 154 and his goal in the 3–1 victory over Bristol City at the Cottage in February eclipsed Johnny Haynes' record of 158, making him Fulham's leading scorer of all time.

Editor's note: Davies is widely credited with breaking the record at Wolves the previous week. At the time Haynes was officially credited with 157 goals and it was only later that this figure was adjusted to 158.

His fourteen goals in twenty-nine league starts emphasised what a good player he still was, and for the sixth time he was Fulham's leading scorer, beating Jezzard's post-war record of five seasons. Fulham finished a creditable fourth, but were defeated in the play-offs by Bristol Rovers. It seemed to be the start of a downward spiral.

His 1989–90 season was truncated badly by a troublesome Achilles tendon injury and other minor knocks which meant that he only started two games prior to February after playing in the first game of the season. He scored in three league games in a row on his return to the side and finished with six goals in total, his lack of appearances affecting Fulham badly. The team scored only fifty-five all season and finished one point and one place above relegation.

Gordon was now thirty-five. Time was finally catching up on him, and he was in and out of the side for most of the 1990–91 season. He had the inevitable purple patch with five in eight games during October and November, but scored just twice more, once in the FA Cup in December, with his final league goal coming against Crewe Alexandra in January in a 2–1 win in front of the Cottage faithful. It was his 178th Fulham goal.

His final Fulham game for the second time around came in March in front of just 3,000 in a 1–3 defeat at Rotherham United. Without Davies in full flow, the team scored a paltry forty-one league goals all season and once again missed relegation by a whisker. Amazingly with only seven goals, Gordon Davies was the club's top scorer for a *seventh* season, a record unlikely to be broken.

At the end of his Fulham career, the club granted him a testimonial match which was played against a Wales XI during the summer of 1991. Even this

Defenders close in, but Gordon still gets his shot in – and scores against Charlton in the FA Cup in January 1981.

was not without controversy as Jimmy Hill and the board allegedly tried to block such an idea, perhaps intimating that Gordon's thirteen years of service at the club had actually been split into two periods of six years and five with two missing in the middle. This would seem to break the general 'rule' prevailing at the time of ten years of continuous service. However common sense prevailed in the end and the match went ahead.

Gordon was convinced that there was enough left in the tank for him to continue with Fulham, but more acrimony arose when Jimmy Hill made a proclamation insinuating that Gordon's legs were no longer up to the rigours of league football at thirty-six. Davies proved Hill wrong by returning to Wales for a season with Fourth Division **Wrexham** where he found the net four times in twenty-two appearances in the 1991–92 season. Included in that season was a sensational 2–1 FA Cup win over reigning league champions and star-studded Arsenal. Davies won the free kick which led to the first goal, a direct shot from former Manchester United player Mickey Thomas and then unselfishly set up the winning goal for Steve Watkin just two minutes later. They also earned a creditable draw against West Ham in the next round.

With the end of his league career coming in 1992, Davies undertook a brief sojourn into management with a move to the unusual setting of Norway and little known club Tornado Måløy Fotballklubb, then in the Norwegian Second Division. It was a difficult set-up there and Gordon was not able to bring in as many players as he would have wanted, so he just set himself the goal of keeping the side in the division. He was offered a chance to play and coach the side, but the chairman had his own ideas for the club and so Gordon departed.

He returned to England with an idea about coaching, but instead assisted old friend Sammy McIlroy for the 1992–93 season, playing non-league football with Vauxhall Conference side **Northwich Victoria**, where he still managed double figures, netting twelve goals in thirty-six games. He also scored a cup final hat-trick against Wycombe, including the winner in

extra time, to land Northwich the non-league version of the League Cup (The Bob Lord Trophy) 5–4 on aggregate, before finally bringing the curtain down on a fifteen-year career at the age of almost thirty-eight.

After retiring, Gordon Davies became a pest control officer for Rentokil. However a few years later, he started running his own pest control company in Northamptonshire where he now lives. He says, 'It's like a football manager in some ways, but I deal with more legs!' Fortunately Gordon still maintains a close contact with Fulham and, for the last twelve years, has had a key role hosting guests in the corporate hospitality suites at Fulham home games.

GORDON DAVIES
Fulham career – all competitions

Season	Appearances	Goals	Home	Away
1977–1978	5	1	0	1
1978–1979	37	11	10	1
1979–1980	43	16	6	10
1980–1981	53	22	13	9
1981–1982	50	25	14	11
1982–1983	44	20	10	10
1983–1984	43	26	17	9
1984–1985	14	6	3	3
1986–1987	24	9	6	3
1987–1988	43	15	9	6
1988–1989	38	14	9	5
1989–1990	24	6	3	3
1990–1991	32	7	5	2
Total	**450**	**178**	**105**	**73**

*Total career **league** appearances–**460**, and **league** goals–**178**.*

Chris Guthrie

Always a handful for defenders, he gave Fulham a tidy return of goals.

Chris Guthrie was an England schoolboy international and a Geordie born in Dunston who joined his home-town First Division **Newcastle United** in 1970. He had an older brother Ron also at the club although they never played in the first team together. Chris was singled out as a young star, but his progress at St James' Park was difficult as he faced the daunting prospect of dislodging the famed duo of ex-Fulham striker Malcolm Macdonald and John Tudor from the team. After just three Newcastle appearances, including a debut against Manchester United, he was allowed to leave in 1972 and join Third Division **Southend United**. He replaced Bill Garner who had recently joined Chelsea. At the time it was a record signing for Southend United.

He found his shooting boots quickly at Roots Hall and in a period of three years netted thirty-five goals in just over 100 appearances. His progress was noted and in 1975 he made a big-money (£100,000) move to First Division **Sheffield United**. He was a replacement for the recently departed and popular Billy Dearden. The Blades were a faltering side at the time but in two seasons in Yorkshire, and sixty appearances, Chris scored fifteen goals. He left in the summer of 1977 for a cut-price £30,000 to join Third Division **Swindon Town**. Although the Wiltshire team finished mid-table, Guthrie added a further twelve goals to his career total.

Chris joined Second Division **Fulham**, themselves going through a transitional period, in September 1978. Fulham paid a large fee estimated at £70,000. Guthrie was seen as the replacement for John Mitchell who had joined Millwall in the close season. Guthrie was a typical number 9. Dark-haired, big and strong, he relished the physical side of the game and never shirked a challenge. He was very good indeed in the air, capable of spectacular headed goals and for a big man was deceptively good on the ground. He never possessed great speed or silky skills but was the ideal foil for the more talented players. Nevertheless he always gave defenders a busy afternoon.

He made his Fulham debut against Millwall at Craven Cottage in a 1–0 victory and scored his first goal for the club at Oldham the following week in a 2–0 victory at Boundary Park. He scored regularly up to Christmas, culminating in a hat-trick in a 5–1 win over Cambridge United on Boxing Day. The goals dried up a little after Christmas but he still finished the campaign as Fulham's top goalscorer with thirteen.

The next season though was disappointing; after netting in the memorable 4–3 win against Birmingham City at St Andrews on the opening day,

Guthrie opens his scoring account for Fulham with this goal, the first in Fulham's 2–0 victory at Oldham in September 1978.

Always in the thick of it, but never down and out.

he scored just once more, against Shrewsbury, before Christmas. Fulham were a struggling and unhappy side that season and Guthrie's style of play did not seem to aid the team. He was also reported to have had disagreements with manager Bobby Campbell. He made his final appearance as a substitute against Burnley in February 1980 before moving on to Third Division **Millwall** in his third £100,000 transfer, and a record for Millwall.

It was an unhappy and unlucky move. Guthrie made just seven appearances for the Lions scoring once, before sustaining a knee injury which effectively ended his league career. There was controversy about the transfer as Fulham maintained they never received the full fee for the player; it was not disclosed whether there were stage payments involved.

After retiring at just twenty-nine, Chris played football with non-league **Witney Town**, before a nomadic period in Holland where he played for **Roda JC**, **Helmond Sport** and **Willem II**, and he also had a short spell in Hong Kong with **Seiko**. His final spell associated with football was as a kit-man under Jim Smith back at Newcastle United.

Chris eventually became an international – at fly-fishing. Whilst playing abroad, he was drawn to fishing for relaxation, and eventually used it for useful employment becoming a professional fishing instructor in the Midlands.

CHRIS GUTHRIE
Fulham career – all competitions

Season	Appearances	Goals	Home	Away
1978–1979	37	13	9	4
1979–1980	18	2	1	1
Total	55	15	10	5

Total career **league** appearances–273, and **league** goals–78.

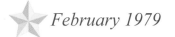

Peter Kitchen

Unlucky marksman signed for a club record fee, but delivered only a few Fulham goals.

Peter **Kitchen** was born in Mexborough in Yorkshire and joined Third Division **Doncaster Rovers** as a youth player. He was spotted by manager Lawrie McMenemy after scoring two hat-tricks in youth games for Yorkshire schools at Belle Vue and he went on to spend seven years there as a first-team player.

He made his debut at the age of eighteen and scored after just two minutes during a 3–0 win over Shrewsbury Town at Gay Meadow and scored again in his second game, a 1–2 defeat against Swansea Town. Despite Rovers struggling in the basement divisions for several years, Kitchen made a name for himself at Rovers, forming striking partnerships with Brendan O'Callaghan (later of Stoke City and the Republic of Ireland) and Mike Elwiss.

He played alongside Elwiss in one of the biggest games for the club at the time when they drew 2–2 at Liverpool in a third-round FA Cup tie in January 1974, with Kitchen scoring one of the goals. It could have been worse for the eventual cup winners as Peter's last-minute shot hit the crossbar; Doncaster lost the replay 0–2. Kitchen went on to attract attention from higher division clubs for several years. In the 1974–75 season he netted twenty-one goals.

He spent a four-day trial at Bobby Robson's Ipswich Town, but apparently did not do enough to impress the future England manager. He had all the attributes except pace, but that may have been enough for Robson not to take the risk.

He remained at Doncaster but, frustrated by their lack of ambition, he eventually asked for a transfer but there were no immediate takers. It did not affect his goalscoring form, however, as in that final season he managed twenty-three league goals. This prompted a bid from **Leyton Orient** in the summer of 1977 for £45,000 which was reluctantly accepted. It was hardly a dream move, as Orient were a moderate side in the Second Division, and Kitchen had the ability for the top flight. He had scored 105 goals for Doncaster in all competitions. Kitchen was seen a replacement for Laurie Cunningham who had joined West Bromwich.

His first season at Brisbane Road was a personal triumph although Orient finished in the lower reaches of the division. He was ever present and scored twenty-one league goals. It was in the FA Cup however that he truly shone. Orient reached the semi-finals of the FA Cup before going out 0–3 to Arsenal, having disposed of First Division Middlesbrough and Chelsea on the way. Kitchen scored in every round except the semi-final including two stunning goals against the Blues to win the replay at Stamford Bridge. He became an instant cult hero at Brisbane Road. He scored fewer

goals the following season but was surprisingly allowed to move to Craven Cottage in February 1979 when **Fulham** bid a then club record fee of £150,000 for him. He was to partner target man Chris Guthrie. He was moderately successful too in the remaining few months of the season with five goals from seventeen starts. He made his debut in a 0–1 home defeat by eventual runners-up Brighton, and scored his first goal in just his second match in a 2–2 draw at Preston.

Peter Kitchen was a good, all-round forward. His ability was sound, and his chief strengths were good control, awareness and an eye for goal. He was always more than an out-and-out goalscorer, and possessed genuine flair and a bit of 'attitude'. He relied much more on skill than a physical approach. It seemed likely from an early age that he would thrive on the bigger occasions. Kitchen was not slow at all; in and

around the box he was extremely sharp, but he was never quick by First Division standards. He sometimes looked rather lazy but like Greaves had an uncanny knack of being in the right place at the right time. His rather large nose earned him a nickname of Cyrano (de Bergerac) and he always sported the trademark Mexican moustache of the late Seventies.

His second season at Fulham though was a complete disaster for both him and the club. He suffered a succession of injuries which restricted his playing to just four starts. With his strike partner Guthrie gone, he could not impress. Fulham's form collapsed alarmingly and they were relegated. Kitchen scored his only goal on the final day of the season and in his final game for the club, a 2–5 defeat at Shrewsbury Town. Fulham gratefully accepted a sizeable bid for Kitchen in the close season of 1980 of £100,000 from Second Division **Cardiff City**.

It's a blur as Kitchen pounces to score. This was his first goal at home for Fulham, in the 3–1 victory over Charlton in March 1979.

He regained his fitness and made his debut for Cardiff in a 4–2 win against one of his former clubs (Leyton Orient) and, although he didn't score in that game, he rediscovered some form and ended the season as the club's top scorer with thirteen league goals and, mainly thanks to scoring five in a 6–0 win over Cardiff Corinthians in the Welsh Cup, nineteen goals in all competitions as Cardiff just avoided relegation on the final day. However his form at Ninian Park did not continue into his second season as the club failed to avoid relegation for the second year running and dropped into Division Three.

He left Cardiff mid-season and was going to return to Doncaster, but was offered pitiful terms by the manager Billy Bremner, so for financial security spent a period in Hong Kong with **Happy Valley**. He returned for a second spell with **Leyton Orient** now

in the Third Division and had another very successful season with the east London side scoring over twenty league goals. In one of his final games he equalled the club goal-scoring record by netting four in a 5–3 win over Millwall but that was not enough to impress manger Frank Clark.

After leaving Orient, he played in the indoor American league with **Las Vegas Americans**, before a brief spell with non-league **Dagenham**. His final stint as a Football League player was a few games with Fourth Division **Chester City**. He had a second spell at **Dagenham** to complete that 1985 season before being released. He retired at thirty-three but made a brief non-league comeback with **Margate** at the age of thirty-nine. Following this, Peter remained in football and took a post with Premiership Wimbledon. He coached as part of their youth development programme and managed the Under-13s and Under-15s for approximately eight years, before leaving the club in 2000.

Peter subsequently worked with a leisure management company in Kent, finally retiring in 2010 to spend time travelling.

PETER KITCHEN
Fulham career – all competitions

Season	Appearances	Goals	Home	Away
1978–1979	17	5	2	3
1979–1980	7	1	0	1
Total	24	6	2	4

*Total career **league** appearances–**438**, and **league** goals–**166**.*

The 1980s

Dean Coney

A skilful player with a good 'goals per game' record, and top scorer for two seasons.

Dean Coney was born in Dagenham and as a youth represented Essex and London Boys. After signing as an apprentice for **Fulham** in April 1980, he turned professional a year later. Following impressive displays in both the junior and reserve sides, manager Malcolm Macdonald took a big gamble and gave Coney his debut in the Third Division aged just seventeen. He did well in the 2–1 win over Newport County and took just four games to get off the mark, in a 2–3 defeat at Carlisle. By the end of the season, he had netted a creditable three goals (in consecutive games).

The following season, 1981–82, Coney immediately established an almost telepathic understanding with Gordon Davies, and helped the principal striker with a number of assists. Coney was now known as Dixie, a reference to the illustrious Dixie Dean from the 1920s. He missed only four games in all and scored nineteen goals in all competitions, second only to the goal-scoring machine Davies. Despite this he scored in only one league game in the first fourteen matches, but had scored in the League Cup. The goals then began to flow regularly albeit usually in singles. He did score twice to knock Second Division Oldham Athletic out the League Cup. At eighteen he was a fully established player. Fulham scored ninety goals that season and the Davies/Coney partnership accounted for virtually half that total. Despite a nervy ending, those goals were enough to promote Fulham from the Third Division.

The 1982–83 season saw Fulham as promotion challengers all season until the painful and eventful final day at Derby, where Fulham lost an 'abandoned' match. Once again the intelligent Davies/Coney partnership was a revelation, although Coney was rather eclipsed in the scoring department by a number

A typical powerful header from Coney. This was a goal in the 3–0 victory over Oldham in the League Cup in November 1981.

of players. He managed four goals in his first ten games, but failed to find the net again in the league after that. Regrettably Dean Coney will also be remembered for a headed miss in the critical home game with fellow challengers Leicester City that might have brought a draw, reducing Leicester's total by two points. The failure to win promotion to the First Division was a major blow to the club.

Dean Coney was not that big or quick but he had a good footballing brain, deft touch, good control and excellent passing ability. If there was one criticism it was that he worked too hard creating goals for other team-mates rather than scoring himself. He was one of the best hold-up players around, bringing others unselfishly into play. He had two good, skilful feet and was a good player in the air. A significant number of Coney's goals were spectacular efforts.

The first half of the next season, 1983–84, was punctuated mainly by injury and a loss of form. Fulham had won just five league games by the end of January, a run that included thirteen league games without a win and were playing poorly. When Coney came back into the side permanently, Fulham won ten of the final seventeen league games with Dean scoring seven in those seventeen games. When he found the net in a 3–0 win at Swansea City in February, it was his first league goal for over fifteen months. Gordon Davies unsurprisingly also flourished; with nine league goals up to January, he hit fourteen in those last seventeen games and Fulham finished creditably in mid-table.

The following season saw Davies leave for Chelsea and Coney found a new strike partner in Leroy Rosenior. He continued to do well and in November was awarded his first England U-21 cap in a goalless draw with Turkey. He had scored nine in twenty-seven games when he was injured in an away match at Shrewsbury which ultimately finished his season.

As the promotion-aspiring team began to fall apart, Rosenior departed to QPR, leaving Coney to carry on virtually alone. He was still playing well and in the September and October of the 1985–86 season won two more England U-21 caps, scoring his only England goal in a 3–0 win over Turkey. Coney missed just five league games and ended the season as leading scorer with thirteen goals in all competitions. It was not enough to save Fulham and they finished bottom of the table and were relegated.

Coney stayed loyal to his first club despite relegation and reunited his partnership with Davies. 1986–87 proved to be another difficult term for Fulham, who finished a disappointing eighteenth. Coney was top scorer again with fourteen goals in all competitions. He scored his final goal for Fulham in a 2–0 victory in April over Newport County, coincidentally the opposition when he made his debut. His final match was the penultimate game of the season, an uninspiring home defeat by Bournemouth.

With the club in turmoil, owner Ernie Clay seemed determined to sell as many players as possible and when Coney's contract expired, he was snapped up

by First Division **Queens Park Rangers** in a double signing with Paul Parker for a combined fee of between £450,000 and £500,000. It was a real giveaway transfer, especially when it is remembered that Parker moved on to Manchester United four years later for £2m. At least Dean Coney got the opportunity to play in the top division.

Coney was at Loftus Road for less than two seasons, managing just seven league goals in forty-eight appearances. A number of these were substitute appearances, but often QPR manager Trevor Francis employed Coney in midfield which was alien to him, so the Rangers crowd never got to see the best of him or the skills of his hold-up play. In his first season at the Bush, though, he did win a fourth England U-21 cap.

Towards the end of that second season, 1988–89, **Norwich City** manager Dave Stringer paid £350,000 for Coney; it was one of their highest ever fees paid at the time. Norwich were enjoying an excellent season and were in with a chance of winning the First Division championship. Stringer felt that Coney would score the extra goals that were needed, though he had failed to score in any of his sixteen games that season for QPR.

His time at Carrow Road was neither happy nor productive. He scored just one goal in his seventeen appearances spanning two seasons. The home crowd never took to him and he was frequently heckled during

Coney played in Hong Kong for a season with **Ernest Borel** in 1990–91, before returning to the UK with non-league **Farnborough Town**, then in the Conference South. He played at Farnborough for six seasons until the completion of the 1996–97 season, the first two seasons as a forward and then as a defender as his pace began to drop. He played almost 150 league games and scored fourteen goals. At the end of that time he was player/manager.

He lost that position and played one final season with **Carshalton Athletic** (1997–98) scoring once in twenty-one games, but he suffered a severe knee injury during that time and was forced to hang up his boots. He returned to Farnborough in 1999 as temporary manager, and then as first-team coach, but it was a time of unsteadiness and Town were relegated. Coney steadied the ship for new owner and manager Graham Westley and stayed on for a while as coach before moving on.

He did some coaching work for West Ham schoolboys, and then became assistant manager to his former Fulham goalkeeper friend Jim Stannard in 2005 at his hometown club and Conference side, Dagenham and Redbridge. Football was only part-time work by then and Coney spent a fair few years working on building sites. Recently arthritis in his fingers has caused that to cease. He is currently employed by Ladbrokes as a manager and is no longer active in football.

matches. Eventually he handed in a transfer request, but he suffered a hernia and a cruciate ligament injury in a reserve match before he was able to find another club. He did not play league football again, and his career was effectively over at twenty-six.

DEAN CONEY
Fulham career – all competitions

Season	Appearances	Goals	Home	Away
1980–1981	7	3	1	2
1981–1982	51	19	8	11
1982–1983	44	7	4	3
1983–1984	29	7	3	4
1984–1985	28	9	6	3
1985–1986	42	13	8	5
1986–1987	45	14	9	5
Total	246	72	39	33

*Total career **league** appearances–276, and **league** goals–64.*

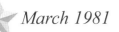
Dale Tempest

Talented understudy who found fame in the Far East.

Dale Tempest was born in Leeds, but grew up in Peebles in Scotland, before coming south where he went to school in Bracknell in Berkshire. He joined the **Fulham** youth squad in January 1980 alongside the likes of Paul Parker, Jeff Hopkins and Dean Coney, becoming a professional in September. He made one substitute appearances in his first 1980–81 season, against Burnley (0–3) in March, aged just seventeen.

Although a talented player, Dale was seen as the primary understudy to both Dean Coney and Gordon Davies, and he predominantly replaced these players during the 1981–82 promotion season. His first goal came in a disappointing 1–3 defeat against Plymouth Argyle in a midweek home match in March. He added a second in a 2–0 win at Chester near the end of the season. In all, he made fourteen appearances that season, although five were as substitute. In the 'nearly' promotion season of 1982–83, he made just three starts and one appearance as substitute, not adding to his goal tally.

His final season, 1983–84, was his most productive. He took part in the first eleven league and cup games, scoring an impressive five goals in the space of six games. The fifth, when he scored in the 3–1 win in the first leg of a League Cup tie against Doncaster Rovers at Craven Cottage, proved to be his final goal.

He needed a cartilage operation and almost immediately sustained a hernia injury and did not play regularly again until the following April. His final Fulham game was the last of the season, a comfortable 3–0 win over Oldham Athletic. In the summer, following the emergence of Leroy Rosenior, he was allowed to move back to his native Yorkshire to join Second Division rivals **Huddersfield Town**. In that final Fulham season he had made sixteen appearances in total.

He was a success at Leeds Road, forming a highly effective partnership up front with Mark Lillis. In his first season there, he netted sixteen goals. He added a further eleven the following season. After Lillis's sale to Manchester City, Tempest was offered a poor contract to continue and turned down the terms, so for the remainder of the season he was loaned to Third Division **Gillingham** where he scored an impressive four goals in just nine games.

His departure from Huddersfield was inevitable and in 1986 he travelled abroad to join Belgian side **Sporting Lokeren**. With regard to the technical side of his game,

Tempest improved and had a decent season. The club were favourites to go down, but instead they had an excellent season and finished by qualifying for the UEFA Cup. This would have continued but after a difference of opinion with the coach over pre-season fitness and training, Tempest moved on again. He had scored four goals in twenty-seven appearances.

His wife had not settled in Belgium and the family returned to the UK where Tempest secured a role with Fourth Division **Colchester United**. In all competitions, Tempest played ninety-six games for them and scored twenty-two goals across two seasons. He made his debut at the start of the 1987–88 season and scored his first goal against Scarborough just two days later. Tempest found the technique a little basic in the Fourth Division and Colchester finished just two above bottom in the 1988–89 season. He scored in his last game too in a 3–1 win over Torquay United.

He then had the opportunity of signing for Stockport County on similar money or going abroad to Hong Kong for a £10,000 signing-on fee plus significantly better wages. For a young man with a mortgage, there was no real argument for staying in the UK.

So he went out east, joined **South China AA**, was top scorer and was offered another contract. The lifestyle was enjoyable so he moved his family there. What was going to be only a short-term venture

became a voyage of discovery lasting almost a decade. It was during this time that, after training, Dale began doing television commentary and then presenting in the evening.

He also went to the Hong Kong Institute and obtained a sports science degree, doing a three-year course in nutrition and biomechanics amongst other disciplines. So after graduating, he became the fitness coach as well as a player.

After two seasons with South China AA, he had two seasons with **Eastern AA**. Following this there was a brief liaison with **Kitchee SC** on a game-by-game

basis, as Eastern had signed Tony Sealy (the former Fulham and QPR forward) but three months later he was back with **Eastern AA** after Sealy was sacked. He played for Eastern for a further three years. He finished his career back where it started with **South China AA** for two years. Totally accurate records are not kept in Hong Kong, but the most reliable figures show that Tempest played around 150 league games and scored 109 league goals. In all competitions, it is believed that Dale netted over 200 goals.

He honed and polished his narration skills when, whilst still playing, he was appointed PR director with

Tempest's first goal for the club was this twenty-yard special against Plymouth in March 1982.

the drinks company San Miguel. So for some of the time in Hong Kong he was a footballer, PR director and TV sports presenter all at the same time.

After seven years in Hong Kong, he qualified through residency to play for the national team, and between 1993 and 1998 played seventeen times for the country, scoring five goals. This included three qualification games for the 1998 World Cup.

In the late Nineties, the football in Hong Kong began to disintegrate when Japan took up the baton. Many 'foreign players' were shown the door. After seventeen years in the professional game, Tempest called it a day and retired aged thirty-five. He had been the club's and the league's leading goalscorer

in the Hong Kong First Division league in five out of the nine years he was abroad and had won seven championships.

So when an offer came to return to the Yorkshire club where he had spent two happy playing years, he came back to Britain and Huddersfield Town to become their marketing and PR manager. After his time at Huddersfield, his presentation and PR skills led to him being appointed by Sky TV as the PR director of Skybet, a position he stills holds, and he is seen regularly on the box as an expert discussing sports gambling. Despite this success, tragedy also hit the Tempest family, when Dale's son was killed along with two others teenagers in a road accident in 2007.

DALE TEMPEST
Fulham career – all competitions

Season	Appearances	Goals	Home	Away
1980–1981	1	0	0	0
1981–1982	14	2	1	1
1982–1983	4	0	0	0
1983–1984	16	5	3	2
Total	35	7	4	3

*Total career **league** appearances–176, and **league** goals–54.*

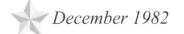

Leroy Rosenior

Good goalscoring in three spells for Fulham and a remarkable managerial record, now a respected TV presenter.

Leroy Rosenior was born in Clapham and joined Fulham as a youth. He was part of the seemingly never-ending conveyer belt of talent that was being unearthed during the Malcolm Macdonald and Ray Harford era. He joined Fulham at the beginning of the 1982–83 season after winning England Schoolboys and England Youth (U-16) honours. In his first season he was the Fulham youth player of the year.

He did not have to wait long for a first-team slot, and he played a single league game in the 1982–83 season at Leicester. He was initially used primarily as a back-up to the Coney/Davies strike partnership, but moved up the pecking order following Dale Tempest's departure to Huddersfield Town.

Following an injury to Coney and with Fulham in twentieth position in the table, Rosenior played his second game in a 0–3 defeat at Oldham in December 1983. His first goals came just nine days later, two splendid efforts against Derby County in a 2–2 draw at Craven Cottage on Boxing Day. His scoring continued and included a brace in a 4–0 win over Cardiff City. A goal in the 5–1 demolition of Manchester City made it eight in just thirteen games. With Rosenior up front, Fulham lost just once in those thirteen games. When Coney was fit again, Fulham played for half that season with three front-line strikers.

He was in and out of the side at the start of the following season, 1984–85. However when Gordon Davies was sold to Chelsea in November, and with Fulham spirits low, Rosenior returned with a stunning hat-trick in a surprise 4–2 victory at Grimsby Town. He remained in the side for the rest of the season, finding goals hard to come by but finishing with seven for the season. His final goal came against Portsmouth in a 1–3 defeat at the Cottage in April, and his final game was in a 1–0 victory over Notts County on the final day of the season.

He was without doubt not the finished article at this point and was quite raw in terms of technique and finesse. But he was a powerful player, athletically built and strong on the ball, and he was also capable of good headed goals. He was also pretty quick on the ground for a tall player.

With chairman Ernie Clay looking to sell players, Rosenior surprisingly departed Fulham on the eve of the 1985–86 season to First Division **Queens Park Rangers** for a reported fee of £100,000. He spent two seasons at Loftus Road and was in and out of the side. He made thirty-eight league appearances in that time, scoring eight goals. His time at QPR included an appearance as substitute in the League Cup final at Wembley in 1986, which QPR lost 0–3 to Oxford United.

Seemingly surplus to requirements at Loftus Road, Rosenior returned to **Fulham** at the start of the 1987–88 season. It was part of the 'giveaway' deal that saw both Dean Coney and starlet Paul Parker depart in the opposite direction, much to the dismay of Fulham supporters. Fulham were now in the Third Division and fighting for their very existence.

That season was the most successful of Leroy's career. He top-scored with twenty-two goals in thirty-nine games and was the mainstay of the forward line alongside Gordon Davies. He scored on the opening day, and had eleven under his belt before October was finished. He scored regularly all season (including four two-goal games). He looked a far more accomplished player now and was selected to play for the England U-21 side. He was also Fulham's player of the year. His final goal of the season came in his final appearance, a 3–1 win at York City.

His goalscoring feats didn't go unnoticed and close to the transfer deadline he was sold again, this time to First Division **West Ham United** for a substantial sum. He scored five goals in nine matches for the Hammers in the few remaining games of that season. He was a regular the following season (1988–89) as well, with eleven goals in thirty-five matches, but the Irons were relegated.

In the next three seasons, however, he managed just eleven starts for West Ham and three goals, his playing limited by a degenerative knee injury. His stay at Upton Park was punctuated by two loan spells. The first took him back once again to **Fulham** still in Division Three in 1990–91. He did not score in his first game but netted in each of the next three. He did not score again in the next seven games and returned to the Hammers. There was also a very brief loan spell with Second Division **Charlton Athletic** in the 1991–92 season. He played just three games and failed to score. He left Upton Park in March 1992 to join Second Division **Bristol City**.

He spent two seasons at Ashton Gate, making fifty-one league appearances and scoring fourteen goals including a hat-trick in his penultimate league game.

In the twilight of his career he was able to 'switch allegiances' internationally and he made a single appearance for the Sierra Leone national side in the African Nations Cup. As his career wound down, he began turning his attentions to coaching and looked after City's reserve and youth sides in the 1994–95 season.

After a very brief playing spell with Hampshire's **Fleet Town** of the BHL Southern Division to keep up fitness, Leroy stepped into management as the player/manager of Southern League Premier side **Gloucester City** in March 1996. Despite severe knee trouble, he continued to play on a 'when required' basis over the next three seasons, latterly as a centre back and also with one emergency appearance in goal! He was a hugely popular and respected manager who led City to the FA Trophy semi-finals and third place in the DML Premier League in 1996–97, defeat on the final day of the season costing them a place in the Football Conference. He then stayed on during the 1997–98 season despite the club's financial problems.

His success at Gloucester led to a return to Bristol City, where he performed a variety of roles over four years from assistant academy director, to reserve and U-21's manager, and finally as assistant first-team coach and caretaker manager. He then made a somewhat surprising decision to return to club management with DML Premier side Merthyr Tydfil. Having failed to help them do enough to avoid relegation, he finally made the well-deserved graduation into league management five months later, taking over the reins in 2002 at Division Three Torquay United.

He took the club to Wembley and an unlikely promotion in 2004, but was unable to keep them there, experiencing relegation on the last day of the season. Following this, key players were sold, and he left the club by mutual consent in January 2006. He was not out of work for long as two months later he was appointed first-team coach at Shrewsbury Town acting as assistant to manager and former Fulham player Gary Peters. However in the close season he was on the move again, headhunted by Brentford chairman Greg Dyke to be manager. It was heralded as a new start for the Bees under a bright, young manager; but it went badly wrong. The job lasted just five months and he left the club by mutual consent in November 2006, after a run of sixteen games without a win.

Six months later Rosenior took charge of the Sierra Leone national side for a friendly against Leyton Orient in May 2007, a game which they won 4–2. It was announced that he would take charge of Sierra Leone for their two imminent African Nations Cup qualifiers.

In May 2007, Rosenior returned to Torquay United as head coach but was reportedly sacked after just *ten minutes* – the shortest managerial reign in the history of English football! This was because at the same time as he was appointed the club was

purchased by a local consortium that installed Colin Lee as chief executive, and Lee then appointed former Exeter City assistant manager Paul Buckle as manager instead.

Since that time, despite being linked to further jobs, Leroy has carved himself a decent television and radio career including *Radio Five Live* and as the presenter of *The Football League Show* which follows *Match of the Day*. He has also covered the African Nations Cup for television. He is a leading anti-racism campaigner in British football and travels the country working as an ambassador for the 'Show Racism the Red Card' campaign. Leroy has a son Liam who is a professional player who made almost 100 appearances for Fulham in the Premier League between 2004 and 2007 and is currently (2013) at Hull City.

LEROY ROSENIOR
Fulham career – all competitions

Season	Appearances	Goals	Home	Away
1982–1983	1	0	0	0
1983–1984	25	8	4	4
1984–1985	31	7	2	5
1987–1988	39	22	8	14
1990–1991 (loan)	13	3	2	1
Total	109	40	16	24

*Total career **league** appearances—**244**, and **league** goals—**73**.*

Tony Sealy

Much travelled front man who scored well at all his clubs, and notched a hat-trick at Fulham.

Although Tony Sealy was born in Hackney, he learned his trade at the famous Wallsend Boys Club, but signed his first professional contract with Second Division **Southampton** in 1977 after two years in their youth scheme. The Saints won promotion as runners-up in 1977–78. He appeared as a substitute for the last ten minutes of the 1979 League Cup final at Wembley, which Southampton lost 2–3 to Nottingham Forest. He found it hard to break through at the Dell after making his debut at eighteen, making only seven league appearances (five as a substitute) in two seasons without scoring.

In 1979 he left Southampton and signed for First Division rivals **Crystal Palace**, then managed by Terry Venables. Whilst there he was sent on loan during his first season to Fourth Division **Port Vale** in February 1980. He spent three months at Vale Park impressing with six goals in seventeen games. Palace were relegated in Sealy's second season, 1980–81. In almost two seasons at Selhurst, Sealy had scored five goals but had made only twenty-four league appearances.

He then moved across from south London to west London, following Venables to Second Division **Queens Park Rangers** for a fee of £80,000. Sealy made his QPR debut in the 3–1 win over Derby County in March 1981 and went on to play sixty-three league games, and scoring eighteen league goals, in a little over two seasons. In February of his first season at Loftus Road, he returned once more to **Port Vale** on a one-month loan, again impressing with four goals in six games; but the club could not afford to secure his services permanently and he returned to Rangers.

In his second season, 1982–83, Rangers won the Second Division championship, and Sealy finished as top scorer with sixteen goals in all competitions, ahead of both Clive Allen and Simon Stainrod. He scored one of the three QPR goals on the plastic pitch that virtually ended Fulham's promotion challenge that season.

In December 1983, he signed a one-month loan with **Fulham**, scoring once in five games. He made his debut in a 0–3 defeat to Oldham at Boundary Park in December. The goal he scored at Brighton earned Fulham a point in a 1–1 draw. Sealy returned to QPR, but the transfer to the Cottagers was made permanent during the close season.

Sealy scored in the third game back with Fulham in a 3–2 victory at Manchester City, but was injured the following week and was out for almost six months. After a couple of substitute appearances he returned with a bang, scoring six goals in four games at the tail end of the season. This included a brace to beat Grimsby Town 2–1 at the Cottage and then a superb hat-trick at Molineux in a 4–0 win over Wolves. The finale saw Fulham finish in a comfortable mid-table position.

Tony Sealy was a stocky player and only five feet nine, and his main attributes were pace, quick feet and an excellent poacher's ability in and around the six-yard box. He could play in the centre but was equally at home out on either flank. He would have been a better player had he not been beset with injury so often in his early career.

Sealy was only at Craven Cottage for just over a year. He started the 1985–86 season as he had finished the previous one with three goals in his first seven games, including, as four months earlier, a brace to beat Grimsby Town 2–1 at the Cottage! He scored his final goal in his last game, a 2–3 defeat against Sheffield United. However, Fulham received a good offer for him, and the urge to travel and play at the top saw him move on and back to the First Division, with **Leicester City** under Gordon Milne. It was a heavy loss for Fulham, though, as they scored just forty-five league goals all season and were relegated.

Sealy scored on his debut and six times in his first fourteen games. He helped Leicester avoid relegation by a single point in 1985–86. However, the Foxes were relegated the next season. During his second season he was loaned to **Bournemouth**, scoring twice in thirteen appearances, helping the south coast club to the Third Division championship under Harry Redknapp. His two seasons at Filbert Street had seen him play thirty-nine games and score seven goals.

In the summer of 1987 he left the shores of Britain to move to Portugal and **Sporting Lisbon**, where he scored four goals in their 1987–88 European Cup Winners Cup campaign. Lisbon finished fourth in the top flight and Sealy added nine goals in twenty-nine appearances. For the final couple of months of the season he moved on to have a short four-game spell with **S.C. Braga**.

He then returned to London, joining his fourth London side, Third Division **Brentford**. Under Steve Perryman, the Bees missed out on the play-offs by four points in 1988–89, but Sealy had managed only twelve games and four goals. In the close season, the nomadic striker was on the move again, joining Swindon Town. However, he never actually appeared for them, moving on swiftly to Third Division **Bristol Rovers**.

Under Gerry Francis, Rovers topped the division in 1989–90, two points ahead of rivals Bristol City. He then played one season of Second Division football with Rovers. In all, he made thirty-seven appearances scoring seven goals. After that second campaign, Sealy moved to Finland for a brief spell with **MYPA**.

On returning to the UK, he rejoined **Brentford**, and they won the Third Division title in 1991–92. Sealy

played eighteen games but did not score. Aged thirty-three, Tony moved to Hong Kong the following year and over the course of four years played with sides **Michelotti**, **Eastern AA** (where he crossed paths with Dale Tempest) and **Hong Kong FC**. He finally stopped playing in 1996 aged thirty-seven, in a career covering fifteen different clubs at home and abroad.

He became player/manager of Hong Kong FC in 1995, a position he maintained until 2002 when he was promoted to operations manager. HKFC became a classic 'yo-yo' club, often winning promotion as Second Division champions, but also often relegated from the top division after failing to establish themselves. Under Sealy, the club won the Second Division championship six times. He has lived in Hong Kong now for over twenty years and at the time of writing has been with the club for eighteen years.

TONY SEALY
Fulham career – all competitions

Season	Appearances	Goals	Home	Away
1983–1984 (loan)	5	1	0	1
1984–1985	13	7	2	5
1985–1986	7	3	2	1
Total	25	11	4	7

*Total career **league** appearances–**261**, and **league** goals–**64**.*

September 1985

Chris Pike

A tall, hard-working striker popular with the Fulham faithful.

Chris Pike was born in Cardiff and began his playing career in the Cardiff Combination League with Park Lawn Football Club of Whitchurch, before moving up to the Welsh Football League with **Maesteg Park** and finally **Barry Town**.

In the summer of 1985, he was given a chance in the Football League when he was signed by Second Division **Fulham**, struggling to cope with the loss of key strikers Gordon Davies, Leroy Rosenior and Tony Sealy. He was a late starter in league football, being over twenty-three when signing for the Cottagers.

He made his Fulham debut in September 1985 in a 2–3 home defeat by Sheffield United. He had some early success, scoring the winner against Shrewsbury Town in a 2–1 victory in October followed by the winner in a 1–0 win over Stoke City at the Cottage a fortnight later. He had also scored in Fulham's 4–2 win at Notts County in the League Cup.

Pike was a tall, rangy forward and an efficient target man. He had a good touch and was, because of his height, a good player in the air. He was an honest, hard worker too and proved to be a popular journeyman with the Cottage faithful.

After a couple of months out of the side, he returned with his best run in the Fulham team. He played eighteen games adding two more goals. The fifth and final goal of his Fulham career came as the winner in a 3–2 away victory at Brighton in April. In the 1985–86 season he had made thirty appearances in all. Regrettably the goals were not enough to prevent Fulham's tumble into the Third Division.

He was not an immediate starter the next season due to injury, and in December spent a period out on loan with Cardiff City, scoring twice in six appearances. An injury crisis meant that he returned to Fulham and he played a further thirteen games that season without adding to his goal total.

Chris remained at Fulham for two more years, but due to injuries and a loss of form he made only three further substitute appearances. Seeing no future for the player, Fulham released him on a free transfer.

In August 1989, Pike returned to Third Division **Cardiff City**, this time on a permanent basis. He returned to the Cottage with his new club in November, scoring as well as Cardiff romped to a 2–5 victory. Both clubs finished the season in the basement area of the division, Cardiff being relegated.

At Cardiff, Pike established a striking partnership with Carl Dale and the two competed for the club's top scorer award at the club for four years, with Pike winning the award for three consecutive seasons between 1989 and 1992, the third season sharing it with Dale. Cardiff were promoted as champions in his final season at Ninian Park. By this time, albeit in the lower division, Pike had scored an impressive sixty-five goals in under 150 matches for the Bluebirds.

Surprisingly, Pike left Cardiff and dropped back to the fourth tier for the 1993–94 season with **Hereford United** scoring a hat-trick that season against Colchester United. Hereford finished in a lowly position, but for Pike personally it was another successful season with eighteen league goals in thirty-eight games.

Early in the following season, 1994–95, Chris joined **Gillingham** and scored thirteen goals in only twenty-seven appearances in his one season there. At thirty-three, he returned to Wales and played non-league football, having three more successful years at his first club **Barry Town**, and scoring an impressive forty-six goals in just eighty-two league games.

After leaving Barry, Pike played for a succession of Welsh clubs, including **Cwmbran Town**, **Bridgend Town**, **Rhayader Town** and **Llanelli**. He was still playing league football aged forty in 2001. Chris is the uncle of Real Madrid's Gareth Bale.

CHRIS PIKE
Fulham career – all competitions

Season	Appearances	Goals	Home	Away
1985–1986	30	5	3	2
1986–1987	13	0	0	0
1987–1988	3	0	0	0
1988–1989	0	0	0	0
Total	46	5	3	2

*Total career **league** appearances–**261**, and **league** goals–**102**.*

Andy Sayer

Another hard-worker who scored useful goals for the Whites.

Andy **Sayer** was born in Brent, and joined local side **Wimbledon**, who were then in the Third Division. He made his debut as a seventeen-year-old making one further appearance that season (1983–84), and Wimbledon were promoted. The following season he played in almost half of their league games and impressed with eight goals.

The next season he found it harder to break into the Dons side, making only seven appearances and not scoring, and to aid his development he went out on loan to Sweden, playing eighteen games for Stockholm's **Vasalund IF** netting three times. Once again Wimbledon were promoted.

The 1986–87 season was probably Sayer's most successful, as he played twenty First Division games for the Plough Lane side, scoring seven goals. He found the next season a lot tougher, but still made nine appearances without adding to his Wimbledon goal total. He spent a short period on loan to Fourth Division **Cambridge United** that season, making five appearances without a goal.

He seemed surplus to requirements with Wimbledon in the First Division, and Third Division **Fulham** jumped in and signed him. He ('Leo' naturally) made his debut on the opening day of the 1988–89 season and made a dream start too with his first goal in Fulham's 2–1 away win over Cardiff City. He scored ten goals in his first seventeen games including two braces in consecutive 5–1 victories.

A few knocks, loss of form, plus competition from Michael Cole saw Sayer's role reduced to a bit-part substitute level, and he added just one further goal after November. Still, he finished the season with eleven goals and was second-highest scorer, just three behind Gordon Davies.

Sayer was small for a striker and was instantly identifiable by his blond hair. Despite his height, he was capable in the air. He was not blessed with great skill or pace, but was a very honest and hard-working player who gave everything for the team, and with his stocky build always tried to deny defenders time and space in which to play.

The 1989–90 season was similar to the previous one with six goals in his first seventeen games, including a brace in a 3–2 win at Crewe Alexandra in September. One of these goals has always courted controversy as it came following a huge kick from Fulham goalkeeper Jim Stannard that was misjudged by his opposite number. Most reports and observers gave the goal to Stannard, but Sayer always claimed he got the last touch, although pictures of the incident seem to suggest that the ball was already over the line before Sayer's toe-poke contribution. Nevertheless, the Fulham statistics have it down as Sayer's goal.

His final game was the 2–4 defeat by Swansea in February 1990, and during that month Fulham surprisingly sold him to same-division rivals **Leyton Orient**. In the remainder of that season, he made ten appearances at Brisbane Road, scoring once. The following season, 1990–91, was disappointing with just eleven appearances for the O's and two goals. That season saw a three-game spell on loan to First Division **Sheffield United**. The 1991–92 season, when he was back at Orient, saw a return of three goals in nine games, but they proved to be his last in league football.

Aged just twenty-six, Sayer dropped out of league football and spent three years with **Slough Town**, the first two of these in the Conference League. He scored on his August debut against Kettering in a 4–2 victory and in that 1992–93 season top-scored with twenty-one goals in all competitions. The next season was tougher and he managed only eight goals, and Slough were relegated to the Isthmian League. However, he made double figures again with ten in his final season, 1994–95. After leaving Slough, he had one season with **Enfield**.

He then moved on to Stompond Lane and three seasons with **Walton & Hersham**. No data is available for his first season (1996–97), but his second was very successful with twenty-one goals from forty matches. The following season he still managed twenty-nine appearances and eight goals for the Swans.

After a year out of football, Sayer's career became fairly nomadic with spells at a number of Surrey football clubs including **Leatherhead**, **Egham Town**, **Tooting and Mitcham United**, **Molesey** and finally **Bisley Sports**. He finally hung up his boots at the age of forty in 2006.

Despite an average career as a player, Sayer has proven to be in demand as a scout. Since moving abroad, he has worked for Mark Hughes at Manchester City and Queens Park Rangers and has been recruited recently by Brendan Rogers to scout for Liverpool, monitoring players in Germany, Holland and Scandinavia.

ANDY SAYER
Fulham career – all competitions

Season	Appearances	Goals	Home	Away
1988–1989	32	11	6	5
1989–1990	31	6	2	4
Total	63	17	8	9

*Total career **league** appearances–149, and **league** goals–37.*

The 1990s

Gary Brazil

Creative forward with the club during difficult times, top scorer for two seasons.

Gary Brazil was born in Tunbridge Wells, and joined First Division Crystal Palace as an apprentice straight after leaving school in 1979. He found it hard getting into the team at Selhurst Park during the time of Terry Venables as manager and left at the end of the season without a first-team appearance.

He turned full professional when dropping down two divisions to join Third Division **Sheffield United** on a free transfer in August 1980. His time with the Blades was very up and down. Although the Bramall Lane club gave him his real break in the game, he was often used as a substitute, played in midfield or used as a winger instead of in his favoured role as a supporting striker.

In nearly five years at Sheffield United, Brazil played only seventy-eight games in all competitions, of which thirty were as a substitute. He did though manage ten goals. The Blades suffered relegation out of the Third Division in that first 1980–81 season under former Fulham scout Harry Haslam. The following season United made an immediate return as champions under former Sunderland man Ian Porterfield. A mid-table finish was achieved in 1982–83, before a second promotion in three years was achieved with a third-place finish in 1983–84.

Deemed not to be up to the rigours of the Second Division, Brazil joined **Port Vale** on loan in August 1984 and made himself popular by scoring three goals

in six Fourth Division appearances – before returning to Sheffield.

Still out of the first-team picture upon his return, he was offered the chance to go on a month's loan to beleaguered Third Division **Preston North End**. Gary scored just once in six matches, but the deal was made permanent at the end of that period. There was disappointment for him, however, as North End were relegated at the end of that season.

The following 1985–86 season was again a disappointment, although Brazil was now a first-team regular and scoring frequently, Preston finished the season one from the bottom of the entire Football League and were forced to seek re-election. Under John McGrath the club won promotion immediately, with Brazil and John Thomas forming a deadly strike partnership. Brazil was voted Preston's player of the year. Season 1987–88 was a consolidating one, although Brazil just missed out on a Wembley appearance, Preston losing to Burnley in the semi-final of the Football League Trophy (Sherpa Van Trophy).

Before the end of the next season, Brazil departed in a £200,000 move to First Division **Newcastle United**. (It was £100,000 cash and midfield player Ian Bogie in exchange.) During his four years at Deepdale in all competitions Brazil had played 202 games, scoring seventy-two goals.

During the remainder of the 1988–89 season, Brazil made just three starts as Newcastle suffered relegation

Brazil's goal at Swansea on the last day of the 1993–94 season was a fine strike, but could not prevent Fulham losing 1–2 and being relegated to the bottom division of the Football League.

from the top tier. The following season he started just five games, as indifferent form and injuries to his back and shoulder limited his appearances. He was also behind Mark McGhee and Mickey Quinn in the strikers pecking order.

After eighteen months on Tyneside, and making only twenty-three appearances, Brazil made a £110,000 move to Third Division **Fulham**. He made his debut in a 2–2 draw at Shrewsbury in September 1990 and scored his first goal in his sixth game, a 2–2 draw with Birmingham City at Craven Cottage. That first 1990–91 season was a disappointing one with Brazil netting just five goals in forty-four games. After December he failed to score at all, as Fulham just about held on to their status.

The following season was much improved. Brazil played in all of Fulham's forty-nine games and finished the season as top scorer with sixteen goals in all competitions. He netted four braces in that season and four goals in the last five league matches. Although not included in these official statistics, he also blasted a hat-trick in Fulham's 6–2 victory over Maidstone United in the Football League (Autoglass) trophy. It was the beginning of a fruitful partnership with Sean Farrell. The club missed out on the play-offs by just four points and three places.

Gary Brazil was not really a front-line striker, often preferring to play off a bigger man. He was also just five feet nine inches which limited his aerial ability to a degree. On the other hand he was an industrious midfield player with his compact play, neat passing, clever ball control and distribution. This meant that he also created a significant number of goals as well.

Season 1992–93 was an indifferent one and due to a succession of niggling injuries he played only four games between November and March. He managed four goals in the last five matches, giving him a total of seven in twenty-seven starts. However the next season, 1993–94, was good for him; he was again ever present, playing in all of Fulham's fifty-one games and for the second time in three years was top scorer with fifteen in all competitions. He also scored in the fateful final game of the season at Swansea that saw the Cottagers relegated to the bottom tier.

Gary missed two months of the 1994–95 season and time was beginning to catch up with him, but he still managed a further seven goals in thirty-six starts, with Fulham finishing two places and three points outside the play-offs. After starting as a regular at the beginning of the next season, he played twenty-four games scoring three times, his final goal being in a 1–1 draw with Barnet at Craven Cottage in November. His final game was in January, a 1–1 third-round FA Cup draw with Shrewsbury Town at Craven Cottage, where he surprisingly received a red card.

Brazil was a fans' favourite, always giving 100% in every game and having a strong bond with the supporters. He also stayed loyal to the club during the worst period of its history. Later in January 1996, he became Fulham's youth team coach, although

still registered as a player. He was one of those rare strikers who scored more Fulham goals away from Craven Cottage than at home.

At the end of that season he left the club after six years, and signed a one-month playing contract with Division Three (fourth-tier) **Cambridge United**, scoring on his debut in a 1–0 win over Barnet. He was substitute following that, and his contract was not renewed and he joined **Barnet** and was a regular there, making nineteen appearances in four months and scoring twice. He then called time on his league career after seventeen years.

In February 1997, he signed for non-league Conference side **Slough Town** and spent one and a half busy seasons there scoring ten goals in sixty-nine appearances. Slough Town also reached the semi-final of the FA Trophy in the 1997–98 season. He finally stopped playing just short of his thirty-sixth birthday.

After retiring, Gary Brazil joined Division Two Notts County as coach in 1999 and then as assistant manager to Sam Allardyce. Following Allardyce's departure to manage Bolton Wanderers in October, Gary Brazil stepped up as temporary team manager. After a promising start to the season, the team faded and finished well short of the play-offs. Brazil was demoted in favour of new manager Jocky Scott, but this reign was short-lived and, after many boardroom clashes, Brazil was reinstated as temporary manager. The appointment lasted only five weeks when Brazil failed to win a game in that time and was replaced by Bill Dearden. He did however remain at Meadow Lane.

In 2004 Brazil became youth team coach at Doncaster Rovers, and after almost three years returned to Fulham, coaching the academy U-18 side. After a very happy and successful five years at Motspur Park, he was appointed as a youth team coach and manager of the Nottingham Forest academy in May 2012. In 2013 he took his Forest colts to the semi-final of the FA Youth Cup.

GARY BRAZIL
Fulham career – all competitions

Season	Appearances	Goals	Home	Away
1990–1991	45	5	3	2
1991–1992	49	16	7	9
1992–1993	30	7	4	3
1993–1994	51	15	5	10
1994–1995	38	7	3	4
1995–1996	24	3	1	2
Total	237	53	23	30

*Total career **league** appearances–**491**, and **league** goals–**123**.*

Kelly Haag

Mostly used as a substitute, he played well and scored some vital goals.

Kelly Haag was born in Enfield and played a starring role in the **Brentford** youth team, looked like one to watch, and in the 1989–90 season made five appearances for the Third Division Bees, though four of these were as substitute. He joined Third Division **Fulham** in the summer of 1990. He scored on his debut as Fulham secured a 2–2 draw at Shrewsbury Town in September. For the majority of the season he was usually a used substitute. He played a few games in the number 10 shirt late in the season and scored a critically important goal against his former employers as Fulham won 2–1 at Griffin Park. He then scored again to earn Fulham another point in a 1–1 home draw with Swansea. These two results helped save the club from relegation that season.

In the 1991–92 season, he scored twice in the opening eleven games, both times as a substitute, including the winner in a 4–3 away victory over Bradford City. His best run in a Fulham shirt came at the tail end of that season when he played thirteen consecutive games in the number 11 shirt. He scored four goals in ten games and in those last thirteen games Fulham won seven and drew four, their most consistent form of the season. His goal against Bradford City at the Cottage in a 2–1 win on the final day would prove to be his last.

His final season, 1992–93, was disappointing, and he did not start a game until almost March, making ten appearances in all, five of those as substitute. He also failed to add to his goal total, his last appearance being in a 3–0 win over Hartlepool United in April. Almost half of Kelly Haag's appearances for Fulham had been as substitute.

After three seasons at Craven Cottage, he left Fulham to join Division Two (third-tier) **Barnet**. He played a full season for the Underhill side making thirty-eight league appearances, scoring eight goals. Barnet finished bottom of the table in the 1993–94 season (and Fulham were relegated too).

After leaving Barnet, he had a short trial at West Ham and then another at Leyton Orient. From that time Haag dropped into non-league football. The most accurate information that can be obtained is that he went to **Sutton United** briefly and then **Woking**. There followed a brief period with **Stevenage Borough** in 1995–96, before a part season at **Dagenham and Redbridge** where he was top scorer with eight goals, but in a season where the Daggers were relegated from the Conference.

From then on information is very scarce, but Kelly seemed to have ended his career with Buckinghamshire and Hertfordshire clubs and could have played at all the following clubs: St Albans City, Baldock Town,

Fisher Athletic, Aylesbury Town, and Ware. It was reported that as recently as 2006 he was playing for St Margaretsbury FC at the age of thirty-six. He is also another former Fulham footballer who became a cab driver.

KELLY HAAG
Fulham career – all competitions

Season	Appearances	Goals	Home	Away
1990–1991	25	3	1	2
1991–1992	36	6	5	1
1992–1993	10	0	0	0
Total	71	9	6	3

*Total career **league** appearances–110, and **league** goals–17.*

Phil Stant

No-nonsense hard man who played for twenty clubs, scoring important goals for Fulham.

One of soccer's great nomads and characters, **Phil Stant** was born in Bolton. His route into professional football came after a career in the military. Stant is a veteran of the Falklands War, serving with 5 Infantry Brigade as part of 81 Ordnance Company, and his experiences in the South Atlantic were the subject of a 2007 ITV documentary, *Falklands 25: A Soldier's Story*.

He was billeted at Aldershot, and his first Football League experience was part-time with Third Division **Reading**, signing from **Camberley Town** in 1982–83. At Reading he netted twice in four games, before going to war. He progressed into bomb disposal, working alongside the SAS, before seriously turning his attentions to football in 1985. His impressive performances for the **Army** team led him to being bought out for £600 by Fourth Division **Hereford United** in November 1986, and he played part of that campaign, scoring four in eleven appearances in all competitions.

Season 1987–88 was a mediocre one, but he missed just seven games, scoring thirteen in all competitions and being top scorer. He really came to the fore the following season, when he scored thirty-two goals in forty-nine matches in all competitions and was top scorer for the club again and top scorer in the Fourth Division. Those goals, however, were not enough to get Hereford promoted.

His goalscoring feats caught the attention of Third Division **Notts County**, and in that summer he secured a move to Meadow Lane for £175,000. It was not a great success, with Stant playing just twenty-two league games and scoring just six goals, but the team did well in that 1989–90 season and were promoted to the Second Division. After promotion, Stant seemed surplus to requirements and he did not play for County again.

He spent the majority of the following season out on loan, with Fourth Division **Blackpool** in September (five goals in twelve games), Fourth Division **Lincoln City** in November (four games and no goals) and Third Division **Huddersfield Town** in January (five games and one goal).

However, he was able to secure a £60,000 permanent transfer to Craven Cottage in February 1991. Although **Fulham** had smaller strikers in Gary Brazil and Gordon Davies, they were desperately short of height and strength in the middle following the departure of Leroy Rosenior to West Ham at Christmas.

Stant gave Fulham what they needed at the time; he was six feet two inches and extremely strong. He was everything you might expect from an Army footballer, a no-nonsense, hard and physical player who put himself about and got in where it hurt, giving defenders a tough time. He was very good with his head and created openings for other players. His build belied a good touch and a keen eye for a goal.

Fulham were in trouble with only two wins from their previous thirteen matches. Stant started in the best possible way by scoring on his debut and it proved to be the winner in a 1–0 victory over Preston North End at the Cottage, and in his next game he scored a point-saving equaliser in a 1–1 draw at Tranmere Rovers. He made it three in four games with a goal that secured a point against Reading at home (1–1). Goals were then hard to come by and it took time for the big man fully to settle in.

But Fulham recovered. Stant's goal against Mansfield Town at home secured another important 1–0 victory and he saved his most important goal until last, the winner in a vitally important 2–1 victory over high-flying Brentford at Griffin Park in April. Fulham won four and drew five of their last eleven league games to stave off relegation and every one of Stant's goals 'counted', meaning that Fulham had eight extra points by the end of the season. Stant played his final game on the last day of the season in a 1–1 home draw with Leyton Orient.

Sadly for Fulham, Stant moved on again in the summer of 1991 after just six months and nineteen games with the Cottagers and he joined Fourth Division **Mansfield Town** for £50,000. He was an immediate success and his twenty-six league goals in forty matches secured promotion for the Stags in the 1991–92 season, just one season after being relegated. He was doing well the following season too, with seven goals in twenty games, but he was on the move once again, this time to Wales when Division Three (fourth-tier) **Cardiff City** had a £100,000 bid accepted.

Stant's eleven goals in twenty-four league games were enough to secure promotion for Cardiff City at the end of the 1992–93 season. In the following season he managed ten goals in thirty-six appearances and had a brief one-month spell back at **Mansfield Town** in March where he played four games scoring once. Stant remained in Cardiff at the start of the 1994–95 season and scored a very impressive thirteen

goals in nineteen games. In his time at Ninian Park he had netted on average a goal virtually every other game.

With this impressive scoring, Stant was a wanted man and he moved back to his native Lancashire with a £90,000 transfer to Division Three (fourth-tier) **Bury** in January 1995. Once again he was an immediate success with thirteen goals in just twenty games. In 1995–96 it was even better as, leading the line and adding a further nine league goals, he saw the Shakers promoted. He was not a regular starter at the beginning of the following season, playing eight games and scoring once. He took a month-long loan move to **Northampton Town** in November scoring twice in five games and then for the second time joined fourth-tier **Lincoln City** for £30,000 in December 1996 when that loan expired.

Once more the goals flowed and Phil rattled in fifteen in just twenty-two games during the reminder of that campaign, but Lincoln were not promoted. Stant was now thirty-four and age was beginning to catch up with him. For once in his career, the goals dried up and in the 1997–98 season he managed just three in twenty-seven appearances for Lincoln, but the second half of the season was spent coaching and assisting caretaker manager Shane Westley. Under Stant's coaching, Lincoln City were promoted on the final day of the season.

In 1998–99, Stant hardly set foot on the pitch making just five substitute appearances on an 'as required' basis. Again he was assistant manager to Westley who departed in November and chairman John Reames took over. Unfortunately Lincoln were relegated at the end of the season.

Back in Division Three, Stant put on his boots again in the 1999–2000 season, making twenty-two appearances for Lincoln (mostly as substitute) and scoring three goals. At the end of that season, Reames handed the manager's role to Stant. Despite being the Imps manager, Stant was still registered as a player.

However, his time in charge at Sincil Bank lasted just thirty matches during the 2000–01 season and, four days after the Lincoln City Membership Scheme's Community Ownership Package for the shareholding of the club was successful, the new board of directors terminated Stant's contract and that of his assistant George Foster, with former Grimsby Town boss Alan Buckley coming in as his successor. In March 2001 he left Lincoln and signed a short-term contract with **Brighton and Hove Albion** where he made seven substitute appearances, scoring once. These were his final appearances in the Football League. He was aged thirty-eight.

His desire for playing was still high and in the 2001–02 season he turned out for no fewer than four non-league sides – **Worcester City**, **Dover Athletic**, **Hayes** plus **Hinckley United** where he linked up with one-time Notts County colleague Dean Thomas and scored twice in seven league appearances, as well as in the Leicestershire Challenge Cup final.

In the summer of 2002, Stant moved back into management being appointed player/manager of **Gainsborough Trinity**. He enjoyed a successful season at the Northolme, leading the club to the fifth round of the FA Trophy whilst securing a mid-table league finish and winning the Lincolnshire Senior County Cup. He was also still very active as a player, making twenty-eight appearances and scoring thirteen goals. He resigned from his post at the end of the 2002–03 season because of outside work commitments.

Three months later, Stant was back in football returning to management with **Ilkeston Town**. Remarkably he was still registered as a player in 2003–04 and made ten appearances for the club scoring once. He finally hung up his boots six months short of his forty-second birthday.

He led Ilkeston Town to promotion to the Northern Premier League Premier Division in the ensuing 2004–05 season but, following a disappointing start to their first campaign at the higher level, Stant resigned in September. He had a further spell with Worcester City in 2007, coaching and assisting manager John Barton.

In a remarkable playing career of twenty-two years, Stant had represented no fewer than *twenty* different clubs. Since his retirement from playing, Phil has concentrated his energies running the Newark & Sherwood College Football Academy whilst he is also a youth development monitor for the Football League.

Stant has written a book about his football and war career called *Ooh Aah Stantona*.

PHIL STANT
Fulham career – all competitions

Season	Appearances	Goals	Home	Away
1990–1991	19	5	3	2
Total	19	5	3	2

*Total career **league** appearances–433, and **league** goals–170.*

Sean Farrell

Elegant all-round striker who regularly hit the target and netted two Fulham hat-tricks.

Sean Farrell was born in Watford. However, he joined Watford's rivals **Luton Town**, then in the First Division, in 1985 as a fifteen-year-old. After impressing during his initial trial, he was invited back to play for the club's youth team in a match against Reading, during which he scored two goals in a 4–2 Luton victory. The club offered him an apprenticeship soon after, and he signed before his sixteenth birthday, turning professional two years later.

He made his First Division debut for the Hatters at eighteen in 1987 and remained with the club for four years, but he was rarely in the side early on, and managed only five appearances in those first three years. During that spell, he spent time out on loan, initially with Fourth Division **Colchester United** in March 1988, making four full and five substitute appearances in two months, scoring just once in a 2–1 win over Halifax Town.

He broke into the Luton first team in the 1990–91 season making twenty appearances. This season included a one-month loan at Fourth Division **Northampton Town** in which he made four appearances, scoring once. In the four-year period in Luton's first team, he managed just one goal.

With David Pleat back as Luton Town manager, the club in relegation danger, and his future looking uncertain, **Fulham** took the striker, initially on a month's loan, in December 1991 to replace Andy Cole who had just completed a three-month loan from Arsenal. But he immediately impressed at Craven Cottage and the loan was cemented with a £100,000 permanent transfer.

Farrell made his debut in a 1–3 defeat at Birmingham City just before Christmas and scored on his home debut in a 2–1 win over Torquay United on Boxing Day. In his fourth game on New Year's Day, he scored a spectacular hat-trick as Fulham registered a fine 3–2 victory over West Bromwich Albion at the Hawthorns. He finished the season with ten goals in twenty-five league games, being second highest scorer behind Gary Brazil, despite not joining the club until four months into the season.

The following season, 1992–93, Farrell missed only twelve games, scoring three times in the first five league matches. He had registered seven before the end of October, but then hit a barren patch and did not score another league goal until almost the end of March. He completed the term in fine style with a second Fulham hat-trick in a 4–0 win over Burnley in the penultimate home game. He finished the season as top scorer with thirteen goals in all competitions as Fulham finished mid-table.

Farrell was a traditional centre forward and, although not blessed with great skill or pace, he was a good all-round professional. He was just over six feet, good with his head and knew where the goal was, many of his goals being long-range shots or lobs. He was strong on the ball and was very good at holding up play and retaining possession. What he lacked in flair he countered by giving everything for ninety minutes. He always played each game with great heart and total effort. He was also a great character and enjoyed his football. He was a positive influence in the dressing room and popular at all the clubs he played for.

In Fulham's relegation season of 1993–94, Sean critically missed almost two months in January and February, and finished with twelve goals in all competitions, once again second only to Gary Brazil. This included a spectacular volley in the 1–3 defeat against Liverpool in the League Cup at Craven Cottage just after coming on as a substitute.

His final goal was against Rotherham United in the last home game in a 1–0 win at the Cottage that gave Fulham a chance to avoid relegation, and his final game was that fateful afternoon a week later with defeat at Swansea. Farrell was happy at Fulham despite the relegation to the fourth division and he made a reluctant move in the close season of 1994 when he moved on and up a division to **Peterborough United** for a fee of £120,000 in 1994.

He opened his account in 1994–95 in the sixth game and finished the campaign with eight goals in thirty-six appearances. He had a better season in 1995–96 with twelve goals in thirty-four games; this included two braces as well as a hat-trick in the FA Cup against Bognor Regis Town. He was doing well at the start of 1996–97 too with four goals in nine starts. He was sent off in what proved to be his final game for Peterborough against Bury and moved again, signing for Division Two **Notts County** in October 1996 for £80,000, where he played for almost five seasons.

After completing that initial season, where County were relegated, Farrell was influential the following one, where his goals helped to propel Notts County back to Division Two as champions in 1997–98. Later in his County career, he sustained a bad knee injury. He was out of the game for eighteen months and had eleven operations. He battled his way back to fitness, but was never quite the same player. In the final season, 2000–01, he made just a handful of appearances, many as a substitute, netting just three times. He was surprisingly released on a free transfer at the end of the season. He had scored twenty-three goals for County in all competitions in ninety-eight games.

Season	Appearances	Goals	Home	Away
SEAN FARRELL *Fulham career – all competitions*				
1991–1992	25	10	3	7
1992–1993	38	13	6	7
1993–1994	39	12	6	6
Total	102	35	15	20

*Total career **league** appearances–286, and **league** goals–76.*

Interest in him was high from his former club Luton, as well as Swansea and Torquay; he eventually opted for a trial at Swindon Town but after two months no formal agreement was forthcoming.

He was quickly snapped up by (then) non-league **Burton Albion** as he knew Nigel Clough, and he played there sporadically for two seasons. His experience was invaluable and Burton were promoted from the Unibond Premier League with Sean's assistance and into the Conference. He had scored twelve goals in twenty-eight games including a hat-trick in an FA Trophy match against Barrow. He made twelve appearances for Burton in the Conference scoring once against Southport. However his knee continued to give him problems, and he spent time out on loan at **Hucknall Town** in 2002 and **Grantham Town** in 2003 in order to try to improve his fitness, but he finally called time on his battle with the condition and retired in 2003.

Whilst at Burton, Farrell went to college and trained as a driving instructor, which is how he earns his living now. He lives in the Nottingham area with his wife and three children.

Mike Conroy

Top scorer for two seasons, he spearheaded the start of our rise from the bottom tier with fine goals.

Mike Conroy was born in Glasgow, but attempted to start his career south of the border with Coventry City in 1983 as a youth player. He did not make much headway at Highfield Road under former Fulham coach Dave Sexton and returned to Scotland on a free transfer with the now-defunct **Clydebank** on the west side of his native home town.

In three years with the part-time Bankies, he made 114 league appearances and scored thirty-eight goals. He arrived just in time to help them claim an unexpected place in the inaugural Scottish Premier League a season later. Therefore Mike got the chance to play two years at the top against some of his Glasgow boyhood heroes. He spent a further season with the Bankies following their relegation from the top flight. In 1987 he joined **St Mirren** in the Scottish Premier Division for a significant fee, but remained there for just ten months, scoring only one goal in ten appearances.

But he caught the eye of the English scouts and returned to England in 1988 to join Third Division **Reading** in a £50,000 deal. He spent three years at Elm Park, but never truly settled there, and his goalscoring deserted him. Although he scored four goals in five games early in the 1988–89 season, he only started a total of nine league games. The following season he scored just two league goals in thirty-four games, one of them being the winner in 2–1 victory at Fulham. The final season, 1990–91, was the worst of them all, when he netted just once in thirty-three games, playing midfield and sometimes even full back under manager Ian Porterfield.

At the end of that season, Conroy moved to Fourth Division **Burnley** for £40,000, where manager Frank Casper saw something in the big Scot, and this is where the most prolific scoring period of his career began. In his two years with Burnley, he scored forty-one goals in 101 appearances in all competitions.

Conroy started the 1991–92 season well and netted in each of his first four games. Injury and a loss of form meant the goals dried up for a while, but he was soon back to scoring form. He reached double figures against Doncaster Rovers at Christmas and in early January he turned in an impressive performance against Gillingham. He scored early but then went on to miss three golden chances in the first half after the Gills had equalised. But after the break he came back and scored twice more for his only hat-trick for the Clarets (4–1). That was during a run when he scored in six successive games. When Conroy scored the only goal in a vital game at Mansfield, he had finally achieved twenty goals in a season, and then went on to score four more in the league plus five more in cup

competitions, a total of twenty-nine. It was the first time a Burnley player had scored over twenty league goals for a quarter of a century. Those goals ensured that Burnley won the Fourth Division championship.

He found goals more difficult to come by in the following season but linked up well with new signing Adrian Heath, and Burnley had a comfortable season in the higher division with Conroy finishing with eleven. One of those goals came in a 5–2 victory over Fulham! Burnley manager Mullen then deemed

Conroy scores the first goal in the 2–1 victory at Swansea in September 1996.

Conroy to be surplus to requirements, and the manager of **Preston North End**, former Fulham player John Beck, paid a transfer fee of £85,000 to take Conroy across Lancashire to Deepdale.

During two seasons Conroy's scoring streak continued with twenty-two goals in fifty-seven appearances. In his first start for Preston in 1993–94 he netted a superb hat-trick in a 6–1 thrashing of Shrewsbury Town. In one game he played alongside a very young David Beckham who was on a month's loan from Manchester United. Beckham and Conroy predictably both scored in the 3–2 win over Fulham.

The 1994–95 season saw him finish top scorer with ten league goals from twenty-five appearances. There was also heartbreak in a play-off semi-final defeat. It was the start of a rise in fortunes for Preston who

were promoted under the auspices of former Fulham defender Gary Peters. Conroy's goalscoring over the previous four seasons attracted **Fulham** manager Ian Branfoot who paid £75,000 to bring him south for a second time to join fourth-tier Fulham in the close season. At that time, Fulham only had the veteran Alan Cork as a central striker.

Conroy made his Fulham debut on the opening day of the 1995–96 season in a 4–2 win over Mansfield Town. He then opened his account in midweek in a 3–0 win over Brighton and Hove Albion in the League Cup. The Scot netted four in his first seven appearances, and his first league goal for the club was the 100th of his senior career. But then the goals dried up and he scored just once more in the league before Christmas. This league form contrasted with a

Mike shares his joy at scoring with Fulham fans who made the journey to Spotland in August 1996.

Concentration against Rochdale in March 1997.

stunning hat-trick put away in the first round of the FA Cup when Fulham turned the form book upside down to demolish higher-level opposition in Swansea City by a massive 7–0.

His next league goal was in the ill-fated 1–2 defeat at Torquay that left The Whites just one off the bottom of the table and facing non-league football. With just two league goals in almost five months, and in a struggling Fulham side, the crowd began to get on his back, leading to some choice 'verbal exchanges' with the Cottage faithful. However, he recovered with four more goals before the season's end and finished on fourteen in all competitions and as top scorer.

During the following season, 1996–97, Conroy was a revelation, scoring in both the opening League Cup games and the opening league victory over Hereford (1–0). By Christmas he had already accrued eighteen goals, mostly singles, but also two braces. As he became a marked man, his scoring rate slowed down and he sustained a nasty injury at Barnet causing him to be not fully fit for five games. His goals were one of the most prominent reasons that Fulham won promotion in that important season. He also managed the vital equaliser in the McAree-inspired 2–1 away victory at Carlisle. He finished once again way ahead as top scorer with twenty-three goals in all competitions. He was also voted player of the year by the supporters.

Conroy was six feet tall and a lithe and agile athlete, capable of scoring and creating goals. He did a lot of work off the ball and opened up the pitch for others. Team-mates would remark on that attribute and how much weight he took from the other forwards. He was also one of Fulham's best headers of a ball. A non-smoking teetotaller he was a popular colleague and a good character in the dressing room. From a sticky start at Craven Cottage, he became a hero due to his efforts in that 1996–97 season.

He started the following season in good form too, with the winner in the 1–0 win over Wrexham on the opening day. He also scored in both League Cup ties with Wycombe Wanderers. In the 2–1 first-leg win at Wycombe, Conroy scored one of the goals that would be talked about at Fulham for decades. Taking Glenn Cockerill's pass out of defence, he spotted the goalkeeper Taylor off his line and took aim from the halfway line beating the goalkeeper with an arrow-like, powerful left-foot lob-shot from fifty yards.

His final Fulham goal was against Blackpool, the club he would ultimately join, in a 1–0 win at the Cottage in October and his final league game was a 1–1 draw with Millwall at the New Den in November. Injuries restricted his appearances that season and he also seemed to be surplus to requirements under the new management team of Ray Wilkins and Kevin

Conroy scores with a flashing header at Cardiff in March 1996. He netted two goals that day, and Fulham romped to a 4–1 victory, the other goals coming from Rodney McAree and Rob Scott.

Keegan recently installed by the club's new owner Mohamed Al Fayed.

He stayed until the 1998 March transfer deadline when he moved to a third Lancashire club, third-tier **Blackpool**, for £50,000. He made fourteen appearances for the Seasiders in 1997–98 and 1998–99 but failed to find the net in the league (though he did score once against Scunthorpe United in the League Cup). In December 1998 he was loaned out to fourth-tier **Chester City** for whom he scored three goals in ten appearances. He returned there, again on loan, a month after his first period expired, but failed to add to that previous total in five matches.

Conroy was on his way back home to Scotland in 1999 and to Airdrie, when the opportunity of a lifetime came knocking. Ex-player and friend Stuart Munro offered him a chance to play in Australia's NSL (National Soccer League). Conroy's wife was from Melbourne and she had wanted to return, so emigration ensued. Initially Conroy had a season at **Carlton**. He had originally signed a two-year contract, but the club fell into financial difficulties and folded. He moved across to **Eastern Pride** in 2000, but after six games and one goal, they too were beset by financial problems and eventually went bust. The coach at Eastern Pride that year was the former Fulham centre back Jeff Hopkins.

Mike Conroy is happily living in a small suburb on the outskirts of Melbourne and now works for a Japanese golf company in charge of logistics. He remains heavily involved in football and is head coach for Melbourne-based side Doncaster Rovers, who play in the Victoria State League Division Three, which is three divisions below the National A-League. He began his coaching career as reserve-team coach at the same club. He remains optimistic that with the facilities there, Doncaster can take the next step up towards the Victorian Premier League.

MIKE CONROY
Fulham career – all competitions

Season	Appearances	Goals	Home	Away
1995–1996	49	14	6	8
1996–1997	48	23	13	10
1997–1998	14	4	3	1
Total	111	41	22	19

*Total career **league** appearances–337, and **league** goals–94.*

Paul Moody

A clever and powerful goalscorer with deceptive skills, he bagged two Fulham hat-tricks.

Paul Moody was born in Portsmouth and originally started his career playing in goal for local Sunday teams. He finally settled on being a central forward player. At nineteen, he was playing parks football when he was spotted by a **Fareham Town** scout. He scored a hat-trick for Fareham reserves and then put away a hat-trick on his league debut against Shepshed. His first season there, 1986–87, turned out to be Fareham's most successful in the FA Trophy, when they reached the semi-finals before losing to the eventual winners Kidderminster Harriers. In two years playing in the Southern Premier League at Fareham, Moody scored twenty-two league goals in sixty-nine games.

In 1988–89 he became **Waterlooville**'s most expensive signing at £4,000. Waterlooville were in the same division as Fareham, and football was very much a part-time activity for Moody who was making his living as a painter and decorator. He was only at Waterlooville for a year when future Fulham manager Ian Branfoot, then at **Southampton**, ensured that Waterlooville received a club record fee of between £40,000 and £50,000 to take Moody to the Dell and catapult him out of non-league football straight to the First Division.

Moody's time in the top flight was very hard and he found it difficult to acclimatise; it was made doubly difficult by the fact that he was vying for a first-team slot with an up-and-coming Matt Le Tissier. He was a late starter at this level being already twenty-three, and in almost three years on the south coast between 1991 and 1994 he made just twelve top-flight league appearances. Sandwiched in this time was a one-month loan at **Reading** where he played five games, scoring once.

In February 1994, Moody got his chance when he signed for second-tier **Oxford United** for £60,000. He netted eight in just fifteen starts in the remainder of the 1993–94 season. Unfortunately it was not enough to prevent Oxford from being relegated. The next season was a 'nearly one' for improving Oxford and they almost reached the play-offs, finishing seventh. Moody's contribution had been impressive with twenty league goals in forty-one appearances.

But it was even better the following season, 1995–96, when Moody scored seventeen league goals, and Oxford were promoted back to the second tier as runners-up. He scored three hat-tricks that season, including one after coming on as substitute in a 5–0 victory over Burnley, all three goals inside fifteen minutes. Oxford then consolidated their position in 1996–97, though Moody, who played in thirty-eight league games, could only manage a further four goals. In three and a half seasons at The Manor Ground, he scored forty-nine goals in just 136 league games.

Popular Paul, now thirty, joined promoted **Fulham** from Oxford United for £200,000 in the summer of 1997 as one of Micky Adams' last buys before his departure from Craven Cottage. He made his Fulham debut in early September 1997 in a 2–0 win over Bristol City at Ashton Gate, and scored a brace in his first home game in the 2–0 home victory over Plymouth Argyle. It was, however, a sombre evening occasion as it was the first home match since the untimely deaths of Princess Diana and Dodi Fayed (son of Fulham's new chairman).

He added a second brace soon after in a 3–1 home win over Oldham Athletic in October. He was then in and out of the side due to niggling injuries and loss of form but came back strongly with a spell of seven goals in five games over December and January. This included a hat-trick in a 4–1 win over Luton Town at Kenilworth Road. These were a shot (in the first minute), a headed goal and a penalty. They were three consecutive goals too, with Steve Hayward getting the fourth. He then missed a month with injury but came back with a spell of four in three games, near the end of the season, that included another brace in a 2–0 win over rivals Brentford at Griffin Park. Fulham ended the league campaign hanging on to a play-off spot.

His and Fulham's season ended on a sour note though when Fulham lost in the play-offs to Grimsby Town 1–2 on aggregate. On a boiling hot day in the first leg Moody was, some say, rather unfortunate to be sent off in the first half of the 1–1 home draw which left Fulham struggling with ten men for the majority of the match. The second leg was lost 0–1 with Fulham once again reduced to ten men. Moody did have the consolation however of ending the 1997–98 season as Fulham's top scorer with fifteen in all competitions.

Paul Moody was six feet three inches in his stockinged feet and was a fifteen-stone beanpole striker much in the mould of Ian Ormondroyd or Peter

This headed goal from Moody secured a point in the match at Oldham in August 1998.

Crouch. He was lean and gangly like Allan Clarke and instantly recognisable with white-blond hair. He was not blessed with great pace or skill and you would not expect to see him running the channels.

However, for such a big man he was a clever player with a deft touch. His sole job was an old-fashioned one, to score goals and to get amongst defenders and unsettle them, which is what he did. He was very brave and strong with good balance and a strong shot; He relished the no-nonsense physical side of the game and he was all elbows and legs which frequently saw his name in the referee's notebook. However, having come up through non-league, he recognised that competitive side of the game, and understood the need to give 100% every game, which is why he remained a popular figure wherever he played.

His aerial power was his biggest asset. He had a great jump and a very good record for scoring goals with his head. When he was not scoring himself, he created many with knock-downs and headers across goal which led to chances for team-mates. This aerial power could also be used with numerous flick-ons for the faster, smaller players.

The following season, 1998–99, he scored in his first match in a 1–1 away draw at Oldham Athletic, but during the following midweek match at home to Stoke City he was badly injured, sustaining a fractured leg following an innocuous fall. The injury caused him to miss the vast majority of the season.

By the time he was fit again and named as substitute for the penultimate game of the season at Walsall, Fulham were already promoted. In the final game against Preston North End at the Cottage, Moody came on as a second-half substitute for Dirk Lehmann and created Fulham history by becoming their only player ever to score a hat-trick as a substitute.

The fact that the goals all came in one half, and in just a thirteen-minute spell, makes it all the more remarkable. They were a shot and a header with a penalty sandwiched in between. The feat is made unique by the fact that it turned out to be Moody's last time in the white shirt of Fulham, as he was on the move again during the close season. In league terms, he had averaged almost a goal every other game with nineteen in forty games.

Fulham had been promoted, Kevin Keegan had left the club to manage England and new manager Paul Bracewell appeared to dispense with Moody's services with indecent haste. By the start of the 1999–2000 season he had joined **Millwall** of Division Two (the third division) for a fee of £150,000.

After a sticky start, in his first season the thirty-two-year-old Moody managed eleven goals in thirty-four games, including a hat-trick in a 5–0 win over Reading. The goals propelled Millwall to fifth place but they were beaten by the only goal in the play-off semi-final by Wigan. In his second season, 2000–01, he scored thirteen goals and this included another hat-trick in the 3–1 win over Wigan Athletic; and against Bristol City (1–2) there was also the almost mandatory sending off. His two years at the New Den had seen him score a total of twenty-four goals in sixty games, again a ratio of almost one in two. His partnership with co-striker Neil Harris saw Millwall finish as champions and promoted back to the second division.

Moody started the following campaign with Millwall, but made just one substitute appearance before being transferred again, back to fourth-tier **Oxford United** for a second spell. Initially it was a month's loan, but the move was made permanent on the expiry of the loan with another £150,000 move.

This penalty goal was sandwiched between a fierce shot and a powerful header to give Moody a hat-trick against Preston in May 1999. He had come on as a half-time substitute, making the hat-trick unique in Fulham's history.

It was a mixed season for him; although he finished as top scorer with thirteen goals from thirty-five league games and his goals helped keep Oxford in the Football League, injuries and age were beginning to tell and he had lost some mobility. He did manage another dismissal as well. He was also feeling the strain of the daily commute from Portsmouth where he still lived. At the end of the season and at thirty-five, he called time on his seventeen-year career and was given a free transfer by Oxford.

He spent the 2002–03 season with **Aldershot Town**, then in the Isthmian League, and scored six goals in nineteen games, even donning the goalkeeping jersey in an emergency, but by now his game had slowed right down, with back injury problems limiting his starts. After Aldershot Town, he spent the next season much nearer home, playing part-time with **Gosport Borough** in the Wessex Premier Division, but even the start of this season was curtailed by injury. One of his first Gosport games was against Fareham Town with whom he had started his career. At thirty-seven, he finally stopped playing.

After finishing his playing career, Moody returned to the painting and decorating trade, looking at courses on interior design and then moving into the business of buying and renovating houses. He still retains a connection with football and after taking coaching badges and qualifications in working with young people, he did scouting work for Fulham in the 2008–09 season. In 2010 he performed the same role for Norwich City, and is now player development coach at Carrow Road.

PAUL MOODY
Fulham career – all competitions

Season	Appearances	Goals	Home	Away
1997–1998	39	15	6	9
1998–1999	8	4	4	0
Total	47	19	10	9

*Total career **league** appearances–**288**, and **league** goals–**106**.*

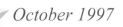

Paul Peschisolido

Fulham's first million-pound player who notched up almost 450 career league appearances.

Paolo Pasquale Peschisolido, more commonly known as **Paul**, was the son of Italian parents who moved to Canada when they were both young. His father was a keen player who encouraged his son and it was always football over ice hockey.

Paul was born in Scarborough, Ontario, and was playing professionally whilst still at school. He was selected to play in all of Canada's three games at the 1987 FIFA U-16 World Championship hosted in Canada. He played for **Toronto Blizzards** in the Canadian Soccer League where he was named rookie of the year in 1989. He had also picked up six caps for the Canadian U-20 side scoring twice. In the following two years, he played in the Major Indoor Soccer League with **Kansas City Comets** being named the league's newcomer of the year, whilst gaining twelve caps for the Canadian U-23 side and netting five goals.

With his Italian roots, and with his father's promptings, he returned to Italy for a year to spend a season with the academy at **Juventus** in 1991, which by his own admission did not work out well.

Homesick and disillusioned, he cut the period short and returned to Canada. Despite this, he made his senior international debut for Canada in a June 1992 Columbus 500 Cup match against Hong Kong, in which he scored his first international goal. The Canadian national team coach and ex-Crystal Palace defender Tony Taylor later took a post in the Midlands and engineered an opportunity, under the new EC rules, for Peschisolido to move to England where, after scoring in both of his trial games, he joined **Birmingham City** of the second division (Division One) in November 1992 for a fee of £25,000.

The young Peschisolido was soon a key player in the Blues team, and was joint top scorer in both the 1992–93 and 1993–94 seasons at St Andrews with a total of sixteen goals in just forty-three games. Unfortunately those goals were not enough to prevent Birmingham City from tumbling into Division Two and into a financial crisis.

Having spoken with **Stoke City** manager Joe Jordan, he elected to stay in the Division One by joining the club for a fee of £400,000 plus a player

On a waterlogged pitch, Peschisolido scores the first goal in the 4–1 victory over Walsall in October 1998.

exchange. Starting with a goal in a 3–2 win over Charlton and two the following week in a 2–0 win at Notts County, he scored thirteen league goals and fifteen in all competitions in his first season at the Victoria Ground, ending up as top scorer. He had added another six goals in twenty games in the 1995–96 season, sometimes playing as an impact substitute, when Stoke, now with financial problems of their own but challenging for a place in the Premiership, surprisingly sold Peschisolido back to **Birmingham City** on transfer deadline day. Birmingham were then back in Division One, and he played just nine games for them, adding a solitary goal to his career tally.

His second spell with the Blues lasted a mere few months as, in the close season of 1996, he was on the move again to Midland rivals **West Bromwich Albion** in a £600,000 deal. He scored just nine minutes into his league debut as Albion won 2–0 at QPR. He ended the season as joint top scorer with fifteen league goals which included a hat-trick in a 3–1 victory at Bury. He started the 1997–98 season with a bang too, with six goals in twelve appearances, before Fulham launched a bid.

It was a sign of what was happening at **Fulham** as, after a transfer bid of £1.1m had been agreed, Peschisolido became the very first third-tier one million pound player, doubling the previous record deal. It was also a sign of Mohamed Al Fayed's intentions for Fulham, as Paul also become Fulham's first £1m signing. Even though it meant dropping down a division, Peschisolido had no regrets.

Predictably he scored on his league debut in a 1–1 draw with Northampton Town; it was the start of an excellent spell of six goals in eight games including a brace in a 3–0 win over Gillingham at Craven Cottage. The goals came fairly regularly throughout the season, mainly in singles, but over Easter in April, he scored a hat-trick in a 5–0 win over a hapless Carlisle United side. He finished the season with thirteen league goals, just two behind top scorer Paul Moody. The season ended sourly for Peschisolido though as Fulham made the play-offs. Going into the second leg of the semi-final game against Grimsby Town level at 1–1, Peschisolido was sent off early in the game for what was described as a late tackle. This hampered Fulham's scoring efforts and they lost 0–1 being therefore denied a place in the play-off final.

After dislodging Dirk Lehmann the following season, 1998–99, and after the first quarter of his season had been blighted by suspension and injury, Peschisolido returned to the side in October and scored five in the next eight league games including a brace in a 2–1 win over Chesterfield. Included in this purple patch was one of the goals of the season at Anfield in the third round of the League Cup, an exquisite curled shot from the edge of the penalty area that arced over the Liverpool goalkeeper, producing an unlikely equaliser. Fulham put up a creditable performance against their opponents who were two divisions above them, but finally bowed out 1–3. Pesch also scored

both the goals that disposed of non-league minnows Leigh RMI in a first-round FA Cup replay.

Although the goals dried up rather after that, he played a crucial role as an impact substitute playing alongside Geoff Horsfield and Barry Hayles. In that season he played thirty-three league games but almost half of them were as a substitute. He finished the season with ten goals in all competitions, behind Horsfield and Kit Symons and just one ahead of Hayles. However he was a valued member of the squad, picking up a championship medal.

At just five feet seven inches, Paul Peschisolido was hardly a target man or likely to win much in the air and his strength was on the ground. Being that size, he had a low centre of gravity and was capable of turning quickly with close control and dribbling skills. He also had an electric burst of pace over ten to twenty yards, which would often take him darting into the opposition penalty box. He was also good with both feet, and scored goals from close in and from outside the area.

Having played out on the wing earlier in his career, he was quite at home playing wide on either wing or in the middle. He could sometimes be enigmatic, and sometimes produced flat, depressed performances, but on other days could fizz through the whole game and be virtually unplayable. He was also ideal as a game changer, and often when the team needed a lift and a goal, the introduction of Peschisolido would usually provide just that. He always gave the game his best efforts and was a popular figure with supporters.

Back in the second tier, life was a lot harder for him in 1999–2000. It started off well with three goals in four matches early in the season, but apart from a goal in a 1–1 draw at Bolton in November, he could not find the net again. He did however score three times in the League Cup. Although he had played in thirty league games that season, 40% had been as a substitute. The Horsfield/Peschisolido front pairing did not seem to catch the eye of the new manager Jean Tigana.

Relations were strained as Tigana made it clear to Peschisolido that he wanted to bring in his own front men and after just two League Cup appearances in 2000–01, the last being an away tie at Chesterfield, Fulham allowed him to be loaned out in November to **Queens Park Rangers**, playing alongside Peter Crouch as a 'Little and Large' combination. As usual, he scored on his debut after just ten minutes in a 1–1 draw with Portsmouth. A second loan period followed at Bramall Lane in January where he scored two goals in five games for **Sheffield United**, once again netting on his debut. The third loan spell of the season came on deadline day in March where he played five games for **Norwich City** but failed to score.

In the summer of 2001 he left Premiership Fulham for Division One **Sheffield United** for a cut-price fee on a two-year deal. Peschisolido spent the best part of three seasons with the Blades, the second of which (2002–03) proved to be eventful. With the help of his goals, United reached the semi-final stage of both the

It looks easy as Peschisolido crashes the ball home for the second goal in the 2–0 victory at Wrexham in November 1998.

FA Cup and the League Cup, whilst also finishing in a play-off place. Peschisolido netted a hat-trick against Gillingham in January, but United did not get promoted. He missed three months with a broken foot and although United had another decent FA Cup run the next season, they finished eighth. Peschisolido was now thirty-two and travelling three hours a day for training so, when an offer came in from **Derby County** on deadline day, the Canadian moved again. By the end of his spell in Sheffield, he had netted seventeen goals in seventy-nine league games, though well over 50% of his United games had been as a substitute.

Paul immediately began to repay Derby as he scored the winner on his debut against Rotherham and then against Watford and twice against arch-rivals Nottingham Forest dragging the Rams clear of relegation. In the 2004–05 season, he contributed nine in all competitions including an FA Cup goal against Fulham (who won 4–2). In the final two seasons (2005–06 and 2006–07), it was much more of a bit-part role, adding a further eight goals over those two seasons in forty-eight appearances. However, his time at Derby finished on a high when he was part of the team that defeated West Bromwich Albion 1–0 in the play-off final and returned Derby County to the Premiership. After this success, he was released by the east Midlands team. He had made ninety appearances and added twenty goals to an already impressive CV.

At thirty-six, Peschisolido signed for League One (third-tier) **Luton Town** on a one-year deal in the close

season of 2007. He played just four league matches and one cup match before an ankle problem kept him out of action. After the injury failed to respond to injections, it was confirmed in December that he would require an operation, ruling him out for the rest of the season. Luton released Peschisolido at the end of the 2007–08 season, following their relegation to the fourth division. Failing to recover fully from his injury, Paul called time on a sixteen-year career.

Initially Peschisolido was linked with a move to non-leaguers Worcester City where his former Birmingham team-mate Richard Dryden was manager, but in January 2009 he was appointed as Jeff Kenna's assistant at League of Ireland club St Patrick's Athletic. However, after just four months there, he resigned citing 'personal reasons'. Three days later, he was confirmed as manager of Burton Albion taking over from caretaker manager Roy McFarland who had taken the club to promotion to the Football League after the departure of Nigel Clough. Peschisolido was in charge of Burton for almost three years; they finished in lower mid-table positions in the first two seasons, but he was relieved of his duties in March 2012, following a winless run of fourteen games which included six successive defeats.

Pesch had a long international career covering twelve years. He won fifty-three caps for Canada, playing qualification games in four different World Cups. He played in twenty-one World Cup qualifiers and three Confederation Cup games. His spells were punctuated by a confrontational relationship with

In October 1998 Fulham lost 1–3 at Liverpool in the third round of the League Cup, but the visitors' goal was a real highlight. From over twenty yards, Peschisolido (at left in the picture) curled the ball into the far top corner of the goal.

former coach Holger Osieck. After a period out of the team, he was recalled by new manager Frank Yallop, once of Ipswich Town, to the Canadian squad in April 2004 at thirty-three. In all, he scored ten international goals, four of them in World Cup qualifiers. He was also sent off in a World Cup qualifier against El Salvador. His final international was a September 2004 World Cup qualification match against Honduras. Paul Peschisolido was inducted into the Canadian Soccer Hall of Fame in 2013.

Paul is married to West Ham vice-chairman and former Birmingham City director Karren Brady who appears on television with Alan Sugar in *The Apprentice*.

PAUL PESCHISOLIDO
Fulham career – all competitions

Season	Appearances	Goals	Home	Away
1997–1998	37	13	10	3
1998–1999	40	10	5	5
1999–2000	36	7	3	4
2000–2001	2	0	0	0
Total	115	30	18	12

*Total career **league** appearances–447, and **league** goals–118.*

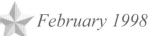

Tony Thorpe

Came to Fulham for £1m, but surprisingly left after three goals in fifteen appearances.

Tony Thorpe was born in Leicester and began his career with Second Division Leicester City's youth team, but failed to break through into the first team, and was transferred to **Luton Town** in August 1992 at the age of seventeen. During his time there he switched from being an attacking midfielder to out-and-out striker, with considerable success.

In season 1996–97 he scored twenty-eight league goals for Luton, who were then in Division Two (the third division), and collected fifty league goals in under five seasons with the Hatters in just 120 games. The goals ratio attracted **Fulham** who were looking for promotion from the same division. To bolster their 1997–98 promotion push, with Paul Moody and Paul Peschisolido already in the squad, Mohamed Al Fayed paid £1m to bring Thorpe to Craven Cottage.

He made his debut in a 1–2 defeat at Blackpool in February. His first goal came on his home debut and gave Fulham three needed points in a 1–0 win over Bristol Rovers. He scored another in the next home match but Millwall were the victors 1–2. His last Fulham goal came a month later, the final goal in a 5–0 drubbing of a dispirited Carlisle United side. He played in all of the final fifteen matches of the season, but only started six of them.

Thorpe was small for a striker, only five feet nine inches, and was more of a goal poacher, at home mainly in the six-yard box finishing off chances. He appeared to have a good touch, but also seemed to be marginally overweight and slightly unfit and seemed to inject little pace into the attack, and although he could certainly not be classed as a failure, he did not seem to fit in with the playing style of that current Fulham line-up.

The Fulham promotion push failed at the play-off stage, and with Keegan now in sole charge it was a real surprise when Thorpe left Fulham after just three months. The club recouped its million-pound outlay when he moved up a division to **Bristol City**.

He took time to adapt at Ashton Gate in the 1998–99 season, and was sent out on loan to **Reading** in February, scoring once in six matches. Then a month later he was loaned back to **Luton Town** where he scored four goals in eight games. City finished bottom and were relegated. The following season, in November, he went back to Luton for a third time, scoring once in four appearances.

He eventually found his feet and some decent form in Bristol, netting another half century of goals in only 128 league games between 1998 and 2002 before he rejoined Luton Town for a fourth time, this time permanently (on a Bosman free transfer) in the summer of 2002.

After fifteen league goals in his first season back at Kenilworth Road, Thorpe left the financially crippled Bedfordshire club for Division Two (third-tier) **Queens Park Rangers** for a cut-price £50,000 fee, after he had threatened to invoke a rule whereby he could move to QPR for free. He scored ten goals in forty-one games in his first season at QPR, helping them win promotion to Division One, but in the following 2004–05 season he was loaned out by Rangers to relegation strugglers **Rotherham United** where he managed one goal in five games, but the Yorkshire side finished bottom and were relegated.

Thorpe was then released by QPR in the close season, and joined third-division (League One) **Swindon Town**, along with another ex-QPR striker, Jamie Cureton. Remaining fit seemed to be a problem and he managed just seven appearances and one goal for the Wiltshire side. Following a permanent transfer, he spent the rest of that 2005–06 season with **Colchester United**. He made fourteen appearances and although he did not score, he helped United to promotion. His former Swindon team, however, were relegated.

Thorpe was released by Colchester at thirty-two and he dropped into non-league football with a very short spell at **Stevenage Borough**. In September of the

2006–07 season, he returned to the Football League with a spell at Blundell Park. He played five games for League Two (fourth-tier) **Grimsby Town**, scoring once, and then signed permanently for the Mariners in January, but he made just one 'permanent' appearance before being released at the end of the season.

He signed for **Tamworth** in the Conference North for the 2007–08 season whilst also signing on for Sunday league side Hockley Rangers in Leicester's Alliance League. After just three months, Thorpe left Tamworth by mutual consent after an eye condition prevented him from playing. The eye was injured when it was scratched on a tile while working and his vision deteriorated with little sign of improvement. However, he went on to join **Barton Rovers** (near Luton) later in the month.

He then signed for **Woking** in September 2008 but was released after just one game following the dismissal of the club's manager. Three days later, he signed for **Brackley Town**. This arrangement lasted just two months due to work commitments, but he did net four in nine games.

He signed for Lincolnshire side **Stamford AFC** in December 2008. He remained with the club until May 2009, where after twelve games and seven goals he became a free agent, finally signing for **Halesowen Town** as player/coach in December 2009. He was appointed player/manager of the club in November 2010 but resigned less than three months later, citing time and family pressures. He then resumed his playing career at **Hinckley Athletic** in the East Midlands Counties League. As at 2012 Tony was playing for Leicester Senior League team **Thurmaston Town**.

Since 2008 he has also been part of the Ingram Soccer Academy, coaching young players, and recently he has gone into the sales business back in his home town of Leicester with initially Millington Travel and latterly Braunstone Cross Road Motors.

TONY THORPE
Fulham career – all competitions

Season	Appearances	Goals	Home	Away
1997–1998	15	3	2	1
Total	15	3	2	1

Total career **league** appearances–*384*, and **league** goals–*136*.

Dirk Lehmann

Flamboyant journeyman striker, but remembered for his ears…

Dirk Lehmann was born in Aachen on the Germany/Belgium border, signing for Bundesliga 1 side FC Koln, without making a league appearance. He moved to Belgian second-tier side **Lierse SK** and over two years made eighteen league appearances with a respectable seven goals. He was almost twenty-four when he made his first senior appearance. He then joined another Belgian side in **RWD Molenbeek**, this time in the First Division, staying just a season with two goals in twenty-six league appearances, plus further UEFA Cup appearances. He then returned to play in Germany with second-tier side **FC Energie Cottbus**, once again staying just a season with only one goal in twenty-four league appearances.

He was surprisingly transferred to Division Two (third-tier) **Fulham** for the 1998–99 season. He made his debut on the opening day of the season in a 1–0 win at Macclesfield, scoring his first goal in midweek in a 2–1 League Cup victory away at Division Three Cardiff City. He then wrote his name into Fulham's folklore by scoring twice in the 3–0 Friday evening home victory over Manchester City, who were favourites to win the division. He also scored an important goal at Southampton that saw Fulham home 1–0 against the Premiership side in the League Cup in September.

That was as good as it got. Dirk was a trier and a good team player. At six feet one he was good at flick-ons and headed efforts. However, after a few games it was apparent that he was a journeyman player with few exceptional qualities in terms of pace, touch or explosive scoring. His most stand-out feature were the ear-rings he used to wear whilst playing which he covered with white sticking plaster for safety.

He netted one further goal, a fine header that gave Fulham a 1–1 draw against non-league minnows Leigh RMI in the first round of the FA Cup in November. It earned a replay and Fulham reached the fifth round. After starting twelve of the first sixteen league games, Lehmann drifted out of the side being used more as an impact substitute. He started just four more games, finishing the season with five goals from thirty-five appearances in all competitions. Although Fulham were promoted as champions, Lehmann could only claim a bit-part role.

Fulham by now had recruited Horsfield and Hayles to complement Peschisolido. After a season at Fulham, Lehmann moved to the Scottish League with **Hibernian**. He scored twice on his debut for them in a 2–2 draw with Motherwell. He played at Easter Road for two seasons, returning a respectable nine goals from fifty-nine matches. He left Hibernian in 2001

under freedom of contract, and returned south, signing for Division Two (third-tier) **Brighton and Hove Albion** under former Fulham boss Micky Adams to play alongside Bobby Zamora. However Adams was replaced early in the season and new manager Peter Taylor did not see the German as pivotal in his plans. He made only three league starts and four substitute appearances for the Seagulls in the 2001–02 season, failing to score. His only goal during his spell at Brighton was in an LDV Vans Trophy game against Swansea City. He was also banned by the FA from wearing the trademark ear-rings during that time.

After just six months on the south coast, he moved back to Scotland joining **Motherwell**, where he was one of the players who negotiated a new contract after the club was placed into administration. In just

This towering header from Lehmann earned Fulham a replay in the FA Cup first-round match in November 1998 against Leigh RMI from the Unibond Premier League.

over a season he made forty-three appearances for Motherwell scoring nine goals.

In the summer of 2003, his nomadic career took him to Japan where he played for a brief spell with second-tier side **Yokohama**, scoring once in twelve games, but he soon returned to his native Germany joining Bavarian League Two side **SSV Jahn Regensburg** in 2004, scoring once in six games, He ended his career the same year, playing lower-league German football with **SC Borussia Freialdhoven 1912**.

At Fulham, due to his German origin and his distinctive moustache, he earned the nickname 'Pornstar' which dogged him for a number of years in football, with many believing that he had been part of the industry and asking him how many films he actually made!

DIRK LEHMANN
Fulham career – all competitions

Season	Appearances	Goals	Home	Away
1998–1999	35	5	3	2
Total	35	5	3	2

*Total career **league** appearances–33, and **league** goals–2.*

Geoff Horsfield

'Feed the Horse' was the cry as he went on to be top scorer for two seasons and a firm Fulham favourite.

Horsfield delights in scoring the first of Fulham's three goals without reply at York in February 1999.

Geoff Horsfield was born in Barnsley, the son and grandson of coal miners. While still a schoolboy he started playing football in the Barnsley Sunday League for a men's team, Athersley Recreation, and the players were often six to seven years older than he was. He had an early rejection when he had an unsuccessful trial with home-town club Barnsley. On leaving school, Horsfield took a college course in bricklaying.

He continued playing football part-time, with **Athersley**, then with **Worsborough Bridge** in the Northern Counties East League. Finally he made the step up to the Football League, turning professional with fourth-tier **Scarborough** in July 1992, and

was given a league debut in March 1993. However, after playing just twelve games and scoring one solitary goal bridging two seasons, he was released and returned to the building sites, whilst still playing part-time football. His father, however, still had high hopes for his son and persuaded him to keep trying. He joined non-league **Halifax Town** in 1994, but after a nine-game spell with the Shaymen without scoring he was once again released.

However Geoff plugged away and rejoined his previous Scarborough manager McHale at **Guiseley**, where his thirty-six goals helped the club to reach third place in the Premier Division of the Northern Premier League in the 1994–95 season. He then moved on

to **Witton Albion** in the 1995–96 season, where he sustained a potentially career-threatening knee injury. After thankfully making a full recovery, he returned to **Halifax Town** for a fee reported as £4,000, making a second debut against Woking in October 1996.

It was not a great season for Halifax, but on the last day of the 1996–97 season and with the club needing to beat Stevenage Borough to avoid relegation from the Vauxhall Conference, Horsfield scored the goal which clinched a 4–2 victory. Horsfield had managed nine goals in that first campaign.

The following season however it was a totally different story. Halifax Town won the Conference title by a clear nine-point margin, thus regaining their Football League status. Horsfield's thirty goals in forty league games, including hat-tricks against Yeovil Town, Telford United and Hereford United, made him that season's Conference top scorer. In all competitions it was thirty-four goals in just forty-seven appearances. Together with team-mate Mark Bradshaw, Horsfield was selected for the England semi-professional representative team, for a match against their Dutch counterparts, but injury prevented him from playing.

Right up to this point, Horsfield had still been working in the building trade, but promotion to the Football League meant he gave up his job to become a full-time footballer. Seven goals in his first ten games in the fourth division were enough to attract a record bid for a Halifax player of £350,000. The bid was from Kevin Keegan, and Horsfield moved up a division, signing for **Fulham** in October 1998.

Horsfield made his debut in a rain-soaked encounter with Walsall at Craven Cottage, coming on as a second-half substitute and scoring with a 'dink' over the goalkeeper to complete the scoring in Fulham's 4–1 victory. He added his second the following week with a headed goal in a 3–2 win over Blackpool. He took a bit of time to acclimatise, and did not score again

in the league until after Christmas. He then hit form with a run of eleven goals in twelve league games that included three braces. This included a magical solo performance in a 4–0 win at Luton Town where he scored twice. In this run, Fulham won eleven and drew the other game. Fulham won the Division Two title by fourteen clear points in 1998–99. Despite joining the team two months after the start of the season, Horsfield was Fulham's top scorer with seventeen goals in all competitions. He was also named in the PFA's Division Two Team of the Year.

'Feed the Horse and he will score' was often heard from inside Craven Cottage. Although Fulham had Paul Peschisolido and later Barry Hayles, the Cottagers had had little aerial power and were lacking a target man after the significant injury to Paul Moody. Horsfield was the template of a centre forward. He was six feet tall, strong and very direct. He was more a throw-back to the Sixties – and a welcome change. He had two good feet and scored goals from close in and outside the box too, and he was very good in the air.

He never gave defenders a moment's peace and his powerful runs and physical style upset defences. He was described as a 'great team player – and one that every team needs'. He could hold the ball up if necessary or turn defenders with his back to goal. Despite his powerful building-site physique, he had an extremely good touch coupled with skilful ball control. With his non-league background, he gave 100% every game and was a great chaser of lost causes. He was described as a 'great lad' both on and off the pitch, and popular with his team-mates. He never forgot his working class roots and always had time for the Fulham supporters.

In Division One (the second division), the Horse found goals harder to come by. He registered two on the opening day of the 1999–2000 season away at Birmingham City in a 2–2 draw, scored in the League Cup at Northampton in a 2–1 win and in the return leg scored his only Fulham hat-trick in a 3–1 victory.

He had scored six goals in the league by November and, as Fulham progressed in the League Cup, few at Craven Cottage will forget the 3–1 win over Premiership Tottenham Hotspur in the fourth round. Horsfield won the match almost on his own, gave England centre back Sol Campbell a chasing he would not forget and scored a magnificent solo third goal with the outside of his foot to clinch the match. Due to injuries and a drop in form, Horsfield missed a third of the season, and scored just one league goal after Christmas but still ended up as top scorer for the second consecutive season with fourteen in all competitions. His final game was a 3–0 victory over Huddersfield Town on the last day of the season.

Jean Tigana was watching his new team from the stands. The only skills lacking from Horsfield's

Watch out, there's a Horse about...

repertoire were pace and mobility. Tigana also thought Horsfield's style was too aggressive for a higher level, seeing the number of cautions he had received. Despite Geoff's two memorable seasons, the manager decided to replace him with Louis Saha, and in the close season rivals **Birmingham City** paid a record £2.25m to capture Horsfield's signature on a five-year contract.

He was top scorer for the Blues in his first season, finding the net on twelve occasions, and his two goals in the second leg of the League Cup semi-final helped the club reach their first major final for nearly forty years. In the 2001–02 season, Horsfield was chosen player of the year both by Birmingham's fans and by his team-mates. His strike partnership with Stern John proved crucial in the unbeaten run which helped Birmingham reach the play-offs, and he scored the equaliser against Norwich City in the play-off final at Wembley, which the club went on to win on penalties to earn promotion to the Premier League. Horsfield had promised a donation to his first club, Athersley Recreation, if he ever reached the Premiership, and a few days after the play-off victory he gave them £25,000 towards improving their ground and facilities. Once again, he had scored twelve goals that season, but also picked up seven cautions that had earned suspensions.

Horsfield's first ever Premier League goal came in the 3–0 September 2002 local derby defeat of Aston Villa. However, he became frustrated by manager Steve Bruce's selection process, as he found himself used as an impact substitute. A late run in the side,

when playing alongside World Cup winner Chistophe Dugarry, produced four wins and a draw in the last six games to ensure the Blues' survival. Horsfield's goal tally in the 2002–03 season was a meagre five.

The following season Horsfield moved down a division to **Wigan Athletic** but, after just three months, having scored an excellent seven goals in just sixteen games, he moved for £1m to same-division **West Bromwich Albion**, who were also in need of a big central striker.

Geoff made his Albion debut in a 0–1 defeat away to Coventry in December, and eventually helped the club to achieve their aim of promotion back to the Premier League. The team laboured in their first season back in the top division, 2004–05, with Horsfield scoring just three goals in twenty-nine league appearances. His contribution on the final day of the season against Portsmouth, however, proved vital to the club's survival. Coming on as a second-half substitute, he scored with his first touch, before setting up a second goal for team-mate Kieran Richardson (now with Fulham). Combined with the results from other matches, including Norwich's 6–0 defeat at Fulham, the 2–0 win ensured Albion's escape from relegation as the first club to survive in the Premier League after being bottom of the table at Christmas.

Horsfield later joined **Sheffield United** and then **Leeds United**, followed by loan spells at **Leicester City** and **Scunthorpe United**.

In October 2008, Horsfield revealed that he had been diagnosed with testicular cancer, and was advised that his playing career was finished. He decided to make his illness public to help spread awareness of the disease, and lent his support to a Premier League-backed project launched in 2009 to promote men's health issues. By December, following successful surgery, he was reported to be considering a return to football, either as a player or in a coaching role, He went on to link up with fourth-division **Lincoln City** managed by his former Halifax Town team-mate Peter Jackson. He played regularly during his time with Lincoln, but scored only the one goal, and at the end of the season the club decided not to renew his contract.

In the summer of 2009 fourth-tier **Port Vale**, managed by former Fulham player and boss Micky Adams, appointed Horsfield as player/assistant-manager. He played in nine games of the season despite needing painkillers for a cracked rib and a cracked bone in his hand. The final of the 2010 Staffordshire Senior Cup was his final competitive game at thirty-seven. When Adams departed, Horsfield

was appointed caretaker for a week. After an uneasy time with new manager Jim Gannon, who was later sacked, he remained at Vale Park as assistant manager. He then concentrated on his coaching qualifications, but eventually walked away completely from active football to pursue business interests in building and property development. He has retained an interest in football in radio media work on Midlands Blue Radio.

Horsfield has not had the best of luck with illness, as he had swine flu in 2009 and had another significant health scare in January 2013, when he had to be rushed to hospital for an operation to remove potentially deadly blood clots on both lungs following an innocuous calf muscle injury.

In March 2013 he agreed to come out of playing retirement to assist the Alvechurch chairman, an old friend, and he joined Midland Football Alliance side **Alvechurch**, until the end of the 2012–13 season, at the age of thirty-nine!

Flying high at Stoke.

GEOFF HORSFIELD
Fulham career – all competitions

Season	Appearances	Goals	Home	Away
1998–1999	34	17	11	6
1999–2000	40	14	8	6
Total	74	31	19	12

*Total career **league** appearances–340, and **league** goals–79.*

The first-ever Premiership goal at the Cottage, August 2001, and it's that man Hayles who scores it.

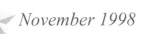 *November 1998*

Barry Hayles

A record signing, a season's top scorer and a firm Fulham favourite with a robust style.

Barrington **Hayles**, better known as Barry, was born in Lambeth and began his playing career with humble Willesden Hawkeye in the early 1990s. He then joined Isthmian League Premier Division side **Stevenage Borough** in February 1994, and impressed in his first two seasons there. His arrival at Broadhall Way started a prolific three-year goalscoring spree that saw the striker net a goal for every two starts he made. A key member of the 1995–96 Conference-winning team, scoring twenty-nine goals in thirty-eight games, Hayles regularly topped the goalscorer charts in the top tier of non-league football.

When the club were denied promotion to the Football League due to ground irregularities, Hayles became tempted to break into league football. In the close season of 1997, after continuing to impress with Stevenage throughout the 1996–97 season, he earned a £250,000 move to the third division of the Football League with **Bristol Rovers**. His final three-year goal tally with Stevenage had been a hugely impressive seventy-three goals in 154 matches.

A late starter entering league football at the age of twenty-five, he impressed immediately at Bristol, scoring on his debut against Plymouth Argyle with a first-half header, and going on to top the division's scoring chart in his first season in league football with twenty-six goals. Rovers narrowly lost 4–3 on aggregate to Northampton Town in the divisional play-offs. After beginning the 1998–99 season brightly with another ten goals in nineteen games, Hayles earned a £2m move to **Fulham**. Once again, he had been able to keep up a ratio of a goal almost every other game with thirty-six goals in seventy-six appearances.

At the time Hayles was Fulham's record signing, and he arrived to join a Fulham side looking like promotion candidates from Division Two (the third tier). He had decent competition for a place with Paul Peschisolido and newly-signed Geoff Horsfield. Initially he looked out of his depth and unrefined, missing a host of chances even with players trying to set him up with a goal. He had made his debut in 2–1 win over Chesterfield and netted in his fourth game, the 4–0 win over Burnley. Single goals began to flow, and he scored the goal that saw Fulham beat Premiership side Southampton in a third-round FA Cup replay. Despite missing a quarter of the season, he finished with nine goals and a championship medal.

Hayles was still far from his best at the start of the following season after stepping up a division. He spent most of the first half of that 1999–2000 season out of the side or as a substitute. Although his pace was evident, there were still a number of unsubtle aspects

about his play and the physical side of his game. He netted in just four league matches contributing a meagre five league goals. He did manage a brace in the 3–0 win at Luton Town in the third round of the FA Cup. His best game of the season was alongside Geoff Horsfield in the fourth round of the League Cup when the pair's aggressive style, hard running and physical effort saw Fulham beat star-studded Premiership side Tottenham Hotspur 3–1. Both Horsfield and Hayles netted on the night.

It was a very mixed season for the London man, as he also picked up two dismissals, a harsh one in the League Cup at West Bromwich Albion where Fulham won 2–1, but also a needless one for a deliberate handball offence during a dismal 0–2 defeat at Sheffield United just after Christmas. He ended the season, as he did the previous campaign, with nine goals. Hayles was called up to the Cayman Islands squad in 2000 for a pair of World Cup qualifying matches against Cuba. He took part in an unofficial

Hayles (second left Fulham player in the picture) nets the opening goal in the 2–0 victory over Blackburn in February 2002.

0–5 friendly defeat against American club side D.C. United but he never played for the Caymans in a full international after FIFA ruled that he did not meet eligibility requirements.

In the 2000–01 season he blossomed under coach Jean Tigana with his touch and finesse improving with every game. It helped of course that he was playing alongside Louis Saha and Luis Boa Morte, but the three players together wreaked havoc amongst opposing defences. Hayles's abrasive bulldozing style perfectly complemented the silky skills of Saha and the searing pace of Boa Morte.

He started well, scoring on the opening day in the 2–0 win over Crewe and he claimed seven in his first eight games including braces in a 4–1 win over Stockport County and a 3–0 win over Gillingham. Another brace followed in a 3–1 win over a physical Portsmouth side in November. Hayles then cemented himself as a fans' favourite by netting a hat-trick in a 5–0 thrashing of arch promotion rivals Watford on Boxing Day. By the turn of the year he had already scored sixteen goals. The pace and flow of goals slowed after that, with other players taking up the reins, but he finished with nineteen in all competitions, though incredibly he was only the third highest scorer. However, he now had his second championship medal in three years.

At only five feet seven, Hayles did not win too many flick-ons or aerial battles but for a man of his size, he scored many headed goals. Having come through non-league, Barry had no fear of the physical side of the game and relished a battle. His main attribute was his pace and robust style. He certainly knew how to get amongst defenders and unsettle their game. As he sharpened his skills at Fulham he also became a calm and clinical finisher, feared by opponents. He would never be the complete player as his first touch and control sometimes let him down, but he made up for these deficiencies with hard-working wholehearted displays that made him so popular with the fans.

Appropriately it was Barry Hayles who scored the first goal at Craven Cottage after the club's promotion into the Premiership, netting the first in a 2–0 win over Sunderland on an emotional summer's evening. Naturally it was another huge step up for Hayles but he coped admirably. Against the best defences, goals were hard to come by, but he netted a notable brace in a 2–0 win over a violent Everton side in December. In just five years Hayles had made his way from non-league football to being the top scorer for a Premiership side.

Sadly that was the pinnacle of his career, as when Tigana decided to purchase Steve Marlet it was Hayles who dropped out. Despite netting twice in the Intertoto Cup including the final itself, and scoring once in the UEFA Cup in Zagreb, he seemed to have become a secondary option. Although he made fourteen league appearances and one cup appearance in 2002–03, only five of them were starts and he contributed just one goal in a 3–0 win at Sunderland. However, with Marlet

No apologies for showing this Hayles goal again. It's one of the author's all-time favourite Fulham pictures. Hayles (nearest to the penalty spot) scores against Everton in December 2001.

misfiring, Barry Hayles was recalled to the Fulham side at the start of the following season, scoring three in the first three games including two in a tremendous 3–0 win at White Hart Lane. His final Fulham goal came in an excellent 3–0 away win at Upton Park in February in a fourth-round FA Cup replay against West Ham. His final game was as a substitute, a forgettable 3–4 home defeat by Blackburn Rovers in April. His total for the season was five.

During his time at Fulham between March 2001 and September 2003, Hayles made ten international appearances for Jamaica, four of which were World Cup qualifiers, but he never scored for the national side.

Fulham now had Brian McBride and Andy Cole, and gave Barry Hayles, at thirty-two, a free transfer and he joined Championship side **Sheffield United** in the summer of 2004. He made just four appearances for the Blades and was only at Bramall Lane for a couple of months, failing to find the net. He moved on swiftly and back to London with another Championship side, **Millwall**, for a nominal fee.

Over the course of two seasons, (2004–05 and 2005–06) Hayles made fifty-five appearances for the Lions scoring sixteen goals which included a hat-trick in a 3–0 Millwall win away at Derby County in his first season. With his enthusiasm and physical style, he became very popular at the New Den. Also like his Fulham predecessors who had joined Millwall (Guthrie and Mitchell) he managed an almost obligatory sending off, at Norwich City, in his second season. Millwall were relegated at the end of that season.

Hayles moved back west when he was signed by Ian Holloway for Championship **Plymouth Argyle** for a fee of around £100,000 prior to the start of the 2006–07 season, and he quickly established himself once again as a supporters' favourite after a highly impressive start which earned him the nickname 'The Ox in the Box'. He scored thirteen goals in his first season for the Pilgrims making him top scorer, but managed another dismissal, against Southampton. In his second season he managed two goals up to Christmas. He had played sixty-two matches for the club.

On New Year's Eve, Hayles moved to **Leicester City** on an emergency loan, which became permanent for a fee of £150,000, Hayles signing an eighteen-month contract. He scored twice in his opening four matches earning Leicester valuable points, but failed to score in the next fourteen, and Leicester were relegated from the Championship at the end of the season.

In August 2008, Hayles now thirty-six moved west for the third time, dropping down a division to join Cheltenham Town on loan for a month, which was extended for a further month in September. He rejoined Cheltenham on loan for a third time in November. Hayles then had a brief ten-match run in the Leicester City first team upon his return, but failed to score a single goal. He nonetheless earned a Leicester medal after the club finished the season as League One champions. Hayles was released at the end of his contract in May 2009.

Barry joined **Cheltenham Town** on a permanent basis during the summer. After making thirty-nine league appearances for the Robins in 2009–10, and adding another seven goals, he was released along with seven other players in May 2010. At thirty-eight, he called time on his league career.

This however did not stop him from playing, and he stayed in the west country, signing for Southern League Premier Division side **Truro City**. He was soon scoring regularly and scored a hat-trick in the top of the table clash between Salisbury City and Truro in February. Truro won 6–0, inflicting Salisbury's first home defeat of the 2010–11 season. In two seasons, Hayles scored twenty-seven goals in seventy-six appearances, twenty of those in his first season. Truro were league champions in that first season.

Due to financial problems at Truro, Hayles joined **St Albans City** in August 2012. He played for the Hertfordshire club for four months during 2012–13 scoring six goals in sixteen games. However, when **Truro City** were sold to new owners, Hayles returned there adding another six goals during the remainder of the season. At the age of forty-one, Barry Hayles is still playing at a good level of football, having signed for **Arlesey Town** in the summer of 2013.

BARRY HAYLES
Fulham career – all competitions

Season	Appearances	Goals	Home	Away
1998–1999	34	9	7	2
1999–2000	43	9	6	3
2000–2001	39	19	13	6
2001–2002	43	12	11	1
2002–2003	24	4	0	4
2003–2004	32	5	0	5
Total	215	58	37	21

*Total career **league** appearances–437, and **league** goals–120.*

The 2000s

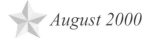

Luis Boa Morte

Charismatic Fulham legend with exceptional pace and a fierce shot.

Luis Boa Morte Pereira was born in Lisbon and started his professional career with Sporting Clube de Portugal (**Sporting Lisbon**) at the age of sixteen in 1994 after being scouted playing for his local team, and he signed professional terms with them at the beginning of the 1996–97 season. He was then sent out on loan to feeder club Lourinhanense for the season. There are few details about his junior playing career at either club. In his one season there he must have impressed as he became one of Arsene Wenger's original signings for **Arsenal**, joining the London club for a fee of £1.75m in the close season.

He made his debut for the Gunners in August 1997 as a substitute against Southampton. During Arsenal's double-winning 1997–98 season he made fifteen league appearances, though only four of these were starts, and he also made four appearances in the FA Cup, three as substitute, although he did not appear in the final itself. He scored two goals for Arsenal that season, both of them coming in a 4–1 League Cup victory against Birmingham City.

The following season, 1998–99, he was a fairly regular member of the Arsenal squad, usually as substitute, in the early part of the season, augmented by a few European Cup appearances including one against Panathinaikos in December, when he scored Arsenal's third goal in a 3–1 victory. His fourth and final Arsenal goal came against Preston North End in a 4–2 FA Cup third-round win. He came on as a substitute as Arsenal won the 1999 FA Charity Shield. His final appearance for Arsenal was as a second-half substitute at Sunderland early in the 1999–2000 season, one of only two appearances that season.

After failing to hold down a regular spot in Arsenal's first team, Boa Morte was signed by Dave Jones at **Southampton** in August 1999 for a fee of around £500,000 with further payments to be based on appearances. In only his second appearance for his new club, away at Middlesbrough in September 1999, he was sent off for handling the ball in the goalmouth near the end of the game, with Paul Gascoigne scoring from the resulting penalty to give the home side a 3–2 win. He scored his only goal for the Saints just before the New Year at Watford. Five months into the season, Jones was sacked and replaced by Glenn Hoddle who dropped Boa Morte from the side. After Hoddle's appointment, Boa Morte made only three further appearances for the south coast club making a total of seventeen in the 1999–2000 season. As at Arsenal, most of these games had been as a substitute.

In July 2000 he had a trial at **Fulham**, following which he moved to Craven Cottage, initially on a season-long loan. As a result the second instalment on the fee due to Arsenal was never paid. Fulham were managed by Jean Tigana who spotted Boa Morte's potential as a right winger and as a replacement for Peschisolido and gave him his opportunity, and it paid handsome dividends. In his first season at Fulham he helped the Whites win the 2000–01 Division One title in style, making thirty-nine league appearances (eighteen as substitute) and scoring twenty-one goals in all competitions, forming a lethal partnership with Louis Saha and Barry Hayles.

He had made his debut on the opening day of the season in the 2–0 win over Crewe Alexandra and scored his first goal in his third league game, after coming on as a substitute in a 4–1 win over Stockport County at the Cottage. He scored five in the first nine league games and scored regularly throughout the season, netting twelve before Christmas. His final return included five braces, an exceptional rate for a winger. The one chink in his armour showed in March when he was sent off for the first time for Fulham against Bolton Wanderers for allegedly spitting. Boa also scored the second Fulham goal at Huddersfield Town in the 2–1 win that guaranteed promotion.

His contributions to the championship-winning season resulted in him being signed permanently in June 2001 for a fee of £1.7m which was paid to Arsenal, despite Southampton's earnest attempts to bring him back to the Dell after the expiry of the loan arrangement. Due to a number of impressive performances for Fulham, Boa Morte was called up to the Portuguese national team, winning his first cap in April 2001 against France.

In Fulham's first two seasons in the Premiership, Boa Morte was not able to replicate his form of the championship-winning season and he found Premiership defences a much harder nut to crack. He played regularly up to Christmas in the 2001–02 season, but found the net just once, in a 1–1 draw at Charlton in early September.

In October he was sent off again. On a soggy afternoon in pouring rain he put a penalty wide against Ipswich Town at the Cottage, was later booked for dissent and was then dismissed for diving – all in the first half. He was sent off again two months later during a violent last half-hour in the 2–0 win over a physical Everton side following an incident which sparked a twenty-man brawl. However this red card was later rescinded by the FA as Boa Morte was the victim of an awful foul. With injuries, he made just three full starts after the New Year. During that season, he scored his first and only goal for Portugal

A typical pile-driver from Boa Morte. This goal came during the Division One promotion season of 2000–01, and was scored against Norwich City in January.

in a 5–1 home win against Angola in November. The game had to be abandoned when the Angola team was reduced to six players.

Boa Morte played more regularly in 2002–03 but once again found the goals that had flowed so easily in Division One hard to come by. His form was better, but he scored just once before Christmas, a consolation in a 1–3 defeat at Villa Park in November. His second goal that season was far more valuable. After Chris Coleman had taken charge, Boa Morte scored the equaliser in a creditable 1–1 draw at Stamford Bridge which helped to haul Fulham away from the bottom of the table and secure safety. Luis had also assisted in the UEFA campaign, scoring in both legs of the second-round ties against Dinamo Zagreb, which helped put Fulham through to meet Hertha Berlin.

Luis Boa Morte was quite tall for a winger, and had two main attributes – exceptional pace and a fierce shot. He could frustrate and delight in equal measure. On a poor day he could be a liability to the Fulham side with poor tackles, verbal antics and aggressive play that saw him frequently in trouble with referees and opponents. On a good day, he was able to turn a match. His passion, physical involvement and determination could see him win matches almost on his own and, at his very best, few Premiership defenders could cope

with his speed and trickery and his ability to take players on. He could play on either wing, or in a more central role, and even as an attacking midfield player if the game demanded it.

He was also a character in the Fulham tradition, fiery, unpredictable, but all smiles, and one whose commitment to the cause and never-say-die attitude endeared him to the Cottage faithful and elevated him to cult hero status. At the end of one season, he threw all his kit into the crowd for the fans, including his shorts! He would be recognised later in his Fulham career by being awarded player of the year and by being made captain. He also earned the nickname 'Dead Snake' following a comical mistranslation of his surname.

In the 2003–04 season, he began to show some of his best Premiership form. He started off in storming style with five goals in the first seven league games including a brace in a 2–0 win against Leicester City. Regrettably the other side of his character came through too, when he was sent off in injury time in the 1–2 home defeat by Liverpool for hacking down Sinama-Pongolle on the halfway line. There followed an in-out period over the next two months, including suspension, but he then firmly established himself in the Fulham team. He scored four in nine games

In action against Crystal Palace in October 2000.

between February and April, including one in a game that secured a draw with Manchester United (1–1) at Loftus Road. He ended the season with double figures, ten in all competitions from thirty-nine appearances. Despite an impressive season at club level, Boa Morte was very disappointed to be left out of his country's squad for the 2004 European Championships on home soil.

The 2004–05 season was similar. Boa Morte tended to score in spurts, with four in four matches early on. Two of these put Fulham 2–0 ahead against Liverpool at Craven Cottage, only for Liverpool to come back with four in the second half. Later in the season he scored in three consecutive matches in April. He ended the season just one short of double figures again. His good form that season attracted interest from Newcastle United in the summer of 2005. At one stage it looked as if he might leave Craven Cottage, but Coleman persuaded him to stay and offered him the team captaincy.

Opinion was divided as to whether the captaincy was a good idea. Although his impassioned style drove Fulham on to greater efforts, many thought his own personal form suffered. Once again he got himself into trouble and was sent off for the fifth time in a Fulham shirt during a drab 0–0 draw with West Bromwich

Albion for two bookable offences, the second of which looked very harsh. The 2005–06 season also included his crowning moment in a Fulham shirt when he scored the only goal in the 1–0 win over Chelsea in March, writing himself into Fulham folklore. He managed seven goals in thirty-seven starts that season, and Fulham survived comfortably in the top flight under his captaincy. The winger was, this time around, part of Portugal's 2006 World Cup campaign in Germany, and he played in the 2–1 victory over Mexico in June, in the group stages of the tournament, as Portugal reached the semi-finals.

His form appeared to dip in the 2006–07 season and his performances by his own standards were jaded, and although he played fifteen league games in the first half of the season he failed to find the net. It was however a major surprise when **West Ham United** came in with a bid of around £5–6m in the January transfer window and Luis Boa Morte, still only twenty-nine, moved to Upton Park, Fulham having signed Clint Dempsey as a younger replacement. His last appearance was as a substitute during an awful 0–0 draw with Watford at Craven Cottage on New Year's Day.

He signed a three and a half year contract. He played his first game for the Hammers in an FA Cup

Boa fires in a typical cannonball shot, but this one, against Tottenham in a Football League Cup match in November 2001, went just wide.

tie against Brighton, setting up two goals. He played against Fulham in his second league game for the Hammers in an entertaining 3–3 draw. He scored his first goal for the club in an important 3–0 away win against Wigan in April.

In season 2007–08, he took part in twenty-seven of the Hammers' Premiership games (many as substitute) but failed to score. Now aged over thirty, he had lost some pace and was generally being used in midfield. He did manage however to pick up another red card. The next season followed exactly the same pattern, and once again he played in twenty-seven of the Hammers' Premiership games but failed to score. At the end of the season, and after an absence of three years, Boa Morte was recalled by manager Queiroz to the Portuguese squad in May and he earned his next cap in June 2009, playing in Portugal's 2–1 win in Tirana against Albania in a 2010 World Cup qualifier. Over a period of eight years from 2001, Boa Morte made twenty-seven appearances for Portugal scoring once.

Opinion on him at Upton Park was pretty polarised. With some he was very popular due to his enthusiastic and hard-working ethic which was at odds with some of the Hammers players at the time, but others saw him as over the hill and a waste of money. He managed to pick up seven cautions during the season.

In July 2009, he picked up a serious injury in a pre-season friendly against Spurs. West Ham were playing in the Barclays Asia Trophy in Beijing. Luis got his studs stuck in the ground, twisted his knee and suffered a cruciate ligament injury. It put him out for nine months. He made his comeback in April 2010, playing forty-five minutes in a reserve team game. Making an appearance in the first team for the first time during that 2009–10 season, he opened the scoring for West Ham against Manchester City in a 1–1 draw in May. It was his first goal for West Ham for over three years.

In June 2010, West Ham chairman David Sullivan announced that Boa Morte had been offered a new deal and Boa signed a new two-year contract. Under manager Avram Grant, he played in a number of positions including full back and played in twenty-two games in 2010–11. He once again failed to score but picked up seven cautions. In August 2011, his contract with West Ham was cancelled by mutual consent. He had netted just twice for the Irons in ninety-one league games in a period exceeding four years, but had accrued an amazing twenty-one cautions and a sending off.

Later that month, Boa Morte signed a two-year contract with Greek side **Larissa**. He thus rejoined former coach Chris Coleman with whom he had worked for four years at Fulham. Boa Morte signalled his intent to help Larissa back to top-flight football in Greece during 2011–12. He provided his first assist in an impressive 3–0 away win over Veria FC in November. However, he left in January 2012, just seven games and six months into his stay, due to financial problems prevailing at the club; manager Coleman would also not remain there much longer. Luis was not out of work for long as during the same month he signed an eighteen-month deal with Johannesburg side **Orlando Pirates** in South Africa. Once again though it proved to be a false dawn. He played only three games for the club and returned to the UK after just four months, the South African club reportedly saying that he simply wasn't good enough and that they had younger and fitter players already there in his position.

In September 2012 Boa Morte joined League One (third division) Portsmouth on trial, but failed to secure a deal, and a month later, now thirty-five, he signed for League Two **Chesterfield** where former Fulham goalkeeper Mark Crossley was a coach. Although he was a model professional and a role model for the younger players, after playing in thirteen matches for the Spireites, his contract was not renewed in January 2013. Since that time he has returned to Fulham, and there may be a future role for the Portuguese star with younger players at Craven Cottage.

LUIS BOA MORTE
Fulham career – all competitions

Season	Appearances	Goals	Home	Away
2000–2001	46	21	11	10
2001–2002	29	2	0	2
2002–2003	45	5	1	4
2003–2004	39	10	6	4
2004–2005	39	9	6	3
2005–2006	37	7	7	0
2006–2007	15	0	0	0
Total	**250**	**54**	**31**	**23**

*Total career **league** appearances–337, and **league** goals–48.*

Louis Saha

The complete striker, catalyst in Fulham's return to the top tier, notching thirty-two goals in a season.

Louis Saha was born in Paris and was a scholar at the French football academy Clairefontaine that produced soccer talent like William Gallas, Nicolas Anelka and Thierry Henry. He joined **Metz** in eastern France at seventeen in 1995, and for two seasons he developed his skills with them. Saha represented France at Under-17 level, and also Under-18 youth level, where he scored six in thirteen games including the winning goal in the 1997 European Under-19 Championship against Portugal.

Despite being six feet tall, Saha began his career out on the wing. He broke into the Metz team at seventeen but was hardly prolific, scoring just once in twenty-one league games in his first season, 1997–98. The

following season he made just three appearances. However that season was split as in January the **Newcastle** manager Ruud Gullit took Saha to Tyneside for a half-season loan with the Magpies. Played predominantly on the wing, Saha made eleven league appearances during that time, scoring just once in a 4–1 victory over Coventry City at St James' Park. He also played and scored in one FA Cup match, the only goal in a fifth-round tie against Blackburn Rovers. Newcastle made the FA Cup Final where they were beaten 0–2 by Manchester United, but Saha was omitted completely from the final squad and he returned to France.

In the 1999–2000 season Saha was again pretty unspectacular in terms of goals with just four goals in twenty-three appearances for Metz. He did however bag eight goals in eight games in the Intertoto Cup. During the last couple of seasons he had however won further French caps at Under-20 and Under-21 levels. Despite the paucity of goals, new **Fulham** manager

Jean Tigana had been alerted to the potential of the young forward and paid Metz £2.1m for his signature in the summer of 2000. Tigana saw the athletic Saha as a prime striker and played him more centrally.

Starting with the number 9 on his back, Saha was an instant success at Craven Cottage. He made his debut against Crewe Alexandra on the opening day of the 2000–01 season and scored a fine goal in a 2–0 home win; he netted a fine solo goal in his second game too as Fulham won emphatically 3–1 at Birmingham City. He then scored twice in the second leg of the first-round League Cup tie against Northampton Town in a 4–1 win. Just five days later the Whites' fans began to see a true star as Saha bagged a first-half hat-trick in a 5–1 demolition of Barnsley.

From then until Christmas everything Saha touched turned to gold, and by the New Year he had already amassed twenty-one goals in two competitions. With assistance from the bustling Barry Hayles and the pace of Luis Boa Morte, Fulham were tearing Division One defences apart and were running away with the title. Inevitably the scoring slowed a little in the second half of the season, but Fulham romped home with the league title and Saha finished his first season with the club with thirty-two goals, the first time a Fulham player had scored over thirty goals in a season since Bedford Jezzard almost fifty years previously. His final goals of the season were two penalties against Wolverhampton Wanderers at Craven Cottage, one scored with the left foot and one with the right. He had netted a hat-trick and six braces in that season's total and was the division's top scorer. He had missed just three league games all season.

In the first season in the Premiership, Saha once again started promisingly. On the opening day Fulham lost 2–3 at Old Trafford, but Saha scored twice, each time giving Fulham the lead, his first goal coming after just three minutes. He then scored in the first home match too, the second goal in a 2–0 win over Sunderland. He was named as the Barclaycard August player of the month in the Premiership. He was a tightly marked player in more ways than one and managed just one further league goal before Christmas, a stunning volley from the edge of the area in a 3–1 home win against Newcastle United.

He had a subdued season compared to the explosive one previously and added only four goals in the second half of the season. This included a brace at Chelsea and a critically important equaliser in a 1–1 draw at former club Newcastle United which helped pull Fulham clear of relegation. In total the 2001–02 season brought him just nine goals, behind Barry

An opening-day equalising penalty against Bolton Wanderers at Loftus Road, August 2002. Fulham won 4–1.

Hayles and Steed Malbranque. He had missed just two league games all season.

Louis Saha looked to be the complete striker, strongly built, superbly athletic, lightning quick and with an explosive shot from either foot. His heading ability was also as good as anything ever seen at Fulham. He could beat players with ease and seemed to be able to score at will. His build enabled him to shield and retain the ball despite the close attendance of his opponents. If he had a chink in his armour it was that he was susceptible to injury.

The second season in the top flight, 2002–03, proved to be a big disappointment for Saha. It started well with a goal in the Intertoto cup and for the third season in a row he scored on the opening day with a penalty in the 4–1 win over Bolton Wanderers, but he was badly injured in the fourth game, the momentous 3–2 win over Spurs at Loftus Road. Following this, he made just one start over the next five months, missing the entire UEFA Cup campaign. Soon after his return, he netted three in four games and finished the season with a penalty at Charlton and a total of only five goals from twenty league games, seven of these as a substitute. At this point, Saha's lustre was beginning to fade somewhat.

But he worked hard on his fitness and started the 2003–04 season with a real fire. For the fourth consecutive season he scored on the opening day in the 3–2 win over Middlesbrough at Loftus Road. He proceeded to score on a regular basis and by mid-January had fifteen league and cup goals, including four braces. Fulham under Chris Coleman were in fourth place in the table at one stage before Christmas and the height of their achievements during that period was an historic 3–1 victory over Manchester United at Old Trafford. Although he did not score, Saha had a fine game and caught the eye of Sir Alex Ferguson once again.

With his spectacular form and goals, the **Manchester United** machine launched a shameless media campaign to unsettle Saha and accelerate a move to Old Trafford. Initially it looked as if he would stay, but United increased their offer and the pressure built daily. In the end, although the truth may never be known, Saha allegedly threatened to go on strike or play badly if Fulham continued to deny him his dream move. It became acrimonious with Saha ostracised and training on his own. Just before the closure of the January transfer window, Fulham received a record fee of £12.3m for Saha and he left for Old Trafford. Louis signed off with a goal in his final game that secured three precious points in a 2–1 home win over Everton. Certainly it was a shame that such a hero had departed under a dark cloud. Even though Saha had left in January, he still finished as Fulham's clear top scorer come the end of the season.

His hot streak of form continued during the remainder of that season; Saha scored on his debut for United against Southampton, and in the next match at Goodison Park scored twice against Everton. Six weeks later he returned to Fulham in United colours and scored a fine goal in a 1–1 draw. In the 2003–04 season he scored seven league goals in his first seven starts but did not find the net again. Strangely Saha was not awarded a full French cap whilst with Fulham, but almost immediately after signing for Manchester United he won an international call-up for the French team, scoring on his debut in a 2–0 win over Belgium; he added a second goal during a friendly with Andorra three months later. He also made the French Euro 2004 squad for the tournament in Portugal, making two substitute appearances in the competition.

The 2004–05 season was a stop-start season for the Frenchman and it was marred by constant injury. Saha never really got going making only fourteen appearances for United and scoring two goals.

Over the summer, Saha suffered another hamstring strain which ruled him out for the first three months of the 2005–06 season. He recaptured his form with six goals in League Cup matches, making him a surprise choice over Ruud van Nistelrooy. He played in the League Cup final too, scoring in United's 4–0 win over Wigan Athletic. In the second half of United's season he scored seven goals (including the obligatory goal against Fulham) and ended the season with fifteen in all competitions. With this upturn in form and fitness, Saha was selected for the French squad for the forthcoming 2006 World Cup and contributed to France reaching the World Cup final with three appearances, but he was suspended for the final itself against Italy after picking up needless cautions against Brazil in the quarter-final and Portugal in the semi-final during a total of just twelve minutes on the pitch.

Saha began the 2006–07 season by scoring after only seven minutes into the first league game (against Fulham, of course). By December he had scored eight league goals in just fifteen starts. He had also scored twice against Celtic and in both legs of the Champions League games against Benfica. From that summer through to December, he was also busy internationally with three friendly games for France and four appearances in the Euro 2008 qualifiers where he scored two further international goals against Georgia and the Faroe Islands. In December, he signed an extension to his contract, but soon afterwards began suffering from more significant injury problems. He ended the season with fifteen goals in all competitions.

The next season he managed only four goals up to Christmas. After New Year's Day the injuries returned to haunt him and he played just four more league games scoring once. The hamstring injury kept him out and he missed the 2008 Champions League final which United won, beating Chelsea on penalties. When he had been fit, Saha had scored an average of a goal every three games for United, but Sir Alex Ferguson had grown tired and frustrated by the consistent absences and during the summer of 2008 Saha moved on to Premiership **Everton** for an undisclosed fee.

Playing on a 'pay as you play' deal in the 2008–09 season, he was unfit joining the Toffees and trained without pay until fit. He made his debut against Hull at the end of September and scored his first Everton goal in November (against Fulham, of course). He netted just six goals all season. In addition he scored two FA Cup goals and assisted Everton in reaching the FA Cup final. Saha played in the final and set a record when he scored after only twenty-five seconds, the quickest FA Cup final goal in history, and the fastest in any competition at the new Wembley stadium.

Saha fires home one of his two goals in the 3–1 victory over Burnley at the Cottage in September 2000.

Saha heads home his goal in the 3–0 victory over Huddersfield Town at the Cottage in November 2000.

Unfortunately for Everton, Chelsea came from behind to win.

Saha scored his first goal of the 2009–10 season against Arsenal, but Everton lost 1–6. Staying quite fit, he went on a run of notching thirteen Premier League goals in twenty-four games, but he did not score again after February. He signed a two-year contract extension with Everton in February 2010, keeping him at the club until the end of the 2011–12 season. Saha was called up to the French squad again by Raymond Domenech in February but was forced to withdraw due to injury.

He missed a month early in the 2010–11 season and failed to score in his first nineteen league games. He broke his duck against Arsenal, and the following week posted his best goal total in English football when he netted four goals for Everton in a 5–3 victory over Blackpool. In March he scored against his old club Fulham yet again, with a low drive from a free kick, but later in the game he was stretchered off with an ankle injury and remained sidelined for the rest of the season.

In the 2011–12 season, although fit, he scored just once in the league for Everton, this as a substitute against Fulham (of course!) at Craven Cottage. He added a single League Cup goal the following week against Chelsea, but it would be his last for Everton, and his final appearance was in a 1–1 draw with Blackburn Rovers in January 2012.

Before the end of the January transfer window he joined Premiership **Tottenham Hotspur** on a free transfer, signing a six-month contract. He made his usual prolific start with three goals in two games, two in a 5–0 demolition of his previous club Newcastle United. He scored once more in an FA Cup game and

it looked as if Saha would be offered a longer deal. It was a big surprise when Spurs decided not to extend the arrangement.

In August 2012, Martin O'Neill signed up Saha on a one-year deal for Premiership **Sunderland**. He made eleven league appearances and three League Cup appearances but failed to score at all in the 2012–13 season. His last match was in early December, and his contract was mutually terminated on transfer deadline day January 2013. The following week, Saha signed a six-month contract with Italian team **Lazio**. He made his debut as a substitute in February in a match against Napoli. He started just once and was a substitute in five other games. Once again Saha was released at the end of the short-term deal. There were numerous press rumours as to where Louis might play next, but in August 2013 he announced his retirement from the game.

LOUIS SAHA
Fulham career – all competitions

Season	Appearances	Goals	Home	Away
2000–2001	48	32	21	11
2001–2002	44	9	4	5
2002–2003	28	7	6	1
2003–2004	22	15	11	4
Total	142	63	42	21

*Total career **league** appearances–332, and **league** goals–112.*

Steve Marlet

Fulham's record purchase – but it didn't work out for player or club.

Steve Marlet was born in Pithiviers, south of Paris, and joined northern Paris lower-league side Red Star when just sixteen after a year with Paris Saint-Germain. He made his debut for **Red Star** at seventeen in 1991–92, and in that first season he made seven appearances scoring once. He was hardly prolific the following season either with five goals from thirty-one games. His third season, 1993–94, was better with nine goals in forty appearances.

He matured as a goalscorer and his final two seasons with Red Star (1994–95 and 1995–96) would be the most prolific in his career, with twenty-seven goals from fifty-nine appearances – almost one every other game. Overall his return for Red Star was good with a goal every three games or so. He was a young hero locally and popular with supporters, in one season helping the tiny club reach the quarter-finals of the French Cup.

His performances with Red Star earned him a move to higher-division **Auxerre**, where he played for four seasons. He scored only three in twenty-four games in 1996–97, but in an injury-hit season netted six in eighteen in 1997–98 including a brace against Monaco. He also took part in the club's UEFA Cup matches. In his final two seasons there, he netted sixteen goals in sixty-five matches – hardly a striker's rate.

However, his performances were enough to secure him a prestigious higher-level move to **Olympique Lyonnais** (Lyon) who were able to purchase Marlet quite cheaply. His first season, 2000–01, saw a more than reasonable return of twelve goals in thirty-one games including a brace against RC Lens. He also performed very well in the Champions League with four goals in eleven games, forming an effective partnership with Brazilian Sonny Anderson. Lyon also won the French Cup that season with Marlet playing alongside future Fulham team-mate Steed Malbranque. During that season and early in the next, Marlet was awarded six French international caps, scoring his first goal for France in a 5–0 win over South Korea.

He had netted one in five the following season, 2001–02, when **Fulham** manager Jean Tigana decided to make Steve Marlet the most expensive purchase in Fulham's history by buying him for an astonishing £11.5m. It was also on a five-year contract. With Fulham finding their feet in their first season back in the top flight, the move caused shockwaves throughout English football. It would be a price tag that would weigh heavily on both the club and the player.

Marlet was twenty-eight and at the height of his career, and the ante was raised with comments about his ability, especially when it was reported that the Fulham coaching management had implied that Marlet would be as good as Arsenal's Thierry Henry, if not better. Marlet was Fulham's marquee signing and was supposed to team up with French compatriot Louis Saha and take Fulham to the next level. However, he had spent a great deal of his playing career on the right wing, seemingly his best position, or as an attacking midfield player behind the main striker 'in the hole'. Fulham fans did not really know what to expect.

Marlet's debut was delayed due to an injury sustained whilst playing for France, but within ten games it was beginning to be clear what Fulham had purchased – a speedy, efficient and tidy footballer and more of a winger, but a player seemingly out of his depth in the pace and rigours of the Premier League, overshadowed by Saha, Malbranque and even Barry Hayles who all outscored him. He was certainly not a central striker, neither was he worth the inflated transfer sum paid. It did not help his cause that Fulham played him in a variety of positions to try and assess the best place to play him.

Marlet made his Fulham debut as a substitute in a 1–3 home defeat by Arsenal in September, and some bad luck followed when he appeared to fracture his knee in the 2–1 home win over Southampton in October and spent the next two months out injured. His return as a substitute just before the end of the year saw him score his first goal for Fulham in a 2–3 home defeat by Manchester United, a simple tap-in from a couple of yards after strong approach work from Rufus Brevett.

The Fulham team in general struggled but Marlet managed four in eleven games towards the end of the season including a screamer in the 3–0 home win over Bolton that secured Fulham's Premiership status. To be fair to Marlet, he also netted three FA Cup goals including the face-saver near the end of a 2–2 draw at lowly Wycombe Wanderers, managed by Lawrie Sanchez, and the neatly-headed only goal of the game at the Hawthorns in the quarter-final that earned Fulham a semi-final clash with Chelsea. In this turbulent season, he won three more French caps scoring a second French goal in the 5–0 demolition of Scotland and had won a place in Roger Lemerre's French squad for the 2002 World Cup.

The Cottagers at times had been poor throughout their first Premiership season, so it might have been difficult to judge Marlet's true worth to the side. He seemed to possess all the basic attributes, but without being outstanding at any of them. He had a decent shot when he used it and was pretty good with headed goals, but all in all he appeared just an average to good player whose languid, almost lazy, style did not really endear him to the home supporters.

The 2002–03 season started pretty well for him. He scored twice in the Intertoto Cup, albeit against lowly opposition, and he scored on the opening day of the league from a penalty against Bolton Wanderers (4–1) and managed three in his first eight games. However, it was to get no better, and his final league goal came in a 1–2 defeat against Blackburn at Ewood Park in November.

He managed to improve his standing at Fulham somewhat with a goal in each of the three rounds of the UEFA Cup during October and November, but during that time he also scored an own goal from a comical mis-cue following a cross from his French compatriot Henry that handed Arsenal a 0–1 victory on a plate at Loftus Road. The following month he was sent off late in the game in an edgy 0–1 defeat at Birmingham City following a late and unnecessary clash with Robbie Savage.

Marlet had been named Steve by his mother as her favourite actor was Steve McQueen, but the Fulham fans saw few 'Bullitt' shots, he did not take part in

Coleman's 'great escape' at the end of that season and the Fulham fans certainly did not see a 'magnificent seven' league goals. He failed to register a goal at all in his final thirteen league games.

Following the sacking of Jean Tigana, new manager Chris Coleman withdrew Marlet from the side that took ten points from the final five league games to survive in the top flight once again. Marlet had scored five goals in the Intertoto and UEFA games that season, but it was not enough to save his London career. Strangely his indifferent form had not seemed to affect his standing with France and he won eight further caps during the season and in the close season, which included two goals in a 5–0 victory over Slovenia.

He played just one further league game for Fulham on the opening day of the 2003–04 season, scoring in the 3–2 home win over Middlesbrough. He had scored just eleven league goals in fifty-four matches. The fallout with the transfer had seismic ramifications for all parties involved. Many suggested it was the most important factor in Tigana losing his job. Fulham would not be so easily persuaded in the future into paying out such huge sums. Steve Marlet's career never recovered.

Fulham chairman Mohamed Al Fayed considered that he had been misled over the transfer and sought High Court justice. The whole transfer was described by judge Elias as murky and the transfer dealings as bizarre, with some aspects possibly amounting to a conflict of interest. However, there was not enough concrete evidence for the judge to find in Fulham's favour and, after withholding some of the transfer fee, Fulham were eventually forced to pay the entire amount.

Marlet engaged in a war of words with Fulham and with manager Chris Coleman. It was evident that he wanted no future at Fulham, and the club wanted him out of the squad. In the end, Marlet was sent out on loan to French side **Olympique Marseilles** with Fulham still having to pay the wages on his contract.

Marlet nets to make the final score 2–3 in the match against Manchester United in December 2001.

Initially the loan was for one season, with Fulham hoping for a permanent deal at the end of it. In what remained of the 2003–04 season, Marlet scored a very respectable nine goals in twenty-three matches for Marseilles, including six in the last eleven matches of the season, but his progress was hampered by injury and he was out for three months. He was also often overshadowed by the efforts and goalscoring power of the emerging talent that was Didier Drogba. Whilst with Marseilles that season he won his final six caps for France scoring twice in those games, in friendlies against Switzerland and Andorra.

Marseilles declined a permanent move at the end of the season, wanting Marlet to do more to earn himself a deal, so Fulham in desperation had no option but to extend the loan to a second season. In that second 2004–05 season Marlet scored seven in thirty-one appearances, but surprisingly Marseilles decided not to offer him a permanent move. He was selected for the French squad to take part in Euro 2004 but was an unused substitute, his French career also seemingly over.

In the end, Fulham cut their losses, cancelled the contract and allowed Marlet to move to **VFL Wolfsburg** in the Bundesliga on a free transfer. The 2005–06 move lasted just a season, with a very poor return of just one goal (against MSV Duisburg) in twenty-one matches. Of those twenty-one games, only six were starts, and he spent the majority of the season on the bench. Marlet was given another free transfer at the end of the season.

He was now thirty-two and joined newly-promoted French Second Division side **FC Lorient**. Once again the move was to last just one season, and after spending most of the time as a substitute he was released for the third time at the end of it. Again he had managed just one goal in twenty-two games and had been unable to shift the front players Gignac and Namouchi.

Now without a club, Marlet considered offers from Israel and Australia. He had a bizarre one-week trial at Ipswich Town in October 2007, playing and scoring in one reserve match. He had trials in the USA with Chicago Fire of the NSL and also with French Second Division side Rheims. None of these opportunities led to offers of employment.

After two years out of the game, Marlet eventually found his way back to the amateur leagues, plying his trade for **FCM Aubervilliers**. He played there for two seasons, taking part in forty-four games and scoring thirteen goals. At the age of thirty-seven in August 2011, Marlet returned in a player/coach role with his first Paris club **Red Star 93**.

After his time at Fulham, Marlet's career did go into decline. It was a dramatic downfall too and a disappointing one for the player and his subsequent clubs. A player who played between 500 and 600 games in all competitions and scored well over 130 career goals over a period exceeding twenty years, consolidated by almost a quarter of a century of caps for his country, cannot be a bad player. It was just a shame so little of his skills were ever apparent during his time with the Whites. Each of Steve Marlet's Premiership goals effectively cost Fulham over £1m.

STEVE MARLET
Fulham career – all competitions

Season	Appearances	Goals	Home	Away
2001–2002	33	9	3	6
2002–2003	44	9	3	6
2003–2004	1	1	1	0
Total	78	19	7	12

*Total career **league** appearances–55, and **league** goals–11.*

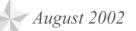

Facundo Sava

Educated Argentinian forward who wore the mask of Zorro.

Facundo Sava was born in Ituzaingó in Argentina, and started his career as a nineteen-year-old with Buenos Aires side **Ferro Carril Oeste** in 1993. Over a three-year spell he netted nine goals in eighty games. He then made a move to famous Argentinean side **Boca Juniors**, but remained there for just one season, making only seven appearances and not finding the net.

He was then sold on to Buenos Aires side **Gimnasia y Esgrima La Plata** in 1997. Facundo remained there for five years, his longest spell anywhere, and he enjoyed one of the most prolific scoring times of his playing career, netting sixty-seven goals in 182 games, a ratio of better than one in three. He was top scorer in his final season there.

In the summer of 2002, Sava was sold to **Fulham** for £2m. It was always considered a controversial move. Many thought that Fulham manager Jean Tigana knew little of the player and that he had been brought in over his head by, it was rumoured, the new director of football Franco Baresi. This was one of the factors that precipitated Tigana's departure towards the end of the season.

There sometimes appeared to be a reluctance by Tigana to start a game with Sava and he was often used as a substitute. There frequently seemed to be congestion up front too as Sava was competing for a striker's place with Louis Saha, Steve Marlet and Barry Hayles. Fulham fans first saw Sava make three Intertoto appearances, but he did not score.

However, he made an impact straight away in the 2002–03 season; in just the second league game, with Fulham two goals down, he came on as a late substitute at Middlesbrough and the Whites netted twice in the last two minutes to earn a point, with Sava securing the equaliser in injury time. In the league, all his goals were important ones. He scored the winner, and his first goal in front of home supporters, with a low shot in a 1–0 victory over Charlton Athletic at Loftus Road in October.

His next goals were the most important. In an impressive display Fulham beat Liverpool 3–2 at Loftus Road and Sava scored twice, deflecting Sean Davis's shot into the net for the other. Some newspapers credited Sava with a hat-trick, but the formal club statistics credit Facundo with just two. He had also played in four UEFA cup games and scored in the third round against Hertha Berlin. Unfortunately it was at the wrong end of the pitch and his mis-cued clearance past Van der Sar proved to be the winner in a 1–2 defeat. A goalless second leg was enough to put Fulham out of the competition.

His fifth goal came before New Year and it was a valuable strike that earned Fulham a 1–1 draw away at West Ham on Boxing Day. Just after New Year, he netted in the 3–1 win over Birmingham City in the third round of the FA Cup. Fulham never lost a match in which Sava scored. He played sporadically for the

Sava scores the only goal of the game against Charlton Athletic in October 2002 during Fulham's sojourn at Loftus Road.

Sava shoots the winner in the 2–1 victory over Bolton Wanderers in December 2003.

remainder of the season, but made only thirteen league starts. It however was an impressive season with six goals in twenty-six games (nine as substitute).

Facundo Sava was a far better player than many gave him credit for. He was almost six feet three and well built. He was comfortable playing out wide or in the middle. He was strong and difficult to dispossess and able to run at defenders. His main skill was holding the ball and opening up the game, bringing others into play with accurate distribution. He always looked a goal creator rather than the main spearhead of the attack. He was a more of a static forward than a mobile one. His headed 'flick-ons' and knock-downs were also invaluable in team play.

In some ways it was a shame that his skills were overlooked, as he will always be remembered for donning the 'mask of Zorro', which he kept in his football sock, when he scored, a tradition that had begun in Argentina. In the second season, however, it was never worn. Many saw it as harmless fun, but often it was ridiculed by other fans and clubs. Sava was an intelligent player, with a psychology degree, and enjoyed his life in London with visits to museums and art galleries.

His second season, 2003–04, was disappointing and he missed a considerable part of the early season with knee and shoulder injuries. He came on as a substitute early in December and scored the winner in a 2–1 home victory over Bolton Wanderers. He rounded off his London career with a win too, coming on as a substitute in 2–1 win over Everton in a fourth-round FA Cup replay at Loftus Road. In all he made just one start with eight substitute appearances. It was true that he lacked pace and some mobility but more significantly he did not appear to be a key player in new manager Chris Coleman's plans.

Therefore it was a sad end to his Fulham career for the colourful and smiling Argentinean. He was offloaded to Spanish Second Division side **Celta de Vigo**, initially on loan. It was then made a permanent move and despite only three goals in twenty-six games, Facundo helped the team secure promotion to the Spanish First Division.

He moved to another Spanish Second Division team, **Lorca Deportivo**, scoring seven times in thirty-eight games. However after just one season he returned to Argentina to play for the famous Buenos Aires side **Racing Club**. In two seasons there he enjoyed the best scoring form of his career with twenty-nine goals in sixty-six games.

His career then became rather nomadic, with a single season with local side **Arsenal de Sarandi** (three goals in twenty-one games) and a single season with **Quilmes** (four goals in twenty-one games) whom he helped achieve promotion to the Argentine Premier Division. He elected not to play in the Premier League but to return instead to his first club **Ferro Carril Oeste**. With Ferro, he played six games in the 2010–11 season scoring twice, before deciding to retire. He played his last game in an away draw against Belgrano in September 2010.

It had been a colourful and exciting career of seventeen years for the South American. In total he had made over 500 appearances in all competitions and scored over 130 goals in a career covering Argentina, Spain and England. Sava had built on his coaching qualifications throughout his playing time and, following his retirement, concentrated full-time on coaching. Eighteen months later, Sava took his first coaching job as head coach at San Martin de San Juan but the appointment lasted just six months before he was sacked. Three months later he was appointed manager of Union de Santa Fe where he remains in 2013.

FACUNDO SAVA
Fulham career – all competitions

Season	Appearances	Goals	Home	Away
2002–2003	33	6	4	2
2003–2004	9	1	1	0
Total	42	7	5	2

*Total career **league** appearances–26, and **league** goals–6.*

January 2004

Brian McBride

**A top scorer and great sportsman,
simply a true Fulham legend.**

Brian McBride was born in Arlington Heights in Illinois. He played football at Buffalo Grove High School and led 'The Bison' to the state championship in 1988, his junior year. During a play-off game, McBride broke his nose in the first half, but came back into the game to score the match-winning goal. In his four years in high school, he scored eighty goals, thirty-three as a senior, despite playing his final season as a defender. In the regional final in his senior season, McBride played in goal, saving penalty kicks and scoring at the other end.

He had an illustrious playing career with Saint Louis University, from which he graduated in 1993 with a degree in secondary education. In his four seasons with the 'Billikens' he played eighty-nine games, scoring seventy-two goals plus forty assists.

Whilst studying, McBride was a 1992 second-team and a 1993 first-team 'All American' player (a national team from all universities). He won his first cap for the USA in 1993.

In 1994, he played briefly for the American minor league side **Milwaukee Rampage**, and in only eighteen games, he scored seventeen goals and assisted with another eighteen. Later in 1994, he left the United States to ply his trade in Germany with Second Division **VfL Wolfsburg**. McBride was making his senior debut at almost twenty-three, coming late into professional football after education. Brian struggled to find playing time with the club and, when the Major Soccer League (MLS) was created, chose to return to play in the United States.

Brian joined **Columbus Crew** for the inaugural season of the MSL in 1996, and played for eight years with them, amassing an impressive seventy-seven goals in 195 games in all competitions. In 1998, he took part in the World Cup in France and scored against Iran, but the States lost all three group matches.

The years with Columbus Crew were punctuated by two loan periods in England. The first came in 2000 when McBride played for Division One (second-tier) **Preston North End**, then managed by David Moyes. While McBride played well for the club, he sat out several games after having a blood clot surgically removed from his arm, which necessitated the removal of a rib to relieve pressure. The clot came as a result of a hard collision that McBride had suffered during his first game with Preston.

In the summer of 2002, McBride took part in his second World Cup finals in Japan and South Korea. This time the USA qualified at the end of the group stage which included a fine 3–2 win over Portugal in which he scored. They were then unluckily knocked out by a single goal by Germany at the next stage. Brian had become the first American to score at two World Cups, a feat subsequently emulated by Clint Dempsey (when at Fulham) and by Landon Donovan.

In the 2002–03 season, Premier League **Everton** were in the middle of a slump and Moyes, now in charge of the Toffees, sought the forward's services. During McBride's three months with the club, he did not disappoint, scoring four goals in eight games, including one on his debut. Everton sought to extend McBride's loan period but the MLS rejected it, preferring a permanent transfer.

In January 2004, Premiership **Fulham** bought thirty-one-year-old McBride's rights from MLS for a bargain £1m. The Cottagers were in desperate need of a presence up front with Marlet gone, Sava out of favour and Saha having just departed for a record fee. Brian made an immediate impact in his first game, coming on as a substitute in a league game with Tottenham at Loftus Road and scoring the winner, albeit a tap-in, to give Fulham a much-needed 2–1 victory. He played nineteen games during the last half of the 2003–04 season, scoring a total of five goals, including a brace on the final day in a 2–0 victory at Bolton Wanderers.

In the following season, with the arrival Andy Cole, McBride played thirty-one league games and six cup games, scoring nine goals. In those thirty-seven appearances, no fewer than twenty were made as an impact substitute. Early in the campaign, Fulham failed to utilise McBride's talents to the full, playing him mainly in League Cup matches. In consequence of that, McBride failed to find the net at all until April, but given a decent run in the side, he scored six league goals in the final nine matches, including a brace in the 6–0 win over Norwich City on the final day. The total also included a fabulous, acrobatic bicycle kick in the 3–1 win over Portsmouth and a bullet-header goal from fifteen yards in the 2–0 victory over Everton, one of the best headed goals seen at the Cottage in the last fifty years. During 2005 he was named in the MSL All-Time Best XI.

In 2005–06, partnering Collins John up front, he played thirty-eight league games and one cup game, scoring ten goals. He started well with four goals in the first seven league and cup matches. He added two further braces, the second of which was in a hugely entertaining 3–3 draw with Aston Villa, highlighted by typical, skilful McBride goals. He did not find the net again after February. McBride's original contract with Fulham was only to the end of that season; however, in March he signed a one-year extension, and he was now a highly popular and much-needed player. It was no surprise when he was named as the club's player of the year.

In the summer of 2006, McBride played in his third World Cup in Germany. The USA did not qualify, but held Italy to a creditable 1–1 draw. McBride was severely bloodied in that group stage match after being elbowed in the face by Daniele De Rossi; he needed three stitches. As a punishment, De Rossi was banned for four matches and fined. McBride then announced his retirement from international football. He had won ninety-five caps for his country and had scored thirty goals. He is currently the fourth highest goalscorer in American international football history.

Season 2006–07 promised much, but eventually turned into a relegation nail-biter for Fulham.

McBride was complemented now by Heidar Helguson and Collins John. Fulham won only twice after mid-December. McBride scored twelve goals that season (all single strikes), and Fulham seemed to be relatively safe but McBride suffered a rare goal drought, not scoring for the last three months of the season, and Fulham were only saved by a late win over Liverpool. McBride's twelve goals, even before his late barren spell, had seen him finish as top scorer, and in February he signed yet another one-year extension. Once again, Brian won the club's player of the year award.

The term 'legend' is sometimes over-used, but in only three seasons Brian McBride had truly earned the honour. Although he had no great pace, he had virtually every other skill available. He was excellent with positional play, astute with headed flick-ons, and had superb chest control and a fine first touch, especially for a six foot striker.

He was strongly built especially in the thighs and was great at hold-up play and holding off opponents. Despite being on the receiving end of a lot of physical fouls, he never once retaliated nor complained to referees. He also never feigned any injury, a refreshing sight to see at the top level. He was often praised for his sporting attitude.

Brian was an accomplished marksman with both feet, and could score from distance and close in. He was also very good at anticipating crosses and could easily and quickly adjust his body position. He was possibly the best header of a ball at Fulham in the last half century with some headed goals being truly spectacular and breathtaking. McBride now had so much titanium plate in his head due to facial injuries sustained whilst playing with such a brave style that he regularly set off alarms at airport security desks.

Finally he had a typical American work ethic, and gave his all for the cause for the full ninety minutes. His battling and hard-working attitude through all adversities endeared him quickly to Fulham fans. Off the field he was as good as he was on it, humble, polite, highly articulate, humorous and very willing to engage with Fulham supporters after games and at social functions.

With such an all-round reputation, he was given the Fulham captaincy at the start of the 2007–08 season. Sadly a disaster was just around the corner, when, in the course of scoring against Middlesbrough in just the third game of the season, McBride dislocated his kneecap and was carried off in acute pain, though still applauding the Fulham crowd! He missed five months of the season and this would have a huge impact on Fulham's season under Lawrie Sanchez and latterly Roy Hodgson.

When Brian did return, his goals were critical, the only goal in a 1–0 win over Everton, the first goal in the 2–0 win at Reading and finally the most important of all, the diving header from a Jimmy Bullard free kick that beat former Fulham goalkeeper Maik Taylor and gave Fulham a head start in the relegation six-pointer against Birmingham City; Fulham eventually

ended up 2–0 victors. It was his final Fulham goal.

The goals kept Fulham up, and McBride's presence had been crucial. Appropriately, his final game was the historic win at Portsmouth that ensured Fulham's survival.

However, during the close season of 2008, McBride, now thirty-six, announced that he would be leaving the UK to return to the United States to play out the sunset of his career in the MLS. Brian had become such a popular figure that the club renamed a bar inside Craven Cottage 'McBride's' in June 2009.

In the summer, McBride was named as one of the three over-age players on the USA Olympic team and served as captain. He made his **Chicago Fire** debut in August 2008, coming on as a second-half substitute against DC United, and scored his first goal against Houston Dynamo. He then scored the first goal in the MLS play-off Eastern Conference championship against Columbus Crew, his former club. However, Chicago lost that game 2–1 and were prevented from being in the MLS play-off final. He scored six in that part season.

McBride then scored seven goals during the 2009 season, and in September 2010 he announced that he would retire in October at the end of that MLS season. He scored his eightieth MLS goal during his final league match before being intentionally substituted, leaving the pitch for a final time to a standing ovation. His sixty-six games with Chicago Fire had brought forth a further nineteen career goals.

In June 2012, aged forty, he was one of several former professional footballers who agreed to come out of retirement to join Wembley FC to play in their FA Cup campaign for the new season. McBride was supported by fellow former internationals Parlour, Keown, Caniggia, Le Saux, plus Seaman (goalkeeping coach) and would be managed by Terry Venables. Wembley were being featured in a television documentary as they endeavoured to help the club play at Wembley Stadium. Sadly, Wembley were knocked out in a replay by Uxbridge.

Back home in 2012, McBride launched and established the Brian McBride Soccer Academy which is based in Lake Zurich, Illinois. This was founded to find and develop the next generation of American football strikers. He has also become the first-ever spokesman for the Central Ohio Diabetes Association. During his playing time, he donated $100 to the association for every goal and assist he tallied for the US national team. He lost a family member to the disease and so the cause remains close to his heart.

BRIAN McBRIDE
Fulham career – all competitions

Season	Appearances	Goals	Home	Away
2003–2004	19	5	1	4
2004–2005	37	9	5	4
2005–2006	39	10	6	4
2006–2007	42	12	7	5
2007–2008	16	4	3	1
Total	153	40	22	18

*Total career **league** appearances–156, and **league** goals–37.*

Collins John

An unfulfilled talent, he was Fulham's top scorer in one bright season.

Collins John was born in Zwandru, Liberia, but his family emigrated to the Netherlands after the murder of his father during the Liberian Civil War. He had two brothers, Paddy and Ola, who also became footballers. Ola recently played against Fulham for FC Twente in the last European campaign and is currently with Benfica.

The striker began as a youth with DES Nijverdal, before moving to **FC Twente** where he made the first team at only seventeen. In just a season and a half, he made thirty-five league appearances scoring an impressive eleven times, and nine in eighteen matches in his second partial season. In that second season, he also began to win international honours with Holland, playing in the Under-21 side.

He was signed by **Fulham** in January 2004 for a fee thought to be in the region of £600,000 where he was introduced to the Cottage faithful by John Collins, his reverse namesake. There was initially a tide of admiration and sympathy for the young footballer who had reached the top after surviving and witnessing such brutalities. He was needed as well as it seemed his youth and pace would complement the other skills possessed by Brian McBride.

His debut for the club came as a substitute against Chelsea at Stamford Bridge in March. His first goals arrived in only his second match, again as a substitute, at the Walkers Stadium where he scored two late goals, as Fulham beat Leicester City 2–0. Forty-eight hours later came another brace, this time at Loftus Road against Blackburn Rovers; unfortunately his evening was spoilt by the team's comical defending that cost Fulham points in a 3–4 defeat. He finished the season with those four goals from only three starts and five substitute appearances. During the close season, he made his senior Dutch debut, appearing in a 2–2 friendly against Sweden in August. He then made his second appearance for the Netherlands when they played in a friendly match against Liechtenstein.

In the 2004–05 season it looked as if things would continue in style. On the opening day, John netted the first goal of the season for the Whites that gave Fulham a creditable 1–1 draw against Manchester City, but he reverted to substitute after starting five of the first six games. Indifferent form and knocks saw him in and out of the side and he scored only once more before Christmas, in a memorable Mark Crossley inspired 4–1 win at Newcastle in November.

The aftermath of a John goal at Charlton in October 2005.

He added two more in the FA Cup fourth-round ties against Derby County. He scored twice more towards the end of the season against Chelsea and Everton but overall his season had seemed an anti-climax. He had played in thirty-four games that season, but twenty were as a substitute.

Things improved for Collins in the 2005–06 season, though he started the season as a used substitute in six of the first seven games. He notched up four goals in those six matches, and one of them, a volley from his weaker foot against Middlesbrough in November, was named goal of the month by the BBC and was in the running for goal of the season. In his first full start, he scored in the 2–3 home defeat by Manchester United. He began to score regularly with a brace against Sunderland in a 2–1 home win in January, followed by another couple in the 6–1 thrashing of West Bromwich Albion in February, and in between he scored Fulham's goal in the depressing 1–2 home defeat by Leyton Orient in the FA Cup.

He netted three more singles before the end of the season in the space of eight matches, including a goal at Anfield in a 1–5 defeat where he was booked seemingly for a brawl in the tunnel after the final whistle. The referee, however, didn't report the incident. John managed to finish the season as Fulham's top scorer with twelve in all competitions. He had appeared in thirty-eight out of the forty-one possible matches, but once again twenty of those appearances had been as a substitute. He was voted Fulham's player of the season.

His career reached its peak in the summer of 2006 when he was part of the Netherlands U-21 squad that won the 2006 European Championship in Portugal. He was still just twenty. In all, John netted four times in nine U-21 games for Holland.

That was as good as it got. John started six of the first seven matches of the following season, 2006–07, but failed to score and returned to substitute. He would only start another three games. His only goal of the season and his last for Fulham came away against Manchester City in a 1–3 defeat in November.

Collins John appeared to have all the attributes to take him to the top: athletic build, pace and strength, an ability to play wide or inside, an eye for goal and a hunger to succeed. However this quickly seemed to dissipate. He was often seen as lazy, unwilling to put any effort into winning the ball back or tracking back. A number of attacks foundered as John was caught offside.

His body language was frequently poor and he appeared to be complaining and gesturing about a perceived lack of service. The initial goodwill towards him from both team-mates and fans seemed to go up in smoke. It was thought by some that being a Premiership footballer had possibly gone to his head, and he thought that he had already 'arrived'. Others considered that he had been further distracted by the bright lights of London.

From this point his career started to unravel dramatically; he was not even seriously considered by new manager Lawrie Sanchez at the beginning of the 2007–08 season. His time at Fulham that season was limited to three substitute appearances. His final appearance was in the exciting 3–3 draw with Tottenham Hotspur at the beginning of September. In 108 games in total for Fulham, he had made sixty-four of those as a substitute (nearly two-thirds!).

John signed for **Leicester City** in October 2007 on a three-month loan deal. He made his debut in a 1–0 defeat against Sheffield United a few hours later, and scored his first league goal in a 2–0 win over Barnsley soon after. John scored his last goal for the Foxes against Colchester United six days later in a 1–1 away draw. He returned to Fulham after making just eleven league appearances for Leicester. In January 2008, he joined **Watford** on a loan deal until the end of the season with the option of a permanent move after that. He struggled with his fitness during his time at the club, making only three starts and two substitute appearances. In April 2008 he returned to Fulham after tearing a thigh muscle. On the 2008 transfer deadline day, he moved to **NEC Nijmegen** on a one-year loan deal, with the Dutch side also obtaining a transfer option.

The next four years followed the same downward spiral. In Nijmegen, John suffered with continual problems. Although he was important as a substitute in two UEFA Cup matches, he failed to make an impression in the Dutch league in 2008–09. After just four months and five appearances, he went on trial at Charlton Athletic but was not offered a contract.

Back in Nijmegen, he was suspended and then demoted to the reserve squad by the manager. In March, John returned to Fulham, as neither NEC nor John saw any reason for continuing the loan. That same month, John requested to train with Dutch side Heracles Almeno alongside his brother Paddy until the end of the season. The request was denied by Fulham, because John had no intention to play for the Dutch club the following season. John now appeared to be out of condition and lacking match fitness.

After being freed by Fulham, he chose to join Belgian Pro League side **KSV Roeselare** signing a two-year contract at the start of the 2009–10 season. He took part in ten of the first twelve games. However, just three months into that arrangement he was suspended and demoted to the reserve squad for disciplinary reasons. Two weeks later, Roeselare terminated his contract after eleven games without a goal. Although there are two sides to every story, John was perceived to be 'difficult' to deal with.

A month later, he joined MSL club **Chicago Fire** during their pre-season training camp with a view to signing before the start of the 2010 MLS season if there had been a successful trial. In March 2010, Chicago Fire signed him on a free transfer, following an endorsement from USA player Brian McBride. Although he scored in only his third game for Fire, he had a disappointing season in the MLS, and after just three goals in seventeen games, John was released

by Chicago in November 2010. Two months later, he joined **Gabala FC i**n Azerbaijan, given another career opportunity by their manager, ex-Arsenal star Tony Adams. After failing to revive his career in Azerbaijan, playing only three games and not scoring, John handed in a transfer request. In the summer of 2011, he went on trial with Nottingham Forest and flew to Portugal with them for a pre-season break but was not offered a deal.

After six months out of football, John signed a one-year contract with Iran Pro League side **Mes Sarcheshmeh** in December 2011. After just four games and without a goal he was released six months later. He attempted a deal with Genclik Gücü S.K. in Northern Cyprus, but the transfer did not materialise.

In desperation, in September 2012 John joined English League Two (fourth-division) side **Barnet**. He made his debut against Plymouth Argyle, but was substituted after just fifteen minutes due to a thigh injury. He also played in the FA Cup against Oxford United. He made only two appearances and played just seventy-five minutes for the club, and after a string of injuries he had his contract terminated by mutual consent in January 2013. In June, he returned to his native Holland and joined league side **Go Ahead Eagles** on trial. Now aged just twenty-seven, his once very promising career already looks over.

COLLINS JOHN
Fulham career – all competitions

Season	Appearances	Goals	Home	Away
2003–2004	8	4	2	2
2004–2005	34	6	2	4
2005–2006	38	12	7	5
2006–2007	25	1	0	1
2007–2008	3	0	0	0
Total	108	23	11	12

Total league appearances to date–112, and league goals–22.

Andrew Cole

Two spells at Fulham, top scorer one season, over 230 career league goals.

Cole could be placed in this book in two places – in the Nineties, when he spent a short period on loan from Arsenal, or here in the 'Noughties' when he spent a full season at Craven Cottage after a permanent move.

Andrew **(Andy) Cole** was born in Nottingham but started his career as a youth player for First Division **Arsenal** after leaving school in 1988, signing professional forms in 1989. He made his only league appearance for the Gunners, aged nineteen, as a substitute in the home match against Sheffield United in December 1990 which Arsenal won 4–1. He also made a substitute appearance against Tottenham Hotspur in the Charity Shield in 1991.

Early the next season he was loaned to **Fulham**, making his debut in a 3–0 win over Swansea City in September 1991. He opened his account the following week with Fulham's first goal in a 2–2 draw at Stoke City. His second goal came in a 3–0 win away at Bolton Wanderers in October. His third was during a 1–2 defeat at home to Stockport County in November, in the last of his thirteen league games on loan.

He returned to Highbury for six months before being sold to Second Division **Bristol City** on transfer deadline day in a £500,000 deal making him, at the time, the club's most expensive signing. He scored eight goals during what remained of the 1991–92 season and during the 1992–93 season he netted twelve in twenty-nine matches.

He was only at Ashton Gate for one calendar year and around deadline day, in one of the shock moves of the season, Division One **Newcastle United** under manager Kevin Keegan (later manager of Fulham) paid City a club record £1.75m to take Cole to Tyneside. It proved an instant success as Cole netted twelve goals in his first twelve games including hat-tricks against Barnsley and Leicester City. This latter came on the final day of the season in a 7–1 victory as the Geordies romped away with the title. By this time, Cole had been awarded three England U-20 and eight England U-21 caps, scoring four times.

Partnering Peter Beardsley (another to join Fulham later on), the lethal pairing took the Premiership by storm. He scored his first goal of the 1993–94 season at Old Trafford and ended the season with an amazing thirty-four league goals. This included four braces as well as hat-tricks against the mighty Liverpool (3–0) in November and Coventry (5–1) in February. He scored a total of forty-one in all competitions, breaking the record set by Hughie Gallacher almost seventy years previously. Cole actually scored in twenty-eight (70%) of *all* the league games. Newcastle finished third, qualifying for the UEFA Cup and putting them back in Europe for the first time in over twenty years. Cole was voted the PFA young player of the year and took the Premier League Golden Boot award.

Cole scored nine Premier League goals in eighteen games at the start of the 1994–95 including six in the opening five games and scored a hat-trick against Royal Antwerp in the UEFA Cup. He also was awarded an England 'B' cap, scoring on his international debut in a 2–0 win over Ireland 'B'. In January, however, Cole was sensationally sold in a shock deal to **Manchester United**, a transfer worth £6m–£7m cash plus £1m-rated Keith Gillespie moving in the opposite direction, setting a new record for the most expensive British transfer. The move caused fury amongst fans on Tyneside, but Keegan was unrepentant. In all competitions, Cole had hit an amazing sixty-eight goals in eighty-four games for Newcastle giving him an average strike rate of four goals in every five games.

Despite joining halfway through that season, Cole still managed to score twelve goals in just eighteen Premier League games for United. This included two braces and in February an incredible five goals in a 9–0 annihilation of Ipswich Town, making him the first player to score five goals in a Premier League game. Because he was cup-tied he missed United's FA Cup final defeat against Everton. In March, he was awarded his first full international cap, in a friendly against Uruguay (0–0).

With such high expectations, Cole's first full season with Manchester United in 1995–96 proved to be troublesome, as he struggled to find his free-scoring form following the return of Eric Cantona after his long suspension. Though Cole scored in four successive games during December, he was heckled by fans and panned by critics alike across much of the season for scoring only thirteen times and missing many goalscoring opportunities. However, he scored the winner in the FA Cup semi-final against Chelsea to send United to Wembley again. He also scored the second goal in United's 3–0 defeat of Middlesbrough on the final day of the season to help them win the Premier League title for the third time in four years. He also played in their FA Cup final 1–0 victory over Liverpool to become part of England's first ever side to achieve the double twice.

Before the start of the 1996–97 season, Cole had to deal with being offered to Blackburn Rovers as bait

in a £12m bid that would have brought Alan Shearer to Old Trafford but the offer was turned down and Shearer opted for Newcastle instead. Despite this, Cole stayed to justify his place at the club. Early in the season, Cole had both legs broken in a reserve game following a crude tackle from Liverpool's Neil Ruddock. He somehow managed to recover by December and still play a part in twenty Premier League games that season. Cole then ended the season strongly with five goals in six games in the league and one in the Champions League. He then scored the title-sealing goal in a landmark 3–1 win for United at Anfield, the scene of his broken legs just half a season earlier, thereby assisting them to their fourth title in five years, and winning another Premier League title medal. In the summer, after a two-year absence, he won his second England cap, against Italy.

Following Cantona's retirement, the 1997–98 season saw Cole emerge as first-choice striker once again, and he discovered his best form for the club, scoring fifteen goals including a spell of eleven in ten matches. Despite this, and rarely for them, United finished trophy-less after a shock FA Cup departure at Barnsley. Cole had also netted five FA Cup goals. He achieved several personal landmarks in this campaign – scoring his first European hat-trick for the club in an away match at Feyenoord, as well as ending

the season as runner-up to Dennis Bergkamp in the PFA Players' Player of the Year award. Despite this accreditation, and being the leading goalscorer in that season with twenty-five in all competitions, Cole was omitted from England's 1998 World Cup squad by manager Glenn Hoddle.

During the 1998–99 season Cole faced stiff competition from new signings Dwight Yorke, Teddy Sheringham and Ole Gunnar Solskjaer but ended up developing an immensely successful partnership with Yorke. Cole and Yorke contributed fifty-three goals between them and were rated as one of the most feared attacking partnerships in Europe. Cole played a key role in the side's unique treble of the Premier League title, FA Cup and UEFA Champions League. He put away seventeen league goals which included five braces, his final league goal being the winner in a 2–1 victory over Spurs on the last day that secured the title for United again. The season also saw him score his 100th Premier League goal.

He scored twice in the FA Cup including the only goal in the fifth-round victory over Fulham, and United defeated Newcastle 2–0 at Wembley. He also scored five goals in Europe which helped seal United's place in the final for the first time in over thirty years. United won the memorable final against Bayern Munich 2–1.

Cole was again the principal striker in 1999–2000 with eighteen league goals in twenty-eight Premier League games. This included three braces and a four-goal haul in a 5–1 victory over his previous club Newcastle United. He collected his fourth Premier League title medal in five seasons, and scored more than twenty goals in all competitions for the third successive season. He also joined an elite group by scoring his 100th goal for the club in a 2–2 draw against Wimbledon. An injury saw his hopes of playing in the European Championship 2000 disappear.

Another Premiership title followed in the 2000–01 season when, despite suffering from an injury that restricted his appearances to only half of the season, Cole scored thirteen goals in all competitions. He netted six in his first nine league games, and also another hat-trick in the qualifying stages of the European Cup in a 5–1 home win over RSC Anderlecht. The goal he scored in the knock-out stages against Valencia made him, at the time, Manchester United's all-time record goalscorer in European competition. In his thirteenth game for England in March 2001, Cole scored his only international goal, in a World Cup qualification match which ended in a 3–1 win over Albania.

The following season saw Cole face extra competition from new signing Ruud van Nistelrooy.

Despite this, he managed to score four goals in five matches early in the season. He was also awarded his fifteenth and final England cap in the 2–2 World Cup qualification draw with Greece at Old Trafford.

He left Manchester United after seven years, signing for Premiership **Blackburn Rovers** after falling behind in the pecking order and into a 'super sub' role. Blackburn paid a fee of £8m, and within two months of arriving at Ewood he had collected a League Cup winner's medal, scoring the winning goal for Rovers in the final against Tottenham Hotspur who were managed by the former England manager, and open critic of Cole, Glenn Hoddle. This victory meant that, in the space of seven seasons, Cole had won all three domestic trophies plus a European trophy. He ended the season with a total of thirteen goals in just twenty games for Blackburn in all competitions, including two on the final day of the season against Fulham. After failing to be selected for the 2002 European Championship squad, Cole announced his retirement from international football.

Rovers finished sixth in the table at the end of the following season, 2002–03, and qualified for the UEFA Cup. That campaign saw Cole reunited with Dwight Yorke, who had signed for Blackburn from Manchester United for £2m in July. By his standards, it was a pretty barren season and he managed just seven goals. This total was enhanced by six goals in the two domestic cup competitions.

Cole also had a frustrating time in the 2003–04 season. It started well with a brace against Wolves on the opening day (5–1), two more in a creditable draw at Chelsea (2–2) and a fifth against Portsmouth, but the goals dried up as Rovers dropped into the bottom half of the Premier League table, finally finishing fifteenth. Cole was the club's top scorer with eleven goals, but his fractious relationship with manager Graeme Souness hit rock bottom after Cole reported him to the PFA accusing him of unfair treatment, and a departure was almost inevitable.

Thirteen years after spending two months on loan at **Fulham**, Cole returned to Craven Cottage for the 2004–05 season, joining them on a one-year contract. He started well with two goals on his home debut that saw the Whites win 2–0 against Bolton Wanderers. He scored four in his first six games. The fourth goal came in a fiery and volatile match at the Hawthorns where Fulham drew 1–1 as, following the dismissal of Papa Bouba Diop, Cole was also sent off following a verbal and physical confrontation with Albion's Neil Clement (son of former Fulham player Dave Clement).

He scored regularly throughout the season and some of his goals were important, including the clincher in a 2–0 win over Spurs at the Cottage, and the only goal of the game that saw Fulham victorious at Norwich. This was followed by a brace against Crystal Palace on New Year's Day. He scored the first in a valuable 2–1 victory at St Andrews and the equaliser that saw Fulham eventually win 3–1 against Portsmouth. He also netted Fulham's final goal of the campaign, the sixth in a 6–0 thumping of Norwich City. He finished as the club's top scorer with thirteen in all competitions and scored one of the goals of the season against Liverpool. Despite this successful season with the Cottagers, he decided to leave the club, as his family wanted to return to the north-west of England.

Cole signed for Premier League **Manchester City** at the beginning of the 2005–06 season and enjoyed a good start to his career at Eastlands with seven goals in his first twelve games. But he added just a couple more and his time at City was truncated by an injury received in February that caused him to miss the last three months of the season. After recovering, and despite signing a new contract, Cole made a strange decision to return south and he signed for Premier League **Portsmouth** on transfer deadline day for an undisclosed fee expected to rise to £1m depending on appearances.

He scored his first league goal for his new club in the 2006–07 season in a 2–0 win at home to West Ham in October plus an inevitable goal against former club Fulham in a 1–1 draw. However, he added only one further goal and struggled to break into Harry Redknapp's side and in March he dropped down a division, signing for **Birmingham City** on loan until the end of the season. Cole returned to Portsmouth after only five appearances in the Midlands and one goal against Wolverhampton Wanderers. Cole was released by Portsmouth at the end of the season.

With his career in decline, Cole signed a one-year contract with Premiership **Sunderland**, reuniting him with Dwight Yorke for the third time. He did not appear in a match in the 2007–08 season until the end of November, his first game being in a 1–7 defeat at Everton. After ten league games without a goal, he was loaned out to Championship side **Burnley**. He scored six goals there, including a fine hat-trick in a 4–2 win at Queens Park Rangers but, after returning to Sunderland, he was released at the end of the season.

In July 2008, Cole signed a one-year contract with Championship **Nottingham Forest**, his twelfth and hometown club. However, after only eleven appearances and no goals into the 2008–09 season, Forest confirmed that Cole's contract had been cancelled by mutual consent at the end of October. Two weeks later, Cole announced his retirement from football, bringing an end to a nineteen-year career. Cole has the satisfaction of being the second-highest goalscorer in Premier League history. In his career, he scored a total of 187 Premier League goals, placing him behind Alan Shearer who netted 260 goals.

After a year out of the game, Cole worked under former Newcastle and Fulham team-mate Lee Clark coaching the Huddersfield Town club's strikers. In 2011 he was invited back by Sir Alex Ferguson to Old Trafford to work with the club's younger players, whilst completing his coaching badges. He is currently working with MUTV as a pundit.

ANDREW COLE
Fulham career – all competitions

Season	Appearances	Goals	Home	Away
1991–1992 (loan)	13	3	1	2
2004–2005	39	13	7	6
Total	52	16	8	8

*Total career **league** appearances–**509**, and **league** goals–**230**.*

Heidar Helguson

Icelandic warrior and penalty-taker, with a Fulham hat-trick.

Heidar Helguson was born in Dalvik, Iceland and started his career in the Icelandic league system with his hometown **UMFS Dalvik**. He began as an eight-year-old and spent six years in the junior and development squads. Amazingly he made his debut for the club's reserve team at only thirteen. He was given his first-team debut in 1993 when he just was fifteen years old. He scored five goals in eleven league appearances in that season and his creditable performances earned him a transfer to **Þróttur** (aka Knattspyrnufélagið Þróttur, or Þróttur Reykjavík) in 1994, aged only sixteen.

In his three seasons playing for Þróttur, Helguson scored thirty-one goals in fifty-one league appearances. He also represented the Iceland U-19 team eighteen times, scoring twice. His eye-catching performances generated interest from several European, English and Scottish clubs and eventually earned him a transfer abroad to Norway where he joined **Lillestrøm SK**.

Heidar arrived at Lillestrøm in the autumn of the 1998 season. He made his first-team debut in October, curiously wearing number 1 on his shirt. In his debut season he managed just two goals, but during the following season, 1999, Heidar became one of the great surprises in Norwegian football when he scored sixteen league goals. Heidar was a very popular player in Norway, and even had his own fan club named *The Helgusonsons*. He scored seven in his first nine games, and his overall total included a four-goal haul in a 6–1 away victory at Stabeck IF, and also three two-goal matches. In his time at Norway, he also won six U-21 caps for Iceland, scoring once.

Helguson then moved to England to join Premiership **Watford** in 1999, with Lillestrøm receiving a transfer fee of £1.5m, a club record for Watford at the time. Manager Graham Taylor signed Helguson midway through the 1999–2000 season to boost the struggling club's striking department. Heidar made an impressive debut at home to Liverpool, scoring in that game and in the next game too, against Bradford City. He scored four more times that season. However, his six goals in sixteen games were not enough to keep Watford up, and the Hertfordshire club were relegated after only one year in the Premiership. He also racked up five cautions in those sixteen games.

Back in the second division (Division One) for 2000–01, Helguson was part of a Watford side that was undefeated for the first fifteen games of the season, topping the league. However, when the side's form slumped at Christmas, Heidar's form also suffered, one of several bouts during his early time at Watford, and he was well below his best for a large percentage of that campaign. At the end of the season, Taylor retired and was replaced by Gianluca Vialli,

who used Heidar as a wing back on occasions, but he still finished the 2001–02 season with nine goals in thirty-seven games in all competitions.

With former Fulham player and manager Ray Lewington in charge of the Hornets for the next season, Helguson showed a marked improvement. Although he did not play until late September due to injury, he finished the season as Watford's top scorer with thirteen goals from thirty-four games, including goals in their run to the FA Cup semi-finals. Helguson's involvement in the first half of Watford's 2003–04 season was curtailed by serious injury, but on his return he put in some notable performances, finishing with nine goals in just twenty-four matches.

The next season, his sixth, was his best in a Watford shirt. Relatively free of injury, he scored twenty goals in all competitions, including three two-goal matches. He picked up the Goal of the Season, Display of the Season and Player of the Season awards. His physical style however had seen him collect no fewer than nine yellow cards. Inevitably, his goal tally brought about interest from Premier League clubs and with Watford needing money, a transfer offer from **Fulham** was accepted. Helguson had scored and impressed when the teams had met in a third-round FA Cup tie at Vicarage Road in January. Helguson was purchased to replace Andrew Cole who had left Fulham after just one season.

Heidar was confined mostly to the substitutes bench at the beginning of the 2005–06 league campaign, as Chris Coleman was experimenting with any two from three of Brian McBride, Collins John and Helguson, but he made his first start and scored his first goal for Fulham in the 5–4 League Cup victory over Lincoln City. He also netted in the third round of the League Cup against West Bromwich Albion in October as Fulham went out 2–3.

He was not given a league start until December, but responded with his best spell as a Fulham player with eight goals from ten games. Linking up well with Brian McBride, he scored goals with head and feet and took Fulham's penalties too (his first two Fulham goals in his first two full starts both came from penalties). As one would expect from an Icelandic player, he was 'ice-cool' from the spot. The eight-goal total included a hat-trick in a 6–1 home win against a hapless West Bromwich Albion side in January. After that, he scored just once more that season, in the final match (a 1–0 win over Middlesbrough). He finished as second highest scorer with eleven, one fewer than Brian McBride and one more than Collins John.

Heidar was a good stop-gap forward for Fulham. He was strong, brave and direct and gave his all, and he was also exceptionally good in the air considering

he was only five feet ten. He always gave defenders a game to remember and was good at creating space for more gifted players. He did though have a number of limitations. He had little pace and his dribbling and balls skills were a little clumsy at the top level. Also he sometimes took the physical side of the game to excess, receiving many warnings and bookings.

The 2006–07 season saw him score (some reports give it as an own goal) on the opening day in a poor 1–5 defeat at Old Trafford, in the 1–2 defeat by Wycombe in the League Cup in September and a third goal against his former club Watford in an exciting 3–3 draw in early October. But he only netted twice more, his final goal being the first in a 2–1 win over Newcastle United at Craven Cottage in early February. His final game was the last of the season, a 1–3 loss

at Middlesbrough. He had taken part in thirty of the thirty-eight league games that season, but almost half of those were as substitute. He had also contrived to pick up no fewer than ten bookings.

In this Fulham team, it looked as if the quality of the Premiership was just a bridge too far for Heidar, and when the Cottagers signed David Healy and Diomansy Kamara in the summer, he left Fulham to join Premiership rivals **Bolton Wanderers** on a three-year contract for an undisclosed fee. He made his Bolton debut as a substitute on the opening day of the 2007–08 season against Newcastle United, and four days later he returned to Fulham for the first time since leaving and got on the scoresheet at the Cottage following a dropped ball howler from Fulham goalkeeper Tony Warner, but Bolton lost 2–1.

It was four months before Heidar got any more playing time, mainly due to injury and some loss of form, but his return was necessary as Bolton had sold Nicolas Anelka to Chelsea earlier that month. His first appearance back in the side was a goalless draw against Fulham where he came off the substitutes bench for the last eight minutes of the game. He scored his first goal for Bolton since coming back from injury four days later against Reading in a 2–0 win. Bolton confirmed in the close season that they had sent Heidar over to Belgium for more surgery in order to have him back for pre-season training.

He played a League Cup game and just one further league game for Bolton in 2008–09, against Fulham in a 2–1 defeat, before he was on the move again. It is an interesting statistic that Helguson played just eight games for Bolton Wanderers and three of those were against Fulham. In November, he joined Championship side **Queens Park Rangers** on an emergency loan and in January 2009 the move was made permanent for an undisclosed fee. He played twenty games in all, and scored five goals including two braces in the first ten games, but he also picked up five cautions. He played in the opening five games of the following season scoring once, before he was loaned out in September, returning to his first club in England, Championship side **Watford**, initially for three months.

He was once again a success at Watford, with five goals in his first four games. In January 2010 the loan was extended for the remainder of the season. The goals dwindled a little, but he ended up with eleven goals in twenty-nine games – and six further cautions.

Returning to Loftus Road, Helguson played regularly for Queens Park Rangers in the 2010–11 season, scoring thirteen goals and helping them to secure promotion back to the Premier League as champions. Heidar featured regularly under manager Neil Warnock the following season, and became a Rangers legend by scoring the winning goal from a penalty in a 1–0 victory against Chelsea. This was Rangers' first win over their west London rivals in over fifteen years. Despite missing most of the second half of the season with a groin injury, Heidar finished as QPR's top goalscorer for the season with nine goals in all competitions, helping them to secure Premier League survival on the last day of the season.

He subsequently joined Championship **Cardiff City** in August 2012 on a one-year contract. He scored seven in his first nineteen games and remained consistently in the Bluebirds' first-team squad all season. He was delighted to take part in the team that won promotion to the Premier League in May 2013. Despite this success, it was a surprise when his contract was not renewed. At thirty-six, Heidar Helguson is currently unattached and without a club after fourteen years in England.

From his time in Norway until 2011, Heidar earned fifty-five caps for Iceland scoring thirteen times.

He made his debut for Iceland in April 1999 during a friendly match against Malta, coming on as a substitute. After playing in a friendly against Spain in August 2006, a long spell outside the national team followed, and Heidar announced his retirement from international football in June 2007. However, in August 2008, he announced a return to international football and was immediately selected in the Icelandic team to face Norway and Scotland a few days later. He scored a goal against Norway in the 2–2 World Cup qualifier. He also scored in the UEFA Euro qualifying match against Portugal in October 2010.

HEIDAR HELGUSON
up to July 2013

Fulham career – all competitions

Season	Appearances	Goals	Home	Away
2005–2006	29	11	7	4
2006–2007	34	5	3	2
Total	63	16	10	6

Total career **league** appearances–**380**, and **league** goals–**114**.

Clint Dempsey

Top-scoring American in the Premiership, with two Fulham hat-tricks.

Clint Dempsey was born in Nacogdoches in Texas and for much of his childhood his family lived in a mobile home environment. His older brother Ryan was offered a trial for the Dallas Texans, an elite youth football club, and he brought along Clinton, who was spotted while passing the time juggling a ball on the sidelines and was signed up. Dempsey became an outstanding member of the Texans at an early age, but had to stop attending due to his family's time and more importantly money constraints, as his eldest sister Jennifer had progressed to becoming a ranked youth tennis player. Several parents of his team-mates with the Texans offered to assist the Dempsey family with expenses and travel, allowing him to rejoin the club.

In November 1995, Jennifer, then just sixteen, succumbed to a brain aneurysm. Dempsey was devastated with the family's loss and later explained that this life-changing event helped him develop a deeper motivation to pursue football, in honour of his sister. He went on to be the captain and top scorer of the Texans. He then attended Furman University studying for a health and exercise qualification whilst becoming a key player for the university's 'Paladins' football team.

After graduation, Dempsey travelled east to Massachusetts to join the **New England Revolution**. In his first season, he missed only one of twenty-four games scoring seven goals. He helped Revolution to the Eastern Conference (league) finals and earned the 2004 MSL Rookie of the Year honour. He also made his senior debut for the USA team in November.

In the 2005 season, Dempsey contributed ten goals and nine assists in twenty-six league games. He also scored the match-winning goal in the Eastern Conference final on his way to an appearance in the MSL Cup final. In 2006, Dempsey added eight more goals, but missed a significant period during the play-offs due to injury. He came on as a substitute in the MSL Cup final, but the Revolution lost their second consecutive final, this time in a penalty shoot-out. In May, Dempsey was named in the USA squad for the 2006 World Cup in Germany. He was the only American player to score a goal in the tournament, with his equalising goal in a 1–2 loss to Ghana.

In December 2006 **Fulham**, under Chris Coleman, offered MSL $4m for the transfer of Dempsey, and he became another American addition to the Cottagers squad which already included US internationals Brian McBride and Carlos Bocanegra. He was granted a work permit as Fulham announced his signing on a long-term deal. At the time this made Dempsey the most expensive American import into the Premier League.

He made his Fulham debut as a substitute in a 1–1 home draw against Spurs in January 2007. Clint's first goal for Fulham in May was most important when, as a substitute, he clipped home a cross which turned out to be the only goal in a home win over Liverpool. This goal effectively saved Fulham from relegation and guaranteed their place in the top flight for the following season. He played his only full game on the final day of the season at Middlesbrough.

Dempsey was not in the starting line-up for the first three matches of the 2007–08 season, but after a long-term injury to Brian McBride, he came into the side as a midfielder/striker and he responded immediately with three league goals in as many games. After a few games without goals, he netted three more in nine games.

After a goal against Spurs over Christmas following the sacking of Sanchez, Dempsey did not score again that season. However, he remained an integral part of the side that initially slipped into danger and then recovered to beat Portsmouth 1–0 on the final day of the season, securing Premier League status for another year. Having scored six goals he ended the season as Fulham's joint top goalscorer with no fewer than three other players. During the close season, Fulham announced that Dempsey had signed a contract

extension which would keep him at the club until the summer of 2010.

Initially it was difficult to pigeon-hole Dempsey into a position. He could seemingly play in midfield and out on either wing, but did not appear to relish the role of an out-and-out striker on his own up front. He could make strong impacts on games, but could just as easily drift out of them as well.

At the start of the 2008–09 season, Clint rarely made the Fulham starting line-up in the first three months under Roy Hodgson, but scored his first goal in a 1–1 away draw at Portsmouth in October after coming on as a substitute. His lack of playing time meant that his place in the USA national team was also in jeopardy. He scored his first home goal of the season in a 3–0 win over Middlesbrough in December and eight days later he endeared himself to the home crowd by scoring his first brace in the Christmas local derby with Chelsea which included a last-minute headed equaliser in a 2–2 draw.

In February, Dempsey scored the first FA Cup goal of his career in a 2–1 home win over Swansea City in a fifth-round replay. He added another brace as Fulham came from a goal down to beat Manchester City 3–1 away from home. Dempsey ended as Fulham's second highest goalscorer that season with eight goals. These goals helped Fulham secure a seventh-place finish in the Premier League, the highest in the club's history, and confirmed their qualification for the newly formed UEFA Europa League for the following season.

Dempsey re-discovered his form in the summer of 2009 with the USA in the Confederations Cup. He scored in the final qualifying match against Egypt, in the semi-final against Spain and in the final against Brazil although the USA eventually lost the match. At the start of the season, Dempsey signed another contract extension to remain with Fulham until 2012–13.

At the beginning of the 2009–10 season, he scored his first goal in European competition when netting Fulham's second goal in a 3–1 win against Amkar Perm in the play-off round. Even if his best position in the side was still unknown, Clint was now more or less a regular player in the side, and saw his best scoring spell in a Fulham shirt over October and November with five goals in five league games including two in a 3–0 home victory over Blackburn Rovers. In January, Dempsey suffered a suspected knee ligament injury in a 2–0 away defeat at Ewood Park and missed the next two months of the season.

In March, he came off the bench in the second leg of the last-sixteen tie with Juventus in the Europa League and, with the aggregate score tied at 4–4, scored a superb winner with a long, curling chip shot over the goalkeeper. Fulham won the game 4–1 and the goal was arguably the most famous in Fulham's history. Clint scored two more league goals that season and in May he replaced Bobby Zamora during the 2010 UEFA Europa Final against Athletico Madrid, thus making history by becoming the first American to appear in a major European final. With seven goals that season, he was third behind Bobby Zamora and Damien Duff.

Dempsey was automatically included in the USA squad for the 2010 World Cup, and became the second American (after Brian McBride) to score in more than one World Cup tournament when he netted the equalising goal against England in the first USA

game. The USA qualified from the group this time alongside England, but were eliminated by Ghana in the first knockout round.

Dempsey was on the substitutes bench for Fulham's early games in the 2010–11 season but under the tutelage of Mark Hughes his established position in the team became 'in the hole' just behind the principal front man. He scored goals regularly throughout the season, mainly singles, but also three braces at Craven Cottage against Wigan Athletic, Stoke City and Bolton Wanderers. By scoring that second goal against Bolton, he became Fulham's highest Premier League

goalscorer with thirty-three. He also became the first USA player to score double figures (for any club) in a Premier League season, beating McBride's previous record of nine, also set whilst at Fulham. Dempsey was top scorer with thirteen in all competitions and was a clear winner as the fans' player of the year.

Dempsey had made significant strides in the season and at the peak of his career had started to look like the complete player. His main attribute was 'coming in late' for high or low crosses to score spectacular goals and he had developed the art of running on to through balls to convert chances. He liked running at defenders, and his pace, touch and control had improved every year. At six feet one inch, scoring headed goals had become his speciality, but he was just as useful at dead-ball free kicks. He had also seemingly become accustomed to the physical side of the English game and often gave as good as he got in aerial or floor challenges.

If the previous season was good, 2011–12 was to prove even more fruitful for Dempsey under more guidance from manager Martin Jol. He had only netted six up until the New Year, plus three in the group stages of the Europa League, but these had included an eighty-fifth-minute winner against Liverpool in December. That goal propelled Dempsey to become the most prolific American goalscorer in the Premier League, overtaking Fulham legend Brian McBride. He also netted the equaliser in the Boxing Day derby against Chelsea, the match ending 1–1.

He really came alight after that, netting hat-tricks in consecutive home matches against Charlton Athletic in the third round of the FA Cup (4–0) and Newcastle United in the Premier League (5–2); these were the first hat-tricks of his professional career. The hat-trick against Newcastle saw him become the first ever USA player to score a hat-trick in the Premier League. He continued to score regularly and grabbed two further braces, at home to Wolves in a 5–0 victory and away at Bolton in a 3–0 win. The strikes at Bolton moved Dempsey past Louis Saha's record of thirteen Premier League goals for Fulham in a single season.

Dempsey became the first USA player to reach the milestone of fifty goals in the Premier League with a free-kick against Sunderland in the last home game of the season. That would be Dempsey's final goal for the club. He played his final match, against Tottenham, the following week.

Dempsey was voted the Fulham player of the year by fans for the second consecutive season. He was the clear top scorer with twenty goals, and had become the first Fulham player to score twenty league and cup goals in a single season since being promoted to the top flight back in 2001. He was also voted into fourth place by the Football Writers' Association as player of the year.

However, clouds were developing and Dempsey wanted one more chance at the 'very top level' and declined any discussions on a further Fulham contract. He also had only one year to go, and he wanted to play in the Champions League. He had become a firm favourite and legend at Craven Cottage but his departure was somewhat acrimonious. There were rumours that he had refused to don the white shirt again and was not included in Fulham's opening fixtures. It looked as if he would move to Liverpool (his 'transfer' being announced on that club's owner's website) but dealings stalled. However, at the eleventh hour on the final day of the transfer window, he departed to **Tottenham Hotspur** for a reported £6m.

He joined Spurs on a three-year contract, but did not appear in his desired Champions League tournament, only the Europa League. His first goal for Spurs was the winner in a 3–2 victory over Manchester United at Old Trafford. He also got a late equaliser against the Red Devils at White Hart Lane. He then scored in a victory over second-placed Manchester City. Despite their outlay, Spurs, with a surfeit of attacking midfield players, rarely selected Dempsey to play unless it was the League Cup, FA Cup or the early rounds of the UEFA competition. Hence he failed to get much of a run in the first team.

In his brief Spurs career, Clint managed to score seven league goals and three cup goals. In April, he scored two goals against FC Basel (who Fulham had beaten twice en route to the final in 2010) in the second leg of the Europa League quarter-final to send the match into extra time. Tottenham eventually lost the match on penalties, and were thus eliminated from Europe. Spurs also failed to qualify for the Champions League on the final day of the season. Despite his sporadic appearances for the north London club, Dempsey still finished as third highest scorer with ten.

In March 2013, Dempsey was given the USA captain's armband by Jürgen Klinsmann for the important World Cup qualifying matches against Costa Rica and Mexico. In June he scored two goals against Germany in a 4–3 win. Those goals were his 34th and 35th for the national team, making him the second all-time leading scorer for the United States, overtaking Eric Wynalda.

Spurs purchased even more midfield players in the 2013 close season, and Dempsey was seemingly surplus to requirements. He still had plenty to offer the Premier League but in August surprised a great number of the football community by electing to return to America with the **Seattle Sounders** in a £6m deal. In September 2013, Clint Dempsey won his 100th cap for the USA and scored from a penalty in a 1–3 defeat to Costa Rica in a World Cup qualifier.

CLINT DEMPSEY
up to July 2013

Fulham career – all competitions

Season	Appearances	Goals	Home	Away
2006–2007	12	1	1	0
2007–2008	40	6	4	2
2008–2009	41	8	5	3
2009–2010	44	9	6	3
2010–2011	42	13	9	4
2011–2012	46	23	18	5
Total	225	60	43	17

Total career **league** appearances–**238**, and **league** goals–**65**.

Erik Nevland

The super-sub Viking legend.

Erik Nevland was born in Stavanger in Norway and started his career at his local football club **Viking FK** (Brede Hangeland's first club). He made his debut aged nineteen for Viking as a substitute for the final four minutes against FK Molde in 1996. In the next season he netted five goals in thirteen games for Viking's second team.

This prompted Old Trafford scouts to act and they took him on trial, where he impressed with three hat-tricks in successive trial matches. He signed for **Manchester United** and was with them for almost three seasons. However, he never managed to fully establish himself in the first team. He made his debut against Ipswich Town in the third round of the League Cup where United went down 0–2. His only appearance in the Premier League was as a substitute against Southampton in January 1998. He participated in the 1998 UEFA European U-21 championship when Norway achieved third place.

His only goal for the United first team was in a League Cup match against Bury in October 1998, which was also his last appearance. In all, he managed just six appearances with the Red Devils of which four were as a substitute. During his time in Manchester he had two loan spells, initially with previous club **Viking** in 1998 where he scored three in eight games and a less successful one in 1999 in Sweden at **IFK Göteborg**, where he made four appearances failing to score. Due to his lack of playing opportunities, he returned to **Viking** on a permanent contract midway through that third season. During his period in England he won twenty-five caps and scored two goals for the Norway U-20 and U-21 sides.

At the end of that season, Viking won the Norwegian Cup final, and a year later Nevland scored twice against Chelsea in the UEFA Cup including the deciding goal, overturning a 1–2 deficit at Stamford Bridge with a famous 4–2 home victory to progress 5–4 on aggregate. He won his first senior international cap in 2001. In his time at Viking, he failed only once to achieve double figures in terms of goals. He scored fifty-four goals in 113 appearances.

In November 2004, he moved to Holland to join **FC Groningen** on a free transfer and became a cult hero. In his first half-season for his new club, he scored sixteen times in twenty matches. Nevland also scored the first ever goal in FC Groningen's new Euroborg stadium. Once again, apart from the final partial season, Nevland netted double figures every campaign, making a total of forty-five goals in ninety-three matches, for the second season an average of a goal almost every other game.

In April 2007, Nevland signed a new three-year contract with FC Groningen and in December he was voted 'Groninger of the Year' by television viewers in that province, in spite of his not having been born there or even in the Netherlands! In January 2008, aged thirty, he signed for **Fulham** for a fee of £1.85m, plus a further 370K if Fulham retained Premier League status, which at the time looked improbable. Nevland had previously worked with new Fulham manager Roy Hodgson at Viking.

In February, he made only his second ever Premier League appearance when Fulham played Aston Villa at Craven Cottage; he played well, getting off to a winning start in a 2–1 victory. Fulham's demotion plight began to look worse, but then Nevland produced some substitute magic. At relegation rivals Reading, Fulham were clinging to a 1–0 advantage when substitute Nevland was put clear in the last minute to score a vital second, consolidating the win. History was repeated three weeks later when Fulham, who were 1–0 ahead against their other relegation rivals Birmingham City, sent on Nevland and again in the last minute he was sent clear to shoot past Maik Taylor to give the Cottagers the vital 2–0 scoreline. In the final game, at Portsmouth, with the scores level and Fulham needing a win, Nevland came on and five minutes later they had scored. He was unlucky not to increase the lead shortly afterwards. In just eight games, he was already a hero in the eyes of the Fulham fans.

The following season, 2008–09, Nevland made twenty-six appearances, but only started six games. Hodgson used Erik almost exclusively as an impact substitute, usually later in the second half replacing tired legs. He added four more goals, three as a substitute, scoring two late goals in a 3–1 victory over Portsmouth and as an early substitute in the 1–0 win over Stoke City. In one of the few games he started, he scored in the 1–3 defeat at Chelsea. All the goals came after Christmas.

Nevland (Erik the Viking) was a pocket dynamo, and at only five feet nine was never going to be the best in the air, but he was a natural goalscorer. He had great anticipation and was always in the six-yard box when required. He was also good at running on to passes and breaking opponents' offside traps. He was clever at positioning, often drawing defenders out of position thus creating space for other forwards. Despite being over thirty, he was still fairly fast over ten to twenty yards. As one would expect from a Norwegian he had a 'cool' head and was renowned for his clinical finishing. He also relished the physical game in England and received a few cautions, but was never daunted by bigger opponents.

After Fulham qualified for Europe in 2009–10, Nevland was again mainly used as a substitute but started more domestic games. He appeared as a half-time substitute in Europe against AS Roma and was sent off within minutes for what looked a pretty innocuous foul as Fulham lost 1–2. He made nine appearances in Europe for Fulham.

At home, he netted in a tempestuous 3–1 win over a nine-man Liverpool, and later in a 3–0 home win over Blackburn Rovers. He scored an FA Cup goal at Accrington Stanley and his last Fulham goal came in a 1–2 reverse away at Everton near the end of the season. His domestic record was twenty-four appearances and four goals. In the European final against Athletico Madrid, Nevland replaced Damien Duff and played the final six minutes of normal time and all of extra time. It was his last game for the Whites. He had appeared for Fulham almost twice as often as substitute as in the starting line-up. He won the last of his eight international caps in 2010.

After making nearly seventy appearances for Fulham, and despite Hodgson's wish to keep him at the club, Nevland once again returned to Norway and **Viking** in June 2010, and was promptly installed as captain. At Viking he played for virtually three more seasons, making over sixty appearances and adding another twenty-two goals to his already impressive total. He retired in 2012 aged thirty-five. His Viking club acknowledges Nevland as their seventh highest goalscorer of all time, with 135 goals in all matches.

Despite his brief time with Fulham, he remains hugely popular for the effort put in, especially during the 'great escape' and, for his part, Erik remains a huge Fulham fan.

ERIK NEVLAND
Fulham career – all competitions

Season	Appearances	Goals	Home	Away
2007–2008	8	2	1	1
2008–2009	26	4	3	1
2009–2010	33	4	2	2
Total	67	10	6	4

*Total career **league** appearances–**53**, and **league** goals–**9**.*

Bobby Zamora

Powerful England international, his goals helped Fulham to a European final.

Bobby Zamora was born in Barking, London. As a youth he played for the famous Senrab Football Club in east London, alongside the likes of John Terry and later Fulham team-mate Paul Konchesky. A West Ham fan, he started at their academy as an apprentice, but was released by the east London club.

At sixteen, he travelled west and joined Division Two **Bristol Rovers** as a trainee under the watchful eye of manager Ian Holloway. After two years, he turned professional and made four league and two cup appearances for them as a substitute early in the 1999–2000 season. He joined non-league **Bath City** on a month's loan in January, and made a huge impression scoring eight goals in six league games. He considered it a strong character-building and very enjoyable experience. After returning to Bristol he was immediately loaned out again, to Division Three (fourth-tier) **Brighton and Hove Albion** for the remainder of the season. He impressed with a spell of six goals in as many games.

During that summer, he made a permanent move to Brighton for £100,000 signing for former Fulham manager Micky Adams. During his tenure on the coast he quickly established himself as a prolific goalscorer. In his first full season, he had bagged over

twenty goals before Christmas, netting an early brace against Rochdale and a hat-trick against Torquay. In total he scored thirty goals in 2000–01. He won the division's Golden Boot award and was included in the Division Three PFA team of the year as Brighton won the championship by a clear ten points.

Undaunted by promotion, Zamora continued with his sensational scoring record, and finished the 2001–02 season with thirty-two goals. Once again he won the divisional Golden Boot award, and he made the Division Two PFA team of the year as Brighton secured a second successive championship. His form saw him break into the England U-21 team, drawing interest from several higher-division clubs.

Division One proved to be a lot tougher, and although Bobby added a further fourteen goals in 2002–03, the Brighton team were relegated after just one season. Zamora left Brighton and Hove Albion as one of the club's top twenty goalscorers of all time. Although a number of his goals came from the penalty spot, he finished with a remarkable eighty-two goals in 136 games.

The relegation had prompted **Tottenham Hotspur** manager Glenn Hoddle to invest £1.5m in the striker during the summer. In the top flight, Zamora endured an unhappy period at White Hart Lane, and he struggled to hold down a consistent first-team berth. He failed to find the net at all in the league and his only goal was a League Cup effort against the club he would join next, Championship **West Ham**. Just four months into the season, Zamora joined The Hammers in a deal which saw Jermain Defoe move in the other direction.

In the 2004–05 season, Zamora scored thirteen goals, including one in the first leg and two in the second leg of the play-off semi-final against Ipswich Town and also the single goal in West Ham's 1–0 victory over Preston North End in the Championship play-off final which promoted West Ham into the Premiership. The next season he made forty-two league and cup appearances and scored ten goals in total as West Ham finished in the top half of the Premier League and reached the FA Cup final, where he received an FA Cup runners-up medal, missing a penalty in the shootout against Liverpool. He signed a four-year extension to his contact early the following season.

He started off the 2006–07 season in fine style, scoring five goals in the first four games, but, as West Ham hit a difficult period and dropped down the table, he did not score again until January. However, he then scored five in seven games in March/April as West Ham's form improved. They managed to pull off an unlikely escape from relegation in the end winning 1–0 at Old Trafford on the final day. He was the Hammers' player of the year. He made only fourteen appearances for West Ham in 2007–08, scoring just one goal, and missed six months of the season with tendinitis.

Despite Zamora being a West Ham devotee, he and team-mate John Pantsil signed for **Fulham** in July for a joint fee of £6.3m, Zamora's being £4.8m of the total. In his first season, he struggled to find the net after scoring an early goal against Bolton Wanderers in a 2–1 win. He scored just twice in thirty-five league appearances during the 2008–09 season. He also managed two FA Cup goals.

At this time Zamora looked an unhappy player, and despite playing with determination he missed several easy goalscoring chances. Eventually the supporters began to become restless, which led to a strained and feisty relationship with the Cottage crowd culminating in several verbal exchanges with the player. In the close season it seemed as if Zamora would leave when Fulham and Hull City agreed a fee of £5m for his transfer, but he decided to remain in London and prove his worth. Despite his indifferent form, Fulham qualified for a Europa League place.

On his Europa League debut, he scored once and set up two goals against FK Vetra to give Fulham a 3–0 away advantage going into the return leg. He opened his 2009–10 Premier League account on the opening day of the season when a Clint Dempsey shot was deflected in off his body in a 1–0 win at Portsmouth. Bobby's form under Roy Hodgson improved no end. Although hardly prolific, he contributed eight league goals (all singles) and of those eight games Fulham won seven and drew the other. He also contributed three FA Cup goals including one against his old club Spurs. But it was in Europe where Zamora really stood out, scoring twice just before half time in the Whites match against FC Basel, their 3–2 victory in Switzerland taking them through the group stages.

Zamora struck the winner in Fulham's Europa League round of thirty-two first leg against Shakhtar Donetsk when Fulham won 2–1. The goal was a powerful strike from outside the box that went in off the underside of the crossbar. Zamora also scored Fulham's first goal in the historic UEFA Europa League comeback against Juventus, which Fulham won 4–1 (and 5–4 on aggregate). He was widely praised for his performance against the Italian stars.

He continued to impress on the European stage by scoring in both legs in a 3–1 aggregate win against Wolfsburg as Fulham progressed to the Europa League semi-finals. Zamora had been playing with injuries, but was a member of the team that played in the European final against Athletico Madrid, although he was substituted before the hour mark to make way for fresh legs. He finished an impressive season with nineteen goals in total.

Zamora now looked to be a complete player of international standing. Although he was capable of scoring with his head and both feet, his main asset was his hold-up play. With superb body strength he was able to keep defenders at bay whilst bringing team-mates into play. He was playing with intelligence too, with accurate passing and control around the edge of the penalty area creating chances for others.

Although he qualified to play for Trinidad and Tobago and was picked to play in a World Cup qualifier against El Salvador during the season, he did not play due to an injury picked up in training. However his form was such that there were calls for Fabio Capello to include him in the England squad and he was watched a number of times. Sadly injury once again prevented him from being included in the provisional squad for the 2010 World Cup. However, he did make his England debut before the start of the following season in a friendly against Hungary at Wembley, coming on as a half-time substitute as England won 2–1.

He started the 2010–11 season in good form, scoring in the 2–2 draw at Blackpool, and twice in the 6–0 League Cup win over Port Vale, and signed a new four-year contract with Fulham which would keep him at the London club until the summer of 2014. The day after signing however, disaster struck when Zamora broke his leg following a poor tackle from Wolves' Karl Henry. He was out for almost six months but, after looking a little rusty on his return, scored four league goals in the final ten games including a couple against Blackpool.

He started the 2011–12 season well too, with three goals in his first four games including one in the 6–0 hammering of Queens Park Rangers. After a dry spell,

he then scored three more times, his last goal coming in a memorable 5–2 win over Newcastle United when he also assisted in three of the others. It turned out to be his last appearance. He also won his second England cap, a full debut in a 1–0 friendly victory over Sweden in November.

Despite unsubstantiated rumours of a rift with Martin Jol, it was somewhat surprising when Zamora joined west London neighbours **Queens Park Rangers** in the January transfer window, his fourth London club. He scored on his debut in a 2–1 defeat to Wolves. He netted once more against Everton but, more significantly, played a vital team role that allowed Rangers to stay in the Premiership on the last day of the season at Manchester City.

The 2012–13 season started promisingly, with three goals in his opening four games. However he sustained a hip injury which kept him out for over two months and he was not fully fit for the rest of the season. He scored once more at Swansea, but missed three matches after a straight red card offence against

Wigan Athletic. Queens Park Rangers were relegated to the Championship at the end of the season. Despite many changes of personnel there during the close season, Zamora was still a QPR player at the start of the 2013–14 season.

BOBBY ZAMORA
up to July 2013

Fulham career – all competitions

Season	Appearances	Goals	Home	Away
2008–2009	41	4	3	1
2009–2010	48	19	12	7
2010–2011	16	7	6	1
2011–2012	29	7	6	1
Total	134	37	27	10

*Total career **league** appearances–**401**, and **league** goals–**132**.*

Andrew Johnson

Quality goalscorer, unlucky with injuries, but a season's top scorer.

Andrew **(Andy) Johnson** was born in Bedford and started his football career as a trainee within the academy of Division One Luton Town. Initially his career was held back by the perception that, at five feet seven inches, he was too small to prosper as a top-level footballer. At just sixteen, Johnson moved to the Midlands to join **Birmingham City**.

In his first two seasons at City he made only four appearances without scoring. He was first capped for England at U-20 level at this time, being selected in the team for the 1999 FIFA World Youth Championship. In 1999–2000 he played twenty-two league games scoring just once. He was a regular in the squad for the next two seasons, making fifty-seven league appearances scoring just seven times. He was voted young player of the season by the Blues fans in the 2001–02 season.

He experienced defeat and personal heartbreak in the 2001 League Cup final, where Birmingham drew 1–1 with Liverpool after extra time. After eleven penalty kicks with the score at 4–4, Johnson missed a decisive penalty, seeing his spot kick saved by the goalkeeper, sending the cup eventually to Merseyside.

In August 2002, Johnson signed for second-tier **Crystal Palace**, surprisingly as a makeweight in the deal that took Clinton Morrison to St Andrews. Johnson was valued at £750,000. The transfer turned out to be an excellent change for both Johnson and the

Eagles. In 2002–03, he was soon a hero with Palace fans notching two consecutive hat-tricks, one in the 5–0 demolition of arch-rivals Brighton and Hove Albion in October and then another at Walsall.

However, manager Trevor Francis continued to rotate strikers, often leaving Johnson on the bench or playing him wide on the right supporting Ade Akinbiyi and Dele Adebola. When Francis left, he was replaced by former Palace star Steve Kember who decided to play Johnson in the role of support striker. Kember was sacked in November, but in spite of all these upheavals Johnson managed fourteen goals in all competitions and was top scorer.

In 2003–04, under the aegis of new manager and coach Iain Dowie, assisted by Fulham's current youth coach Kit Symons, Johnson's all-round game improved and he ended the season as top scorer in Division One with thirty-two goals in all competitions. Palace were promoted to the Premier League for 2004–05 and Andy was named as Palace's player of the year.

There was some criticism of Johnson in that seven of his season's goals (almost 25%) had come from the penalty spot, many of those spot-kicks won by himself for fouls. He earned a reputation with some for 'diving' whilst others countered that he was just too quick for the division's defenders who could not handle his pace and speed of turning or his ability to shield the ball.

It's Little and Large, as Johnson tries to make headway against Blackburn's Chris Samba.

Palace's return to the higher echelons of football lasted just one season and they were relegated. However, for Johnson it had been another season of triumph. He was the highest scoring English player with twenty-one goals and the second highest scorer overall in the Premier League. Johnson's tally of twenty-one Premier League goals was the most ever scored by a Crystal Palace player in the top flight and for the second consecutive season he was Palace's player of the year.

His goalscoring form attracted the attention of the England manager Sven Goran Erikson, though Johnson's detractors persisted with noting that almost half of his goals came from penalties rather than open play (a record for the Premier League); he had won seven of the penalties himself.

Palace were relegated on the final day of the 2004–05 season and Andy requested a transfer. Palace chairman Simon Jordan was hugely critical of Johnson's agent for pressurising the player into handing in the transfer request. However, Johnson eventually signed a five-year improved contract with a pledge to help the Eagles regain their place in the Premier League. He had also been included in the PFA's team of the year.

By this time, Johnson had already won his first England cap, against Holland in February replacing Wayne Rooney on the hour. In the summer of 2005, he won his first full cap playing against the USA.

(*Craven Cottage alert:* Fulham's Zat Knight came on as a substitute, and both England goals came from current Fulham player Keiran Richardson.)

Johnson was soon playing alongside Clinton Morrison, who had rejoined Palace from Birmingham. Johnson started the 2005–06 season impressively with six goals in the first seven league games. He and Morrison quickly became Dowie's first-choice pairing. But after Crystal Palace's failure to return to top-flight football, speculation about Johnson's future at the club began to mount with a transfer to a Premier League club seeming highly likely. He had been top scorer in all of his four seasons at Selhurst Park contributing eighty-five goals.

With Dowie no longer at Palace, a move seemed inevitable. **Everton** secured Johnson with an £8.6m bid; it was reported that he was one of Everton's best paid players. It was a record purchase for Everton and a record sale for Palace.

Johnson netted his first goal for Everton on his debut in a 2–1 win over Watford at the start of the 2006–07 season, and ended the campaign with eleven league goals and twelve in all competitions, making him Everton's top scorer. There were still persistent suggestions regarding 'simulation' which manager Moyes was forced to defend. Johnson's form was good enough to see him earn a further five England caps during that season.

The hat-trick match ball from the QPR game.

The next season he scored just six goals in thirty-two appearances, though this was augmented by four in Europe. He picked up his eighth and final England cap against Germany in November, but never scored an international goal.

In July 2008, Everton accepted an offer of 'an eight-figure sum' from **Fulham** for Johnson. It was reported that problems had arisen from his medical, prompting a possible renegotiation of the fee, but the protracted move was finally concluded in early August, the player signing a four-year contract for an undisclosed fee, thought to be in the region of £10.5m. With potential add-ons, it would have made him Fulham's most expensive purchase.

He made his debut for the club in the 2008–09 season in a 2–1 win over Bolton Wanderers when fully match fit in September. Johnson did not make the greatest of starts as he was sent off against West Ham in September for two innocuous bookable offences. He scored his first and second Fulham goals against Wigan Athletic in October in a 2–0 victory. The majority of Johnson's goals came in a three-month period from November when he scored eight. He finished the season on ten from thirty-six appearances. It is interesting that Fulham had won seven and drawn one of the eight matches in which Johnson had scored.

At the start of the 2009–10 season there were more problems when Johnson sustained a shoulder injury following a crude body-check from an Amkar Perm defender early in the European qualification matches. Then, due to a troublesome knee problem, he missed a large number of matches, including the last four months of the season. He made only thirteen appearances in all, only nine of these in domestic fixtures, and all of his three goals came in the preliminary stages of the European competition.

The knee problem persisted over the close season and Johnson also missed the first three months of the 2010–11 season, trying to regain fitness. After October he gingerly found his way back in the team, playing in twenty-nine games (almost half of these as substitute) and adding just three more goals, but again Fulham were unbeaten in the three games in which he contributed goals.

He finally seemed to be over his injuries and made a good start to the 2011–12 season, scoring eight goals in thirteen matches in the preliminary European stages. He scored twice at the qualification group stage and added two braces against Odense and Wisla Krakow. But he was dismissed again for two needless bookings away at FC Twente where Fulham lost 0–1. In one match in October, Johnson scored his only Fulham hat-trick in the 6–0 massacre of west London rivals Queens Park Rangers, but it would prove to be the only league game he scored in that season and his goals were his last in domestic competition for the club. It kept up the record that Fulham never lost domestically when Johnson scored.

Andy played his last game in a 0–3 home defeat by Swansea in March. He had made just twenty league appearances that season and fewer than 100 domestically in his four years at the club. Johnson's contract at Fulham expired in June 2012 and he was released. As with Fulham's other big signing, Steve Marlet, each of Johnson's domestic goals cost Fulham a hefty price, in this case over £650,000.

In June 2012 Johnson signed for Premiership **Queens Park Rangers** on a two-year contract, linking up again with Bobby Zamora. He made his debut as a substitute in the first game of the season at home to Swansea City. After only three league games the injury hoodoo struck again as it was announced that Johnson would probably miss the majority of the 2012–13 season with a cruciate ligament injury. He recovered and was in the QPR squad for the 2013–14 season.

ANDREW JOHNSON
up to July 2013

Fulham career – all competitions

Season	Appearances	Goals	Home	Away
2008–2009	36	10	6	4
2009–2010	13	3	3	0
2010–2011	29	3	0	3
2011–2012	33	11	9	2
Total	111	27	18	9

*Total career **league** appearances—**380**, and **league** goals—**114**.*

The 2010s

Dimitar Berbatov

Elegant, languorous Bulgarian striker, Fulham's top scorer in 2012–13.

Dimitar Berbatov was born in Blagoevgrad in Bulgaria to parents who were both professional athletes. His father Ivan was a footballer with Pirin and CSKA Sofia while his mother Margarita was a handball player. He began his footballing career with his home town club **Pirin Blagoevgrad** as a fifteen-year-old where he was instantly identified as a star in the making with a tremendous scoring rate for both the junior and reserve sides.

At seventeen, he joined the youth squad of his father's former club, **CSKA Sofia**. He signed his first professional contract with the club and made his debut during the 1998–99 season, at the age of eighteen. He won the Bulgarian Cup with CSKA at the end of that season, where he had scored three goals in five games. He had also netted three in eleven starts in the league. Berbatov's first experience in Europe came in September 1999 in a 2–0 defeat against Newcastle United up against his boyhood hero Alan Shearer.

It was during that 1999–2000 season that he began to make his name as a goalscorer, scoring sixteen goals in thirty-four league and cup matches. He made five appearances for the Bulgarian U-18 and U-21 sides, scoring an average of a goal a game. Incredibly he also made his first senior appearance for the Bulgarian national team in a 1–0 friendly victory over Greece.

At the age of eighteen Berbatov was allegedly kidnapped, following a training session, by a Bulgarian criminal, who unsuccessfully attempted to convince the young striker to sign for the club he owned, FC Levski Kjustendil. A spell of nine goals in eleven games during the first half of the 2000–01 season plus seven goals in four European games was enough to persuade German club **Bayer Leverkusen** to pay £1m to sign Berbatov on a four-year contract in January 2001. At the time of his transfer he had managed a ratio greater than a goal every other game for CSKA. By this time he also had his first international goal in a 2–3 friendly defeat against Chile in February 2000. By October he had also played in seven World Cup qualification matches adding five goals.

Berbatov played for the club's second team at first, but after scoring six goals in seven appearances was promoted to the first-team squad, despite being sent off in his last reserve match. He made his first-team debut in the USA in a 4–3 MSL pre-season friendly win against American side D.C. United, scoring a hat-trick. His league debut came in February, as a substitute in a 4–1 victory against FC Köln. Berbatov found himself being used as a substitute by manager Berti Vogts, making six appearances but not finding the net as Leverkusen finished fourth, qualifying for the following season's UEFA Champions League.

During the 2001–02 campaign, Berbatov registered fourteen domestic goals and two in Europe including a goal in a 4–2 win over Liverpool in the Champions League quarter-final. After a slow start in the league he managed six in eight matches towards the end of the season and also scored his first senior hat-trick in the domestic cup competition in a 3–2 away victory against VfL Bochum.

It was ultimately a season of disappointment for Bayer Leverkusen. They reached the Champions League final and, in that game against Real Madrid, Berbatov came on as a substitute in the first half, but Leverkusen lost 2–1, thanks to a brilliant goal from Zidane. They were also runners-up in the Bundesliga and losing finalists in the DFB-Pokal (Cup) thus completing an unusual treble of runners-up finishes and keeping their nickname 'Neverkusen' intact.

Berbatov established his place as the first-choice centre forward during the 2002–03 season, netting his team's goal against Manchester United in the Champions League in September. It was a big learning curve for him and in terms of goals a disappointing one with just six in all domestic competitions. By October, he had played in six European Championship qualifiers for Bulgaria scoring five goals as they qualified for the finals.

During the 2003–04 season, he scored sixteen goals in thirty-four league appearances, including thirteen in the last eighteen games, plus a further three cup goals. In the summer he played in the European Championship for Bulgaria. It proved to be the only major tournament he would take part in. He did not score and Bulgaria lost all three group games.

His final two seasons saw a rising awareness of his talent. In 2004–05 he netted twenty goals in the Bundesliga which included four braces and a hat-trick in the final league game of the season against Borussia Mönchengladbach. He also scored five Champions League goals and one in the domestic cup (26 in total). By October the following season, he had played in nine World Cup qualification matches scoring seven goals.

In the 2005–06 season he scored in the opening five matches and finished with twenty-one goals which included fifteen in the final fifteen games. This late run included two braces and a hat-trick against FC Kaiserslautern. He began to be monitored by a number of top English and European sides.

During the close season of 2006, **Tottenham Hotspur** reached an agreement with Bayer Leverkusen for Berbatov's transfer for a fee of £10.9m, which made him the most expensive Bulgarian footballer ever. He rejected Manchester United in order to work

with Martin Jol. After he was granted a British work permit the transfer was completed in July. He opened his Spurs account in his second game and on his home debut in a 2–0 win over Sheffield United.

He took a while to adapt to the Premier League but still managed twelve goals all season including four in the final five fixtures. He scored his first FA Cup goals when coming on as a second-half substitute against Fulham and netting twice as Spurs won 4–0 at Craven Cottage.

But it was in Europe in the UEFA Cup where he shone, with seven goals in eight ties, before Spurs were eliminated at the quarter-final stage. He ended the 2006–07 season with twelve league goals, and won both the Tottenham Hotspur player of the season award and a place in the PFA Premier League team of the year. Between September 2006 and November the following season, he would also play eleven Euro qualification matches scoring six goals. He had also now been appointed captain of his country, a position he would hold until his final international game.

During the 2007–08 season, goals were hard to come by, but Berbatov scored his first Premier League four-goal haul in December in a 6–4 win over Reading.

Spurs reached the League Cup final in February 2008, and Berbatov scored the equalising penalty as Tottenham went on to win the game 2–1 after extra time. He ended the season with fifteen league goals and three in domestic cups. Spurs were again in the UEFA Cup and Berbatov added five goals but Spurs were eliminated at the last-sixteen stage.

Before the start of the 2008–09 season, **Manchester United** began to court the player and there were allegations that manager Alex Ferguson had used the media to unsettle the player. Ongoing rumours of a substantial bid apparently affected Berbatov and he was omitted from the Spurs team for the games against Sunderland and Chelsea during August 2008. Inevitably he moved to Old Trafford, costing United £30m, with Berbatov signing a four-year contract.

Berbatov's first two goals for the club came in the 3–0 win away against Aalborg BK in the Champions League group stage in September. He netted his first league goals in Manchester United colours during a 4–0 victory over West Bromwich Albion. Generally he struggled for league goals and, apart from a purple patch of four in four games in mid-season, he could only manage nine in the league.

Berbatov scored two goals against West Bromwich Albion on his home debut, the second being this penalty calmly put away.

He also missed a penalty against Everton in a semi-final tie that ultimately cost the Red Devils an FA Cup final place. He scored twice against Celtic too in the Champions League and played in all the matches including the final where United lost 0–2 to Barcelona. He had, however, picked up his first League Championship medal. Between September 2008 and October the next season, Berbatov also played eight World Cup qualification matches scoring five goals, which included a hat-trick in a 6–2 win over Georgia.

Berbatov struggled to make a decent impact during the 2009–10 season as well, but managed twelve league goals, although some displays were uninspiring. He failed to score in Europe or in any domestic cup competition. There was some media speculation that Berbatov would leave Manchester United during the close season, but this was denied by Alex Ferguson. He also played his final match for Bulgaria in March.

If that season had been disappointing, the next was totally different. Berbatov started the 2010–11 season in fine style scoring in four of the opening five games, only failing to net against Fulham. Contained within that spell was his first hat-trick for Manchester United in his team's 3–2 home win over arch-rivals Liverpool; the second goal, an overhead kick, became a contender for the Premier League's goal of the season. It was the first treble by a Manchester United player against Liverpool in over sixty years.

Two months later, he equalled a Premier League record by scoring five goals in a game during United's 7–1 home victory over Blackburn Rovers; he was the first non-Englishman to net five in a Premier League match. Berbatov netted his first goals of the 2011 calendar year with his third hat-trick of the season in a 5–0 thumping of Birmingham City in late January. This made him the first United player since Ruud Van Nistelrooy eight years earlier to score three hat-tricks in the same season. In December, he was named Bulgarian footballer of the year for a record seventh time.

As top scorer in the Premier League in 2010–11 with twenty goals, Berbatov was a member of the PFA team of the year alongside Carlos Tevez. He also shared the Premier League Golden Boot award with the same player. Surprisingly, he was left out of the squad completely in May as United reached the Champions League final. Without him United were beaten 1–3 by Barcelona. However, he now had his second League Championship medal.

The relationship between club and player appeared strained, and for the first half of the 2011–12 season he started sporadically, either not being in the team at all or being on the substitutes bench. In November, he ended his long run without a goal in the Champions League by scoring the equaliser in a home game against Benfica in a 2–2 draw. He proved a point during December with a spell of seven goals in five games. Included in this spell was a hat-trick in a 5–0 win over Wigan Athletic on Boxing Day, his fourth for United and his fifth in the Premier league. During the January transfer window, there were rumours of a move back to Germany with Bayern Munich, but that never materialised. After January, he drifted out of the side again and finished the league campaign with just those seven goals.

On the final day of the transfer window in August 2012, Berbatov was reunited with his former manager Martin Jol when he signed for **Fulham** on a two-year contract for a fee rumoured to be £4m. Fulham had been lacking a tall striker since the departure of Bobby Zamora the previous season.

He made his debut as a half-time substitute in a game at West Ham where Fulham lost 0–3. Two weeks later he made his home debut scoring twice in a 3–0 win over West Bromwich Albion. He then scored once at Reading and registered two more in a fine display at Arsenal; both matches finishing as 3–3 draws.

He scored regularly for the rest of the season including a spell where he scored in four consecutive games which included a brace against Queens Park Rangers and the winner in a surprise 1–0 victory at White Hart Lane against former club Spurs. In all he scored fifteen goals in his first season, was top scorer and was named as Fulham's player of the season. At the time of printing this book he remains a vital member of Fulham's squad.

Berbatov has remained an enigma during most of his time in England, sometimes looking a world-beater and sometimes looking average. He can be aggressive and full of running in one match and then seemingly lethargic and one-paced the next. He has been variously described as brooding, surly and moody, but he also has a cheery personality.

He is capable of great goalscoring bursts which will be followed by a number of games without a goal. His languid, laid-back style has often been criticised as lazy and his manner and demeanour as arrogant, but those who know him say this is not the case. His main style is a calm and unhurried way of playing, never panicking when in possession.

Despite his tall frame, Berbatov appears to prefer the ball at his feet, and he is noted for his immaculate control and accurate passing. He has superb technical ability and impeccable touch. He plays the classic deep-lying forward role rather than the target man.

Outside of football, he lists his hobbies as drawing and basketball. He is skilful with a pencil and is known for his caricature drawings of his team-mates. He is a

sponsor of children's charities in his native Bulgaria, supporting five care homes. He is also the founder of the Dimitar Berbatov Foundation, which helps young people to develop their talents.

In 2009, after scoring twice in a friendly match against Malta, Berbatov had scored forty-eight international goals which made him the highest scoring Bulgarian of all time. He retired from international football in May 2010. There were a couple of attempts to persuade him to return and Berbatov seemed receptive, but in September 2012 he re-affirmed his decision to quit the international football scene.

DIMITAR BERBATOV
up to July 2013

Fulham career – all competitions

Season	Appearances	Goals	Home	Away
2101–2013	35	15	8	7
Total	35	15	8	7

Total career **league** appearances–**211**, and **league** goals–**90**.

They also wore the Centre Forward's Shirt

Apart from those players described in detail within the main body of the book, these are the others who have worn the hallowed 'number 9' shirt for Fulham since the war. These are *league* game statistics before the Premiership era of squad numbers. We have called these players our bronze stars.

 Strikers – and these twenty-five take the book up nicely to the magical figure of 100 players.

Player	First season wearing the number 9	Comments
Cyril Grant	1946–47	*Was part of the deal that took leading scorer Ronnie Rooke to Arsenal. He didn't settle at Fulham, scoring four in fourteen games before moving to Southend.*
Jimmy Jinks	1948–49	*Signed from Millwall, stayed just eighteen months, scoring three goals in eleven games before moving on to Luton Town and then Aldershot.*
Alf Stokes	1959–60	*Scored at an amazing rate at Tottenham over five years, notching up forty goals in sixty-five games. Never established himself at White Hart Lane, but won an England U-23 cap there. Joined Fulham for a significant fee and scored six goals in fifteen appearances early on, but faded badly, not looking fit, and within two years had joined Watford.*
Turlough O'Connor	1967–68	*Signed from Irish side Bohemians along with Jimmy Conway. His only appearance for Fulham was at Sheffield Wednesday in the FA Cup. Returned to Ireland a season later.*
Steve Camp	1975–76	*Joined Fulham from non-league Leatherhead and made five league appearances without scoring. Moved to Peterborough United.*
Andy Thomas	1982–83	*Spent time on loan from Oxford United and could have been the missing piece in the jigsaw for the promotion-chasing side that season, but chairman Ernie Clay refused to sanction the purchase. Scored twice in four appearances.*
Trevor Lee	1984–85	*Only one appearance for the club. Also his last appearance in league football.*
Paul Fishenden	1985–86	*Made three appearances for the club whilst on loan from Wimbledon. Found some success with Crewe later in his career.*
Michael Cole	1988–89	*Signed from Ipswich Town and scored four goals in forty-eight appearances. Dropped out of league football after leaving Fulham.*
John Watson	1989–90	*Signed from Dunfermline Athletic. He made twelve appearances without scoring, although he managed two cup goals. It was his only spell in English football.*
Iain Dowie	1989–90	*Five appearances whilst on loan from Luton Town; scored one Fulham goal and was also sent off in the same match. Found success at Southampton and West Ham and later managed three London clubs. Currently a regular sports presenter.*
Steve Milton	1989–90	*Former West Ham apprentice; joined Fulham from non-league Whyteleafe and made fifty-eight league appearances over two seasons scoring nine league goals. Dropped out of league football after leaving Fulham.*

Francis Joseph	**1990–91**	*Nomadic former Wimbledon and Brentford striker. Nearing the end of his career he made four appearances for Fulham without scoring, but managed one League Cup goal.*
Phil Gray	**1990–91**	*Played three games whilst on loan from Tottenham. Did not succeed at Fulham, but had a significant career with Luton Town and Sunderland, winning twenty-six caps for Northern Ireland.*
George Georgiou	**1991–92**	*Joined from non-league Wembley and made just four appearances without scoring.*
Rob Haworth	**1993–94**	*Came through the Fulham juniors, and over two seasons made twenty-one appearances, most as a substitute, scoring once. Dropped out of league football after leaving Fulham.*
Alan Cork	**1994–95**	*Experienced marksman with a long career behind him. Part of Wimbledon's 'Crazy Gang' for whom he scored 145 goals. He was a member of the Wimbledon team that beat Liverpool in the FA Cup final in 1989. Scored three in fifteen games for Fulham, but concentrated mainly on a coaching role. He was assistant manager to Micky Adams during the successful 1996–97 promotion season.*
Mark Stallard	**1994–95**	*Four appearances whilst on loan from Derby County; scored a hat-trick against Exeter City in his final game.*
Carl Bartley	**1994–95**	*Came through the Fulham juniors, made just one league appearance.*
Rory Hamill	**1995–96**	*Northern Ireland schoolboy and youth international, signed from Portstewart. Made forty-eight appearances scoring nine goals.*
Christer Warren	**1996–97**	*Joined on loan from Southampton. Scored on his debut and assisted the Micky Adams promotion winning squad. Made ten further appearances but without scoring. Found success later at Bournemouth.*
Kyle Lightbourne	**1997–98**	*Joined on loan from Coventry City after a prolific spell with Walsall. Scored two goals in four appearances before moving to Stoke City. An international with Bermuda.*
Kevin Betsy	**1998–99**	*Joined from non-league Woking for £80,000 and made fifteen appearances scoring once, against Millwall. Never truly established himself during the period when Fulham ascended the leagues, but found some success later at Barnsley and Oldham.*
Karl Heinz Riedle	**1999–2000**	*Experienced German international player who joined Fulham from Liverpool to add experience to the promotion-seeking side. Was already a veteran aged thirty-five on joining the club, having won forty-two international caps. Scored six goals in thirty-five appearances for Fulham, before assisting Roy Evans as caretaker Fulham manager for a short spell, prior to the appointment of Jean Tigana.*
Peter Möller	**2000–01**	*Five appearances whilst on loan from Real Oviedo in Spain; scored one goal in those games, against QPR. Seventeen caps for Denmark.*

Midfield Players who, on occasions, have worn the number 9 shirt.

Player	First season wearing the number 9	Comments
David Nelson	1946–47	*The other player with Grant who was part of the deal that took leading scorer Ronnie Rooke to Arsenal. Like Grant, he didn't settle, scoring only two in twenty-three games before moving to Brentford where he made over 100 appearances.*
Bobby Brennan	1950–51	*Normally an inside forward, but very occasionally played in the centre. Scored thirteen goals in seventy-three appearances before moving to Norwich City.*
Stan Brown	1962–63	*Although he played in every outfield position for Fulham and was the ultimate 'utility' player for over ten years, Stan actually started his career as a centre forward. He scored six goals in his first nineteen league games for Fulham, the highest scoring spell of his career. Scored sixteen goals in 353 games before joining Colchester United.*
Mark Pearson	1965–66	*Former Busby Babe, signed from Sheffield Wednesday. Normally an inside forward. Scored seven goals in fifty-eight appearances before joining Halifax Town.*
John Margerrison	1978–79	*Played in every position in the forward line after joining on a free transfer from Tottenham, but was really a wide midfield player. Played just one game at centre forward on the opening day of the 1978–79 season. He scored, but Fulham lost 1–3. Scored nine goals in seventy-one games before joining Orient.*
Sean O'Driscoll	1980–81	*Signed from Alvechurch; played in most forward line positions in his early Fulham career, before settling into the number 4 shirt. Scored fourteen goals in 148 games before joining Bournemouth.*
Wayne Kerrins	1985–86	*Another utility player who played in a number of different shirts including both full backs and half back. His first full start for Fulham was at centre forward. Made sixty-six appearances but only scored once. Dropped out of league football after short-term loans with Port Vale and Orient.*
Kenny Achampong	1986–87	*Scored on his debut in February 1985. Normally a wide midfield player, or on the right wing wearing 7 or 8. Played just a couple of games as a number 9. Scored fifteen goals in eighty-one appearances before joining Charlton Athletic.*
Kevin Hoddy	1987–88	*Midfielder who played in every forward line position in a brief career; he played centre forward for just one game. Made twenty-two appearances for Fulham but only scored once. He dropped out of league football after leaving Fulham.*
Justin Skinner	1987–88	*Capable midfield creator who had a decent career at Fulham including penalty-taking. Played centre forward for just one game. Scored twenty-three goals in 135 games before joining Bristol Rovers.*
Gary Barnett	1988–89	*Useful midfield player who could play on both wings or as an inside forward. He started at centre forward for the first two games of the 1988–89 season. Had two spells with Fulham. Scored a very respectable thirty-one goals in 182 games. Had further success at both Huddersfield Town and Leyton Orient.*

Leo Donellan	**1989–90**	*Signed from Chelsea, a competitive player who could play in any position from full back to midfield and forward. Played two games at centre forward during his final season. Scored four goals in seventy-nine appearances. Dropped out of league football after leaving Fulham.*
Jeff Eckhardt	**1990–91**	*One of the great utility players. Signed from Sheffield United, Eckhardt played in virtually every outfield shirt, and played well in all positions. Normally a full back or central defender, he was often called into defensive midfield too. He also scored more than his fair share of goals. Played a couple of games at centre forward for two short periods. Scored twenty-five goals in 249 games and had further success with both Stockport County and Cardiff City.*
Peter Scott	**1991–92**	*Came through the Fulham youth team. He was a combative midfield player who could play in defence or midfield on both sides of the pitch. Scored his fair share of goals. Played a couple of games at centre forward in his final season. Sent off three times in his Fulham career, but scored twenty-seven goals in 277 appearances. Later spent time with Bournemouth and then Barnet.*
Mark Cooper	**1992–93**	*Midfield player with a nomadic career who had a brief spell with Fulham, and played a couple of games at centre forward. Played ten games without scoring. Moved on to Huddersfield Town after only four months at the Cottage.*
Mark Kelly	**1992–93**	*Journeyman midfield player, signed from Cardiff City, who played in several positions at Fulham. Played one game in the number 9 shirt. Scored only two goals in sixty-four appearances. Dropped out of league football after leaving Fulham.*
Ara Bedrossian	**1992–93**	*Wide midfield player who could play in other positions. He made his first six starts in the number 9 shirt. Joined from Cypriot club AP Limassol. Played forty-two games but scored only one goal. He was an international player for Cyprus. Dropped out of league football after leaving Fulham.*
Michael Mison	**1993–94**	*More of a central defensive midfield player, he played in a number of positions. Played his first full game at centre forward, but settled further back in the team. Scored five goals in fifty-five appearances. Dropped out of league football after leaving Fulham.*
Nick Cusack	**1994–95**	*Another utility player, extremely capable of playing in many positions. Started his Fulham career in the number 9 shirt scoring seven league goals including a hat-trick in the last league game of the season. Later in his career settled into a midfield/defence role. Scored fourteen goals in 116 appearances before enjoying further success with Swansea City.*
Danny Bolt	**1995–96**	*Came through the junior ranks. In a brief career, played mostly on the wing, but made one appearance in the number 9 shirt, in an FA Cup game. Scored two goals in thirteen appearances. Dropped out of league football after leaving Fulham.*
Wayne Collins	**1997–98**	*More of a wide midfield player/winger, he played a handful of games in the number 9 shirt. Signed from Sheffield Wednesday, he made fifty-eight appearances and scored four goals. Joined Crewe Alexandra after leaving Fulham.*
Steve Hayward	**1999–2000**	*Normally an inside forward who could play wide. Played three games at centre forward. Signed from Carlisle, he was a skilful hard-working player with excellent passing. Made 115 appearances scoring seven goals. Moved on to Barnsley.*

Wingers who have worn the number 9 shirt.

Player	First season wearing the number 9	Comments
Johnny Campbell	1949–50	*Joined from Belfast Celtic, scoring only four goals in three years. Retired from football due to ill health and died aged just 45.*
Jack MacDonald	1951–52	*Primarily a left winger, who cost a club record £12,000 in 1948. Played a few games at centre forward towards the end of his three-year Fulham career. Moved to Southampton in 1952.*
John Taylor	1957–58	*Played four games on loan from Newcastle whilst completing national service in London.*
Cliff Jones	1969–70	*Veteran former Spurs Welsh international winger who played one game in the number 9 position. Retired after his time at Fulham.*
Brian Greenaway	1980–81	*Came up from the Fulham youth team. Mainly a winger on either side of the pitch, but could play anywhere in the front five, and played three matches at centre forward. Dropped out of league football after leaving Fulham.*
Ronnie Goodlass	1980–81	*An out and out left winger from Den Haag; played one FA Cup game at number 9. Moved on to Scunthorpe United.*
Julian Hails	1991–92	*Came up from the Fulham youth team. A recognised wide player, but could play in any of the five forward positions. Played sporadically at number 9. Had later success with Southend United.*
Peter Baah	1992–93	*Signed from Blackburn Rovers at the age of 19. Made forty-nine appearances for the Cottagers, scoring four goals. Dropped out of league football after leaving Fulham.*
Carl Williams	1995–96	*Came up from the Fulham youth team. Played a few games in the 1995–96 season, making one appearance at number 9.*
Rob Scott	1997–98	*Signed from Sheffield United. A clever inside forward who helped Fulham considerably towards promotion in 1996–97. Lost his place under the Wilkins/Keegan regime, eventually joining Rotherham United. Made eighty-four appearances scoring seventeen goals.*
Leon McKenzie	1997–98	*Made just one start whilst on loan from Crystal Palace.*

Central Defenders who have worn the number 9 shirt.

Player	First season wearing the number 9	Comments
Gordon Brice	1954–55	*Played just one game at centre forward during his Fulham career.*
John Dempsey	1965–66	*The former youth player was tried experimentally at centre forward by manager Buckingham, and scored two league goals and a League Cup hat-trick, but was returned to centre half within a couple of months. Later had considerable success with Chelsea, and was an Eire international.*
John Richardson	1972–73	*Could have been included as a forward, midfield player or defender, a utility player formerly with Millwall and Brentford who could play in virtually any position. Made seventy-one appearances scoring six goals, including one on his debut and two in a televised match against Bristol Rovers. Moved to Aldershot.*
Steve Hatter	1979–80	*Made one stop-gap appearance at number 9.*
Tony Gale	1980–81	*Played a few games in that season wearing the number 9 shirt, but it was part of a midfield role.*
Gavin Nebbeling	1992–93	*Made one stop-gap appearance at number 9.*
Danny Cullip	1996–97	*Made one stop-gap appearance at number 9.*

Full Backs who have worn the number 9 shirt.

Player	First season wearing the number 9	Comments
Gary Peters	1980–81	*Signed from Reading, and played a handful of matches in the number 9 shirt. Was quite often moved forward for a more aggressive midfield role, and scored a few goals, but was never really a goalscorer or centre forward. Moved on to Wimbledon.*
John Marshall	1983–84	*Long-serving player who came through the youth team. It is hard to categorise where to put John Marshall as, like a couple of other Fulham players, he played in virtually every outfield position. But his main role was as an attacking full back on either flank or as a wide midfield player. Played with the number 9 on his back on a few occasions early in his career. Played his whole thirteen-year career with Fulham, and was for many years afterwards a member of the backroom staff.*
Martin Pike	1990–91	*Signed from Sheffield United. Essentially an out-and-out left back. Early in his Fulham career played wide on the left in the number 11 shirt. Played just a couple of games in the number 9 shirt. Scored a fair number of goals from the full back position.*
Mark Taylor	1995–96	*Youth player on loan from Middlesbrough; made the first of his seven appearances at number 9.*
Matthew Lawrence	1996–97	*Played one game in the number 9 shirt.*

Premiership Squad Number 9s

Apart from the players detailed in the book, the following players have held the 'squad' number 9 during the Premiership era.

Player	Season allocated the squad number 9	Comments
Michael Brown	2005–06	*Signed from Spurs. A midfield player who was handed the captaincy by Chris Coleman. Unloved, tough-tackling ball winner. Although he played number 9 and made over forty appearances, he never scored a Fulham goal.*
David Healy	2007–08	*Plucky Irish striker signed from Leeds United, who had a decent pedigree, and was unlucky in his season at Craven Cottage. Played thirty league games scoring four league goals and six in total, making him joint top scorer in the 2007–08 season with three other players. Moved on to Sunderland.*
Stefano Okaka	2009–10	*Striker signed on a half-season loan from AS Roma. Struggled to fit into the Fulham side, scoring twice in eleven appearances. Returned to Roma at the end of the season. Signed for Parma and is currently on loan at Serie 'B' team Spezia Calcio.*
Orlando Sá	2011–12	*Stop-gap striker signed from Porto, he had difficulty with the pace of the English game. Played seven games, scoring once at Norwich. His contract was terminated and Sá signed a three-year contract with Cypriot First Division club AEL Limassol.*

Arthur Rowley hit seven goals in two consecutive weekends in the 1948–49 season, four against Bury, followed by three against Plymouth Argyle. Steve Earle scored eight goals over three games in the space of twelve days in the 1969–70 season, five against Halifax Town, followed by three against Stockport County – both games away from home. Johnny Haynes scored seven goals over five games in the space of fifteen days in the 1958–59 season, three against Sunderland, followed by four against Lincoln City.

Only twice since the war have two players scored hat-tricks (or better) in the same match, Roy Bentley (3) and Roy Dwight (3) in the 6–3 win over Port Vale in the 1956–57 season and Graham Leggat (4) and Bobby Howfield (3) in the 10–1 destruction of Ipswich Town in the 1963–64 season.

Following Trevor Chamberlain's FA Cup hat-trick against Newcastle United in 1955–56, there was a forty-year wait for the next FA Cup hat-trick, which was scored by Mike Conroy against Swansea City in 1995–96.

The promotion season of 1958–59 saw no fewer than seven hat-tricks, all of them in league matches.

Graham Leggat's treble against Ipswich Town in December 1963 in just three and a half minutes is the fastest hat-trick in the history of the First Division/Premiership.

John Dempsey's hat-trick in October 1965 against Northampton Town in the League Cup followed an experiment by manager Vic Buckingham of playing a centre half (centre back) at centre forward. It was his first game at number 9. He scored two further league goals, but was back at centre half within weeks.

In the League Cup the gap between hat-tricks was a mere twenty-eight years – from Steve Earle's against Cambridge United in 1971 to Geoff Horsfield's against Northampton in 1999.

After Tony Sealy's hat-trick against Wolves in April 1985, it was almost seven years before the next one, from Sean Farrell against West Bromwich Albion on New Year's Day 1992.

Mark Stallard scored his hat-trick against Exeter City in October 1994 whilst on a month's loan from Derby County. It was the last of his four games for the club. He didn't score in the previous three, and returned to Derby.

Paul Moody scored his treble against Preston North End in May 1999 after coming on as a half-time substitute – the only Fulham player in history to do so.

There is some debate regarding Heidar Helguson's treble against West Bromwich Albion in February 2006. One of the goals was a deflection. Some newspapers credited Helguson with just two goals and one own goal. The official Fulham statistics register it as a hat-trick.

After Heidar Helguson's hat-trick against West Bromwich Albion in February 2006, it was just short of five years before the next one, when Diomansy Kamara netted three in the FA Cup third-round tie against Peterborough United in January 2011.

The scoring of four hat-tricks in season 2011–12 (Clint Dempsey twice, Pavel Pogrebnyak and Andy Johnson) was the first time that this had happened in a single season for over half a century. They came in the space of just five months.

By scoring a hat-trick in consecutive home matches in 2011–12 (Charlton Athletic and Newcastle United) Clint Dempsey became the first Fulham player to do so for sixty-three years, emulating Arthur Rowley in January 1949.

Pavel Pogrebnyak scored in his first three Fulham league games including a hat-trick in his second home game, against Wolves.

Fulham have not managed a hat-trick away from home for fifteen years.

Gary Brazil scored a hat-trick in the 6–2 victory at Maidstone United in the Autoglass Trophy during 1991–92.

Although they were long-term stars and significant goalscorers for Fulham, Bobby Robson, Rodney Marsh, Jimmy Conway, Les Barrett and Dean Coney never scored a Fulham hat-trick.

Post war, three Fulham players have scored five goals in a game, Bedford Jezzard, Jimmy Hill and Steve Earle. Eight players have scored four goals in a game, Bedford Jezzard and Graham Leggat (both twice), Arthur Rowley, Roy Dwight, Johnny Haynes, Allan Clarke, John Mitchell and Gordon Davies. It is thirty years since any player scored four goals in a game for Fulham.

As well as his hat-tricks, only Bedford Jezzard has also scored four and five goals in a game.

Since the war only three out of eighty-four of our 'hat-trick heroes' have finished up on the losing side, and these were all at home: Trevor Chamberlain in the epic 4–5 FA Cup tie in 1955–56 against Newcastle United, Graham Leggat in the 3–6 league defeat by Aston Villa in 1965–66 (Fulham were two down and Leggat scored three to put Fulham ahead, but Villa came back with four) and Gordon Davies in the 3–5 defeat by Chelsea in 1983–84.

Our 'favourite' opponents have been Swansea Town, and during a period of only four seasons in the Fifties between 1953 and 1957 Fulham scored four hat-tricks against them.

And, finally, Fulham's favourite day for hat-tricks is Boxing Day, which has seen five post-war trebles: Trevor Chamberlain (1956), Bobby Howfield and Graham Leggat (1963), Chris Guthrie (1978) and Barry Hayles (2000).

More Statistics

"He uses statistics as a drunken man uses lampposts – for support rather than illumination."
– Andrew Lang, 1937

Well, we hope not, but we have used statistics in our tables in the best way we can to show the most prolific strikers at Fulham and in the league. Like all statistics there will be some 'outliers' (or 'outsiders') in the data who distort the figures somewhat, but we consider that makes it all the more interesting. There is no rigid mathematical definition of what constitutes an outlier; determining whether or not an observation is an outlier is ultimately a subjective exercise – so there!

All statistics in these tables refer to the post-war era, i.e. from 1946.

Fulham's Best Strike-rate Players

Both the highest figure in 'goals per game' and the lowest figure in 'games per goal' indicate the best strike rate. A figure of 0.5 in 'goals per game' indicates a strike rate of one goal every two games – as does a figure of 2 in 'games per goal'.

Thus, it can be seen that Roy Dwight scored 0.71 goals per Fulham game, which is a goal every 1.4 Fulham games.

The table includes substitute appearances, and these can distort figures somewhat for goalscorers. Sometimes the player may have been on the pitch for eighty minutes and sometimes for only ten minutes.

Statistics are up to the end of the 2012–13 season.

Only our fifty principal strikers are included.

	Fulham Goals – all comps	Career League Goals	FFC Goals per Game	FFC Games per Goal	Career Goals per Game	Career Games per Goal	Total Fulham apps	Total League apps
Roy Dwight	57	85	0.71	1.40	0.55	1.81	80	154
Allan Clarke	57	223	0.57	1.75	0.44	2.29	100	510
Bedford Jezzard	154	154	0.50	1.99	0.53	1.90	306	292
Graham Leggat	134	138	0.48	2.09	0.48	2.07	280	285
Louis Saha	63	112	0.44	2.25	0.34	2.96	142	332
Dimitar Berbatov	15	90	0.43	2.33	0.43	2.34	35	211
Geoff Horsfield	31	79	0.42	2.39	0.23	4.30	74	340
Paul Moody	19	106	0.40	2.47	0.37	2.72	47	288
Gordon Davies	178	178	0.40	2.53	0.39	2.58	450	460
Joe Gilroy	11	8	0.39	2.55	0.33	3.00	28	24
Maurice Cook	97	159	0.39	2.56	0.36	2.77	248	441
Malcolm Macdonald	5	191	0.38	2.60	0.51	1.95	13	372
Teddy Maybank	19	39	0.38	2.63	0.28	3.54	50	138
Mike Conroy	41	94	0.37	2.71	0.28	3.59	111	337
Leroy Rosenior	40	73	0.37	2.73	0.30	3.34	109	244
Sean Farrell	35	76	0.34	2.91	0.27	3.76	102	286

	Fulham Goals – all comps	Career League Goals	FFC Goals per Game	FFC Games per Goal	Career Goals per Game	Career Games per Goal	Total Fulham apps	Total League apps
Steve Earle	108	118	0.33	3.03	0.30	3.31	327	391
Trevor Chamberlain	64	59	0.31	3.19	0.32	3.17	204	187
Rodney Marsh	28	171	0.31	3.21	0.42	2.39	90	408
John Mitchell	60	75	0.31	3.23	0.30	3.35	194	251
Andrew Cole	16	230	0.31	3.25	0.45	2.21	52	509
Vic Halom	25	131	0.30	3.28	0.29	3.45	82	452
Arthur Stevens	124	110	0.30	3.33	0.28	3.51	413	386
Dean Coney	72	64	0.29	3.42	0.23	4.31	246	276
Bobby Zamora	37	132	0.28	3.62	0.33	3.04	134	401
Chris Guthrie	15	78	0.27	3.67	0.29	3.50	55	273
Barry Hayles	58	120	0.27	3.71	0.27	3.64	215	437
Clint Dempsey	60	65	0.27	3.75	0.27	3.66	225	238
Phil Stant	5	170	0.26	3.80	0.39	2.55	19	433
Brian McBride	40	37	0.26	3.83	0.24	4.22	153	156
Paul Peschisolido	30	118	0.26	3.83	0.26	3.79	115	447
Heidar Helguson	16	114	0.25	3.94	0.30	3.33	63	380
Viv Busby	36	74	0.25	3.97	0.25	4.07	143	301
Peter Kitchen	6	166	0.25	4.00	0.38	2.64	24	438
Andy Johnson	27	114	0.24	4.11	0.30	3.33	111	380
Steve Marlet	19	11	0.24	4.11	0.20	5.00	78	55
Johnny Haynes	158	147	0.24	4.16	0.25	4.04	658	594
Gary Brazil	53	123	0.22	4.47	0.25	3.99	237	491
Roger Cross	10	84	0.22	4.60	0.32	3.17	46	266
Bobby Robson	80	133	0.22	4.63	0.23	4.38	370	583
Luis Boa Morte	54	48	0.22	4.63	0.14	7.02	250	337
Collins John	23	22	0.21	4.70	0.20	5.09	108	112
Jimmy Conway	76	68	0.21	4.74	0.21	4.84	360	329
Les Barrett	90	75	0.18	5.46	0.17	5.76	491	432
Jimmy Hill	52	51	0.18	5.71	0.14	7.04	297	359
Facundo Sava	7	6	0.17	6.00	0.23	4.33	42	26
Erik Nevland	10	9	0.15	6.70	0.17	5.89	67	53
Frank Large	3	208	0.11	9.33	0.37	2.70	28	562
Johnny Byrne	2	171	0.11	9.50	0.41	2.42	19	414
Alan Warboys	2	136	0.10	10.50	0.28	3.52	21	479

Potential outliers. *It should be noted that players such as Malcolm Macdonald, Joe Gilroy and Dimitar Berbatov are high on the above list as they played a relatively small number of Fulham games, whilst players such as Johnny Haynes, Bobby Robson, Les Barrett and Jimmy Conway are a lot further down the list. It's harder to keep up a high scoring rate over 300–600 games.*

Fulham Hat-tricks (or better) by Season

	Player	Goals	Opponents		Competition		Date
1946–1947	Doug McGibbon	3	Plymouth Argyle	3–1	League	Home	January 18th
1947–1948	Doug McGibbon	3	Brentford	5–0	League	Home	August 21st
1947–1948	Arthur Stevens	3	Bristol Rovers	5–2	FA Cup 4th	Home	January 24th
1948–1949	Arthur Stevens	3	Queens Park Rangers	5–0	League	Home	October 2nd
1948–1949	Arthur Rowley	4	Bury	7–2	League	Home	January 15th
1948–1949	Arthur Rowley	3	Plymouth Argyle	6–1	League	Home	January 22nd
1951–1952	Jeff Taylor	3	Middlesbrough	6–0	League	Home	January 19th
1952–1953	Bedford Jezzard	3	Rotherham United	4–1	League	Home	February 18th
1953–1954	Bedford Jezzard	4	Derby County	5–2	League	Home	October 10th
1953–1954	Bedford Jezzard	3	Plymouth Argyle	3–1	League	Home	December 25th
1953–1954	Jeff Taylor	3	Grimsby Town	5–5	FA Cup 3rd	Away	January 9th
1953–1954	Johnny Haynes	3	Luton Town	5–1	League	Home	February 20th
1953–1954	Bedford Jezzard	3	Swansea Town	4–3	League	Home	April 19th
1954–1955	Bedford Jezzard	3	Swansea Town	5–1	League	Home	April 20th
1955–1956	Bedford Jezzard	4	Barnsley	5–1	League	Home	August 27th
1955–1956	Johnny Haynes	3	Notts County	4–3	League	Away	September 15th
1955–1956	Bedford Jezzard	5	Hull City	5–0	League	Home	October 8th
1955–1956	Trevor Chamberlain	3	Newcastle United	4–5	FA Cup 4th	Home	January 28th
1955–1956	Roy Dwight	3	Liverpool	3–1	League	Home	April 7th
1955–1956	Trevor Chamberlain	3	Doncaster Rovers	4–0	League	Home	April 21st
1956–1957	Roy Dwight	3	Swansea Town	7–3	League	Home	September 8th
1956–1957	Arthur Stevens	3	Grimsby Town	3–1	League	Home	October 13th
1956–1957	Roy Dwight	3	Notts County	5–1	League	Home	November 24th
1956–1957	Trevor Chamberlain	3	Doncaster Rovers	7–2	League	Home	December 26th
1956–1957	Roy Dwight	3	Swansea Town	5–4	League	Away	January 12th
1956–1957	Roy Dwight	3	Port Vale	6–3	League	Home	February 9th
1956–1957	Roy Bentley	3	Port Vale	6–3	League	Home	February 9th
1957–1958	Roy Dwight	4	Sheffield United	6–3	League	Home	September 18th
1957–1958	Jimmy Hill	5	Doncaster Rovers	6–1	League	Away	March 15th
1958–1959	Maurice Cook	3	Stoke City	6–1	League	Home	August 23rd
1958–1959	Johnny Haynes	3	Sunderland	6–2	League	Home	September 3rd
1958–1959	Johnny Haynes	4	Lincoln City	4–2	League	Home	September 17th
1958–1959	Graham Leggat	3	Middlesbrough	3–2	League	Away	October 25th
1958–1959	Johnny Haynes	3	Leyton Orient	5–2	League	Home	February 14th
1958–1959	Jimmy Hill	3	Sheffield Wednesday	6–2	League	Home	March 27th
1958–1959	Johnny Haynes	3	Rotherham United	4–0	League	Home	April 25th
1959–1960	Graham Leggat	3	Manchester United	3–3	League	Away	November 7th
1959–1960	Graham Leggat	4	Leeds United	5–0	League	Home	February 27th
1960–1961	Graham Leggat	3	Bolton Wanderers	3–0	League	Away	October 22nd
1960–1961	Graham Leggat	3	Leicester City	4–2	League	Home	November 12th

1960–1961	Maurice Cook	3	Wolverhampton W	4–2	League	Away	April 29th
1961–1962	Maurice Cook	3	Sheffield United	5–2	League	Home	March 17th
1962–1963	Maurice Cook	3	Sheffield Wednesday	4–1	League	Home	September 19th
1963–1964	Graham Leggat	4	Ipswich Town	10–1	League	Home	December 26th
1963–1964	Bobby Howfield	3	Ipswich Town	10–1	League	Home	December 26th
1964–1965	Dave Metchick	3	Birmingham City	3–1	League	Home	September 2nd
1965–1966	Graham Leggat	3	Aston Villa	3–6	League	Home	September 18th
1965–1966	John Dempsey	3	Northampton Town	5–0	League Cup 3rd	Home	October 13th
1965–1966	Steve Earle	3	Northampton Town	4–2	League	Away	April 23rd
1966–1967	Graham Leggat	3	Leicester City	4–2	League	Home	December 27th
1966–1967	Allan Clarke	3	Newcastle United	5–1	League	Home	February 4th
1967–1968	Allan Clarke	4	Workington	6–2	League Cup 3rd	Home	October 16th
1969–1970	Steve Earle	5	Halifax Town	8–0	League	Away	September 16th
1969–1970	Steve Earle	3	Stockport County	4–1	League	Away	September 27th
1971–1972	Steve Earle	3	Cambridge United	4–0	League Cup 1st	Home	August 17th
1973–1974	Viv Busby	3	Sheffield Wednesday	4–1	League	Home	February 2nd
1976–1977	John Mitchell	4	Orient	6–1	League	Home	May 7th
1977–1978	John Mitchell	3	Notts County	5–1	League	Home	September 17th
1978–1979	Chris Guthrie	3	Cambridge United	5–1	League	Home	December 26th
1979–1980	Gordon Davies	3	Birmingham City	4–3	League	Away	August 18th
1979–1980	Gordon Davies	3	Leicester City	3–3	League	Away	September 22nd
1983–1984	Gordon Davies	3	Chelsea	3–5	League	Home	October 8th
1983–1984	Gordon Davies	4	Manchester City	5–1	League	Home	March 17th
1984–1985	Leroy Rosenior	3	Grimsby Town	4–2	League	Away	November 17th
1984–1985	Tony Sealy	3	Wolverhampton W	4–0	League	Away	April 27th
1991–1992	Sean Farrell	3	West Bromwich A	3–2	League	Away	January 1st
1992–1993	Sean Farrell	3	Burnley	4–0	League	Home	April 24th
1994–1995	Mark Stallard	3	Exeter City	4–0	League	Home	October 15th
1994–1995	Nick Cusack	3	Rochdale	5–0	League	Home	May 6th
1995–1996	Mike Conroy	3	Swansea City	7–0	FA Cup 1st	Home	November 11th
1997–1998	Paul Moody	3	Luton Town	4–1	League	Away	January 24th
1997–1998	Paul Peschisolido	3	Carlisle United	5–0	League	Home	April 13th
1998–1999	Paul Moody	3	Preston North End	3–0	League	Home	May 8th
1999–2000	Geoff Horsfield	3	Northampton Town	3–1	League Cup 1st	Home	August 24th
2000–2001	Louis Saha	3	Barnsley	5–1	League	Home	September 10th
2000–2001	Barry Hayles	3	Watford	5–0	League	Home	December 26th
2002–2003	Steed Malbranque	3	Charlton Athletic	3–0	FA Cup 4th	Home	January 26th
2005–2006	Heidar Helguson	3	West Bromwich A	6–1	League	Home	February 11th
2010–2011	Diomansy Kamara	3	Peterborough United	6–2	FA Cup 3rd	Home	January 8th
2011–2012	Andy Johnson	3	Queens Park Rangers	6–0	League	Home	October 2nd
2011–2012	Clint Dempsey	3	Charlton Athletic	4–0	FA Cup 3rd	Home	January 7th
2011–2012	Clint Dempsey	3	Newcastle United	5–2	League	Home	January 21st
2011–2012	Pavel Pogrebnyak	3	Wolverhampton W	5–0	League	Home	March 4th

Fulham Hat-tricks (or better) by Player

In alphabetical sequence.

		Goals	Opponents		Competition		Date
1956–1957	Roy Bentley	3	Port Vale	6–3	League	Home	February 9th
1973–1974	Viv Busby	3	Sheffield Wednesday	4–1	League	Home	February 2nd
1955–1956	Trevor Chamberlain	3	Newcastle United	4–5	FA Cup 4th	Home	January 28th
1955–1956	Trevor Chamberlain	3	Doncaster Rovers	4–0	League	Home	April 21st
1956–1957	Trevor Chamberlain	3	Doncaster Rovers	7–2	League	Home	December 26th
1966–1967	Allan Clarke	3	Newcastle United	5–1	League	Home	February 4th
1967–1968	Allan Clarke	4	Workington	6–2	League Cup 3rd	Home	October 16th
1995–1996	Mike Conroy	3	Swansea City	7–0	FA Cup 1st	Home	November 11th
1958–1959	Maurice Cook	3	Stoke City	6–1	League	Home	August 23rd
1960–1961	Maurice Cook	3	Wolverhampton W	4–2	League	Away	April 29th
1961–1962	Maurice Cook	3	Sheffield United	5–2	League	Home	March 17th
1962–1963	Maurice Cook	3	Sheffield Wednesday	4–1	League	Home	September 19th
1994–1995	Nick Cusack	3	Rochdale	5–0	League	Home	May 6th
1979–1980	Gordon Davies	3	Birmingham City	4–3	League	Away	August 18th
1979–1980	Gordon Davies	3	Leicester City	3–3	League	Away	September 22nd
1983–1984	Gordon Davies	3	Chelsea	3–5	League	Home	October 8th
1983–1984	Gordon Davies	4	Manchester City	5–1	League	Home	March 17th
1965–1966	Clint Dempsey	3	Northampton Town	5–0	League Cup 3rd	Home	October 13th
2011–2012	Clint Dempsey	3	Charlton Athletic	4–0	FA Cup 3rd	Home	January 7th
2011–2012	Clint Dempsey	3	Newcastle United	5–2	League	Home	January 21st
1955–1956	Roy Dwight	3	Liverpool	3–1	League	Home	April 7th
1956–1957	Roy Dwight	3	Swansea Town	7–3	League	Home	September 8th
1956–1957	Roy Dwight	3	Notts County	5–1	League	Home	November 24th
1956–1957	Roy Dwight	3	Swansea Town	5–4	League	Away	January 12th
1956–1957	Roy Dwight	3	Port Vale	6–3	League	Home	February 9th
1957–1958	Roy Dwight	4	Sheffield United	6–3	League	Home	September 18th
1965–1966	Steve Earle	3	Northampton Town	4–2	League	Away	April 23rd
1969–1970	Steve Earle	5	Halifax Town	8–0	League	Away	September 16th
1969–1970	Steve Earle	3	Stockport County	4–1	League	Away	September 27th
1971–1972	Steve Earle	3	Cambridge United	4–0	League Cup 1st	Home	August 17th
1991–1992	Sean Farrell	3	West Bromwich A	3–2	League	Away	January 1st
1992–1993	Sean Farrell	3	Burnley	4–0	League	Home	April 24th
1978–1979	Chris Guthrie	3	Cambridge United	5–1	League	Home	December 26th
2000–2001	Barry Hayles	3	Watford	5–0	League	Home	December 26th
1953–1954	Johnny Haynes	3	Luton Town	5–1	League	Home	February 20th
1955–1956	Johnny Haynes	3	Notts County	4–3	League	Away	September 15th
1958–1959	Johnny Haynes	3	Sunderland	6–2	League	Home	September 3rd
1958–1959	Johnny Haynes	4	Lincoln City	4–2	League	Home	September 17th
1958–1959	Johnny Haynes	3	Leyton Orient	5–2	League	Home	February 14th
1958–1959	Johnny Haynes	3	Rotherham United	4–0	League	Home	April 25th

2005–2006	Heidar Helguson	3	West Bromwich A	6–1	League	Home	February 11th
1957–1958	Jimmy Hill	5	Doncaster Rovers	6–1	League	Away	March 15th
1958–1959	Jimmy Hill	3	Sheffield Wednesday	6–2	League	Home	March 27th
1999–2000	Geoff Horsfield	3	Northampton Town	3–1	League Cup 1st	Home	August 24th
1963–1964	Bobby Howfield	3	Ipswich Town	10–1	League	Home	December 26th
1952–1953	Bedford Jezzard	3	Rotherham United	4–1	League	Home	February 18th
1953–1954	Bedford Jezzard	4	Derby County	5–2	League	Home	October 10th
1953–1954	Bedford Jezzard	3	Plymouth Argyle	3–1	League	Home	December 25th
1953–1954	Bedford Jezzard	3	Swansea Town	4–3	League	Home	April 19th
1954–1955	Bedford Jezzard	3	Swansea Town	5–1	League	Home	April 20th
1955–1956	Bedford Jezzard	4	Barnsley	5–1	League	Home	August 27th
1955–1956	Bedford Jezzard	5	Hull City	5–0	League	Home	October 8th
2011–2012	Andy Johnson	3	Queens Park Rangers	6–0	League	Home	October 2nd
2010–2011	Diomansy Kamara	3	Peterborough United	6–2	FA Cup 3rd	Home	January 8th
1958–1959	Graham Leggat	3	Middlesbrough	3–2	League	Away	October 25th
1959–1960	Graham Leggat	3	Manchester United	3–3	League	Away	November 7th
1959–1960	Graham Leggat	4	Leeds United	5–0	League	Home	February 27th
1960–1961	Graham Leggat	3	Bolton Wanderers	3–0	League	Away	October 22nd
1960–1961	Graham Leggat	3	Leicester City	4–2	League	Home	November 12th
1963–1964	Graham Leggat	4	Ipswich Town	10–1	League	Home	December 26th
1965–1966	Graham Leggat	3	Aston Villa	3–6	League	Home	September 18th
1966–1967	Graham Leggat	3	Leicester City	4–2	League	Home	December 27th
2002–2003	Steed Malbranque	3	Charlton Athletic	3–0	FA Cup 4th	Home	January 26th
1946–1947	Doug McGibbon	3	Plymouth Argyle	3–1	League	Home	January 18th
1947–1948	Doug McGibbon	3	Brentford	5–0	League	Home	August 21st
1964–1965	Dave Metchick	3	Birmingham City	3–1	League	Home	September 2nd
1976–1977	John Mitchell	4	Orient	6–1	League	Home	May 7th
1977–1978	John Mitchell	3	Notts County	5–1	League	Home	September 17th
1997–1998	Paul Moody	3	Luton Town	4–1	League	Away	January 24th
1998–1999	Paul Moody	3	Preston North End	3–0	League	Home	May 8th
1997–1998	Paul Peschisolido	3	Carlisle United	5–0	League	Home	April 13th
2011–2012	Pavel Pogrebnyak	3	Wolverhampton W	5–0	League	Home	March 4th
1984–1985	Leroy Rosenior	3	Grimsby Town	4–2	League	Away	November 17th
1948–1949	Arthur Rowley	4	Bury	7–2	League	Home	January 15th
1948–1949	Arthur Rowley	3	Plymouth Argyle	6–1	League	Home	January 22nd
2000–2001	Louis Saha	3	Barnsley	5–1	League	Home	September 10th
1984–1985	Tony Sealy	3	Wolverhampton W	4–0	League	Away	April 27th
1994–1995	Mark Stallard	3	Exeter City	4–0	League	Home	October 15th
1947–1948	Arthur Stevens	3	Bristol Rovers	5–2	FA Cup 4th	Home	January 24th
1948–1949	Arthur Stevens	3	Queens Park Rangers	5–0	League	Home	October 2nd
1956–1957	Arthur Stevens	3	Grimsby Town	3–1	League	Home	October 13th
1951–1952	Jeff Taylor	3	Middlesbrough	6–0	League	Home	January 19th
1953–1954	Jeff Taylor	3	Grimsby Town	5–5	FA Cup 3rd	Away	January 9th

Fulham's Top Goalscorers by Season

	Player	Total	League	FA Cup	League Cup	Note
1946–1947	Ronnie Rooke	13	13			
1947–1948	Arthur Stevens	15	11	4		
1948–1949	Bob Thomas	23	23			
1949–1950	Bob Thomas	11	10	1		
1950–1951	Bob Thomas	14	14			
1951–1952	Bedford Jezzard	8	8			
1952–1953	Bedford Jezzard	35	35			
1953–1954	Bedford Jezzard	38	38			
1954–1955	Bobby Robson	23	23			Joint top scorer
1954–1955	Bedford Jezzard	23	23			Joint top scorer
1955–1956	Bedford Jezzard	27	27			
1956–1957	Roy Dwight	26	25	1		
1957–1958	Roy Dwight	24	22	2		
1958–1959	Johnny Haynes	26	26			
1959–1960	Graham Leggat	20	18	2		
1960–1961	Graham Leggat	23	23			
1961–1962	Maurice Cook	19	15	4		
1962–1963	Maurice Cook	15	15			
1963–1964	Graham Leggat	16	15	1		
1964–1965	Rodney Marsh	17	17			
1965–1966	Graham Leggat	15	15			
1966–1967	Allan Clarke	29	24	3	2	
1967–1968	Allan Clarke	27	20	2	5	
1968–1969	Brian Dear	7	7			
1969–1970	Steve Earle	23	22		1	Joint top scorer
1969–1970	Jimmy Conway	23	21		2	Joint top scorer
1970–1971	Les Barrett	18	15		3	
1971–1972	Steve Earle	14	11		3	
1972–1973	Steve Earle	15	15			
1973–1974	Viv Busby	11	11			
1974–1975	Viv Busby	18	11	6	1	
1975–1976	John Mitchell	10	10			
1976–1977	John Mitchell	22	20		2	
1977–1978	John Mitchell	9	9			
1978–1979	Chris Guthrie	13	13			
1979–1980	Gordon Davies	16	15		1	
1980–1981	Gordon Davies	22	18	3	1	

		Total	League	FA Cup	League Cup	
1981–1982	Gordon Davies	25	24		1	
1982–1983	Gordon Davies	20	19		1	
1983–1984	Gordon Davies	26	23		3	
1984–1985	Ray Houghton *	11	8	2	1	Joint top scorer
1984–1985	Robert Wilson *	11	11			Joint top scorer
1985–1986	Dean Coney	13	12		1	
1986–1987	Dean Coney	14	10	2	2	
1987–1988	Leroy Rosenior	22	20	1	1	
1988–1989	Gordon Davies	14	14			
1989–1990	Clive Walker *	15	13	1	1	
1990–1991	Gordon Davies	7	6	1		
1991–1992	Gary Brazil	16	14		2	
1992–1993	Sean Farrell	13	12		1	
1993–1994	Gary Brazil	15	14		1	
1994–1995	Simon Morgan *	12	11	1		
1995–1996	Mike Conroy	14	9	3	2	
1996–1997	Mike Conroy	23	21		2	
1997–1998	Paul Moody	15	15			
1998–1999	Geoff Horsfield	17	15	2		
1999–2000	Geoff Horsfield	14	7	1	6	
2000–2001	Louis Saha	32	27		5	
2001–2002	Barry Hayles	12	8	2	2	
2002–2003	Steed Malbranque *	10	6	4		
2003–2004	Louis Saha	15	13	2		
2004–2005	Andrew Cole	13	12		1	
2005–2006	Collins John	12	11	1		
2006–2007	Brian McBride	12	9	3		
2007–2008	Clint Dempsey	6	6			Four-way split
2007–2008	David Healy	6	4	1	1	Four-way split
2007–2008	Diomansy Kamara	6	5		1	Four-way split
2007–2008	Danny Murphy *	6	5	1		Four-way split
2008–2009	Andy Johnson	10	7	3		
2009–2010	Bobby Zamora	11	8	3		
2010–2011	Clint Dempsey	13	12		1	
2011–2012	Clint Dempsey	20	17	3		
2012–2013	Dimitar Berbatov	15	15			

* Statistically unusual season where the top goalscorer or the joint top goalscorers were not 'strikers' and therefore outside the scope of this book.

Fulham's Top Goalscorers by Total Goals in a Season

	Player	Total	League	FA Cup	League Cup	Note
1953–1954	Bedford Jezzard	38	38			
1952–1953	Bedford Jezzard	35	35			
2000–2001	Louis Saha	32	27		5	
1966–1967	Allan Clarke	29	24	3	2	
1955–1956	Bedford Jezzard	27	27			
1967–1968	Allan Clarke	27	20	2	5	
1956–1957	Roy Dwight	26	25	1		
1958–1959	Johnny Haynes	26	26			
1983–1984	Gordon Davies	26	23		3	
1981–1982	Gordon Davies	25	24		1	
1957–1958	Roy Dwight	24	22	2		
1948–1949	Bob Thomas	23	23			
1954–1955	Bobby Robson	23	23			Joint top scorer
1954–1955	Bedford Jezzard	23	23			Joint top scorer
1960–1961	Graham Leggat	23	23			
1969–1970	Jimmy Conway	23	21		2	Joint top scorer
1969–1970	Steve Earle	23	22		1	Joint top scorer
1996–1997	Mike Conroy	23	21		2	
1976–1977	John Mitchell	22	20		2	
1980–1981	Gordon Davies	22	18	3	1	
1987–1988	Leroy Rosenior	22	20	1	1	
1959–1960	Graham Leggat	20	18	2		
1982–1983	Gordon Davies	20	19		1	
2011–2012	Clint Dempsey	20	17	3		
1961–1962	Maurice Cook	19	15	4		
1970–1971	Les Barrett	18	15		3	
1974–1975	Viv Busby	18	11	6	1	
1964–1965	Rodney Marsh	17	17			
1998–1999	Geoff Horsfield	17	15	2		
1963–1964	Graham Leggat	16	15	1		
1979–1980	Gordon Davies	16	15		1	
1991–1992	Gary Brazil	16	14		2	
1947–1948	Arthur Stevens	15	11	4		
1962–1963	Maurice Cook	15	15			
1965–1966	Graham Leggat	15	15			
1972–1973	Steve Earle	15	15			
1989–1990	Clive Walker *	15	13	1	1	
1993–1994	Gary Brazil	15	14		1	
1997–1998	Paul Moody	15	15			

		Total	League	FA Cup	League Cup	Note
2003–2004	Louis Saha	15	13	2		
2012–2013	Dimitar Berbatov	15	15			
1950–1951	Bob Thomas	14	14			
1971–1972	Steve Earle	14	11		3	
1986–1987	Dean Coney	14	10	2	2	
1988–1989	Gordon Davies	14	14			
1995–1996	Mike Conroy	14	9	3	2	
1999–2000	Geoff Horsfield	14	7	1	6	
1946–1947	Ronnie Rooke	13	13			
1978–1979	Chris Guthrie	13	13			
1985–1986	Dean Coney	13	12		1	
1992–1993	Sean Farrell	13	12		1	
2004–2005	Andrew Cole	13	12		1	
2010–2011	Clint Dempsey	13	12		1	
1994–1995	Simon Morgan *	12	11	1		
2001–2002	Barry Hayles	12	8	2	2	
2005–2006	Collins John	12	11	1		
2006–2007	Brian McBride	12	9	3		
1949–1950	Bob Thomas	11	10	1		
1973–1974	Viv Busby	11	11			
1984–1985	Robert Wilson *	11	11			Joint top scorer
1984–1985	Ray Houghton *	11	8	2	1	Joint top scorer
2009–2010	Bobby Zamora	11	8	3		
1975–1976	John Mitchell	10	10			
2002–2003	Steed Malbranque *	10	6	4		
2008–2009	Andy Johnson	10	7	3		
1977–1978	John Mitchell	9	9			
1951–1952	Bedford Jezzard	8	8			
1968–1969	Brian Dear	7	7			
1990–1991	Gordon Davies	7	6	1		
2007–2008	Clint Dempsey	6	6			Four-way split
2007–2008	David Healy	6	4	1	1	Four-way split
2007–2008	Diomansy Kamara	6	5		1	Four-way split
2007–2008	Danny Murphy *	6	5	1		Four-way split

Statistically unusual season where the top goalscorer or the joint top goalscorers were not 'strikers' and therefore outside the scope of this book.

Fulham's Top Goalscorers   *Only our fifty principal strikers are included.*

	Fulham Goals – all comps	Career League Goals	Career Goals per Game	Career Games per Goal	Total Fulham Appearances	Total League Appearances
Gordon Davies	178	178	0.39	2.58	450	460
Johnny Haynes	158	147	0.25	4.04	658	594
Bedford Jezzard	154	154	0.53	1.90	306	292
Graham Leggat	134	138	0.48	2.07	280	285
Arthur Stevens	124	110	0.28	3.51	413	386
Steve Earle	108	118	0.30	3.31	327	391
Maurice Cook	97	159	0.36	2.77	248	441
Les Barrett	90	75	0.17	5.76	491	432
Bobby Robson	80	133	0.23	4.38	370	583
Jimmy Conway	76	68	0.21	4.84	360	329
Dean Coney	72	64	0.23	4.31	246	276
Trevor Chamberlain	64	59	0.32	3.17	204	187
Louis Saha	63	112	0.34	2.96	142	332
John Mitchell	60	75	0.30	3.35	194	251
Clint Dempsey	60	65	0.27	3.66	225	238
Barry Hayles	58	120	0.27	3.64	215	437
Roy Dwight	57	85	0.55	1.81	80	154
Allan Clarke	57	223	0.44	2.29	100	510
Luis Boa Morte	54	48	0.14	7.02	250	337
Gary Brazil	53	123	0.25	3.99	237	491
Jimmy Hill	52	51	0.14	7.04	297	359
Mike Conroy	41	94	0.28	3.59	111	337
Leroy Rosenior	40	73	0.30	3.34	109	244
Brian McBride	40	37	0.24	4.22	153	156
Bobby Zamora	37	132	0.33	3.04	134	401
Viv Busby	36	74	0.25	4.07	143	301
Sean Farrell	35	76	0.27	3.76	102	286
Geoff Horsfield	31	79	0.23	4.30	74	340
Paul Peschisolido	30	118	0.26	3.79	115	447
Rodney Marsh	28	171	0.42	2.39	90	408
Andy Johnson	27	114	0.30	3.33	111	380
Vic Halom	25	131	0.29	3.45	82	452
Collins John	23	22	0.20	5.09	108	112
Paul Moody	19	106	0.37	2.72	47	288
Teddy Maybank	19	39	0.28	3.54	50	138
Steve Marlet	19	11	0.20	5.00	78	55
Andrew Cole	16	230	0.45	2.21	52	509
Heidar Helguson	16	114	0.30	3.33	63	380
Dimitar Berbatov	15	90	0.43	2.34	35	211
Chris Guthrie	15	78	0.29	3.50	55	273
Joe Gilroy	11	8	0.33	3.00	28	24
Roger Cross	10	84	0.32	3.17	46	266
Erik Nevland	10	9	0.17	5.89	67	53
Facundo Sava	7	6	0.23	4.33	42	26
Peter Kitchen	6	166	0.38	2.64	24	438
Malcolm Macdonald	5	191	0.51	1.95	13	372
Phil Stant	5	170	0.39	2.55	19	433
Frank Large	3	208	0.37	2.70	28	562
Johnny Byrne	2	171	0.41	2.42	19	414
Alan Warboys	2	136	0.28	3.52	21	479

Fulham's Top Appearances

Only our fifty principal strikers are included.

	Total Fulham Appearances	Total Fulham Goals	FFC Goals per game	FFC Games per goal	Total League Appearances	Career League Goals
Johnny Haynes	658	158	0.24	4.16	594	147
Les Barrett	491	90	0.18	5.46	432	75
Gordon Davies	450	178	0.40	2.53	460	178
Arthur Stevens	413	124	0.30	3.33	386	110
Bobby Robson	370	80	0.22	4.63	583	133
Jimmy Conway	360	76	0.21	4.74	329	68
Steve Earle	327	108	0.33	3.03	391	118
Bedford Jezzard	306	154	0.50	1.99	292	154
Jimmy Hill	297	52	0.18	5.71	359	51
Graham Leggat	280	134	0.48	2.09	285	138
Luis Boa Morte	250	54	0.22	4.63	337	48
Maurice Cook	248	97	0.39	2.56	441	159
Dean Coney	246	72	0.29	3.42	276	64
Gary Brazil	237	53	0.22	4.47	491	123
Clint Dempsey	225	60	0.27	3.75	238	65
Barry Hayles	215	58	0.27	3.71	437	120
Trevor Chamberlain	204	64	0.31	3.19	187	59
John Mitchell	194	60	0.31	3.23	251	75
Brian McBride	153	40	0.26	3.83	156	37
Viv Busby	143	37	0.26	3.86	301	74
Louis Saha	142	63	0.44	2.25	332	112
Bobby Zamora	134	37	0.28	3.62	401	132
Paul Peschisolido	115	30	0.26	3.83	447	118
Mike Conroy	111	41	0.37	2.71	337	94
Andy Johnson	111	27	0.24	4.11	380	114
Leroy Rosenior	109	40	0.37	2.73	244	73
Collins John	108	23	0.21	4.70	112	22
Sean Farrell	102	35	0.34	2.91	286	76
Allan Clarke	100	57	0.57	1.75	510	223
Rodney Marsh	90	28	0.31	3.21	408	171
Vic Halom	82	25	0.30	3.28	452	131
Roy Dwight	80	57	0.71	1.40	154	85
Steve Marlet	78	19	0.24	4.11	55	11
Geoff Horsfield	74	31	0.42	2.39	340	79
Erik Nevland	67	10	0.15	6.70	53	9
Heidar Helguson	63	16	0.25	3.94	380	114
Chris Guthrie	55	15	0.27	3.67	273	78
Andrew Cole	52	16	0.31	3.25	509	230
Teddy Maybank	50	19	0.38	2.63	138	39
Paul Moody	47	19	0.40	2.47	288	106
Roger Cross	46	10	0.22	4.60	266	84
Facundo Sava	42	7	0.17	6.00	26	6
Dimitar Berbatov	35	15	0.43	2.33	211	90
Joe Gilroy	28	11	0.39	2.55	24	8
Frank Large	28	3	0.11	9.33	562	208
Peter Kitchen	24	6	0.25	4.00	438	166
Alan Warboys	21	2	0.10	10.50	479	136
Phil Stant	19	5	0.26	3.80	433	170
Johnny Byrne	19	2	0.11	9.50	414	171
Malcolm Macdonald	13	5	0.38	2.60	372	191

Player	Fulham Goals– all comps	Career League Goals	Career Goals per Game	Career Games per Goal	Total League Appearances
Roy Dwight	57	85	0.55	1.81	154
Bedford Jezzard	154	154	0.53	1.90	292
Malcolm Macdonald	5	191	0.51	1.95	372
Graham Leggat	134	138	0.48	2.07	285
Andrew Cole	16	230	0.45	2.21	509
Allan Clarke	57	223	0.44	2.29	510
Dimitar Berbatov	15	90	0.43	2.34	211
Rodney Marsh	28	171	0.42	2.39	408
Johnny Byrne	2	171	0.41	2.42	414
Phil Stant	5	170	0.39	2.55	433
Gordon Davies	178	178	0.39	2.58	460
Peter Kitchen	6	166	0.38	2.64	438
Frank Large	3	208	0.37	2.70	562
Paul Moody	19	106	0.37	2.72	288
Maurice Cook	97	159	0.36	2.77	441
Louis Saha	63	112	0.34	2.96	332
Joe Gilroy	11	8	0.33	3.00	24
Bobby Zamora	37	132	0.33	3.04	401
Trevor Chamberlain	64	59	0.32	3.17	187
Roger Cross	10	84	0.32	3.17	266
Steve Earle	108	118	0.30	3.31	391
Andy Johnson	27	114	0.30	3.33	380
Heidar Helguson	16	114	0.30	3.33	380
Leroy Rosenior	40	73	0.30	3.34	244
John Mitchell	60	75	0.30	3.35	251
Vic Halom	25	131	0.29	3.45	452
Chris Guthrie	15	78	0.29	3.50	273
Arthur Stevens	124	110	0.28	3.51	386
Alan Warboys	2	136	0.28	3.52	479
Teddy Maybank	19	39	0.28	3.54	138
Mike Conroy	41	94	0.28	3.59	337
Barry Hayles	58	120	0.27	3.64	437
Clint Dempsey	60	65	0.27	3.66	238
Sean Farrell	35	76	0.27	3.76	286
Paul Peschisolido	30	118	0.26	3.79	447
Gary Brazil	53	123	0.25	3.99	491
Johnny Haynes	158	147	0.25	4.04	594
Viv Busby	37	74	0.25	4.07	301
Brian McBride	40	37	0.24	4.22	156
Geoff Horsfield	31	79	0.23	4.30	340
Dean Coney	72	64	0.23	4.31	276
Facundo Sava	7	6	0.23	4.33	26
Bobby Robson	80	133	0.23	4.38	583
Jimmy Conway	76	68	0.21	4.84	329
Steve Marlet	19	11	0.20	5.00	55
Collins John	23	22	0.20	5.09	112
Les Barrett	90	75	0.17	5.76	432
Erik Nevland	10	9	0.17	5.89	53
Luis Boa Morte	54	48	0.14	7.02	337
Jimmy Hill	52	51	0.14	7.04	359

Notice how prominent Malcolm Macdonald, Johnny Byrne, Rodney Marsh, Phil Stant, Peter Kitchen and Frank Large become with goalscoring success at other clubs despite their relative failure at Fulham – and amazingly they are all above Louis Saha, who had great success at Fulham but was not so prolific elsewhere in his career.

League Careers *of our fifty principal strikers* by Total Goals

Player	Fulham Goals – all comps	Career League Goals	Career Goals per Game	Career Games per Goal	Total League Appearances
Andrew Cole	16	230	0.45	2.21	509
Allan Clarke	57	223	0.44	2.29	510
Frank Large	3	208	0.37	2.70	562
Malcolm Macdonald	5	191	0.51	1.95	372
Gordon Davies	178	178	0.39	2.58	460
Rodney Marsh	28	171	0.42	2.39	408
Johnny Byrne	2	171	0.41	2.42	414
Phil Stant	5	170	0.39	2.55	433
Peter Kitchen	6	166	0.38	2.64	438
Maurice Cook	97	159	0.36	2.77	441
Bedford Jezzard	154	154	0.53	1.90	292
Johnny Haynes	158	147	0.25	4.04	594
Graham Leggat	134	138	0.48	2.07	285
Alan Warboys	2	136	0.28	3.52	479
Bobby Robson	80	133	0.23	4.38	583
Bobby Zamora	37	132	0.33	3.04	401
Vic Halom	25	131	0.29	3.45	452
Gary Brazil	53	123	0.25	3.99	491
Barry Hayles	58	120	0.27	3.64	437
Steve Earle	108	118	0.30	3.31	391
Paul Peschisolido	30	118	0.26	3.79	447
Andy Johnson	27	114	0.30	3.33	380
Heidar Helguson	16	114	0.30	3.33	380
Louis Saha	63	112	0.34	2.96	332
Arthur Stevens	124	110	0.28	3.51	386
Paul Moody	19	106	0.37	2.72	288
Mike Conroy	41	94	0.28	3.59	337
Dimitar Berbatov	15	90	0.43	2.34	211
Roy Dwight	57	85	0.55	1.81	154
Roger Cross	10	84	0.32	3.17	266
Geoff Horsfield	31	79	0.23	4.30	340
Chris Guthrie	15	78	0.29	3.50	273
Sean Farrell	35	76	0.27	3.76	286
John Mitchell	60	75	0.30	3.35	251
Les Barrett	90	75	0.17	5.76	432
Viv Busby	37	74	0.25	4.07	301
Leroy Rosenior	40	73	0.30	3.34	244
Jimmy Conway	76	68	0.21	4.84	329
Clint Dempsey	60	65	0.27	3.66	238
Dean Coney	72	64	0.23	4.31	276
Trevor Chamberlain	64	59	0.32	3.17	187
Jimmy Hill	52	51	0.14	7.04	359
Luis Boa Morte	54	48	0.14	7.02	337
Teddy Maybank	19	39	0.28	3.54	138
Brian McBride	40	37	0.24	4.22	156
Collins John	23	22	0.20	5.09	112
Steve Marlet	19	11	0.20	5.00	55
Erik Nevland	10	9	0.17	5.89	53
Joe Gilroy	11	8	0.33	3.00	24
Facundo Sava	7	6	0.23	4.33	26

ASHWATER
PRESS